ISLAM AFTER LIB

FAISAL DEVJI
ZAHEER KAZMI (Editors)

Islam After Liberalism

HURST & COMPANY, LONDON

First published in the United Kingdom in 2017 by
C. Hurst & Co. (Publishers) Ltd.,
41 Great Russell Street, London, WC1B 3PL
© Faisal Devji, Zaheer Kazmi and the Contributors, 2017
All rights reserved.
Printed in the United Kingdom

The right of Faisal Devji, Zaheer Kazmi and the Contributors to be identified
as the authors of this publication is asserted by them in accordance with the
Copyright, Designs and Patents Act, 1988.

A Cataloguing-in-Publication data record for this book
is available from the British Library.

ISBN: 9781849047012

This book is printed using paper from registered sustainable
and managed sources.

www.hurstpublishers.com

Printed and bound in Great Britain by Bell and Bain Ltd, Glasgow

CONTENTS

CONTENTS

RESISTANCE

ACKNOWLEDGMENTS

This book has its origins in the 'Beyond Muslim Liberalism' workshop held at St Antony's College, Oxford in March 2014. In addition to our chapter writers, we would like to thank the following workshop participants who gave papers not included in this volume, or acted as discussants and session chairs: Madawi Al-Rasheed, Mohammed Bamyeh, Alastair Crooke, Michael Freeden, Kevin Fogg, and Nilufer Gole. The workshop was supported by the Economic and Social Research Council (ES/J003115/1) and hosted by the Asian Studies Centre at St Antony's College, Oxford.

Faisal Devji and *Zaheer Kazmi*

LIST OF FIGURES

INTRODUCTION

ISLAM AFTER LIBERALISM

Faisal Devji and *Zaheer Kazmi*

The relationship between Islam and liberalism has been a subject of scholarly as much as popular debate for at least a century and a half. Its progress sometimes hailed and at other times found wanting, this relationship has been marked by the unchanging and even stereotypical terms in which it has been debated, including issues such as the separation of church and state, the status of women and the rights of non-Muslims. Each of these issues serves as a litmus test to measure the liberalism of Muslim individuals as well as societies, and each is also drawn from the real or imagined history of liberalism in Europe. However, as a historical and variable phenomenon, liberalism does not in fact possess a normative definition but constitutes a family of shifting and overlapping ideas having to do with the freedoms of property and contract, speech and movement, or of rights and representation.

The freedoms that have come to define liberalism differ in time and place, so that among its Muslim supporters as much as enemies, for instance, private property and contract law have rarely been controversial (though they might be for those Muslims who identify as socialists). Moreover, the categories 'Islam' and 'liberalism' are not in fact so distinct from one another, and it is even possible to argue that proponents of the latter have always relied upon

1

the former's recalcitrance, against which its own progress is to be defined.[1] After all, religion, understood as a sociological (rather than theological) category common to all peoples, emerged during the nineteenth century together with liberalism, which could then function if separated from other entities such as 'politics'.[2] Islam, therefore, came to be redefined as a noun or proper name instead of a verbal form describing a certain set of practices.[3] As the property of its adherents, it could now be seen as an identity that, whether it had to be opposed or protected, might only be conceptualised in liberal terms as an interest.

In its earliest form, the relationship between Islam and liberalism was defined by imperial politics. Already in the 1930s, the influential Indian philosopher and poet Muhammad Iqbal noted how the questions that were of interest to his colonised Muslim compatriots, as well as to their British rulers, had to do with the former's loyalty to Islamic authorities outside India, their views on jihad or messianism, and the interpretation of certain verses from scripture. Such questions, therefore, which have again become familiar in our own day, first came to define the relationship between Islam and liberalism in the nineteenth century:

> Does the idea of Caliphate in Islam embody a religious institution? How are the Indian Muslims and for the matter of that all Muslims outside the Turkish Empire related to the Turkish Caliphate? Is India *Dar-ul-Islam*? What is the real meaning of the doctrine of Jihad in Islam? What is the meaning of the expression 'from amongst you' in the Qur'anic verse: 'Obey God, obey the Prophet and the masters of the affair (i.e., rulers) from amongst you'? What is the character of the tradition of the Prophet foretelling the advent of Imam Mehdi? These questions and some others which arose subsequently were, for obvious reasons, questions for Indian Muslims only. European imperialism, however, which was then rapidly penetrating the world of Islam was also intimately interested in them. The controversies which these questions created form a most interesting chapter in the history of Islam in India.[4]

But however important they might otherwise be, European and later American views on the relationship between liberalism and Islam do not always define the ways in which Muslims themselves have thought about this relationship.[5] Indeed, during the nineteenth and early twentieth centuries, non-European thinkers often did more to universalise liberal freedoms than those who came to stand as the patron saints of these virtues. Men like John Stuart Mill, for example, rejected the idea that such freedoms could exist outside very specific and invariably Western social contexts, and in this sense their ideas of liberty were highly particularistic, often being defined by the privilege of race, religion or civilisation, in addition to the seemingly more acceptable one of history, conceived as a number of stages that all peoples had to traverse, but in whose path some were more advanced than others.[6] And so it took Asian or African intellectuals to criticise the racist and civilisational distinctions of Western liberalism and insist upon the universality of its freedoms.

In some very real sense, then, liberalism was given its historical potential and indeed reality by colonised populations, and its freedoms were therefore only made into universal ones with the dismantling of Europe's empires after the Second World War and the enshrining of development and modernisation theory as supposedly global and inclusive ideals. Even when international institutions such as the United Nations were established during this period, they had to be forced by the former colonies grudgingly admitted as members to adopt liberal ideals and principles for all.[7] And yet the relationship between Islam and liberalism has always been spoken about with reference to some founding European event only distantly connected to such modern ideas of freedom, like the Renaissance, Reformation or Enlightenment, that Asian or African societies were meant to replicate in order to achieve both their modernity and their liberty.

In other words, a number of distinct and sometimes disconnected historical narratives, ranging from the recovery of Greco-Roman philosophy, the emergence of Protestantism or the dominance of reason have gone into conceptualising the relationship between liberalism and Islam. When Muslims referred to these founding events, they did so in their own ways, and not necessarily in order to remain faithful to some European original.[8] Indeed, it is the political ambiguity of such references that is striking, with a single issue capable of holding diametrically opposed meanings. One way in which non-Europeans laid claim to these founding events, for example, was to argue, with varying degrees of historical accuracy, that they were only made possible due to the influence of (in this case) Islam's scientific and philosophical tradition—itself the inheritance of European antiquity.

Whereas Muslim reformers of the nineteenth century, such as the celebrated Indian leader Syed Ahmed Khan, used this argument to urge upon their coreligionists a friendly attitude towards Europe's liberalism, others in the following century saw this history as one of theft and malice. Having supposedly relied upon Islamic learning to achieve its dominance, then, Europe was understood as having gone on to subordinate Muslim societies, depriving them of the opportunity to develop their own legacy of learning. This story was repeated by the leader of al-Qaeda, Ayman al-Zawahiri, in an online interview in 2008.[9] And what is interesting is the fact that both his anti-Western account, and the pro-Western one from which he drew it, presumed a relationship between Islam and European liberalism so intimate that Muslims had to recover their true selves from it—which is how Zawahiri, like Syed Ahmed a century before, justified al-Qaeda's reliance on Western technology. Naturally, what these two men understood by terms like Islam, liberalism or the West differed, but it is the narrative of intimacy they shared that is fascinating in its very ambiguity, showing how difficult it is to distinguish liberal or pro-Western accounts from their opposites.

In the nineteenth century, when liberalism crystallised as an ideology, albeit a multifarious one, and almost simultaneously came to the notice of non-European thinkers, such economic, social or political reality as it possessed in their lands was to be found largely in colonial contexts. Indeed, in some ways the colony represented liberalism's ideal, its state being legitimised as neutral and disinterested precisely because it was run by an alien power. And this state's frequently glorified character as a third party also turned colonised subjects into interests, whose internecine quarrels could only be arbitrated by it in a kind of social contract, one that allowed them to assume political universality by identifying with the government.[10] Whether or not such a state recognised some element of political representation, in other words, it was able to instantiate, better than any democracy, many of the classical traits of a liberal order. These included government neutrality, subjects defined by their differing interests, and the contract that brought them all together in a pragmatic rather than natural or indeed national way. And the recognition by colonised intellectuals of this connection meant that while anti-imperialist figures like Jawaharlal Nehru sought to fulfil the liberal promise he thought characterised Britain's mission in India, others like M.K. Gandhi saw liberalism as itself part of a system of colonial oppression.

Precisely because they were colonial subjects, however, and thus deprived not only of political responsibility but also forbidden to use its terms, nineteenth-century Muslims under British, French or Dutch rule were compelled to think about liberalism in cultural or religious terms. Indeed, by minimising if not eliminating pre-colonial forms of profane or monarchical authority, and excluding the use of political language, to say nothing of political demands among its subjects, the colonial state ended up expanding the role played by Islam in the societies it ruled. But even the few independent Muslim powers, like the Ottoman Empire, seem to have encouraged the making of liberal claims in the name of Islam once they became self-consciously modern or Europeanised—with the state-sponsored pan-Islamism of the Sublime Porte, for example, understood as a project of Muslim unity and equality in the face of rival claims to Christian as much as Muslim loyalties by European empires.

Such independent countries as Turkey and Iran also appropriated liberal forms of politics during their respective constitutional reforms and revolutions of the nineteenth and early twentieth centuries, although these struggles to delimit executive power or guarantee citizenship rights did not necessarily entail European-style secularism. Indeed, these constitutional movements have arguably informed 'religious' parties more than 'secular' ones in both countries.[11] Whatever this tells us about the more general relationship between religion and liberalism, in much of the Muslim world it implied the largely theoretical and in fact exegetical adoption of liberal ideals among Muslims, with great debates occurring over ostensibly irrelevant issues like the status of women or slavery in the Qur'an, jihad as a purely defensive war hedged by various rules, the republican form taken by the early Caliphate, and so on.

For a variety of reasons, then, liberalism became a subject of cultural and religious, rather than political debate among a number of colonised Muslim intellectuals. It might even be the case that these men discussed liberal values more intensely than their Christian peers in Europe and America, not least because Islam—like Catholicism in earlier times—was often seen as posing a kind of obstruction to modern forms of polity. Today, we seem to have returned to this situation, except now the cultural-religious focus of liberal debate has the postcolonial development of Islamic states and forms of militancy as its context—to say nothing about the 'War on Terror'.[12] But it is also possible to argue that this mode of thinking about the possibility, or failure, of liberalism in the Muslim world results from the fact that its values have never, since colonial times, possessed a political dimension but only ever a cultural-religious one. In other words, while Islam has been shot through with liberal ideas for nearly two centuries, the frequently 'secular' and authoritarian states in which it exists have not always been so, which of course makes the 'cultural' debate about Muslim liberalism a largely misplaced one.[13]

Despite all the ink spilt on describing Islam's 'political' character, not least by Muslims themselves, it is striking how lacking in politics its modern manifestations can be. Take Islamism, for instance, the most important form of political religion in our time. Of its three great founding figures, only Ayatollah Khomeini was able to establish a polity in the name of Islam, though he did so by subordinating the sacred law to the sovereign will of Iran's revolutionary leader, who was able to reinterpret and even supersede it for reasons of expediency or public welfare.[14] Whether or not it was made easier to accept by Iran's Shi'a faith, whose clergy claimed to represent the awaited Imam, this form of sovereignty was dynamic and embodied in the state. The Sunni founders of Islamism, Syed Abul Ala Maudoodi in Pakistan and Sayyid Qutb in Egypt, on the other hand, were deeply mistrustful of sovereignty, which they saw as a power that humans would wield to subordinate religion and impose upon their fellows various kinds of tyranny, whose lack of divine sanction would also force them to rely on violence.

Qutb and Maudoodi, then, sought to proscribe sovereignty's popular form in democracy (where people might decide to overrule scripture), monarchy or dictatorship (whose rulers would try to control Islam), and ideology (fascism and communism also aimed to subordinate religion). They conceived their task as being to limit and even roll back the inroads of the colonial state, as well as what they saw as its postcolonial successor, and to make of Muslim society a kind of self-governing entity guided by religious experts—almost a version of communism as the withering away of the state, or Gandhi's version of anarchism as self-rule. Maudoodi had in fact been an admirer of the Mahatma early in his career, and both men were much taken by Lenin's vision of a stateless society. This was why sovereignty had to be reserved for God, and the task of governance was simply to manage matters within the limited scope permitted by the sacred law. Clearly a non-political vision, despite its use of categories like state, constitution or republic, Islamism has in practice either had to work alongside dictators and dynasts, or act opportunistically and sometimes violently to claim a sovereignty it otherwise disavowed—being unable to theorise and so institutionalise it.[15] It might well be Islamism's attempt to evade or supersede politics, in other words, which makes it so open to the use of coercion and violence.

Islam's long-standing relations with liberalism in all of its many definitions, then, have been intimate for well over a century now, but they have also been politically very ambiguous. Indeed, if anything, this relationship has been defined by its cultural-religious, which is to say its non-political nature. But if this did not prevent Muslim thinkers from engaging with liberal ideas, neither has it stopped them from criticising these notions.[16] In the first half of the twentieth century, for example, the non-political or even anti-political desire for a stateless and self-governing society emerged from a creative engagement with anarchist or communist thought, as to some degree did Gandhi's contemporary vision of *swaraj* or self-rule. But by that century's end, the Islamist denial of sovereignty—or rather its reservation for God—was increasingly being interpreted in the newly dominant terms of neoliberalism, as a form of economic or social management shorn of old-fashioned politics. This is what seems to be happening in places like Malaysia or Turkey, as well as in Western Europe and North America, with their highly commoditised and market rather than family or state-regulated forms of Islamic identity and practice. In a different way, some of the Persian Gulf's principalities are increasingly imagined and run as corporations, responsible to various grades of shareholders rather than citizens. A society such as Dubai's, for instance, is supposed to be defined by its good governance, with such forms of 'Islamic law' as it upholds also defined non-politically as part of Emirati 'culture'.[17]

With Muslim migration to Europe and, to a lesser extent, North America, following the Second World War, Islam's engagement with liberalism shifted to include novel contexts in which Muslims were now also minority citizens within secular and liberal democracies, as well as being newly decolonised peoples in their countries of origin. And yet for many decades after large-scale immigration first began, starting in the 1950s to Europe and only in the 1970s to North America, it would be incorrect to identify these populations as Muslims in any strong sense. For while Islam was certainly their religion, it was not the primary category used to define these groups, either by the immigrants themselves or by the states in which they had settled. Instead, they were identified by nationality and race. This was particularly remarkable in countries like Britain and France, which in colonial times had frequently deployed religion to identify their subjects.[18] This all changed in the 1980s, in the aftermath of the Iranian Revolution. Especially important was the Rushdie Affair, which became the first global manifestation of Muslim solidarity and protest.

While the postcolonial predicament of Muslims produced a bifurcated global reality, dividing them by political geography initially in terms of nationality and race, and then by religion, ongoing developments in the meaning and import of liberalism in the West have complicated this picture. Foremost among these developments have been debates about the relative merits of 'multiculturalism' and 'assimilation', which have dominated European as well as North American public policy concerns about the ideological content of political liberalism. Meanwhile, in international relations, 'globalisation'— understood as shorthand for the rise or resurgence of classical or neoliberalism in the world economy—has been coupled with increasing military interventions in the name of liberal democracy, both in places like the former Yugoslavia, and in Muslim-majority countries like Afghanistan and Iraq. These issues have come to dominate Western foreign policy concerns and have had a significant impact on the self-images of liberalism.

Alongside these developments, liberal Islam emerged as a staple of scholarly and public debate, dating at least from the Islamic Revolution in Iran, and it has since gone through several iterations in meaning. During the 1980s, for example, Albert Hourani's reissued *Arabic Thought in the Liberal Age*, and Leonard Binder's *Islamic Liberalism*, focused largely on the legacy of the modernism of late nineteenth- to early twentieth-century Muslim reformers such as Muhammad Abduh and Rashid Rida.[19] The early obsession with rationality, and its often narrow, juristic character that preoccupied many of these thinkers during the colonial period, has also left a legacy among present-day Muslim liberals. While later theorists of Islamism, such as Maudoodi and Qutb, sought to apply the concept of God's sovereignty within the institutional context of the nation-state, this 'first wave' of Muslim liberals emerging in the nineteenth century had already begun to set the foundations for a synthesis of Islamic law and the liberal state.

It was only after the Cold War that Muslim liberals themselves came to the fore in scholarly and public policy debates. Among the more prominent have been Rachid Ghannouchi, Tariq Ramadan, Bassam Tibi, Abdolkarim Soroush, Farid Esack, Asef Bayat, Omid Safi, and Abdullahi An-Na'im. At the same time, the notion of an 'Islamic Reformation' has also gained currency in Western academic circles, where many Muslim liberals now worked. Since 9/11, questions about Islam's compatibility with liberalism have entered global public policy, media and scholarly debates in a far more encompassing way than ever before. While key events in the recent past, such as the fallout from the Rushdie Affair, had already given such questions renewed focus—including in regard to the growing communal demands of Muslims as religious minorities in the West—they have proved to be a mere prologue to the avalanche of interest in the relationship between Islam and liberalism since 2001. One could reasonably argue that the question of 'Muslim liberalism', its nature and limits, has become the principal conundrum underlying much critical discourse, scholarly or otherwise, in the Western public sphere.[20]

The rise of transnational forms of Islamist militancy in the twenty-first century—epitomised by al-Qaeda and, latterly, Islamic State (ISIS, ISIL, Da'esh) and their ubiquitous presence as existential threats to the liberal state in media and policymaking circles—has also significantly skewed discussion of the nature of liberal Islam as the necessary 'moderate' antidote to Islamist 'extremism'. It is because the discourse of liberal Islam has become so decisively subsumed by prevailing Western state narratives of 'counter-extremism' since 9/11 that its meaning has at once become both estranged from the complexity of its long history and constrained by the crude limitations of its present role in defeating terrorism. In this regard, the present volume also seeks to address the limits of Muslim liberalism as a variegated discourse and practice that has become identified with the perceived need for Muslims to tamp down on violence in the name of their religion. This has created a binary of 'Muslim liberalism versus Muslim militancy' where the construct of Muslim liberalism is inextricably tied to the security and stability of Western liberal democracies.

The intellectual hegemony of liberal Islam has also placed limits on any alternative, even nonviolent vision of Islamic thought and practice that challenges the liberal state. This has been in no small measure a consequence of the state's role in the construction of 'moderate' Islam and the immense governmental resources ploughed into the counter-extremism agenda, which has helped commodify it. This has also bolstered institutional orthodoxies that have little room for the free expression of 'heretical' religious tropes and impulses. In this way, rather than expanding the sphere of Muslim liberty, Muslim liberalism can act as a disciplining force, buttressing religious orthodoxy together with the authority of the state.

Islam's subordination to the political exigencies of the liberal state has had a peculiar influence on the historically non-political, or cultural-religious, implications of a belief in the pre-eminence of God's sovereignty. In the bifurcated political geography of global Islam today—where Muslims make claims on states in both majoritarian and minority contexts—we see a similar progression towards the assimilation of liberal democratic forms governing the language of political possibilities, from the evolution of the Muslim Brotherhood in the Middle East to the confessional claims of Muslim minorities in the West. It is in this sense that the disagreements reformist-minded Muslims—Islamist or otherwise—may have with liberalism belie the philosophical ground they share with it. For, even as they seek to synthesise, adapt to, or critique Western liberalism, they cannot exit its language and categories. In this way, Muslim liberals have accepted the institutional parameters of the West's liberal modernity (the state, rule of law, representative democracy, human rights) even as they seek to contest them.

Whatever their differences, Muslim liberals tend to regard state authority as a critical guarantor of a free society, and conceive Islam as being congruent with the values of secular liberal democracy. They also see Islamic religious authority, grounded in some institutional form, as being elemental to a virtuous Muslim society. The result has been that reformist trends in Islam today have become predicated largely on their correspondence with the political theory and practices of Western liberal democracies. This is the benchmark against which their realisation has increasingly come to be measured, and is evident also in recent scholarly works that seek to bridge 'Islam' and the 'West' through a synthesis between the political theories of Islam and liberalism.[21] This synthetic search for an Islam that accords with the broad ethical and institutional parameters of liberal democracy informs one of four related themes in the current volume, which seek to address Islam's engagement with liberalism and its limits.

Islam and the liberal state

The first of these themes has to do with the possibility of a Muslim politics beyond Islam's correspondence with the liberal state. Is the liberal-democratic state, in its variant forms, the inevitable end-point for any form of Muslim politics beyond violence? This is not, of course, what the early ideologues of 'political' Islam envisaged in their attempts to theorise Islam's relationship with the postcolonial nation-state. God's sovereignty trumped that of the people so that a secular compromise with the popular will was a conceptual impossibility. The way in which Islamist movements such as the Muslim Brotherhood have since evolved, towards the acceptance of certain key institutional practices of the liberal state such as popular elections and economic liberalism, may suggest, however, that Islam's journey towards liberalism is somehow inevitable. It is also fair to say that, despite disagreements over specific policies, Muslims in Western liberal states have largely accepted the parameters of liberal citizenship.

All this is not to assert that, beyond forms of Islamic activism that privilege violence, the vexed issue of God's sovereignty is now settled, and that Muslim politics have found a neat way of accommodating to political liberalism. There are several ways in which departures from this increasingly dominant narrative peddled by Muslim liberals suggest otherwise: in the resilience of non-political forms of Islam that focus on allegedly atavistic modes of religious piety in a society that remain 'quietist'; in anti-political currents of Muslim protest against both the centralising tendencies of Islamist parties and the encroachment of neoliberal ideologies; and in critical dissenters among liberal reformists who question conventional or dominant modes of liberalism.[22]

Critical departures from liberalism

The category of 'critical' or radical dissenters from liberalism leads us to a second underlying theme in the volume: Are Muslim critiques of liberalism themselves parasitic on Western critiques of it? And how have Muslim liberals attempted to co-opt non-violent but more radical forms of critique that question liberalism's premises? Forms of liberalism that trace their origins to the 'Enlightenment' have long been a focus of internal criticism in the West, focusing in particular on the hegemonic tendencies inherent in liberal conceptions of progress, reason, rationality and impartiality. Muslim critics situated within 'postcolonial', 'post-left' and 'critical' responses to liberalism draw on these Western traditions of critique.[23] In this way, it could be said that even in contesting liberalism's influence on Islam, intellectual possibilities for the Muslim world are still being read through a Western optic.

This intellectually parasitic relationship leads to alternative forms of Western intellectual hegemony, which have arisen largely as a by-product of the long-standing Euro-American critical engagement with liberalism and adapted to Muslim contexts. Thus, as if in direct dialogue with Andrew March's synthesis of Rawls and Islam, Wael Hallaq's *The Impossible State* draws on the correspondence between critical theorists and Islam.[24] This has also been evident in the adoption of Western anarchist and counter-cultural modes of critique by Muslims.[25] The difficulty in exiting Western liberalism, even when criticising it, points to underlying questions about Islamic authenticity that have reasserted themselves in the public sphere with force in recent years, and to which we now turn.

'Moderate' and 'extreme' Islam

The issue of what constitutes an 'authentic' expression of Islam has become tied inextricably to contending notions of 'moderate' and 'extreme' Islam since 9/11. While this division is largely a political construct driven by the domestic concerns of Western states, at its heart lies a deeper question about the core foundation of liberalism—that is, how 'free' are Muslims to be Muslim? In reflecting on the context of this question, it is no accident that the idea of 'subversion', so common during the Cold War, has again gained currency in Western policy circles. This has most recently expanded to include the emerging notion of 'non-violent extremism' in the UK.[26]

There is a double irony here. On the one hand, one of the main axes of debate about the liberal state in the West today concerns the public's perception of it as a surveillance state with increasingly authoritarian tendencies. On the other hand, it has sometimes been Muslim liberals who, in contesting jihadi terrorism by recourse to more traditional and centralised forms of

11

Islamic authority, have been complicit in aiding and abetting the growth of this surveillance state. The debate over 'moderate' and 'extremist' Islam is thus fundamentally about ownership, not only of 'true' Islam but over the very meaning of freedom. In this regard, conceptions of *Muslim* liberty and their multiple possibilities can be paradoxically constrained by the advocacy of liberals. To some extent, this far-reaching liberal narrative—which has come to determine Muslim 'authenticity' in the public sphere—has had the added effect of relegating much non-violent protest to the realm of aesthetics rather than politics.[27]

Islam and the language of liberalism

The problem of authenticity points to a more fundamental issue in addressing Islam's engagement with liberalism—the analytical concepts, language and prisms we adopt to make sense of this relationship. What, if anything, is distinctive about liberal Islam? Muslim liberalism is often described as the result of a happy coincidence between the values of Islam and those of the West (or, more specifically, the liberal-democratic state): cue the mining of Islamic intellectual, political and cultural history by Muslim liberals for the apparently abundant evidence of this entirely coincidental link.[28] Earlier, we discussed how, by universalising liberal precepts more comprehensively, Muslims exhibited the promise of liberalism more fully than their colonial masters. But this is not, of course, normally what Muslim liberals mean today when they talk of liberal Islam. Rather, what this juxtaposition of coinciding values reveals is the extent to which Muslim liberals have internalised Western narratives of liberalism—for they have come to see their progressive visions of Islam as assimilating, in some way, to a historically embedded and contingent Western liberalism.

Seeing liberal Islam as synthetic or composite, however, also suggests an active ideological process at work. This has often involved making comparisons stick between liberal concepts, such as consensus, consultation and rationality, and those deemed similar in Islamic thought, such as *ijma'* (consensus), *shura* (consultation) and *aql* (reason). In these practices, 'liberal' concepts unavoidably become the criteria through which to measure the value of 'Islamic' ones. This colonisation of Islamic thought by the language of liberalism also exposes the underlying ideological dimensions of liberal Islam—as a discursive construct that can be mobilised for a variety of ends in the service of divergent interests.[29]

Liberal Islam's ideological malleability may help us to understand how liberalism has been differentially adopted and adapted by Muslim reformist ideologues and movements. A common accusation levelled at Islamists, for example, is that they are 'double-speaking', using liberal categories instrumentally only to achieve the power to enforce shari'a, which is their ultimate strategic objective.[30] But this may have as much to do with the multi-textured, malleable nature of liberal concepts than with their abuse. Perhaps more importantly, however, it reveals how Muslim liberalism is inherently self-limiting, in that to do anything more than use liberal categories instrumentally in the service of Islam would be to diminish or annihilate its own essential or 'authentic' character.

The contributors to this book offer a spectrum of views and disciplinary approaches to the question of Islam's long-standing relationship with liberalism. They range from the historical and conceptual, to the contemporary and empirical. While the various issues that arise from this relationship have increasingly come to preoccupy policymakers, and the global media continues to be fixated by them, developments in academia have also mirrored, responded or else accommodated them. To this extent, the present volume might also be read in the context of ongoing debates about the nature of comparative understanding within, for example, the emergent sub-disciplines of global or world history and comparative political thought.[31] By offering some challenging alternative perspectives on the pivotal global relationship between Islam and liberalism, the volume aims to enhance our understanding of its nature, complexity and trajectory.

The book is in four parts. Part One, 'Origins', revisits the first wave of Muslim liberalism in the 19th and early 20th centuries, forged in the age of empire. These chapters offer new readings of the period that move beyond conventional historical accounts of intellectual developments in both the Arab world and British India. Part Two, 'Debates', explores some of the limitations of key concepts and themes associated with study of Islam in the West, both within and outside the academy. The chapters in this section address a wide range of methodological and interpretative issues and debates, and include historical, philosophical, sociological as well as ideological reflections.

Part Three, 'The State', offers a series of country- and region-focused case studies of the contemporary Muslim world (Indonesia, Iran, the Gulf, and America). Each chapter maps divergent local encounters with liberalism addressing state-citizen relations in the context of globalisation, and how liberalism has come to be refashioned by Muslims within their own particular socio-political and historical contexts. The final part of the book, 'Resistance', ends with a focus on the place of liberalism, its contestation and re-workings in Muslim counter-narratives to the liberal state, which also depart from conventional or orthodox narratives of Muslim resistance. From the politics of race and nation in the Nation of Islam, to art and aesthetic production as a form of protest in Pakistan, to the neoliberalism of 'Post-Islamism', these final chapters illustrate the variety of creative and critical engagements between Islam and liberalism that are covered in this volume.

ORIGINS

1

ARABIC THOUGHT IN THE LIBERAL CAGE

Hussein Omar

No scholarly work looms larger over the history of Muslim liberalism than Albert Hourani's *Arabic Thought in the Liberal Age* (1962).[1] Following Hourani, historians and lay commentators alike have located the origins and essence of 'Muslim liberalism' in the thought of the ascendant Egyptian bourgeoisie of the late nineteenth century. In particular, they focused on the ideas of the former mufti Muhammad 'Abduh and his disciples, including the lawyer Ahmad Lutfi al-Sayyid and the man Hourani celebrated as 'Egypt's first feminist', Qasim Amin. Even as assessments of the movement's merits or lack thereof have varied in the past six decades, scholars remain captive to Hourani's terms of analysis. While the historiography has imposed an ideal, archetypal liberalism on to these figures, shaping them into avatars of 'liberal Islam', this categorisation, as I will show, was predicated on a highly selective reading of their writing in isolation from their actions, obscuring the complexities of, and the contradictions within, their thought. And though some have issued empirical correctives to his work, Hourani's conception of liberalism itself remains unchallenged and the investments that shaped his canon have not yet been examined. As the story that Hourani told has become ever more entrenched, few have questioned the ideas, individuals and institutions it has come to eclipse. Hourani's text itself played a role in obscuring, as the introduction to this volume suggests, the more eclectic and heterodox aspects of nineteenth-century Muslim thought, as we shall see, which have sometimes been treated as inchoate or debased versions of more immaculate contributions.

Hourani has been rightly celebrated for overturning the 'patronizing, moralistic and essentialist Orientalist tradition of judging texts and their producers according to the most stringent criteria of Western "humanism" and "liberalism"', which, in Israel Gershoni's words, is 'an ahistorical, ideal-type kind of test that very few intellectuals in the West would have successfully passed'.[2] However, as unmoralising and unessentialist as Hourani's account was, it proposed an alternative ideal-type—where words were divorced from action, the sophisticated was favoured over the vernacular, and the complete and speculative was considered to the exclusion of the fragmentary and the practical—that now bears the weight of orthodoxy. Hourani's attempt to distil constitutive elements for liberal theory required him to guard the boundaries between political ideas (abstract, normative and lofty) and political practice (mundane, consequentialist, tactical). He considered the former worthy of study while dismissing the latter as belonging to the narrative history of events. This distinction between ideas and events is reflected in the types of sources Hourani used, favouring formal and abstract treatises over the fragmentary ideas embedded in newspaper articles, speeches, debates, diary entries and letters. It is precisely to the latter type of source that I will turn in order to complicate our picture of 'Muslim liberal' thought.

Aside from the fact that a normative split between political theory and political practice is patently Eurocentric—as it is a distinction virtually nonexistent in the Egyptian context—it has also created certain optical illusions. These include the assumption that political theory determines political practice, and not vice versa, which has led historians to overstate the importance and influence of a few 'great men'. Because Amin, for example, wrote in the recognisable and Eurocentric form of the treatise, which intellectual historians typically study, Hourani designated him the 'first feminist'. But Amin's ideas were not particularly novel, even if the genre he chose for them was; others had expressed similar ideas in various media for at least a decade before.[3] Such assumptions about theory and practice, I argue, have led historians to locate the essence of Muslim liberalism within the thought of the small, self-contained group of 'isolated men' known as 'Abduh's circle, bearers of a 'moderate' Islam.

It was the British proconsul in Egypt, Lord Cromer, who first referred to an 'Abduh 'school of thought'.[4] Cromer considered his 'friend' the shaykh to be an 'enlightened' religious scholar, 'animated with liberal sentiments', and his students to be no less than the 'Girondists of the Egyptian national movement'.[5] The proconsul expressed hope that the group would form an 'indigenous' bulwark against the ascendant double danger of fanatical pan-Islamism and Anglophobia.[6] As he was against direct colonial interference in matters of religion, Cromer argued that cultivating the 'moderate' (liberal, elitist and Girondist) Islam that 'Abduh represented was the only means by which the 'fanatical' (violent, populist and Jacobin) could be defeated, as I will examine in the first section of this chapter. Indeed, by the late summer of 1907, members of 'Abduh's circle including Lutfi al-Sayyid had established a political party that they called Hizb al-Umma. It stood in opposition to the group of nationalists whom Cromer and other British observers alleged to be 'fanatical'. This latter group, which soon formed its own political party al-Hizb al-Watani, was presided over by the charismatic lawyer–editor Mustafa Kamil until his untimely death in 1908. Its ideas were further shaped by the writings of the socialist Shaykh 'Abd al-'Aziz Jawish. For historians, the two groups have come to represent two irreconcilable 'schools' of nationalism and are seldom examined as part of a single intellectual tradition.[7] While Hizb al-Umma was 'moderate' or 'liberal', al-Watani was 'fanatical'; the leadership of Hizb al-Umma was enlightened, but that of al-Watani was 'violent'. Hizb al-Umma was secularising and progressively 'Egyptianist', while al-Watani was religiously inspired and regressively Ottomanist or pan-Islamic.

While Hourani lauded the liberal thought of Hizb al-Umma, revisionist historians have been less positive in their assessments. Scholars such as Leila Ahmed have seen in al-Hizb al-Watani a radical, authentically Muslim alternative to the 'derivative' and Western ideas of Hizb al-Umma.[8] Such scholars have linked the espousal of liberal ideas among intellectuals with socioeconomic and pecuniary ambition.[9] Having been enriched by British agricultural reforms, the bourgeois 'Abduh group had an interest in prolonging the occupation, which they did by promoting theories about Egypt's backwardness and arguing for the necessity of British tutelage until the country was ready for self-rule.[10] Scholars such as Walid Kazziha have further criticised these lackeys of liberalism for their elitism and their hopeless infatuation with the West.[11] In mimicking the European middle classes, Egyptian liberals asserted civilisational superiority over their social inferiors, while instrumentally advancing their careers. In doing so, they recycled and propagated orientalist representations of their people as backward.

Liberal reform, some scholars have argued, was no more than a cover for an anti-political, colonially sponsored 'official Islam' that denigrated and suppressed the mystical, 'traditional' faith of the subaltern population. The co-opted middle classes were the colonial state's native agents; they domesticated religion, disciplined bodies and reduced Egyptians into self-interested, monadic individuals.[12] Other scholars, such as Abdeslam Maghraoui, have objected that the norms 'liberals' propagated, despite their universalistic pretensions, were abstracted from a particular, parochial moment in Western European history and were therefore ill-suited to Egypt's 'culture'.[13] Ignoring the contingencies that generated those norms, bourgeois intellectuals attempted to impose them upon their own society, which they had come to regard as inferior and deficient. When their lower-class compatriots were not receptive, they disseminated their ideas by violent and necessarily 'anti-democratic' means, chastening their stubborn countrymen into docility.

Whether celebrating or condemning the figureheads of 'Muslim liberalism', historians have frequently advanced certain problematic assumptions. Sometimes they use 'liberal' as a euphemism for 'Western'. Often, scholars treat liberalism as a coherent and clearly delineated ideology with a set of essential traits, even if they disagree on what these are.[14] To capture its essence, which existed before 'its own self-conscious formulation', they created intellectual genealogies that retrospectively identified theoreticians as 'liberal'—without asking whether these men themselves would have recognised such accounts.[15]

What made the 'Abduh circle, in Cromer's words, a 'school of thought', and how precisely its ideas were different from those of its rivals, are questions that historians have failed to consider. Being a disciple of the mufti was no predictor of an individual's political proclivities, as we will see in the second section of this chapter in the gender debates provoked in 1899 by Qasim Amin. Attributing to these debates the paradigmatic essence of the liberal Muslim position retroactively, and to some extent arbitrarily, imposes lines of intellectual ascent and descent on people who actively denied such lineages.[16] It claims for historians a better understanding of the ideology they describe than 'those who played a fundamental role in its propagation'.[17] The notion that an "Abduh school' had a monopoly over such arguments, and produced them by coherent speculation, obscures the fact that these ideas were becoming hegemonic among political actors of all classes, be they 'Abduh's friends or his enemies, landed aristocrats or ambitious lawyers, self-ascribed 'moderates' or 'extremists'. If one is to overcome the 'great man' model of intellectual history, it is necessary to see the so-called protagonists of liberal Islam as shaped by, and not exclusively the shapers of, the historical dynamics of their age.

As critical as political actors were of colonial modes of identification and representation at the beginning of the twentieth century, modern and contemporary historians have sometimes been less sceptical. This chapter rejects the uncritical acceptance by historians, with their taxonomical impulse, of forms of identification that have their origins in the colonial archive, and instead focuses on the modes of argumentation employed by historical actors themselves. The polemical labels that were first used by colonial administrators— 'moderate', 'liberal', 'fanatical'—would, in time, be adopted, subverted and deployed by Egyptians across the political spectrum. Classifying individuals as liberal or illiberal fails to distinguish between modes of self-fashioning and the doctrinal content of their arguments, obscuring the extent to which liberal arguments were made by many who did not identify as such. As I will show in the third section of the chapter, intellectuals made statements about the place of personal liberty in their political visions that are seemingly at odds with how they have been categorised by contemporaries and historians alike.

Lutfi al-Sayyid, for instance, argued that national and personal emancipation was impossible to attain without the institution of full personal liberty, while thinkers such as Talaat Harb disagreed, arguing that it was to be achieved not by individual autonomy but by submission to God. How ought one to read these statements? Should they be interpreted as statements of belief, pointing to mutually irreconcilable visions? Did the former represent a liberal position and the latter an illiberal or even anti-liberal one? Using Saba Mahmood's characterisation of liberalism, which she claims is uniquely able to link 'the notion of self-realisation with individual autonomy', one might be tempted to argue that they did represent irreconcilable positions.[18] Yet those that made seemingly antagonistic statements understood themselves to be united in a single political struggle, and indeed Harb, whom Leila Ahmed refers to as an 'Islamist', went on to join the 'liberal' Hizb al-Umma. How do we make sense of this? As I will argue, it is only by rejecting the distinction between political thought and political practice—and its attendant requirement to partition text from action, to distinguish strategy from belief—that these apparent contradictions may be resolved.

This chapter also aims to show that intellectuals such as Lutfi al-Sayyid and Jawish were far from the hapless receptacles of colonial logics that postcolonial studies has often claimed them to be.[19] The relationship between liberalism and empire that appears as one of necessity in the work of Uday Mehta was already being intuited or posited by Egyptian political actors.[20] Far from recycling the ideas they sought to overturn, intellectuals responded to and refuted the powerful colonial representations of the 'subject races'—allegedly fanatical, self-interested, greedy—of which Egyptians were considered the prime example. As these representations were crucial to imperial governance, anticolonial thinkers recognised the need to engage in a subtle process of subverting them: appropriating the words of colonial elites, overturning their logics and investing their pronouncements with novel meanings. By doing so, anticolonial activists tirelessly set out to topple the racial hierarchies that cast long and dark shadows over their lives.

Such activists understood that there could be no repudiation of the hegemonic imperial project without a rethinking of the basic metaphysics of humanity upon which it had been erected. Their contemplative passages on the Qur'an and human nature were not just the facile, spiritual musings of oriental mystics, but rather essential to the process by which they began to imagine novel political alternatives to those of imperial hegemons. As I will discuss in the final section of the chapter, through the rewriting of apologetic and sacred history, they imagined a new de-essentialised subject. In this way, Egyptian intellectuals articulated many of the key insights of a postcolonial critique of Eurocentric modernity over half a century before these ideas appeared in the academic field of postcolonial theory.

Moderates and fanatics

The notion that topical debates, such as those surrounding women's rights, could capture the essences of duelling visions of Islam—whether liberal, modernist and moderate, or radical, conservative and fanatical—has its origins in the colonial archive itself. Muslim 'moderation' and 'fanaticism' were polemical labels that were first used by British officials to identify their friends and enemies, and were later adopted by Egyptians themselves.[21] In order to understand their limitations as characterisations of the political debate, one must turn to the contentious moment that produced them.

The representation of Muslims as fanatical was foundational to the British project in Egypt. According to imperial officials, it was 'fanaticism' that prompted the 1882 British bombardment of Alexandria and the seventy-year occupation that followed. Had Britain been defeated in Egypt, 'the lives of Christians in *all* Mussulman states would have been in danger'.[22] According to Cromer, 'Urabi, the leader of the revolutionary movement, was a religious extremist and unconscious Jacobin who had aroused 'race hatred and fanaticism': as non-Muslims were murdered or fled the country, 'Urabi proposed that their property be confiscated and redistributed.[23] By contrast, the British state would act as a purely administrative 'machine': neutral, disinterested and, as such, solely capable of guaranteeing the safety and property of all Egypt's subjects.[24] By arbitrating fairly between the interests of the country's various socio-religious groups, Britain insisted that when its mission had been fully realised, Egypt's inhabitants would finally come to see that there had been no true conflict between them and their colonial overlords.

From the 1890s onwards, fanaticism was the chief mode through which Egyptian resistance to British reform—supposedly technocratic and apolitical—was interpreted. Cromer believed that the mass of Egypt's population were naught but political 'ciphers', 'too apathetic, too ignorant and too little accustomed to take their initiative to give utterance in any politically audible form to their opinions even when they have any'.[25] 'Islamism of the past and of the present' had created an amoral society built on 'unalloyed self-interest'.[26] Because they understood nothing but economistic self-interest—and as such were fundamentally apolitical—the peasants could be won over by the British through greater prosperity. Having suffered abuse at the flail of morally and financially bankrupt despots, the peasants would embrace British administrative reform as they realised it perfectly aligned with their own needs.[27] When it did not work out as planned, opposition to the reform programme was explained away as the product of irrational fanaticism or the self-interested malice of the middle classes. If fanaticism was the prism through which difference with, and opposition to, their rational economistic project was understood, 'moderation' became the term by which the British identified those who were quiescent to it. Lutfi al-Sayyid would write that the allegation of fanaticism was 'a political principle', equivalent to Britain's 'doctrine of free trade'.[28] The British invoked fanaticism to justify inhibiting the introduction of parliamentary institutions in the summer of 1906 and refusing to decrease the number of British troops in Egypt in April 1908, as well as to manipulate shareholder confidence in the Egyptian market after the crisis of 1907.[29]

It was in 1907, with the establishment of political parties, that 'moderacy' and 'fanaticism' entered the lexicon of Egyptian politics. Among the first to be established was Wahid Bey's Egyptian Liberal Party (Hizb al-Ahrar), which celebrated Cromer as the first just and merciful ruler 'since the days of Omar and Saladin'.[30] In its view, Cromer was a father to Egyptians who had 'given them personal and religious liberty, and [instilled] in the hearts of all liberal-minded individuals, a debt of gratitude ever-lasting'.[31] The Egyptian Liberal Party's explicit mission was to battle the 'mischief' of the nationalists, whose 'dangerous propaganda' had 'aroused racial and religious animosities'.[32] Behind the 'veil of Pan-Islamism and patriotism', their incitement turned Egyptians against each other as well as 'against the Occupation', threatening to undo its good deeds and catapult Egypt back into 'that state of tyranny, corruption and despotism which prevailed prior' to it.[33]

Prompted by the establishment of the Egyptian Liberal Party, various political groups issued manifestos, drew up bylaws, and opened formal membership within weeks. As they attempted to distinguish themselves from their rivals, political actors engaged with the taxonomies that had long been used to describe them. Although the two main parties had for some time existed as informal groups—Kamil's group used al-Hizb al-Watani to describe themselves in the mid-1890s, and 'Abduh's disciples had been called Hizb al-Imam (Party of the Imam)—it was only in 1907 that they formally established themselves as political parties. Observers, then as now, have often confused the Egyptian Liberal Party with Hizb al-Umma on the grounds of the latter's self-proclaimed 'moderacy', a word that is, and was, sometimes used as a synonym for 'liberal', but there were important differences between their ideas. Hizb al-Umma declared a moratorium on discussing the relative benefits and drawbacks of the occupation, even though within less than a year it would become stridently anticolonial.

While Wahid Bey adopted the language of liberalism, making it synonymous with pro-imperialism, and while the Hizb al-Umma described itself as 'moderate', the National Party proudly embraced the label of 'extremism'. Kamil expressed contempt for his adversaries' 'moderation'; it was but a distraction that merely reinforced the British discourse of Egyptians' fanaticism. Nationalists were accused of extremism, Kamil explained, 'because we claim the rights and the independence of Egypt', and 'we remind England of ... her promises and her pledges'.[34] In Kamil's view, the label of 'extremism' was being used to silence the movement. If they continued to be labelled as extremists simply for calling for independence, then true nationalists must proclaim their 'pride' in the name and hope that all Egyptians would become extremists as well.[35] Kamil derided Hizb al-Umma's self-identification as moderate as a euphemism for 'fear, cowardice, falsehood and the employment of two attitudes, two policies and two tongues'.[36] Moderacy was a 'dolorous humiliation' that was breaking the nation into factions.[37]

If 'moderacy' and 'fanaticism' were above all polemical modes of identification, not characterisations of antagonistic political ideas, how might we better conceptualise the differences that sometimes made the two parties into bitter rivals? This is no easy task, for even those most intimately acquainted with them found it difficult to articulate their disagreements; indeed, days after Hizb al-Umma announced its programme, accusations flew in the Watani newspapers that they themselves had advocated the same programme all along.[38] Despite his party's reputation for harbouring revolutionary intentions and pan-Islamic proclivities, Kamil was as unequivocal as his 'moderate' rivals in his rejection of both. He considered revolution to be illegitimate even if directed at legitimate ends; the 1882 uprising was treasonous, although it had risen in defence of Ottoman sovereignty.[39] Accusations that his party hoped to spark a revolution were merely enemy propaganda.[40] Kamil's view was strikingly similar to that of his adversaries. In the newspaper *al-Garida*, his rival Lutfi al-Sayyid explained that he did not reject revolution on theoretical but on pragmatic grounds. The failed Russian and Persian uprisings taught that revolution should be avoided, for its likely failure would merely result in more oppression and enslavement, setting back Egypt from its goals.[41] Kamil claimed that along with being labelled 'revolutionary', his party had been slandered with accusations of espousing pan-Islamism.[42] Yet '[driving] out the English in order to surrender our country to Turkey as a simple Turkish province' was anathema to him. The notion that the Egyptian people 'merely wish[ed] to change masters and not to win independence' was an insult.[43] No educated Egyptian would espouse 'replac[ing] one yoke by another', for this would hinder the development of 'a national consciousness' and condemn the Egyptian people to further slavery.[44]

Al-Hizb al-Watani continued to espouse nonviolence after Kamil's death. Shaykh 'Abd al-'Aziz Jawish, who became the party's chief ideologue and editor of its newspaper, *al-Liwa'*, has been considered—by colonial officials and historians alike—the personification of the 'violent', 'religiously fanatical' politics of the Watanists. Yet this 'extremist' would maintain his predecessor's line on nonviolence, even if he had a voyeuristic fascination with assassinations, armed struggles and revolutions elsewhere, such as the Committee of Union and Progress (CUP)'s takeover in Turkey and the assassination of Curzon Wyllie in India. Watching them from afar, Jawish judiciously avoided incitement to such anti-imperial action at home, even if the British constantly accused him of doing so. Jawish, despite being characterised by Hourani as a 'violent orator', argued for 'Peaceful War'.[45] For Jawish, recent global action—such as the Swadeshi movement, or the Chinese boycott of American goods[46]—demonstrated that Egyptians could still attain 'all that they desire by peaceful means, without requiring the destruction of lives and the tainting of the earth with human blood'.[47]

If not through an appeal to moderation or violence, revolutionary intentions or pan-Islamist proclivities, how then can we conceptualise the differences between the two parties? The picture is complicated by the mistaken notion that Hizb al-Umma was merely a formalisation of the school of thought espoused by 'Abduh's disciples. That 'Abduh's circle had previously described themselves as 'Hizb al-Imam' (Party of the Imam), morphologically similar to *umma*, adds to the confusion. As much as it might have given Hizb al-Umma legitimacy for it to seem identical to, or descended from, the imam's 'school', such a claim had little basis in reality. On a purely empirical level, a tight connection between the "Abduh school' and their political affiliations is difficult to establish. For instance, some of the individuals most strongly opposed to the anti-veiling position would become members of the 'liberal' Hizb al-Umma, and some critics of the veil would join al-Hizb al-Watani. Talaat Harb, Amin's most fervent 'Islamist' critic, did not join the allegedly religiously inspired al-Hizb al-Watani Party, but instead became a member of Hizb al-Umma and a columnist for its newspaper. By contrast, Jawish, also an 'Abduh disciple, did not join the political party purported to represent 'Abduh's ideas but its rival, al-Hizb al-Watani.

The notion that Hizb al-Umma was the political expression of the 'Abduh school is a powerful myth. Even those figures whom historians have assumed to be the chief ideologues of Hizb al-Umma, such as Qasim Amin and Ahmad Fathi Zaghlul, had in fact fiercely opposed it.[48] Although his brother Sa'd Zaghlul rejected membership, a number of historians would later accuse him of having secretly supported it, exclusively on the grounds that he had been one of 'Abduh's closest friends and disciples.[49] Amin himself had in fact refused to join the party or subscribe to its paper, *al-Garida*, which he regarded with great suspicion until his death. Belying the claims that Amin was a British lackey, which have circulated uncritically, we see that Amin expressed deep admiration for Kamil's politics, despite their disagreements over the veil.[50] Amin described Kamil's funeral, only two months before his own, as one of two moments in which he heard Egypt's heart beat: 'the spirit of solidarity [rose] brilliantly above the heads of people on the streets and roads'.[51]

Personnel aside, it is difficult to identify any distinct intellectual features of an 'Abduh 'school of thought'. Hourani alleged that the 'Abduh school was defined by its espousal of *ijtihād* (the rational interpretation of texts by laymen), rather than the *taqlīd* (tradition) of conservative clerics.[52] But 'Abduh's political critics used his methodological innovations (*ijtihād*) against him in order to reach perfectly opposite conclusions.[53] Sacred texts could have as many interpretations as they had readers; it was precisely *ijtihād* that had led Amin to read the Qur'an in one way and Harb to read it in another. It is very telling, for example, that when in 1906 Harb reissued his book on the necessity of the veil—the first edition sold out—he appended to it certain pro-veiling fatwas attributed to 'Abduh, who had previously been seen as the paradigmatic critic of the veil.

If 'Abduh's method and writings could be used to argue certain things and their exact opposite, it is only through a historiographical sleight of hand that the 'Abduh school appears as having a coherent and distinct ideology, and as evolving into Hizb al-Umma. This sleight of hand ascribes an unchanging essence to Hizb al-Umma and projects it backwards, not only concentrating the 'liberal' project in the hands of a few, but also granting them a monopoly over it. It postulates an insoluble connection between individuals' views on social issues such as veiling and their formal political affiliations. This link is presented as a logical necessity, even though it never appeared as such to its proponents. It also ignores the fact that an individual's politics may change, or appear to. It is to the apparent shapeshifting of one paradigmatic 'liberal,' Qasim Amin, that we now turn.

The liberation of Qasim Amin

Qasim Amin's *Liberation of Women* (1899) has been regarded as a foundational charter of the 'Abduh group, and by extension, of Muslim liberal thought. Amin, a pupil of 'Abduh who worked as a judge, had become somewhat famous for his 1894 book-length rebuttal of the Duc d'Harcourt's scathing tract, which had attributed Egypt's civilisational decline to Islam.[54] Amin repudiated d'Harcourt's claim that Egyptian women were enslaved by arguing that all 'that we as men can do, they women are able to do as well, as they do'.[55] While Amin's first book was widely acclaimed in Egypt, his second book proved controversial, for it now seemed to criticise Islam rather than defend it. In the *Liberation of Women*, Amin denounced the 'superstitious' customs of veiling and the segregation of women, which, he argued, made them singularly unprepared for mothering nation-building sons. Why had the venerable judge Amin seemingly backtracked on his previous political commitments? Why did he abandon the refutation of orientalist depictions of Islam and instead become a major propagator of them? Such concerns filled the

Egyptian press for months. The resultant furore unleashed by the book's pub-lication prompted over thirty ripostes; by Amin's death in 1908 he had been socially disgraced and politically ostracised by all but a very few.

One of his critics, Harb, the future father of economic nationalism, feared that Amin's text might not bring about the desired national emancipation but instead provoke further imperialist intervention. He argued that Amin's rep-resentation of Muslim women echoed those of European orientalists. Europe had long wanted to put an end to 'backwards' Muslim practices, he wrote, 'to bring the Eastern and Western worlds closer to one another' in order to make the former subservient to the latter. Harb pointed to the deposed khedive as a cautionary tale: Isma'il was so enamoured with Europe that he wanted Egypt to become part of it. He encouraged women to walk barefaced in the streets, so that there would seem to be less to distinguish Egypt from Europe, and in doing so, Isma'il set the stage for the country's colonisation.[56] As with the abolition of slavery in the Ottoman Empire, Europeans would claim that Muslim women were not free, as a pretext to forcibly 'liberate' them in the name of humanitarianism. Harb explained,

> You see ... the strange compassion they have towards Eastern women, and the ways they lament her situation. Despite [the rights she has according to the shari'a] ... they persist in believing that the Muslim woman is miserable, as though she had appointed them as defender of her rights, or as though they wanted all the world's women to become miserable and debased—due to excessive and broad liberties—like the [Western woman].[57]

It was only by maintaining cultural difference that Egypt could ward off further imperial incursions. Although Harb's book-length response would draw on religious texts, its stated mission was political.

Another of Amin's most scathing critics was al-Hizb al-Watani leader Mustafa Kamil. But Kamil's objection was neither to Amin's orientalism nor to his hidden class motivations (as Leila Ahmed has suggested), but to the 'absolute liberty' that he advocated.[58] Kamil was appalled that Amin's support-ers thought that 'the freedom of women, with whatever harm it brings—even adultery—is preferable to the oppressive veil'.[59] He countered, 'Freedom that kills honour is by far more evil than a veil which kills vice.' It was better, he claimed, 'for a man to feel that he is dying and being buried than it is for him to see a female relative ... committing adultery'. Comparing Egypt with the United States, Kamil concluded that 'the freedom that women know there is not appropriate for Egypt and other Islamic nations because of the difference in manners and customs between them'.[60] Kamil did not foreclose the possibility of women's emancipation entirely; he suggested deferring it until women and men, through proper education, were morally equipped to handle it, and the state became powerful enough to maintain morality and regulate relations between the sexes.

Historians have described Amin's argument as liberal and that of his opponents as illiberal. For some, like P.J. Vatikiotis, Kamil represented a stubborn, residual, irreformable Islam, while Amin presented a radical, regenerative possibility. For Leila Ahmed, inspired by Frantz Fanon and Edward Said, the reverse was true.[61] Ahmed argued that the debate was fierce not because Amin's books were radical or progressive—arguments about the necessity of educating women had been made for at least a decade—but because Amin was recycling orientalist claims about Muslims, as well as calling for the transformation of Muslim society along the lines of a Western model.[62] Speaking in a 'native' (and upper-middle-class) voice, Amin merely indigenised long-held orientalist beliefs about Egypt's cultural inferiority, of which the veil had become the most recently charged symbol. Amin was not only a 'son of Cromer and colonialism' but 'thoroughly patriarchal' as well.[63] 'Unfortunately,' Ahmed writes, 'his assault on the veil' represented 'the internalization and replication of the colonialist perception.'[64] Amin thus merely reproduced, unwittingly, the categories and logics of knowledge that had made colonial power possible and imaginable in Egypt.

Ahmed's account, however, does not explain why only five years after Amin staunchly defended Islam in 1894, he would then appear to attack it. Scholars have never considered why Amin might have accepted certain aspects of orientalist representation while rejecting others. It seems implausible that having devoted such celebrated energies to repudiating European representations of Islamic backwardness, Amin would suddenly begin to repeat the forms of thinking that he had forcefully rejected not long before. This seeming change in position requires explanation. It is clear that this was no mere slip of the intellect.[65] It is also clear that Amin's switch from defender to condescending critic of Islam could not have merely been a ploy that allowed the author to ingratiate himself with his colonial overlords. There is little in Amin's biography to suggest he had reason to abandon his previous intellectual commitments so dramatically. In other words, there must be some underlying coherence to Amin's project, some internal logic to his work.

That Amin wrote his first book in French and his second two in Arabic provides one clue to understanding that logic. It is not just that Amin had two very different audiences in mind, but that he understood something profound about the relationship between power and knowledge that had made possible certain forms of imperial rule. I am suggesting that Amin intuited the tremendous import of simultaneously rejecting orientalist representations that legitimated colonial rule in Egypt, while also insisting on the importance of self-critical reflections on his society. That he did so in different languages suggests, to me at least, that the author was being carefully strategic. He did not want his self-critical thought to be abused, for pernicious ends, by Egypt's foreign critics, who might use it as evidence of the country's backwardness as they advanced their own political agendas.

Scholars who have insisted that Amin's liberal position was anti-nationalist have treated Kamil's response to him as genuinely nationalist. Ahmed, for example, argues that Kamil represented a more 'authentic' feminism, one that was truly anti-imperial and grounded in the Islamic heritage.[66] But an examination of his line of argumentation shows greater intellectual intimacy between Kamil and Amin than has been acknowledged. And further, Ahmed's argument can be sustained only through a very partial reading of Kamil's thought. In his voluminous writings, speeches and letters, one can see that Kamil's ontology was not fundamentally different from Amin's. He did not oppose Amin's social Darwinist claims nor his racio-civilisational hierarchies. Moreover, both men shared a belief in their nation's backwardness, even if they disagreed on how to overcome it. In other words, Kamil too accepted some of the basic premises of orientalist representation. Furthermore, it is unclear why Amin's anti-veiling position should have the particular class valence that Ahmed and Walid Kazziha ascribe to it, since its fiercest critics belonged to the exact same class as he did.[67]

The characterisation of Kamil's thought as Islamic, in contrast to the secularising 'Abduh circle, ignores the fact that Kamil asserted the importance of cultural difference, not theology. Kamil's 'Islam' was a disenchanted mode of communal identification, neither a faith nor a set of embedded ritual practices. Formulated in opposition to and despite colonialism, it appeared to emerge from the depths of an immaculate and inviolate past. Yet Kamil's notion of Islam as a culture—a set of manners and customs—owed as much to colonial thought as did Amin's. His insistence on conditionally deferring the liberation of women until his compatriots were sufficiently educated was a disagreement not with Amin's aims, but with his process. Like his rivals, Kamil believed that political emancipation could not be achieved until man emancipated himself from his passions. It was only through the mastery of one's desires and habits that man could become rational and therefore truly liberated. As I will explore in the next section, far from being illiberal, Kamil's argument and its underlying assumptions were similar to those of his critics, even if his conclusions were fundamentally different.

The debate surrounding women's emancipation cannot illustrate the unbridgeable divide between 'liberal' and 'illiberal' varieties of Islam; rather, what it does suggest is that a notion of a 'liberal Islam', defined as a series of topical stances—such as against veiling or polygamy—rather than as a procedural mode of political argumentation or abstraction, might obscure more than it illuminates. It risks muddling the content of intellectuals' ideas with their political positions, confusing our own analytic categories with theirs, and ultimately reproducing polemical taxonomies that belong to the colonial archive.

The metaphysics of freedom

Though they disagreed on many issues, Hizb al-Umma leader Lutfi al-Sayyid and his al-Hizb al-Watani counterparts Kamil and Jawish shared a deep concern with metaphysics. While these preoccupations appear to confirm Partha Chatterjee's oft-repeated claim that anticolonial nationalists operated, above all, in 'the domain of the spiritual', on closer examination it becomes clear that such 'spiritual' meditations were inseparable from their concerns with the 'material'.[68] In other words, the anticolonial activists' extensive investigations into human nature were necessary for beginning the process of imagining alternative political futures to those mapped out by the British. All three men understood that the Cromerian economistic project, which posited self-interest as the fundamental and universal principle upon which to erect a political order, could be rejected only if the notion of human nature upon which it was predicated was itself reconsidered, refuted or reimagined. For all three, even realism about politics needed metaphysical consideration, because it was predicated on coming to terms with man's true nature and his inevitable tendencies.

Like Harb before them, these three intellectuals turned to the topic of slavery—abolished in Egypt during their lifetimes—to articulate their ideas on the metaphysics of Muslim freedom.[69] According to colonial administrators, both slavery and 'the problem of women'—clearly linked in the writings of Harb—were the domains in which Muslims' alleged barbarism was most manifest; discussions of these two topics, in turn, became the basis upon which Muslim intellectuals made their case for political sovereignty. All three intellectuals argued that a man could not willingly agree to be a slave, for man was a mere custodian of his freedom, the true ownership of which was God's alone. To give away one's freedom to a master or king—or even to the state—was thus a blasphemous act. On the basis of this claim, they opposed any form of liberal argument that valorised procedure over content, arguing forcefully against a belief that illiberal actions could be tolerated so long as they were shown to be procedurally liberal.[70]

For Kamil, the author of an 1892 treatise on Roman slavery, it was the Abyssinians' successful resistance against the Italian invasion of 1895–6 that demonstrated beyond doubt that freedom was not something that could be taught or learnt but was, rather, inborn in all humans. The proof, according to Kamil, was that the Abyssinians were neither tutored in 'Western science and education' nor civilised, unlike the Egyptians, who had been exposed to modern forms of knowledge for at least a century.[71] This was unequivocal evidence that the will to freedom was not nurtured but innate and that British claims to the contrary ought to be rejected. It was these very same claims about Egyptians' servile nature that had provided the British with a discursive ploy to further justify the former's enslavement.[72]

While Kamil's argument was generated by secular history, his successor, Jawish, would make a similar set of claims through theology. Born in Alexandria in 1876, Jawish succeeded Kamil as the editor of the nationalist organ al-Liwa' in 1908.[73] It was during his time as lecturer in Arabic at Oxford that Jawish first encountered bigotry against Islam. In response to his Oxford students' characterisation of Islam as a religion of slavery, polygamy and divorce, Jawish formulated the book-length apologia *Islam: The Religion of Freedom and Instinct*.[74] Drawing upon history and theology, Jawish forcefully argued against hegemonic colonial claims that Muslims were slave-like as a result of their particular racio-cultural constitution. His anti-orientalism, like that of Lutfi al-Sayyid, was closely linked to a particular political project, one that rejected the racial hierarchies of colonial rule that understood Egyptians to be essentially and constitutionally irreformable. Indeed, he and Lutfi al-Sayyid both understood that the orientalism of Lord Cromer had successfully disguised a prescriptive project of political subjugation in the clothes of a value-neutral description. Both intellectuals realised that to change the world, they first had to describe it anew.

For Jawish, Islam did not 'contradict human instinct'; rather, it was the purest reflection of it.[75] As a pedagogue, Jawish contended that it was bad forms of acculturation which, like religiously prohibited acts of bodily mutilation, alienated children from their instincts. Were a child 'left alone without

Judeo-Christian acculturation ... he would find himself, by his instincts, Muslim'. For this reason, he argued, 'Islam considers children—even those born to non-Muslim parents—to be Muslim until they reach an age old enough to make their own choices.'[76] The initiation of newborns into Christianity, Judaism or Zoroastrianism is done without their consent; and, because Muslims view sin as uninheritable, these children could not be held accountable for their parents' bad choices.[77] Only a free adult choice would count as an act of apostasy.

History could prove what theology could only theorise. Beginning with a discussion of Socrates' method—he believed its true heirs were the Muslim mystics—Jawish explained that the pre-Christian world was tolerant and religiously plural. It was Constantine's conversion to Christianity that had inaugurated a long era of repression.[78] After Constantine, Christians came to employ horrifying methods of punishment, from inquisition to impalement, to prevent apostasy. Their popes opposed the most enlightened of thinkers—Copernicus, Rousseau and Voltaire—and burnt their books in public. But a fortuitous brush in the twelfth century with the teachings of the 'liberator of minds', the Qur'an, removed their 'veil of ignorance'.[79] The Christian world emancipated itself by embracing the ideas of Aristotle, which arrived via the Arabs, and those of Averroes, who insisted on the compatibility of faith and philosophy as different avenues to the same truth. It was the proximity of Europe to the people of the Qur'an that had led not only to the scientific revolution but to the Protestant Reformation. Islam had bequeathed Protestantism with its democratising tendencies—freedom, equality and anti-clericalism—not the other way around.

Invoking 'Abduh's distinction between a heavenly Islam as protected by God and secular life as corrupted by bad humans, Jawish argued that it was not the faith itself but some of its misguided followers that had allowed monstrous acts of human bondage to come into existence. One should not mistake the terrible habits of the Turks in the Caucasus or of the Sudanese, who 'capture slaves and display them in markets like animals', as reflecting anything about the faith itself.[80] Islam is 'innocent of the crimes' tyrants commit, Jawish wrote; it is 'pure of the abominations and profanities that they've plastered onto it', for its true mission was to protect the innate freedom of man. As a faith, it had made equal all nations, 'with no distinction between races or colours, offering total equality between black and white, the nomadic and the urban, flock and shepherd, men and women, Christians, Jews, and Muslims'.[81] By contrast, the 'Nazarene religion did not forbid the possession of slaves, and

33

throughout history Christian countries ... had no problem with enslaving whomever they wished and using them however they wished'.[82] According to Jawish, slavery in Christian lands became obsolete only once there was no economic benefit to be gained from it. Although these crimes 'existed in every age of ignorance' and in all civilisations, it was the white Christians of the United States who were responsible for the worst violations of all.[83] Having taken ownership over 'the black nation', they procreated with its members but refused to recognise their own offspring—as Islam would have forced them to—instead buying and selling them like livestock.

The critique of orientalist representation that appeared in Edward Said's 1978 masterpiece was already being expressed by anticolonial activists like Jawish half a century earlier. Writing decades before Jacques Derrida and Michel Foucault questioned the relationship between representation and domination that Said so famously articulated, Jawish interrogated that very same relationship upon which imperial rule rested. While this relationship often appears in scholarly works as a problem visible only to us as historians from the privileged vantage of the present, it was a central preoccupation of historical actors at the time. If Egypt had indeed been colonised by representation, then its decolonisation had to undo the relationship between the words and things upon which its colonisation had been premised. In doing so, Jawish was not engaging in a facile apologetic, but rather asserting that Muslims held the universal capacities for self-rule that his colonial oppressors persistently denied him. Although Jawish's polemical treatise took as its apparent subject North America, it is not difficult to see the parallels with the British state in Egypt. In an editorial of June 1908 that would earn him his eviction from Hourani's liberal pantheon, Jawish addressed a group of Copts:

> You have spent thirteen hundred years in a Moslem land, where you have increased and multiplied and waxed fat in wealth and riches. If for but one quarter of that time you had lived with the English, you would have become even as the Redskins of America ... If you were the lieges of King Leopold, the hair of your heads would have been used to make ropes with, your skins would have been turned into the soles of shoes, and your bodies would have been beaten with rods ... Had you been living in Ireland, the British would have discarded you like shoes and dragged you out of your houses, humiliated and oppressed.[84]

Nine days later, when Cossacks bombarded the newly elected parliament in Tehran, thereby ending Persia's three-year constitutional experiment, Lutfi al-Sayyid offered his own reflections on freedom. He wrote furiously against the shah's sword-wielding henchmen, who 'spilt the blood of innocents', people whose only sin was to demand that the nation be sovereign.[85] Those events—in which patriots were 'hauled into the depths of prisons like criminals'—intensified Lutfi al-Sayyid's beliefs on the nature of human liberty, which he had only tangentially articulated in the past. He argued along Jawish's theological lines that 'liberty is an innate gift granted by God to every individual', and therefore no 'human being can despoil another of his liberty'. The nation, as 'a collective of individuals', ought to be free. By extension, no individual in this collective can surrender his liberty, because to do so 'would imply possession in the first place'. Freedom, being the property of God, was not a human 'possession'. It was 'neither the property of the person in whom it dwells' nor that of anyone else. Consequently, no individual could voluntarily give it away. Lutfi al-Sayyid reasoned that 'Any such gift would be truly void ... In this way no king could claim that his people are slaves to him even if they give him their liberty as a gift.'[86]

Because man was merely the custodian of his liberty, to forsake it was, paradoxically, the one voluntary act that Lutfi al-Sayyid believed to be in principle illegitimate. Such practices of wilful enslavement were prevalent among all classes. Men behaved like 'salon dogs' that seek the approval of their masters, abandoning their beliefs simply to satisfy the authorities.[87] Accustomed to receiving instruction from above, had Egyptians lost the capacity to judge right from wrong? The tyranny of the khedive and his British accomplices was reflected in every single aspect of society, and therefore it was 'impossible to talk of social problems and political ones as distinct', Lutfi al-Sayyid argued, for one produced the other.[88] Egypt's educational systems interpolated political tyranny downwards into society, having been built on blind subservience.[89] In the *kuttāb* (mosque schoolroom), ignorant schoolteachers murdered their students' 'instinctive liberty' through insults and punishments; in the Jesuit schools, the masters forced boys to 'kiss the ground'.[90] This self-abasement could be overcome only through reviving the principles of the Muslim faith, by instilling submission to God and not to man.

Lutfi al-Sayyid wrestled with a dilemma: Would ending tyranny, through the immediate enactment of self-sovereignty, be sufficient as a means of emancipation, or would it merely expose Egyptians to the very same dangers—military and imperial—that had produced tyranny in the first place? Either way, he was certain that self-rule would be rendered meaningless were it not accompanied by a programme wherein individuals would learn to rule their passions. By 1907, it had become clear that the colonial state could not be relied upon to enact any such programmatic reform in education, and had failed to accomplish its self-declared mission.[91] Instead of preparing Egyptians for self-rule, Cromer had 'create[d] graduates for government employment'.[92] How could schools create liberty-loving subjects if they were mere 'factories' for 'producing tools for the implementation of orders of their seniors in government'?[93] If the neglect of education was a tyrant's attribute, then Cromer was the most recent in a long succession of despots dating back to the pharaohs. Cromer 'did nothing to education but corrupt it'.[94]

In a review of *Modern Egypt*, Cromer's 1908 book, Lutfi al-Sayyid argued that Cromer had misdiagnosed Egypt's problems by attributing them to Islam. Employing the very same lazy methods of reasoning he ascribed to Egyptians, Cromer had made his claims about Islam after a few 'conversations with orientals'.[95] With neither evidence nor argument, Cromer merely parroted Stanley Lane-Poole's dictum that 'the Islamic religion' was a completely failed culture, concluding that it was 'not receptive to reform for it would not remain Islam after its reform'.[96] This put Egyptians in a bind, since by Cromer's logic a refusal to disavow their faith was akin to endorsing a state of perpetual pupillage under the British Crown. Further, Cromer's attribution of such 'Muslim malaise' had allowed him to endlessly defer the promise of self-rule. Egypt, Lutfi al-Sayyid wrote, had come to realise that the attribution of an abiding and defective subjectivity to Egyptians formed the basis of British arguments for the deferral of evacuation. Yet the malaise or dysfunction that gripped the country had been actively produced by colonial rule itself, not by some intrinsic feature of Egypt's racio-religious constitution. What appeared to be a pure description of an objective reality was now revealed to be a prescription for their continued political subjugation. The nation had now awoken to the truth 'unadorned': Britain's interests were irreconcilable with those of Egypt.[97]

Against Cromer, Lutfi al-Sayyid argued that there was nothing about the essence of Islam that was despotic. The conceptually confused proconsul had mistaken the actions of a few with the constitution and culture of the many, just like 'Mr. Gladstone and Montesquieu' before him.[98] Lutfi al-Sayyid attacked Montesquieu's claims that 'Christian religion strengthens moderate government' and that the 'Mohammedan faith strengthens despotism.' While Christianity does not specifically dictate how states should be governed, Christian clerics have historically facilitated tyranny: popes and priests declared the sacredness of kings, stifling their subjects, who were constantly told that 'good or evil is from God'. The only sustained political theory derived from the Bible was that of Jacques-Bénigne Bossuet, whose 'deformed politics' defended absolute monarchy on theological grounds.[99] Was that the 'moderate government' Montesquieu was referring to?[100] By holding up Montesquieu and Bossuet as exemplars of 'Christian' thought, Lutfi al-Sayyid gave lie to Cromer's belief that there was something essential about Christian civilisation that had led to a system of good government. It was only by butchering European history, by erasing Christian clerics' support for absolutist monarchs, that men like Cromer could sustain their ahistorical claims about the essential backwardness and irreformability of Islam. Islam was not the cause of tyranny, but the means by which one could attain salvation from it. 'Islamic democracy' was superior to that of Aristotle or Rousseau, Lutfi al-Sayyid contended.[101] It was precisely by re-educating Egyptians in the true principles of their faith that democracy could be achieved.

By insisting that it was contingency, not essence, and history, not nature, that had made Egyptians fallen in the past, Lutfi al-Sayyid asserted that they were reformable as subjects and would once more rise in the future. But it remained to be seen how the politician and his colleagues might go about convincing people of their true interests when they were seemingly unable to recognise them. Lutfi al-Sayyid observed:

> We see that each person calling for independence is educated. ... If education spreads then the necessary result will be that more people will call for it. Is it not then that education—assuming that independence will only happen when there is a critical mass of people calling for it—will be the sole cause for independence?[102]

But the current system of education—a 'factory for government functionaries'—inculcates self-interest, and the exchange thereof, in order to realise the colonial state's economistic vision for Egypt.[103] As Lutfi al-Sayyid observed, this mechanical production of functionaries and the transformation of human relationships into contractual ones would bring about neither self-rule nor happiness for the nation. One needed to extend one's ethnographic gaze across Europe to see the negative effects of political regimes that privileged self-interest. Lutfi al-Sayyid invited readers to compare English churches with Latin ones to see the effects of Britain's economism on Christianity. Anglicans stripped their churches of ornamentation, and of the love, forgiveness and compassion central to Catholicism. They imposed upon it a culture of exchange, contract and property, making all its interactions mercantile and harsh. The relationship between the shepherd and his flock had mutated into that of 'the coal merchant and his clients'. Lutfi al-Sayyid mused that prayers were 'like a business transaction, with neither confession nor forgiveness'.[104] It was precisely this regime of self-interest that had to be overcome.

Although labelled a 'classic liberal', Lutfi al-Sayyid strove to transcend liberal categories of self-interest and exchange.[105] And while he feared that socialism would lead to a new form of slavery, it was the colonial vision of economistic freedom of exchange and contract that he feared most acutely. He implicitly criticised Kamil and Jawish for denying the psychological power, and the irreconcilability, of individuals' inevitable tendency towards self-interest. Instead of denying the truth of man's selfishness, he argued, one had to harness its power, to align self-interests with national interests, so that the two would become indistinguishable. When individuals learn to rule their passions and attain 'the characteristic of self-autonomy', the autonomy of the nation would follow 'without delay'.[106] This was the sole guarantor against future tyrants.[107] It was an idea similar to Kamil's on the emancipation of women: individuals must first learn to master themselves through a process of ethical self-disciplining in order to make possible other forms of liberation. For both Lutfi al-Sayyid and Kamil, no tyranny was more dangerous than that of man's unruly, intractable, spirit. One might overturn any number of political regimes, but so long as man remained incapable of ruling himself, he would remain forever incarcerated, and thus a slave.

This view was fundamentally different from that of Harb, who embodied a line of nativist thought that insisted that Egypt's enemy was to be located externally, not internally. Harb had defended the prescription of the face veil because it clearly marked the difference between the Egyptian and her European mistress. An erosion of that difference would amount to an erosion of the Egyptian nation itself. Difference had to be continually reproduced, such that the line between Self and Other would not fade. But Lutfi al-Sayyid feared that Harb's nativist approach might effect an unravelling in the fabric of the nation. Would the nation remain intact if the enemy was defeated? Moreover, in a world in which the so-called sovereign was hamstrung by imperial imperatives, who could determine who the enemy would be? If it fell to the struggle of each individual, surely nothing but chaos would ensue. This was a perennial and constitutive problem within the tradition of Muslim political thought: Did the Qur'anic imperative of commanding good and forbidding evil fall on the individual or ought the task fall to some sovereign-appointed figure lest chaos ensue?

Critics of Harb's nativism argued that having a shared enemy was the only thing that made Egypt's diverse inhabitants become friends. But did the nation need to wait for a stranger to threaten its borders in order to rise 'like one man'? What if the true enemy was internal to Egypt and to every Egyptian, an enemy against whom he had to struggle daily? The commitment of *al-Garida*'s editors to the struggle against the self through a process of autocritique is captured in the quotation they printed beneath the masthead: 'He who carefully examines the truth and makes his peace with it even if it is painful at the first instance, will be happier when criticised by people than if praised by them.' The aphorism was a quotation from the eleventh-century Andalusian polymath Ibn Hazm, available to Egyptians in print since 1905.[108] It was the duty of the newspaper, self-critical and self-reflexive, to identify the internal enemy, which Lutfi al-Sayyid argued was self-interest, the crude egoism of every individual. Conversely, the public good was the common friend of all. The sacred union between Muslims and non-Muslims could only be born if each individual recognised that he harboured within himself the common enemy. It was only when man waged continuous jihad against his own inner antagonist that he would find oneness in the national body politic.

In Lutfi al-Sayyid's reasoning, although the nation was itself natural, national unity was not: it had to be continually produced and reproduced. Unaware as he might have been of the cultural construction that made imagined communities appear natural, Lutfi al-Sayyid understood that merely belonging to a community was very different from being willing to die in its defence, and he contemplated how the latter might be induced. To breed men who would willingly die for the nation, Lutfi al-Sayyid insisted on the necessity of a political education, for only then would the Egyptian subject truly understand where the public good lies, and sacrifice his life and property in the defence of the state.[109] He accused his opponents in al-Hizb al-Watani of valorising cultural difference between nations, and not sufficiently appreciating individual difference within the nation of Egypt itself. Lutfi al-Sayyid rejected the Watanist notion of the nation as a single party on the grounds of its disagreement with human nature. Of the phrase 'the nation is a single party', he wrote, 'there are no words more beautiful'. But this was an unrealisable ideal: those that demand that '12 million must think as one' were surely 'ignorant of human nature'. Even as all Egyptians were united by the love of a single goal—independence—they were so different in nature that it was impossible for them to achieve those ends as a single party.[110] Lutfi al-Sayyid celebrated the eclecticism that formed individual desire: some princes willed large fortunes to their cats; a pasha willed a large sum of money to the dogs of Istanbul; Alfred Nobel created a place for people to commit suicide free of pain or torture.[111]

These examples of human difference were evidence for him that the struggle to produce a national unit had to come from within. Each individual had to wrestle against his internal agonist, since any externally imposed unity would entail a degree of coercion. It was only through internal struggle that the nation could come into being. In contrast to tyranny, which caused servility, Lutfi al-Sayyid argued that the internal struggle against one's ego ought to be celebrated. Invoking the mystical ideal of losing oneself in God, he praised the Sufi who 'drowns in horizons much greater than his own', ridding himself of the 'filth of the material' in order to enjoy the purity of nakedness. It was in this way that an individual should relate to the nation, such that he would become a servant to it. He had to overcome his personal interests, forget and annihilate his Self for the interests of the corporate whole. Instead of denuding a man of his capacity to make moral judgements—as enslavement was bound to do—it allowed him to transcend the pursuit of 'lowly and common pleasures, and replace them with eternal beautiful ones'.

The exemplar of this practice for Lutfi al-Sayyid was his old friend Qasim Amin, who, in the first of his two controversial Arabic works, had emphasised the importance of internal jihad. Amin was the paragon of this daily battle waged against personal interest in favour of the common good:

> Qasim Amin ... was a Sufi in his beliefs ... I have not seen or read a writer as great as him, someone who leant towards the sacralisation of love or the extolment of adoration to the same extent as did Qasim's delicate and sensitive soul, which would lose itself every day in the attempt to make sense of this unknown truth, such that he became a believer in platonic love [al-hawā al-'udhrī], which is evidence for the nobility of his spirit and a step on the route to perfection ...[112]

Comparing Amin to 'Umar ibn Abi Rabi'a,[113] Lutfi al-Sayyid writes that nothing could be veiled—an appropriate metaphor for a man devoted to unveiling—from his sharp gaze. His blazing thought could illuminate that which was murky. Amin believed that the truth of human knowledge always contained error, just as error always contained some degree of truth. As a judge, Amin was as deeply committed to understanding human responsibility as he was to understanding culpability. As a result of his profession, he believed that attributing responsibility correctly was difficult, and in fact beyond human capacity, because man could never be entirely autonomous. Instead 'human beings inherited their akhlāq [ethics], their nerves, their tarbīya [upbringing], their belief (its strength or weakness), and all the psychological conditions that make a sinner commit a sin'.[114] After many years, Amin concluded that 'forgiveness' was the single means towards human perfectibility, and ought to be the chief goal of one's upbringing.

In his description of Amin, and in other passages, Lutfi al-Sayyid conceives of ethics not as a set of regulatory norms or ideas, but as a set of activities embedded in a communitarian way of life. It is thus unsurprising that, once retired from political life, Lutfi al-Sayyid would go on to translate Aristotle's *Ethics* as well as his *Politics*. Indeed, contra the claims of post-secular scholars such as Talal Asad, modernist Muslims like Lutfi al-Sayyid did not advocate the replacement of 'Kantian' notions of moral autonomy in place of an 'Islamic' neo-Aristotelian communitarian model.[115] Instead, they recognised that the anticolonial struggle could not be fought against colonial hegemons' representations of their subjects alone, but required a fundamental rethinking of the categories of self and self-interest on which the very representations had been constructed.

Lutfi al-Sayyid ferociously argued against the claim that Egypt was mimicking Europe. He noted that many of his countrymen had 'mocking' and 'tepid' responses to the establishment of political parties, which he attributed to their belief that participation in political life or membership in parties was 'but an imitation' of civilised nations, and thus somehow inauthentic. 'If,' Lutfi al-Sayyid explained, 'this were an artificial movement, the members of this party would have failed in their meeting and the goals to which they aspire would have collapsed', since nature only allows what is natural to survive.[116] The historical march towards political modernity, as he saw it, was universal. It was not particular to Europe, as many an orientalist has insisted, and indeed Lutfi al-Sayyid pre-empted a rebuttal to the claim—advanced by postcolonial scholars such as Chatterjee—of the 'derivativeness' of anticolonial nationalism.[117] It was imperial rule that was unnatural, since it interrupted that inevitable march. He therefore came to oppose British imperialism not because it had transformed the Egyptian everyman, contra Timothy Mitchell's claims, but precisely because it had not.[118] He and Qasim Amin agreed that Egyptian law had provided the platform for full political liberty. But the British government was predicated on a notion of negative liberty—the absence of external restraints to action—rather than on a positive project of disciplining Egyptians' minds and bodies such that they may be equipped to take up the reins of self-rule.

For both Lutfi al-Sayyid and Amin, full emancipation could not come about simply through the institution of some new legal regime.[119] An imperial project of moral betterment could not succeed through the instrument of the law alone. What was needed was a sweeping educational and moral disciplining; only this, and not the law, would unlock Egyptians' inner capacities. Both intellectuals rejected the notion that the law could provide secular redemption or salvation, contrary to Samera Esmeir's recent claims.[120] Indeed, far from endorsing the law as an instrument of moral reform, Amin, Lutfi al-Sayyid and others pointed to its very limits. It was not enough for British colonial administrators to proudly declare that they had granted the Egyptians absolute personal liberty, Lutfi al-Sayyid reasoned. The package of reforms that had named personal liberty as the objective had largely been successful; so much so that the parents of young men had decried the new freedoms as a form of fanaticism. Moreover, Egyptian laws were more lax than those of virtually any European country. For example, unlike German law, it did not forbid suicide. As Lutfi al-Sayyid explained, 'Where German law punishes attempts at suicide, Egyptian law allows man to do with himself as he pleases.'[121] But this form of liberty, nothing more than the absence of external impediments to action, was not sufficient. This 'fanaticism' for freedom in Egyptian law could never be a substitute for the programme of moral discipline that the government ought to undertake. It was only by 'devoting attention to political life'—not through the legal reforms aimed at personal liberty or the economic reforms for material prosperity—that a government could succeed in its self-avowed mission of preparing the nation for self-rule.[122]

The paradox of the liberal cage

When I speak of the 'liberal cage', I mean to convey that the questions asked and answered a century ago remain ineluctable to Muslims today. Early twentieth-century intellectuals were caught between two contradictory but equally powerful modes of colonial representation: one cast Muslims as essentially tyrannical and in need of liberation from themselves, and the other as lacking the will to be free and therefore unworthy of the rights guaranteed to their fellow men. Both of these claims had provided justification for imperial domination. In order to reject the forms of subjugation that they legitimised, intellectuals first needed to refute their substance. Then, as now, intellectuals found that they were incapable of wresting themselves from endless cycles of orientalist representation and refutation.

The figures examined here appealed to two antithetical strategies, with some figures vacillating between them. The first form of refutation argued that the lack of freedom in Islam was mere misrepresentation. Describing difference as deficiency, imperial agents universalised the parochial experience of the West and imposed it on the rest. This was precisely Harb's argument against women's desegregation. It is an argument that was revived, almost a century later, by Talal Asad, Uday Mehta and Saba Mahmood, among others.[123] Harb maintained that the cynical imperial impulses that hid behind a mask of humanitarianism—for instance, in the case of the abolition of slavery—ought to be resisted. Muslims' particular culture, theology and history should provide the basis for resisting the West's compulsion to make the world in its image. Even as Harb—and some would argue, Mahmood—implied that the slave did not want to be freed, such an argument was made, paradoxically, to advance the cause of national freedom.

Recognising that masters had long used the claim that slaves did not want to be free to justify their subjugation, intellectuals such as Lutfi al-Sayyid perceived that this first strategy, typified by Harb, was self-defeating. Most importantly, they argued that it was necessary to distinguish between the content of the values promoted and the 'concrete', nefarious imperial agents that advocated them. Individuals across the political party divides recognised that their unsatisfied demands—for representation, for access to education, for press freedom—could not be made in terms of particularity or Muslim difference but only by appeal to the universal rights shared by everyone, yet from which, they correctly pointed out, their people had been excluded. Instead of denying the validity of such rights wholesale, they highlighted the incoherence of limiting universal rights to particular subjects. Muslims were not foreign to the universal desires—such as that for freedom—shared by their European counterparts, and as Kamil argued, any denial of this universal desire would merely reinforce the claims that had made colonialism possible in the first place.[124] Despite Cromer's assertions to the contrary, Islam was a faith, not a culture, and therefore a reformed, 'liberal Islam' was no ontological impossibility.

These two responses, when taken out of the imperial context that produced them and divorced from the hegemonic claims against which they were formulated, suggest substantive disagreement about the metaphysical nature of man upon which a political vision should be built. The first response claimed that Muslim happiness was not realised by freedom but by submission to God, whereas the second argued that Muslims—like their brothers and sisters elsewhere—were innately freedom-loving. One can see how they might be mistaken for pointing towards sparring political projects, one illiberal, the other liberal. One might even be tempted to conclude that Harb himself was illiberal, and that Kamil, Lutfi al-Sayyid and Jawish were liberal. But to do so would be to privilege words shorn of action. Instead, if 'liberal' is to have any analytic utility at all, it is best understood as a characterisation of an argument, not of an individual. Although they made competing arguments, it was not because they were advocating mutually irreconcilable visions of emancipation. On the contrary, their aspiration to Egyptian sovereignty was identical. By recognising that we cannot create a taxonomy of the liberal and the illiberal on the basis of such claims alone, we can grasp how and why it is that those who made mutually antagonistic arguments understood themselves to be united in a single political struggle.

To speak of Arabic thought 'in the liberal cage' is to recognise that the historiography inspired by Hourani's seminal text has imposed an ideal, archetypal 'liberalism' on figures such as Lutfi al-Sayyid and his associates. They were reimagined not only as a distinct school of thought but also as avatars of 'liberal Islam', a transformation that was predicated on a highly selective reading of their writings that has served to obscure the complexities and even contradictions within their thought. Evaluating this thought against a Western liberal canon is similarly problematic. As Duncan Bell has argued, there was no single 'liberal' position when it came to virtually anything, not least of all empire; one could identify canonical figures that fiercely opposed it as easily as one can find central, foundational figures that argued for its necessity.[125]

As we have seen, inclusion within the so-called "'Abduh school of thought' did not lead to a single set of opinions. Although Hizb al-Umma was dismissed or lauded—then as now—for its strategic, self-proclaimed 'moderacy', its ideas are difficult to categorise. By 1908, they were as aggressively anti-imperial as those of their adversaries. Lutfi al-Sayyid may have at times appealed to liberal norms, but so did his 'extremist' rivals across the political spectrum. Indeed, those very liberal norms could be evoked to praise the colonial state or to advance a thoroughgoing critique of it. Instead of asking how these ideas project the narrow interests of a 'few selfish capitalists'[126]—an analysis that is too instrumental to be plausible—we might ask how they transcend them. Instead of speculating on the hidden motivations behind these arguments, we might ask why they had become compelling in places far from where they were first suggested. And instead of suspiciously interrogating individuals' intentions, we might ask how it is that those who had previously been so enamoured of empire became such fierce critics of it.

To speak of the liberal cage is to appreciate that liberal modes of argumentation were becoming hegemonic among all politically engaged Egyptians, regardless of class background or interest. Leila Ahmed and, later, Talal Asad have sought to expose Amin's colonial mimicry, his inauthenticity, and his putative class interests, in order to re-evaluate the privileged position in which he has long been placed. The desire to uncover a shameful and foreign genealogy for Amin's ideas, however, makes it difficult for both scholars to see that Amin was primarily responding to a lively local debate, not merely parroting the 'pious pronouncements of British imperialists'.[127] Amin's ideas had long circulated elsewhere—in articles, back pages and pamphlets written by authors (some of them women) who were neither middle class nor French-educated. These marginal authors, largely written out of history, were often rooted in, and appealed to, various Muslim traditions, making it impossible to characterise them as 'secular' or secularising. Amin was simply one in a long series of commentators who did not spark the debate but rather entered it in full progress. A more serious effort to decentralise Amin and other intellectuals like him would begin with this fact and would attempt to understand him not as an innovator, but as an astute observer. The elite intellectuals examined in this chapter did not merely co-opt subaltern 'energies' in the service of imported and alien projects imposed from above but were fundamentally shaped by 'subaltern political commitments' from below.[128] If anything, from 1908 onwards Hizb al-Umma was attacked by its opponents not for espousing liberal norms, but for promoting ideas that were not liberal enough.[129] To recognise this is to acknowledge how central—indeed, inescapable—these arguments were becoming, at multiple levels of society, in the growing movement towards national sovereignty.

2

CORRUPTING POLITICS

Nadia Bou Ali

The *Nahḍa* intellectual movement (1798–1939) has had a long-standing influence in Arab thought and continues to be a topic of contentious debate between liberals, Islamists, and Marxists. *Nahḍa* ['renewal'] discourse was symptomatic of the onset of liberal modernisation in the Ottoman Empire and the consolidation of capitalist relations: intellectuals in the Arabic-speaking lands of the Empire were focusing their attention on the task of redefining society's foundations by formulating a distinctly culturalist discourse based on the coupling of conceptions of internality and authenticity with morality. Although it is well established in scholarship that the Nahḍa was largely liberal in economic and political terms, there has been scarcely any focus on the co-incidence of liberalism with the rise of a concept of Arab culture and morality. Culture, *adāb*, in the Nahḍa worldview was understood in relation to the necessary reform and cultivation of habit, *'āda*, for the advancement of civilisation, *tamaddun*. The refinement of internal faculties, habits and needs, were intertwined with recognizing society as an external institution, and this was the precondition of the emergence of nationalist discourse.

Since then, the Nahḍa has been the paradigm through which the question 'what does it mean to be Arab?' has been asked and answered. The word *adāb* as it emerged in formative Nahḍa works was used to signify culture in broad terms.[1] In its modern instantiation, culture cannot simply be read as a 'Europeanisation' of the conceptual universe of societies the world over, but as what 'has served to de-Europeanize the concepts that constitute the now global thought forms of modernity'.[2] The object of cultural discourse 'is a historically determinate form of human subjectivity' that is ultimately 'grounded in structures of social practice'[3] specific to capitalist society. In a society that is organised around commodity production and exchange, the individual subject is split between two roles, one of practical activity (the liberal pursuit of private interests in civil society) and the other of a practical activity through which the individual strives to tame nature and to achieve a unity with the social totality (culture).[4] This split subjectivity is precisely the thing whose wholeness culture attempts to restore, yet culture proves to be excessive, sacrificial and transgressive of economy: its utility or value appear to lie in its precise functional uselessness. Thus, it becomes necessary to define culture, to attempt to capture it, and to identify its functions or purposes. This quest was the primary Nahḍa pursuit.

'Arab culture' in its Nahḍa formulation expresses the tensions inherent in the formation of a universal form of consciousness from a particular position. The Nahḍa was neither an imported discursive body of thought nor an 'alternative modernity'. Rather, Nahḍa is saturated with the contradictions and incommensurability of capitalist modernity in its liberal form. Despite the multiple critiques of liberalism for its cultureless universality, the relationship between culture and liberalism requires further elaboration for they both seem to emerge as an antinomic pair of capitalist social forms. It is the site of politics or the political that remains to be determined, and in order to get there we must be able to ascertain the retreat of politics, its scarcity in both liberalism and culturalism. This chapter tracks the path of this retreat in Nahḍa discourse.

The Nahḍa carried within it the fantasy of attaining 'the good life' in which atomistic liberal individualism allowed individuals to be perceived as free to engage in relations of commodity exchange and to be confronted by society as an external entity. However, the pursuit of private interest needed to be complemented by a fantasy of achieving a higher subjective unity with the social totality—in other words, a unity between one's internal desires and their symbolic function in society. This fantasy betrayed moments of excess, of the inability of liberal subjectivity to fully fold in on itself. Thus, the logic of antinomy cannot be so tightly bound, for there are moments in which subjectivity becomes possible precisely because of its failed interpellation.[5] In other words, culture can never really achieve a unity between the subject and the social totality despite offering that possibility. Buṭrus al-Bustānī's 1860 translation of *Robinson Crusoe*[6] and his invocation of the story as the ideal of liberal individualism was complemented by Aḥmad Fāris al-Shidyāq's translation of parts of *Don Quixote*: with the former we have the retroactive anticipation of civil society and a society of exchange and with the latter a tragicomic escape from the symbolic order that leads to Quixotian madness. In other words, there cannot be culture without excesses and untamable elements. It is this dialectic of culture and its untamable excesses, I will argue, that emerges in Nahḍa as a duel between global consciousness and universal consciousness in a particular position. These forms of consciousness are distinct: 'for global consciousness, conflicts are generated through external differences between cultures and societies whereas universality ... signifies the possibility of a shared opening to the agitation and turbulence immanent to any construction of identity, the Unheimlichkeit or uncanniness internal to any and every space we call home'.[7]

Claiming that there is a universalist impulse in Nahḍa requires some elaboration, given the tenacious history of the concept of universalism and the over-abundance of its critique as a discourse inhabited by the white, male, dominant subject position. The political importance of the various critiques of universalism is unquestionable for they address the oppressive, racist, sexist and other partial interests that have laid claim to universalism over the past centuries. However, the question remains of how to articulate a pure particular position without contrast with a universal. Rather than dismissing the concept of universalism altogether while promoting a shaky universality of difference in its place, it is important to consider universalism as the inherent attribute of any particular lifeworld: the sole obstacle to the closure of a life world as a totality. In other words, universalism only emerges from a particular life world when it becomes evident that there is an unresolvable tension, a deadlock in the identity of the particular life world that can no longer be resolved through its own terms.

While the exclusionary aspects of liberalism have been emphasised by many scholars, the heterogeneous nature of liberalism and its openness to plural identity formations remains to be considered. Andrew Sartori's work on the concept of culture in Bengal provides a critical engagement with the assumption that liberalism excludes culture: 'the culture-concept has never been incompatible with liberal thought, even when that liberalism grounded itself in the object historical processes of civilisational development. "Culture" could supplement the more classically liberal, negative conception of *emancipation from* the illegitimate exercise of State authority, with the positive conception of subjective freedom as a *capacity to*.'[8] Although liberalism is the main ideology of capitalist modernity, the presence and persistence of other contrasting ideologies is not something that can be dismissed. By claiming that liberalism is both universal and exclusionary, critics of liberalism remain grounded in cultural analysis. Even the harshest critics of liberalism wash up on the shores of anti-Eurocentrism, resorting to the argument of 'leave us our culture'; what is missed in these analyses is a distinction between the false universality of capitalism, which pivots around four fundamental concepts enumerated by Marx (freedom, equality, property and 'Bentham'), and the universality of modernity. The false universality of liberalism functions as a negative force that purports to destroy particularity, yet in fact sustains it and eternalises its various forms around the globe—that is, it renders the distinction between the particular and universal a merely formal one.[9] As capitalism subsumed various societies around the globe, conflict was increasingly presented in terms of differences between cultures and societies. However, the important site of difference that postcolonial thought has largely overlooked is within culture and identity. I want to argue that the uncanniness of identity emerged in Nahḍa early on: when identity came to be seen as inadequate, increasingly foreign, and when the familiar came to be recognised as ultimately strange. Humanism in the late nineteenth century, under the spread of the concept of 'civilisation', presented itself as opposed to particularities, which then required a separation of spheres: the internal cultural world was to be cultivated and reformed, while the state administered the world of politics. This in turn set the stage for the emergence of nationalism—the universality of humanism being linked to the emergence, not the overcoming, of national particularisms. This is in contradistinction to a concrete universality, whose dictum would be the unsettling of particular identity from within, rather than its ossification from without.

One of the distinctive traits of liberalism is the relegation of culture to a realm that is 'natural' and outside politics. The split liberal subject is meant to maintain culture, religion, faith and all other 'idiosyncrasies' within the private realm, while the public is where the subject attains autonomy, freedom and independence. Although this interpretation of liberalism deserves the critiques that have been posited against it, it is not entirely accurate to claim that modernity's sole universalism has been liberal politics. The critique of universalism that emerges from that of liberalism risks dismissing responses to the oppressive capacities of modernity that also carried universalist claims. Moreover, the limits of the 'emancipatory' aspect of liberalism have been exposed by fundamentalist ideologies, and it is the absence of a radically conceived politics amid the deadlock between fundamentalism and liberalism that remains the decisive factor in the present day. Against postcolonial positions on the matter, the emancipatory potential of recognising the contingency of one's own communitarian identity cannot remain unnoticed in historiography. It is thus important to argue that although it was a form of cultural politics, the Nahḍa also carried within it an anxiety for real universality, one that emerged from the recognition that as a modern Arab subject you are no longer fully yourself. Nahḍa thinkers sought to define themselves as both Arab and human, as the anxious participants in a universal history. Their anxiety emerged from the desire for a modernity that seemed incommensurate with the attempt to maintain a cultural identity. The cost of doing so was the outright recognition and public disclosure of the uneasiness of fully identifying as Arab.

The Janus-face of language

Arabic in Nahḍa thought was seen as a *sign* of human civilisation and a means for the preservation of the self. Although much time and effort was invested in ordering the language by compiling lexicons, dictionaries and encyclopaedia, the obsession with language as the 'mirror of the *umma*' created hostility to instrumental conceptions of language as a tool for communication or as a commodity language. Nahḍa sources abound with descriptions of the work on language as the diving into a 'bottomless sea'[10] from which there would be no return. Shidyāq for one proclaimed, 'My greatest ambition has been to dive deep into the sea of this language.'[11] The Arabic language's 'aesthetic secrets, its wisdom, and the artistry of its making are to be brought out of concealment'.[12] However, just as the sea reveals its presence and conceals its content from the spectator, the sea of language is revealed to the student of Arabic and concealed from them because of its bottomless expanse. To elucidate this point further, I am suggesting here that this form of desire for language, in which it is never to be fully attained, actually resists its transformation into an object of national pedagogy. Shidyāq's desire for Arabic, 'the means to all the sciences [*al-'ulūm*] of this world and the hereafter',[13] signifies the turn of Arabic from a language of elsewhere, of an imagined past, to a language of the self as an other, to a 'language like no other'.[14] Often, Shidyāq would exclaim that, as he attempted to conquer language, it conquered him, a fateful defeat that offered him and his contemporaries a sense of enjoyment or *jouissance*. The closer one came to Arabic, the farther it appeared to be and the more it seemed to penetrate them from an elsewhere, speak through them rather than the other way around. In this particular instance of identifying the self in the image of Arabic, the subject believes in the fantasy of a community defined by a language that is neither here nor there: an unconscious sea of language that cannot be mastered. Arabic, which was meant to be the grounds of support of the particular self, was a language foreign to spoken vernaculars, existing only in the written form. In their attempts to master it, Nahḍa intellectuals proclaimed their failures one after the other. Shidyāq aptly captures this in his claim, 'as I sought to conquer the language I was defeated, and it conquered me'.[15] And just as there is something about Arabic that makes it unique and unattainable as an object of desire, there is something about being Arab that makes modernity seem farther away with every step closer to it.

If language was the looking glass through which the Arabs could catch a glance of a singular identification from within the interstices of communal identification, where does the image that is in the mirror actually come from? There is a curious dissociation between an image and the mirror it appears on; in a sense, the image that is in the mirror always exists *in* something else. The oft-deployed metaphor of Arabic as a mirror expresses an anxiety about boundaries, about interiority and exteriority. The act of writing under this form of investment in the language permeated the nineteenth century in the form of public texts (journalistic essays, treatise, books and works of fiction). But writing somehow disentangled language from presence, and thereby from its role as a tool of communication. Language was made to act as a Janus-faced creature with a public and private face. Moreover, language became the mediator between the interior and the exterior: it was the signifier of indeterminacy rather than a reflection of a unified identity. The empire of Arabic did not coincide with any real subject with which it could be identified, remaining an impossible object.

This discourse on *lugha* (Arabic) in Nahḍa sources was supplemented with a focus on morality. Indeed, it can be argued that morality preceded politics in the Nahḍa. While liberal utopians like Adam Smith, John Stuart Mills and others sought to get rid of moral temptations and to establish a form of value-free politics, Nahḍa intellectuals perceived politics as corrupting morality. They constantly referred to politics, *siyasa*, as a corrupting realm compared with morality or *adab* as a realm of self-cultivation.[16] Al-Bustānī's *Nafīr Sūrriyya* (a series of eleven nationalist pamphlets published after the 1860 war of Mount Lebanon and Damascus) carried within them a series of moralising statements for society. Al-Bustānī urged his fellow countrymen to abjure the blind and vengeful passions that he thought had led to the 1860 war and replace them with sympathy, compassion and love. For al-Bustānī, the war was a 'natural and ... moral catastrophe, *al-kharāb al-ṭabīʿī wal-adabī*', and political crisis could only be addressed by moral reform. Dismissing any possibility of justice beyond divine judgement, al-Bustānī acted as a moral realist, and instead of questioning the core of what constituted political legitimacy in society, al-Bustānī as well as his contemporaries concerned themselves with habits, emotions and morality.

On habits and needs: a haunted liberalism

Many Nahḍa thinkers approached the question of politics in ways similar to David Hume and against Thomas Hobbes. They were more involved in contemplating habits, emotions, morals and sociality than representation, legitimacy, justice and the social contract. As such, political community was regarded only as a *means* for the formation of civil society. Under the definition of human, *insan*, in the nineteenth-century Arabic encyclopaedia, *Dāʾirat al-Maʿārif*, the emphasis is placed on the human as a social being.[17] While animals behave according to habits, the human is a sentient being who has to tame his habits. The encyclopaedia entry adopts St Augustine's definition of the human as 'a rational soul that functions through earthly ephemeral organs'.[18] The human is thus defined by rational and creative capacities that can only be cultivated in a social setting. 'If it had not been for society, the human would be the weakest and feeblest of creatures.'[19] As such, the human can only exist for and in society: that is the universal trait of being human. 'Society shapes the human the most, it is the source that provides him with ideas, principles, and habits.' These, according to the encyclopaedia entry, are the factors responsible for the emergence of different races and types (*ajnas*) of human beings.[20] 'It is in this way that individual existence, *al-ʿisha al-khusūsiyya*, and communal existence, *al-ʿisha al-umūmiyya*, are intrinsically linked and inseparable from each other.'[21] This version of virtue ethics grounds morality in the cultivation of society as an organic whole and stands at a distance from the Enlightenment critique of Aristotelian ethics, which seeks to ground ethics in a form of reason that cannot be limited by a social context.

Moreover, the relationship between the public and the private in Nahḍa reveals many of the tensions of the liberal political project. The community remains the core of Nahḍa politics, while individuals merely provide the means for sustaining it. This is where the sacrificial core of liberal politics presents itself: by which the means for one individual life belong to another, and thereby, life comes to be defined by the moral values of thriftiness, parsimony and contentedness. Shidyāq called for parsimony in sexual relations and consumerism alike.[22] His arguments against polygamy that were considered avant-garde for his time were in fact based on an economic logic: multiple marriages slow down the productivity of the man and his social use, diverting him from pursuing beneficial and efficient acts.[23] In fact, Shidyāq posed this argument in an article entitled 'On the Principles of Politics and Other Matters (Reward and Punishment)'. Under the heading of politics, the essay propounds a pre-modern, pre-social contract conception of punishment and retribution and affirms the right of the sovereign to punish. Shidyāq begins his analysis with the role of the state, *al-dawla*: 'the essential principle of politics is that the state is knowledgeable of the conditions of its citizenry, whereby it punishes those who are evil and corrupting while it rewards those who are good and charitable'.[24] Thus, punishment was more effective in governance than reward, and the monarchical state's role was to single out for reward those of its citizenry who have a 'natural propensity and instinctual faculty for creative activities'. Shidyāq's proposition is based on his belief that 'individuals are like metals, carrying their essential traits within them from birth'. From this, he concludes that the state must find a mechanism to identify these traits and develop them so that the individuals who carry them take up roles in governance. 'My personal contention is that humankind is instinctively evil and corrupt';[25] if humans are left to their own will, without education and guidance, they would be blind to the glory of creation and 'place their faith in a cow because it benefited them or a serpent because it frightens them'.[26] The retreat of the figure of the sultan with the beginning of Ottoman disintegration was replaced by the people (a collection of individuals with essences) who in turn demanded testing and measurement for them to be healthy and fit for society,[27] 'kingdoms and nations are like bodies, rarely can one be found free from affliction'.[28]

Measuring the level of knowledge and cultivating it is what Jacques Lacan has referred to as the discourse of the university, which supplants the old master's discourse.[29] The object of the university discourse[30] is not simply the 'accumulation and deployment of knowledge concerning *bodily life*' but an extra element, a 'strange and material presence of the disappearing king'.[31] This shift in the social discourse depicted in Shidyāq's writing exposes the 'bareness of human communities'[32] as they attempt to cover their nudity; their exposure in modernity, for it is in the very efforts to single out an original state for a community that it appears that it is impossible to identify one. It is thus not surprising that Shidyāq argues that the motto for sociality should not be 'do unto others as you would have them do unto you' but rather 'know thyself'.[33]

Shidyāq's perception of human nature, the role of habits in society, the necessary corruption of politics, led him to propose reform and adaptation, *islāḥ wa ta'dīl*, as temporary solutions for society. There are only temporary solutions for Shidyāq, which all rely on habits and conventions that are in turn themselves ephemeral. If the people ought to aid the state in fulfilling its aims, as he claimed, then we can see the body of the king living on among the people through a displacement of authority. But the aim of preserving wellbeing leads to a deadening of oneself; the aim of knowing oneself is not to criticise authority but to obey it. 'Humankind is instinctively evil and corrupt', hence one must recognise one's own limited knowledge: to 'know thyself' rather than to 'think for oneself'. Questioning certain habits (polygamy, consumerism, imitating European ways, attitudes towards women, indolence and unproductivity, the gluttony of aristocrats, ornate language that lacks real meaning, etc.) goes hand in hand with knowing oneself: it is a new form of biopolitics that the Nahḍa discourse instils. Self-knowledge assumes that one can reflect upon the very subject doing the reflecting. Even in the Nahḍa work on Arabic, it was largely assumed that one could somehow step outside language to confirm that it could indeed express a truth about the world in which one existed. The irony of Nahḍa thought is that the criticism of habit and tradition, as well as language, was only possible by exiting them. Irony, as Paul de Man suggests, is a process of duplication of the self, a specular structure within the self, which muddles the relationship with history. Irony arises precisely when the subject can no longer recognise itself as a historical subject.

Shidyāq maintained that the material processes of consumerism and commodification estranged humankind from its elevated status among other creatures. Wreathing against nineteenth-century liberal modernity evidently produced a discourse of morality: the problem was that modernisation only made people 'evil, repugnant, desiring, stubborn, envious, spiteful, cruel and aggressive, fearful and rash'.[34] Modern civilisation was 'like bitter water, the more you drank it the thirstier you would become'.[35] Shidyāq's autobiographical novel *Al-Sāq ʿala al-sāq* depicts his own bodily and physical contortions that arise from his inability to inhabit any space of representation in modernity. He appears in the book, in more ways than one, similar to the German Daniel Paul Schreber,[36] a body of excitable flesh, eroticised at every encounter yet impotent, unable to capture the cause of his desire. It is surely no coincidence that the very same liberal Ottoman reform that Shidyāq himself promoted in his politics itself exceeded his own abilities to inhabit his reformism. Shidyāq's own response to the question posed by the Nahḍa discourse was to make himself into a book in al-Saq: the autobiography's central character Faryaq (the author's fictional double, a compound of the names Fāris and Shidyāq) made his proper name common again. It is the answer to the parasitic nature of words, for language with Shidyāq appears as 'a verbal parasite, a parasitical cancer from which there is no escape'.[37] The symptomatic repetition of phonemically similar words in the book to be interrupted by abrupt sounds like 'shh!shh!', 'tiff!tiff!', 'azwa!azwa!', tell of the attempts to silence speech in the mind. Shidyāq's emptying out of words in the middle of dark nights, his 'blackening of the sheets of paper in the darkest of nights' were an attempt to liquefy language, an attempt to puncture a hole into the symbolic order of habits, meanings and signification. He thus represents the limits of the Nahḍa discourse, the limits at which Nahḍa as a discourse of progress begins to crumble and crack.

In contrast to the individualistic and atomised conceptions of liberal political thought, the subject in the Nahḍa discourse was perceived as an essentially social being, a creature of habit. The problem with modernisation, however, was that habit suddenly got in the way of social life. Soon after the eruption of war in Mount Lebanon and Damascus, Buṭrus al-Bustānī gave a public speech in Beirut to the Syrian Society for the Sciences. The speech's content reveals the obsessive-compulsiveness underlying the modern concept of society. Al-Bustānī defines society, *al-hayʾa al-ijtimāʿiyya*, as being based on 'the fulfillment of the needs of individuals as well as the abetting of their fears'.[38] Human happiness, according to him, can only be attained by the satisfaction of needs. This satisfaction can only proceed from the division of labour, with al-Bustānī providing an extensive Smithian analysis of society.[39] The logic of his analysis is that society's political and economic transformations reduce human relations to those of need, and that these are essentially more progressive than those of tribal and 'savage' societies. The latter, according to al-Bustānī, have fewer needs, rendering their mutual relations weak and their societies lacking in unity and civilisation. 'One person cannot be a farmer, harvester, teacher, baker ... alone,' he argued, even a simple bread loaf requiring many different kinds of labour to produce. Al-Bustānī referred to the story of *Robinson Crusoe* to illustrate this point.[40] The measurement of progress by the satisfaction of needs is tied to the increase of needs themselves; the problem, however, is that needs have an insatiable desire; they do not cease to multiply and increase in capitalist modernity.

Habits, for al-Bustānī, are to be separated from taste and judgement: they can only be accounted for by their benefits and disadvantages for those who bear them. Al-Bustānī drew out a comparison of the habits of the Arabs and Europeans, addressed to a burgeoning bourgeoisie in Beirut. He espoused a form of cultural relativism that relies on neutralising these habits (food, drink, clothing, hair, social conventions) and making them judgement-free. For al-Bustānī, the question is: How do habits fit into a society, and do they advance or detract from its good? If the habits of the Europeans have instilled in them a civilisation that the Arabs covet, what is to be said about the difference in habits between the two? He argued that the adoption of European habits in eating, speaking, socialising, the mixing of the sexes, fashion and clothing is a mere pretence, for it takes the superficial aspect of European societies while not recognising its essence. But what is this core to which al-Bustānī is referring? It is the recognition of the needs of modern society, as well as the means of satisfying them. The response to this cultural face-off, according to him, was 'neither to proclaim all that is Arab as good and all that is European as evil, for both these positions are prejudiced and harmful'.[41]

Al-Bustānī categorises needs into the following types: natural needs (food, clothes and shelter), mental needs (books, philosophical tools), social needs (interaction, bonding), moral needs (charity), religious needs (faith and the practice of religion), political needs (the selection of a number of representatives to safeguard the order, wealth and lives of the population), and complementary needs (music, luxury, coffee, tobacco). This variety of needs can only be satisfied by the law of supply and demand: the latter in turn can only be fulfilled in a society founded upon the division of labour. The satisfaction of these different needs, and so of different kinds of people, according to al-Bustānī, is the only possible source of happiness. His criticism of extravagant displays of wealth and luxury through the law of supply and demand is similar to Shidyāq's discourse of parsimony and thriftiness and both are afflicted with the miserly ideal that haunts liberal regimes.

The encyclopaedic perception of needs necessitated a global vision of human existence: the circle of needs and their means of satisfaction begins with the family and gradually expands in circumference until it encompasses all of humankind. Individual rights in this perspective are reduced to the satisfaction of needs, which is in turn the necessary basis of human sociality. Not surprisingly, what is unaccounted for in this logic is any mention of the notion of freedom. Sociality does not appear to be based on the respect for the possibility of freedom, but for an innate set of needs. Thus, the question of individual autonomy and independence do not figure in this definition of the human. This reduction of man to a social animal can be defined as a realist fantasy, one in which nothing is taken into account except the existing reality of a society being gradually sucked into a mercantile and consumerist economy.

Furthermore, this conception of humanity is ultimately apolitical: the social is divorced from the political. Shidyāq's essay, *Principles of Politics* (*Fī 'usūl al-siyāsa*), focused on the state's biopolitical disciplinary power and its ability to channel the faculties of its people into socially and economically productive activities. Politics, for Shidyāq, essentially meant an organic harmony between the state and its people. Both he and al-Bustānī discussed the institution of hereditary power as something that needed to be reformed in order for the legitimatisation of authority to live on. Al-Bustānī argued in his writings that the rule of law must prevail over all, despite differences in religion and creed. However, although he did call for a separation of religion from politics, his definition of both departs from any strict separation between public and private. Al-Bustānī defined religious authority as *ri'āsa*, sovereignty, and political authority as *siyāsa*, politics. The separation between the two forms is necessary because the former is 'related to eternal and unchanging internal beliefs' while the latter is 'ephemeral, depends on time and place, in constant flux, and open to reform'.[42] In Nahḍa thought as well as nineteenth-century Ottoman governance, political reform was a means of liberal modernisation, while the refinement of habit and the cultivation of the individual were perceived as the essence of civilisation. 'The Human is not made in the image of a sponge that imbibes all the wealth and a resource of the world, rather the Human has been created in the image of giving tree that grows gradually and bears fruit.'[43] Politics as such was understood as transient and corruptible, while morality must be cultivated from an inner self on to the outer world.

Contrary to the fake and mimetic civilisation that Nahḍa intellectuals thought to seduce Arabs, real civilisation was essentially a moral project, one that had to be cultivated within the self internally, in order for it to shine out in the external world. This self-cultivation, however, required a commitment to the specific habits of a people, because habits, according to al-Bustānī, are gained over time and through repetition. Moreover, habits are visible and bodily: those having to do with facial hair, hygiene and cleanliness, parsimony and thriftiness, mannerisms of eating, hospitality, gender roles, clothing and dress, social conduct, oratory, speech and writing. Habits are embodied material forms that take shape in response to these needs and desires, and that do so spontaneously, unconsciously and socially. If, as al-Bustānī and Shidyāq tell us, habits are generated by needs and instilled through unconscious processes of repetition and experience, then what is the significance of placing the burdens of modernity on to the cultivation of habits? Further, how can habits be protected from the expansion of the circle of needs caused by capitalist social relations?

Instead of describing this focus on habits as emerging from an orientalising colonial encounter, I argue that this form of debate was symptomatic of an anxiety generated from the contestation between reason and the passions. By prioritising passions over reason, habit over thought, the Nahḍa narrative addresses its readers in affective terms. Believing in the ways of modern civilisation was not enough for the progress of society, according to these Nahḍa thinkers, for believing can easily give way to a form of superficial mimesis, one in which the essence of modernity goes unnoticed: this essence being the promise of satisfactory fulfilment of human needs and desires. But it is this very promise of satisfaction or enjoyment and its constant failure that drives modern civilisation and produces an even more excessive demand for enjoyment. Shidyāq proposed that the satisfaction of desires produces a series of impressions stored in the brain in the form of imagination.[44] These impressions are largely constituted by memory and past experience. Human reasoning, for Shidyāq, is entirely based on sensorial experiences stored in the memory; in other words, judgement and understanding and other synthetic functions are not accounted for in this perspective. Words cannot have meanings independently of the objects they signify, but it is Shidyāq's very own words that escape him. In his texts, we see a massive factory of production of signifiers and chains of signifiers that are no longer anchored in a signified, wave of homonyms, metonyms and homophonies listed page after page.

The human in this Nahḍa discourse is a creature of habits, one beholden to a repetition compulsion, a swinging pendulum between hysteria and obsession. Ultimately, one who can choose but is not essentially free, being morally bound to the principles of good conscience or the demands of the symbolic order. The dissociation of habit from taste, and thereby from the faculty of judgement, is an important but understudied facet of Nahḍa thought. Habit, as al-Bustānī explained, is equivalent to second nature, *'adat al-mar' tab'uh al-thānī*,[45] and one that cannot be changed, except by death, *'ādatun fil badan lā yughayīruhā ila al-kafan*.[46] Addressing the question of habits requires one to look towards the very limits of subjectivity: death itself. The subjectivity that emerges in Nahḍa discourse is one that must awaken from a pre-reflexive, non-thinking existence in which the fusion between interiority and exteriority goes un-interrogated. This awakening, the realisation of the self in objective reality, becomes the very content of subjectivity. Nahḍa discourse is haunted by inescapable anxieties: How can the subject, the form, become its own content? The sense of self-awareness that overtook Arab thought in the nineteenth century can be read as an example of the rise of universality from a particular life world. This universality depended upon a splitting of the self, for how can habit be the ailment and the cure at the same time? How can the self dwell in particular sites yet beseech a universal subjectivity? The focus on bodily habits such as eating, what people wear, how they style their hair, as well as gestures and mannerisms in Nahḍa works can be seen as an attempt to subordinate the body, to silence it, cover its nudity and primordial exposure. Self-preservation, however, usually comes at very high costs, 'the paradox at work here is, in short, that the defense mechanisms cultures use to protect against a primordial exposure—to cover our nudity—serve in the end to redouble this exposure and thereby to "fatten" the flesh of creaturely life'.[47]

The notion of freedom poses itself here as a necessary point of discussion. It is worth noting that, as a topic, freedom did not receive much attention in these debates on habit and manners. The nineteenth-century encyclopaedia defines *ḥurrīyya*, liberty, by positing it as antithetical to slavery and subjugation: 'being free from conditions of oppression that limit one's ability to act in desired ways and to choose between different things'.[48] In the encyclopaedia, liberty is categorised as being of two types, the 'internal and the external'.[49] Under the category of internal freedom, emphasis is given to the freedom of conscience, an idea that was central to John Locke's essay on tolerance. Internal liberty consists of the freedom of choice, freedom of will, moral freedom (freedom to choose between good and evil) and freedom of conscience. External liberty, on the other hand, is divided into the following types:

> natural freedom (the freedom to act in the world that is in accordance with the human's essential social character), civil freedom (human ability to act in accordance with law and government), political freedom (the freedom to enjoy rights provided by the state to all citizens), physical freedom (the freedom to move one's

body without restraint), intellectual freedom (the freedom to express political, religious, and moral opinion), religious freedom (freedom to believe in any religion), freedom to practice any religion, journalistic freedom, individual freedom, freedom of profession, freedom to trade and commerce, maritime freedom, national freedom (freedom of any nation to gain independence from another nation).[50]

The entry concludes by postulating that 'there is no real liberty in this world because all the aforementioned types of liberty are in fact constrained in one way or the other and are not truly free'.[51] It is important to note that an essential aspect of liberal thought is missing in this classification, which is to say the liberty of property. In fact, this view of liberty seems to be more invested in its 'internal' forms, such as the freedom of conscience, while the freedom of the physical body is categorised as an external one. 'The lack of liberty in human beings, which is the central trait that separates them from animals, along with the faculties of language and reason, leads to the loss of their humanity.'[52] What is interesting about this discussion of liberty is that it describes the realm of necessity, one defined by the distinction between animal and human: liberty is what separates the latter from the former and defines humanity; there is a social essence to liberty. In the same encyclopaedia entry, liberty is seen to exist in degrees: 'it is of a higher degree in adult individuals than it is in a child, and it is weaker in cases of inebriation, illness, and madness. Liberty may be entirely lost to some, it may be strengthened by education and moral guidance as well as observation and practice.'[53]

So although there are two general categories of liberty, internal and external, the determining factor for its growth as a distinctly human trait is in the external social world, that of the senses. If the social world determines the degree of liberty, as well as the habits that support it, then the Nahḍa discourse can be seen as advocating a familiar position—that it is for people's own good if they freely change their habits. Habits become the nexus of thinking of subjectivity and time: changing habits is meant to anticipate a different kind of future by harnessing the potentialities of the present. The discussion of habits by Nahḍa intellectuals has been too hastily dismissed as a self-orientalising form, or a by-product of colonial self-hatred. However, once read as contingent debates in a time of radically changing socio-economic conditions, the focus on habits can be seen as an attempt to economise the forces of society and stoke its reserves for times to come. Rather than read the discourse on habits as a reflection of the desire for a Western modernity, my argument here is that it is an expression of the anxiety underlying modern subjectivity: one in which the subject comes to misrecognise itself. Anxiety arises from a threat to the unity of the subject. Once seen in this light, the invocations of mirrors (language as a mirror) in nineteenth-century Arab texts, serving as attempts to unify the self, cease to be curious metaphors and become explanatory devices.

The retreat of politics

The dissociation of politics from society has been understood as a central trait of liberalism, and it is indeed called for by many Nahḍa intellectuals. However, this dissociation excluded the central tenet of liberal governance, which is the consent of the governed—another theme that is missing in Nahḍa sources. Political representation remains limited to a relationship within which the state is defined as the spirit of the people, rather than the other way around.[54] The spirit is essential to the functioning of the body: the latter cannot exist without the former. Often, Nahḍa intellectuals lamented the corruption of the times they lived in, and proclaimed it a result of politics, *siyāsa*. Politics was perceived as a corrupting realm, one that needed to be addressed by the reform of the Arabs through the cultivation of good habits and morality. It was as though politics was a source of corruption that needed to be kept at bay so that society could pursue its true interests and fulfil its liberty.

The implications of the Nahḍa conception of habit on the thinking of subjectivity and the meaning of political action are significant: when individual habit is shaped by accommodation to external forces, as an internal feature it becomes elevated into a disposition, the defining trait of an inner essence. Thus, habits that are mandated by the external world become internal faculties that define individuals: subjectivity emerges from its own disappearance. Moreover, habits have the power to conceal the source of their origin, and appear as natural traits. The Arab's moustache appears as a natural trait for the Arab, just as the European's hairless face is natural to the European. Nahḍa intellectuals often invoked this example to explain that the difference in habits (here the reference is to facial grooming) was natural only insofar as it was cultural. 'Things in themselves cannot carry contradictory features; contradiction and difference are the results of forces of habits and differences in tastes.'[55] This same reasoning is used to explain the difference between primitive societies and civilised ones: the less civilised and less modern a society is, the less it has needs and the means for satisfying them. The essence of the human is therefore a social one—universal nature is always a second nature, while habits are the originary essence of humankind.

Politics came last in the Nahḍa, for it was a realm that could not be theorised without the elucidation of the power of habits at both its ends: among the governed and the governors. Politics as a site of agonistic conflict, one experienced by Nahḍa intellectuals through wars and the rise of sectarianism, proved to be a complicating factor for a society formed by habit. As we have seen, underneath the harmonious appearance of the subject as a creature of habit, is a mechanism for the splitting or erasure of subjectivity: the internal world is essentially constructed on the outside, made to predict the external world and to be instantiated by it. Action in the world is not meant to make an individual consider their plurality, but rather seeks to reinforce an image of the individual as a self-identical subject. This sociological determinism, one that largely defined Nahḍa thought, entailed a not-so-clear distinction between the public and the private, as well as between emotion and reason. Habits blur this distinction: for one cannot will away a habit by reasoning, nor can it be controlled in public.

By writing about habit, Nahḍa intellectuals took on the role of thinking about a seemingly natural thing and subjected it to an intellectual interrogation. Some habits appeared objectionable while others seemed commendable. The focus on habits needs to be read as a commentary on the meaning of social action, as well as something that reveals the anxiety underlying modern subjectivity. Habits are at the core of defining the meaning of society in Nahḍa thought and are central components of thinking about social action. There is little distinction made between social action that is historically developed (farming, industry) and natural (eating and digesting). Even eating habits, in al-Bustānī's analysis, evolved historically, with the only natural entity in his analysis being human sociality. Listed as matters of habit in Nahḍa literature was everything pertaining to social action: labour and productivity, indolence, speech, writing, marriage, sex, consumption, customs, eating, drinking, walking, music and clothing. Habits impinge on the body, transform it, guide it and manipulate its movements. Moreover, they are the cause of both virtue and vice. The absence of a discussion of the faculty of reason proves to be a departure from more familiarly liberal conceptions of subjectivity. It is only through self-cultivation and the refinement of habit that an individual's rational faculties may come to mature. But happy endings remained far from the truth in Nahḍa texts. Thus most of the population, *safalat al-ʿāmma*, was destined to remain in ignorance. Their ignorance was a corrupting factor for society as a whole, yet freedom was not the solution but instead a gradual transformation of habits.

Nevertheless, in this discourse there was recognition of the limitations of the economy for society, and the limits of living a life in service to the desire for goods. Shidyāq often complained about the abundance of consumable objects: the more one consumed, the less useful one became. The contradictory ethics of political economy: acquisition, work and thriftiness, on the one hand, and good conscience and virtue on the other, did not escape scrutiny. In fact, we can read the focus on habits and morality as an expression of the tensions generated by this universal contradiction; the contradictory core of liberal politics. For how can one be free and virtuous at the same time? How can the luxury of good conscience and virtue be commensurate with a life of freedom? It is as if these Nahḍa writers accepted that it was only through individual self-renunciation that society might flourish. For it is only through sacrifice that one becomes a social being, and only through relationships of bondage that sociality can be instituted. By defining society as a necessary form by which needs are to be satisfied, Nahḍa thinkers promoted a psychology of the passions that recognised the core of the subject to be in response to the question: What do you desire of me? In contemplating the meaning of humanity, Shidyāq wrote:

> It is this same human who is the source of all civilisation, of all art and creation, who does what the wolves would not do to their own whelps. For he desires to drink the world dry and swallow it all to its end ... he who refuses to share with his brother even a little bit of what he owns! I have often thought of this false civilisation [al-tamaddun al-bāṭil]—that surely had not been the state of the ancients—and I have found that it is the reason for evil and animosity; for immersion in sadness and worry; for consumption and over-expenditure; for backstabbing and treason; for competition, diffidence, and wars. Civilisation burdens the self with the greatest costs and constant imminent threats.[56]

The corresponding Nahḍa conception of the fate of mankind was bleak: unhappiness, lack of freedom and endless toil and labour. Politics mirrored these miserable conditions: it was perceived as the normative condition that seeks to subordinate the moral world of subjects. Morality, on the other hand, was seen to be in a constant struggle with habits: the reform of both only being possible through vigilant self-awareness. The function of habit as an unconscious form necessary for the function of consciousness only served to complicate the desire to locate the self in reality and create the conditions of possibility for subjectivity. What emerges from this Nahḍa awakening to self-awareness is a kind of haunting: the Nahḍa is haunted by a possibility that has not yet been actualised.

3

ILLIBERAL ISLAM

Faisal Devji

On 19 July 1927, some twenty years before Britain departed its Indian empire, a celebrated poet, philosopher and sometime politician rose to speak on the floor of the Punjab Legislative Council. Muhammad Iqbal, who would in future be acclaimed the spiritual founder of Pakistan though he died nearly a decade before its creation, addressed the following words to his fellow councillors in Lahore:

> Well, it may be so, yet the talk of a united nationalism is futile and will perhaps remain so for a long time to come. The word has existed on the lips of the people of this country for the last fifty years and like a hen it has cackled a great deal without laying a single egg.[1]

Taken from his speech opposing a resolution to fill government positions by competitive examination, without reserving a certain number of places for caste or religious groups, Iqbal's remark displays a distrust of any politics that assumed the existence of an Indian nation. Such distrust was not uncommon at the time. It was expressed, though for very different reasons, by groups as diverse as the British government, the Hindu Mahasabha and the Muslim League, as well as by Dalit or Untouchable and Dravidian or South Indian

65

movements, all of which sought at various times to contest or limit the idea of nationality propounded by the Indian National Congress. Whether or not the partisans of Hindu, Muslim, Dalit or Dravidian forms of nationality thought, as did Iqbal in the passage quoted above, that a united Indian nation was a future possibility, they all based their distrust of it on the grounds of political reality. Given the historically entrenched and often legally sanctioned nature of the differences and disparities between various caste, religious and other groupings, how was it possible to think about the political representation and interaction of India's various parties in the absence of nationalism as a unifying factor? Could a workable set of political relations emerge in such a situation? What kind of state would they give rise to?

Indian nationalism was distrusted by men like Iqbal not only as a bad idea but also as an unrealistic one, and it was to avoid the political consequences of this idea that such men questioned the very language upon which Indian nationalism was based. In essence, this was the procedural language of liberalism, made up of a few fundamental categories including interest (the basic political fact of liberalism), representation (the institutional organisation of interests) and contract (the relationship between interests), all of which were to be legitimated and guaranteed by a national state. If there was no Indian nation, of course, interests could only be autonomous and formally unrelated entities, representation could only be organised on transient and ephemeral grounds, and contractual relations could only be held together by merely contingent imperatives.

Naturally, the kind of state that governed such a situation could only be some replica of the British Raj.

This possibility raised serious questions about the representation and interaction of India's political units for Iqbal, as indeed for many of his countrymen, in the four or five decades before the partition of India in 1947. Unfortunately, this entire period is today held hostage by the fact of this partition, so that it is only permissible to pose the following kinds of questions in the historiography: Was the division of India inevitable? Did a Muslim nation actually exist before the creation of Pakistan? These retrospective questions are not particularly interesting. They certainly do nothing to illuminate the vibrant political culture of India before partition, which subjected the basic categories of liberal thought, interest, representation and contract to an unprecedented interrogation. And it is important to note that it was over these procedural categories, rather than over some merely academic definition of nationhood, that Indian political debate occurred during this period.

I am interested here in the category of representation, which I will argue was taken up so variously and by such multifarious groups in British India, especially religious ones, as to be quite different from the traditional form of representation in Europe. In fact, the whole lexicon of liberalism was expanded to breaking point in the Indian Empire, undergoing there perhaps its severest political test in the effort to manage the representation and contractual agreement of conflicting regional, linguistic, religious and caste interests of continental proportions.

It might well be the case that no group in British India stretched the liberal category of representation as far as did the Muslims, particularly those associated with the Muslim League. Here we have a gargantuan population of some 70 million that was conceived of as a national minority. And what kind of minority? One dispersed throughout the country, belonging to different sects, ethnicities, language groups, social classes and professions. No wonder that the leaders of the Indian National Congress found it so difficult to take the claims of such a group for representation seriously. Particularly so when this claim for representation did not stop at separate Muslim electorates and administrative zones, but entailed demands that went beyond the demographic strength of the Muslim population. For instance, demands for parity with the Congress in constitutional decision-making, as well as for weightage, a principle according to which Muslim or Hindu populations in certain regions were to be given legislative seats in excess of their proportional share in the population so as to allow them to constitute politically effective majorities or minorities there.

Muslims justified these demands by pointing to the important role they played in India's history, one that was out of proportion to their numbers. Even now, argued the League, Muslims continued to play this role by their disproportionate representation in the imperial army. Finally, however, the demand for disproportionate political representation was justified to prevent poverty and backwardness from depriving Muslims of the fruits of democracy. For in a purely demographic democracy, Muslims supposedly ran the risk of being crushed by a hostile Hindu majority. Such justifications, then, all began from the brute facts of demography but moved beyond them to other ways of conceiving representation. Whatever the merits of this position, which would, in Iqbal's phrase, ensure the substance of democracy even at the expense of its conventional form, it very clearly brought the language of liberalism to breaking point. And this was the case, argued Iqbal, because the realities of India demanded a radicalisation of liberal categories. So in his presidential address to the All-India Muslim Conference in March 1932, Iqbal had this to say about the nature of India's struggle for freedom:

> The present struggle in India is sometimes described as India's revolt against the West. I do not think it is a revolt against the West; for the people of India are demanding the very institutions which the West stands for. Whether the gamble of elections, retinues of party leaders and hollow pageants of parliaments will suit a country of peasants for whom the money-economy of modern democracy is absolutely incomprehensible, is a different question altogether. Educated urban India demands democracy. The minorities, feeling themselves as distinct cultural units and fearing that their very existence is at stake, demand safeguards, which the majority community, for obvious reasons, refuses to concede. The majority community pretends to believe in a nationalism theoretically correct, if we start from Western premises, belied by facts, if we look to India. Thus the real parties to the present struggle in India are not England and India, but the majority community and the minorities of India which can ill-afford to accept the principle of Western democracy until it is properly modified to suit the actual conditions of life in India.[2]

Iqbal makes three points here that question the liberal enterprise of Indian nationalism. The national struggle, he says, exists not between India and Britain, but between India's majority and minority communities, with the latter standing to lose all their historical and juridical privileges in a singular nation-state. Furthermore, the kind of democracy espoused by the nationalists works to the advantage of the urban and educated classes they belong to, because its freedoms of interest, representation and contract are characteristic of a money economy that is foreign to India's peasant majority. And finally, the nationalist project not only ignores but actively subverts the religious landscape of India. Politically, then, Iqbal followed the Muslim League, supporting either a federal India divided into Hindu and Muslim majority provinces, or a united India with a system of separate electorates and weightage.

Unlike Muhammad Ali Jinnah, who would end up founding Pakistan as the League's president, Iqbal did not support these options for purely negative reasons, because the special historical and constitutional conditions of India did not permit the creation of a unitary nation-state there. Rather, he saw the League's curious politics of representation in an entirely positive light because they seemed to stave off the nation-state in its liberal incarnation. Iqbal opposed this latter for several reasons, disapproving, for instance, of its glorification of territorial belonging and its metaphysical rather than merely functional division of society into public and private realms, on the same model, he thought, as the Christian separation of the material and the spiritual. Thus the following passage from Iqbal's 1930 presidential address to the Muslim League:

> Europe uncritically accepted the duality of spirit and matter probably from Manichaean thought. Her best thinkers are realising this initial mistake today, but her statesmen are indirectly forcing the world to accept it as an unquestionable dogma. It is, then, this mistaken separation of spiritual and temporal which has largely influenced European religious and political thought and has resulted practically in the total exclusion of Christianity from the life of European states. The result is a series of mutually ill-adjusted states dominated by interests not human but national. And these mutually ill-adjusted states after trampling over the morals and convictions of Christianity, are today feeling the need of a federated Europe, i.e., the need of a unity which Christian church-organisation originally gave them, but which instead of reconstructing it in the light of Christ's vision of human brotherhood they considered it fit to destroy under the inspiration of Luther.[3]

Iqbal maintained that territorial belonging, in the populist form it assumed with the nation-state, destroyed or at the very least enfeebled all ethical or idealistic imperatives in political life, making for an international regime of parochial and so continuously warring interests: a condition he thought was brought into being with the Protestant Reformation, whose individualisation of religion and revolt against the universality of the Roman Catholic Church spiritually ushered in the reign of the nation-state. Moreover, territorial belonging led to the dominance of property over all the relations of social life, such that all interests became interests of ownership. Indeed, the nation-state could even be characterised by a mode of knowledge for which the world was composed entirely of things that had to be grasped proprietorially, by discursive reasoning alone.

Representation, then, whether epistemological or political, was the very model of discursive reason because it grasped both persons and objects as forms of property, to be weighed, counted and worshipped not only in the practices of democracy but also in those of knowledge as such. This criticism of the liberal nation-state is of course similar in many respects to its Marxist analysis, something that Iqbal recognised and wrote about, dedicating a number of fine verses in admiration of Marx, Lenin and bolshevism. Indeed, for Iqbal, communism was religion's (and especially Islam's) only rival in the criticism of a liberal state and its order of representation, although he thought it infinitely worse than the latter. Communism, according to Iqbal, by transferring all property to the state, actually made it an even more oppressive presence in public life, and even more destructive of ethics as conviction and ideal. In this sense, he thought that atheistic materialism necessarily smuggled back into everyday life the very functions of property that it ostensibly criticised.[4]

As far as the liberal order of the nation-state was concerned, its unhappiness for Iqbal was made possible by the metaphysical division of society into public and private realms, with the ideal, the spiritual and everything that was not tied to property being confined to a private life in which it could function only as ineffective moralism and mere ideal. And it was this specifically metaphysical division of liberal society into public and private that posed the greatest danger to the citizen's life, for it transformed political relations into a set of instrumental transactions by robbing them of what Iqbal variously called idealism, conviction or faith, as in the following passage from one of the lectures delivered in 1934 and collected under the title *The Reconstruction of Religious Thought in Islam*:

> Humanity needs three things today—a spiritual interpretation of the universe, spiritual emancipation of the individual, and basic principles of a universal import directing the evolution of human society on a spiritual basis. Modern Europe has, no doubt, built idealistic systems on these lines, but experience shows that truth revealed through pure reason is incapable of bringing that fire of living conviction which personal revelation alone can bring. This is the reason why pure thought has so little influenced men, while religion has always elevated individuals, and transformed whole societies. The idealism of Europe never became a living factor in her life, and the result is a perverted ego seeking itself through mutually intolerant democracies whose sole function is to exploit the poor in the interest of the rich. Believe me, Europe today is the greatest hindrance in the way of man's ethical advancement.[5]

Iqbal therefore deplored the liberal state as a soulless system of interests driven entirely by the greed for ownership, and feared that the formation and representation of India's religious groups as interests in its terms would end up eliminating whatever remained of the ideal or ethical in them, thus giving way to the malign instrumentality of discursive reason that he saw operating in imperialism, communism and fascism alike. The extreme gravity of this situation, in the years leading up the Second World War, is made very clear in the New Year's message Iqbal broadcast in January 1938 from the Lahore station of All-India Radio:

> The rulers whose duty it was to protect and cherish those ideals which go to form a higher humanity, to prevent man's oppression of man and to elevate the moral and intellectual level of mankind, have in their hunger for dominion and imperial possessions, shed the blood of millions and reduced millions to servitude simply in order to pander to the greed and avarice of their own particular groups. After subjugating and establishing their dominion over weaker peoples, they have robbed them of their possessions, of their religions, their morals, of their cultural traditions and their literatures ...

As I look back on the year that has passed and as I look at the world in the midst of the New Year's rejoicings, it may be Abyssinia or Palestine, Spain or China, the same misery prevails in every corner of man's earthly home, and hundreds of thousands of men are being butchered mercilessly. Engines of destruction created by science are wiping out the great landmarks of man's cultural achievements.

The world's thinkers are stricken dumb. Is this going to be the end of all the progress and evolution of civilization, they ask, that men should destroy one another in mutual hatred and make human habitation impossible on this earth?[6]

For all these reasons, great and small, Iqbal celebrated the lack of national identity in the Indian Empire and approved of the curious forms that the language of liberalism assumed there, because he thought that India could develop a new political language of world-historical importance. He had this to say about India's exemplary political role in his presidential address to the Muslim League in December 1930:

India is Asia in miniature. Part of her people have cultural affinities with nations in the east and part with nations in the middle and west of Asia. If an effective principle of co-operation is discovered in India, it will bring peace and mutual good will to this ancient land which has suffered so long, more because of her situation in historic space than because of any inherent incapacity of her people. And it will at the same time solve the entire political problem of Asia.[7]

Islam occupied a privileged role in this world-historical project, especially in India, where an infinitely diverse and dispersed Muslim minority allowed it to become purified of the kind of regional, linguistic, racial or class identity that might otherwise permit Islam's representation as a liberal interest. Indeed, the fact that the Muslims of India constituted a political interest of some sort despite their diversity and for apparently idealistic motives made them intractable to the propertied order of a liberal state, or so Iqbal seemed to suggest in his 1930 address to the Muslim League:

It cannot be denied that Islam, regarded as an ethical ideal plus a certain kind of polity—by which expression I mean a social structure regulated by a legal system and animated by a specific ethical ideal—has been the chief formative factor in the life history of the Muslims of India. It has furnished those basic emotions and loyalties which gradually unify scattered individuals and groups and finally transform them into a well-defined people. Indeed it is no exaggeration to say that India is perhaps the only country in the world where Islam as a society is almost entirely due to the working of Islam as a culture inspired by a specific ethical ideal.[8]

For Iqbal, it was the abstract nature of Muslim cohesion that made it into a concrete force. Islam's very unreality became the most potent of realities, born of the sheer vulnerability of its abstraction, or so he claims in a newspaper article of 1934 written to counter the new religious movement of the Ahmadis:

> Islam repudiates the race idea altogether and founds itself on the religious idea alone. Since Islam bases itself on the religious idea alone, a basis which is wholly spiritual and consequently far more ethereal than blood relationship, Muslim society is naturally much more sensitive to forces which it considers harmful to its integrity.[9]

It was of course precisely as this sort of entity that Islam was threatened by liberalism, which was what finally made Iqbal's engagement with the nation-state into much more than a merely parochial, and certainly more than a theoretical enterprise, indeed into a life and death struggle. For the kind of Islam Iqbal described, however aberrant it might be politically, had to stand against liberal nationalism if it was to survive at all. Which meant that no matter how benign the latter's intentions, a liberal order could only triumph in India by eliminating Islam as a social reality. And this meant that the claims of Iqbal's Islam put liberal representation itself as an inclusive process into question, exposing it instead as a practice of violence:

> It is my belief that Islam is not a matter of private opinion. It is a society, or if you like, a civic church. It is because present-day political ideals, as they appear to be shaping themselves in India, may affect its original structures and character that I find myself interested in politics. I am opposed to nationalism as it is understood in Europe, not because, if it is allowed to develop in India, it is likely to bring less material gain to Muslims. I am opposed to it because I see in it the germs of an atheistic materialism which I look upon as the greatest danger to modern humanity.[10]

Such are the broad political outlines of what I call the crisis of representation in British India. Whether or not Iqbal engaged in any special pleading for his community, it is clear that his criticism of liberal representation was consistent. Unlike many other such criticisms, it was also realist, for Iqbal accused precisely the liberal state of idealism by calling attention to the non-liberal actualities of political life in India. So in his presidential address of 1930 to the Muslim League, he quotes Ernest Renan's famous essay on nationalism, pointing out that nationality is not some fact of nature but a political project neither suited nor acceptable to India:

> 'Man', says Renan, 'is enslaved neither by his race, nor by his religion, nor by the course of rivers, nor by the direction of mountain ranges. A great aggregation of men, sane of mind and warm of heart, creates a moral consciousness which is called a nation.' Such a formation is quite possible, though it involves the long and ardu-

ous process of practically remaking men and furnishing them with a fresh emotional equipment ... The formation of the kind of moral consciousness which constitutes the essence of a nation in Renan's sense demands a price which the peoples of India are not prepared to pay.[11]

It was on the basis of such realities that Iqbal went on to re-think the relations of social difference in India beyond simply calling for separate electorates, weightage or federation. Indeed, the reality that Iqbal dealt in could only be approached by a thinking that abandoned the ephemeral and opportunistic calculations of party politics, which was, in his words, 'incapable of synthesizing permanence and change in a higher political concept' and thus 'driven to live from hand to mouth'.[12] What kind of thought, then, approached the realities of Indian politics, as Iqbal saw them, to conceive of social difference outside liberal categories? Religion, precisely because it was the one phenomenon not proving amenable to the liberal imperative of nationalism in India, offered the only position from which the latter's order of interest, representation and contract might be countered.

Much like his contemporary, Gandhi, Iqbal wanted to turn to the advantage of Indian politics the very problem of religion that history had bequeathed it. Like Gandhi, Iqbal intended to do this by inserting religion into public life in such a way as to limit the instrumental violence of liberal politics and make place in it for what he called conviction, idealism or ethical life. One way of doing this was to continue the colonial system of separate electorates and weightage, although it forestalled the liberal categories of nationalism in a merely negative way while at the same time giving rise to communal acrimony. Another way of approaching the problem (which, let us be clear, was one not of Muslim or even minority interests, but precisely the possibility of disinterest in a liberal order) was to work towards a federation that would allow for the expansion of religion's ethical or idealistic qualities in public life. As far as Islam was concerned, Iqbal proposed the following solution in his 1930 presidential address to the Muslim League:

> I therefore demand the formation of a consolidated Muslim state in the best interest of India and Islam. For India it means security and peace resulting from an internal balance of power; for Islam an opportunity to rid itself of the stamp that Arabian imperialism was forced to give it, to mobilize its law, its education, its culture, and to bring them into closer contact with its own original spirit and with the spirit of modern times.[13]

The political bondage of India has been and is a source of infinite misery to the whole of Asia. It has suppressed the spirit of the East and wholly deprived her of that joy of self-expression which once made her the creator of a great and glorious culture. We have a duty towards India, where we are destined to live and die. We have a duty towards Asia, especially Muslim Asia. And since 70 millions of Muslims in a single country constitute a far more valuable asset to Islam than all the countries of Muslim Asia put together, we must look at the Indian problem not only from the Muslim point of view but also from the standpoint of the Indian Muslim as such.[14]

Just as Gandhi ended up making a compromise with liberalism by relinquishing his attempt to keep India within an empire, Iqbal, too, compromised with the liberal spirit of nationalism by grudgingly acceding to a territorial form of political order. Iqbal described what this new political order might look like in his presidential address of 1932 to the All-India Muslim Conference, situating it in the historical context of nationalist agitation and religious conservatism in India:

These phenomena, however, are merely premonitions of a coming storm, which is likely to sweep over the whole of India and the rest of Asia. This is the inevitable outcome of a wholly political civilization which has looked upon man as a thing to be exploited and not as a personality to be developed and enlarged by purely cultural forces. The peoples of Asia are bound to rise against the acquisitive economy which the West has developed and imposed on the nations of the East. Asia cannot comprehend modern Western capitalism with its undisciplined individualism. The faith which you represent recognises the worth of the individual, and disciplines him to give away his all to the service of God and man. Its possibilities are not yet exhausted. It can still create a new world where the social rank of man is not determined by his caste or colour, or the amount of dividend he earns, but by the kind of life he lives; where the poor tax the rich, where human society is founded not on the equality of stomachs but on the equality of spirits, where an untouchable can marry the daughter of a king, where private ownership is a trust and where capital cannot be allowed to accumulate so as to dominate the real producer of wealth. This superb idealism of your faith, however, needs emancipation from the medieval fancies of theologians and legists. Spiritually we are living in a prison house of thoughts and emotions which during the course of centuries we have woven round ourselves.[15]

It is important to note here that Iqbal's solution to India's religious problem was intensely patriotic without being in the least nationalist, since its granting of political power to Muslims was meant to make them more rather than less modern as well as Indian by ridding their religion of the stamp of Arab imperialism, and even going so far as to give India a world-historical role in the making of a new Asia. Though a Muslim solution, it was also one that presupposed and indeed called for the equal if not greater participation of Hindus in its enterprise, for the establishment of Islam in the public life of India automatically brought into being the presence there of Hinduism as well. While he did not write much on the political role of Hinduism, Iqbal made it abundantly clear that he thought nationalism and its liberal dispensation were if anything more dangerous for Hindus than they were for Muslims, since 'the process of becoming a nation is a kind of travail, and in the case of Hindu India involves a complete overhauling of her social structure'.[16] More than this, Iqbal was adamant that religious toleration was in fact only true of those who were themselves Hindus or Muslims. So in an exchange with Jawaharlal Nehru, after quoting Edward Gibbon's dismissal of tolerance as an attitude either of indifference or of weakness, Iqbal writes the following:

> It is obvious that these types of tolerance have no ethical value. On the other hand they unmistakably reveal the spiritual impoverishment of the man who practices them. True toleration is begotten of intellectual breadth and spiritual expansion. It is the toleration of the spiritually powerful man who, while jealous of the frontiers of his own faith, can tolerate and even appreciate all forms of faith other than his own. Of this type of toleration the true Muslim alone is capable. His own faith is synthetic and for this reason he can easily find grounds of sympathy and appreciation in other faiths. Our great Indian poet, Amir Khusro, beautifully brings out the essence of this type of toleration in the story of the idol-worshipper. After giving an account of his intense attachment to his idols the poet addresses his Muslim readers as follows:
>
> Ay ke za but tanah ba Hindu bari
> Ham za we amuz parastish gari
> [You who condemn the Hindu's idolatry
> Learn from him the ways of worship]
>
> Only a true lover of God can appreciate the value of devotion even though it is directed to gods in which he himself does not believe.[17]

Like Gandhi, therefore, Iqbal believed that faith alone could recognise itself in others and so be taken seriously without being represented and thus destroyed in a liberal order of interest and contract. While we have been looking thus far at the ways in which Iqbal thought such recognition might be possible in the historical and political realms, it is in his strictly philosophical and literary work that this recognition receives its lengthiest analysis. And much like Gandhi, again, for Iqbal philosophy and literature were important because they were democratic, being not only themselves part of everyday life but also dealing each in its own way with the problems of everyday life. This was of course especially true of Iqbal's poetry, which enjoyed enormous popularity at all levels of society even in his own day. How, then, did Iqbal reflect upon what I have been calling the crisis of representation in the philosophy and literature of everyday life?

The visible and the invisible

> I do not wish to mystify anybody when I say that things in India are not what they appear to be.[18]

This sentence, from Iqbal's 1930 presidential address to the Muslim League, is just one of many statements he made about what we might call the invisible realities of Indian politics. What could this language signify for a man who spent his whole career inveighing against the mysteries and raptures he thought had sapped India's peoples of all sense of reality? I want to argue that Iqbal called invisible those everyday social relations that were not represented in the categories of liberalism and thus not amenable to its politics of interest and contractual agreement. Such relations, however, did not simply exist in some space beyond these categories, but rather formed with them a kind of relationship, so that Iqbal always referred to them together, with the Qur'anic tag 'the visible and the invisible', as in the following passage from his presidential address of 1932 to the All-India Muslim Conference:

> In view of the visible and invisible points of contact between the various communities of India I do believe in the possibility of constructing a harmonious whole whose unity cannot be disturbed by the rich diversity which it must carry within its bosom. The problem of ancient Indian thought was how the one became many without sacrificing its oneness. To-day this problem has come down from its ethical heights to the grosser plane of our political life, and we have to solve it in its reversed form, i.e., how the many can become one without sacrificing its plural character.[19]

Interestingly, Gandhi was also in the habit of using the phrase 'points of contact' to refer to relations between Hindus and Muslims, claiming for example that whatever its strictures on pagans or polytheists, he was unable to condemn the Qur'an because its teachings on subjects like prayer, forgiveness or justice also belonged to Hinduism. So to reject the Qur'an would be to reject a great deal of the Bhagavad Gita as well, both texts as well as their adherents thus possessing a great many points of contact. But what were Iqbal's invisible points of contact, and how could they even be described politically without being betrayed in the process? The quotation above, dealing with politics as a process of philosophical reversal, furnishes us with a clue. In it, Iqbal reverses Hegel's celebrated statement in the *Phenomenology*, where he describes the problem of ancient thought as the movement from particular to universal and that of modern thought as a reversed movement from the universal to the particular. Whereas Hegel maintained that contemporary thought and politics had to begin with the idea of the universal (for instance, the nation-state), which alone gave meaning to particularity (for instance, classes, races and religions all regarded as interests), Iqbal insisted on deferring the moment of universality in order to liberate social and other particularities from its domain. In the nation-state, this meant relying upon social relations that were invisible because they were unrepresented in the language of citizenship. Invisible social relations were important because, unlike interests, they attended to the singular nature of particulars, making one neither equivalent nor substitutable with another.

While this discussion of invisible social relations might seem arcane, it is important to remember that, for Iqbal, such relations were far more real than the abstractions of liberal thought, with which they nevertheless interacted. One of the ways this occurred was in the practice of everyday life, at least that part of it that was not consumed by the language of representation, interest and contractual agreement. In the passage quoted above, Iqbal suggests translation, between the political and the philosophical, the particular and the universal, the ancient and the modern, as a metaphor by which to conceive this sort of practice. Such a practice made relations between the visible and invisible thinkable only in the language of translation, almost as a kind of conversion, one whose transformative operation precluded the substitutions and equivalences of representation. After all, translation permitted intimate relations between different languages without calling for their representation, in fact by destroying representation altogether in a sort of conversion.

And translation plays a large part in Iqbal's work, from his translations of English and German poetry into Urdu to his translations between Asian and European thought. But what interests me particularly is Iqbal's effort to think through the relations between Hindus and Muslims by using the metaphor of translation. Proud of his own Brahmin ancestry, Iqbal delighted in translating Hindu and Muslim terms one into the other, for instance by referring to Rama in one of his poems as the 'Imam of India', and so playfully converting the Hindu deity into a great Muslim prelate. Given the exacerbated religious sensitivities of his times, especially over issues like conversion, Iqbal's playful translations embody a politics that deserves our attention.

In a letter of 1921 to the eminent orientalist Reynold Nicholson, who had translated his long narrative poem the *Asrar-i Khudi* (Secrets of the self) into English, Iqbal noted that reviews of this translation had either attributed an exclusively Muslim character to his work or, on the contrary, linked it exclusively to European thought. Rejecting both these opinions, Iqbal made the following remark: 'It is unfortunate that the history of Muslim thought is so little known in the West. I wish I had time to write an extensive book on the subject to show to the Western student of philosophy how philosophic thinking makes the whole world kin.'[20]

The book Iqbal imagined writing was not meant to represent Muslim thought as something external, but rather to make it available to the West as thought in a purely internal sense. It was this translation of difference into thought that made the whole world kin, and it did so by depriving difference of all its alien particularity, historical and ethnographic, so that it might be apprehended without the mediation of the Hegelian universal. Thought in Iqbal's sense moves beyond an order of representation to one of conversation since it takes the form of kinship. Indeed, for Iqbal, the universe itself was a collection of subjects engaged in an infinite conversation—this being the only way in which it could have meaning for ethical life.[21] Philosophy manifestly acknowledges this kinship by making historically impossible conversations possible between thinkers from completely different periods and contexts, in this way relinquishing the representation of their particularities for a translation into thought.

The conversational nature of philosophical thought directly links it to the relations of everyday life. For example, Hindus and Muslims could not conduct their daily interactions by continuously representing each other in liberal fashion as Hindus and Muslims, but only by destabilising if not altogether relinquishing representation and translating their relations into the languages of commerce or sexuality or friendship, each one presupposing the singularity rather than equivalence of the parties concerned, and each therefore deferring the moment of Hegelian universality. For it is the very proximity of the interlocutor in conversation that deprives him of visibility and therefore prevents his being grasped, defined and classed as an interest.[22] This closeness makes for relations between persons that might be philosophically incomplete or unsystematic and socially prejudiced or stereotyped, since without the moment of universality they exist only partially and as fragments. Such closeness, however, also makes for a conversation without the visibility of representation, and one that is both philosophical and mundane. It is this kind of conversation that characterises Iqbal's politics of translation.

Having revealed the virtues of liberal representation, including even historical and sociological particularity, to be abstractions of and impediments to relations of social proximity, it was left for Iqbal to demonstrate the salience of his politics of translation. This he did primarily in his poetry, which was and continues to be enormously popular in the Indian Subcontinent and much beyond. It is evident that Iqbal made use of the kind of philosophical translation I have been describing in the many poems where he sets up conversations among the most disparate historical characters, who are able to relate one to the other not because they all agree or have the same thoughts, but precisely because they have been denuded of the historical or sociological particularity that makes them prey to the universal. And this translation of difference into thought by no means renders the former less historical; in fact, the opposite is true. In his epic Persian poem, the *Javid Nama* (Book of eternity), for instance, Iqbal has Pharaoh speak to Lord Kitchener, among other curious combinations, and this not only shows in an almost virtuosic fashion how historical differences can become kin by being translated into thought, but also how the very scandal of a conversation between such characters makes the reader even more aware of their historical differences.

More interesting in some ways than these conversational pieces are those poems in which Iqbal performs a complete translation of difference, which is thus apprehended as such without representation and without any exotic particularity being left over from the process. A poem like 'Aftab' (The sun), from Iqbal's first collection of Urdu verse, the *Bang-e Dara* (Call of the caravan-bell), translates the *Gayatri*, a Sanskrit hymn to the sun, in such a way that without an authorial parenthesis it is impossible to identify it as one. There is no attempt at capturing what for the Urdu language would be the exotic or ancient flavour of the original by any peculiar use of syntax or borrowing from commonly understood Sanskrit vocabulary. Apart from a single poem, 'Naya Shivalaya' (The new temple), from his brief period of infatuation with Indian nationalism, all of Iqbal's verse dealing with non-Muslim subjects performs a complete translation. Among these are the biographical poems 'Swami Ram Tirth', 'Ram' and 'Nanak', all from *Bang-e Dara*. Also present in this first Urdu collection are several untitled poems of a satirical nature in which the Hindu and Muslim communities are represented by a cow and a camel respectively. The absurd conversation these beasts conduct in Iqbal's verses has the effect of sending up representation itself, as well as its processes of substitution and equivalence, in an even greater absurdity.

Yet there is still something representative in the very titles given to many of these poems, which mark them out as 'Hindu' or 'Sikh' insofar as they are separated from other poems marked similarly as 'Muslim'. After his first Urdu collection, then, Iqbal stops partitioning his poetry religiously and puts Hindu and Muslim terms in much greater proximity. So in the *Javid Nama* not only do figures like the Buddha and Bhartrihari appear side by side with Muslim personalities, but they interact even more invisibly. For example, in the *Javid Nama* a narrator moves from planet to planet, seven in all, meeting various historical and mythical characters. The plan of this work is always compared both to Dante's *Divine Comedy* and to the legend of Muhammad's ascent through the seven heavens, the *miraj*. A more likely model might be Nizami's Persian epic, the *Haft Paykar* or Seven bodies, where a hero is similarly depicted travelling not from planet to planet so much as from medieval clime to clime, each under the influence of a particular planet. Iqbal, then, modernises this plot by introducing planetary travel. But this whole genealogy of influences and models changes when we consider that one of the first figures Iqbal's narrator meets, who will be his guide to the planets, is Jahan-Dost or World-Friend, a literal translation of the Sanskrit Vishvamitra, who was the spiritual guide of Rama, hero of the epic *Ramayana*. If Jahan-Dost is, as Iqbal told some of his friends, the sage Vishvamitra, then the *Javid Nama* is a kind of *Ramayana*, which is also a narrative of search and travel.[23]

But in what does all this secrecy result? Has it moved past the criticism of political representation to become just an elaborate literary game? Not quite. What appears to us as a difficult and elaborate literary game was in fact Iqbal's attempt to perform his criticism of representation by writing about Hindus and Muslims in a completely different yet entirely comprehensible and even popular way. The role of the Hindu in Iqbal's writing is of some importance, so much so that it cannot be detached from that of the Muslim, to which it relates as thought, the thought of difference as such. The thought of ancient India, particularly as it is manifested in figures like Krishna (in the *Bhagavad Gita*) and the Buddha, Kapila and Bhartrihari, Ramanuja and Shankara, weaves its way in and out of Iqbal's philosophical work, even that which deals explicitly with Islam. But it does so in a very specific way. On the one hand, there are detailed comparisons between Hindu and Muslim thinkers, for instance in the introduction of the *Asrar-i Khudi*, where Iqbal praises Krishna's philosophy of action in the *Gita* and lauds Ramanuja's commentary on it, but is highly critical of Shankara's apparently beautiful but purely theoretical interpretation. The latter's enormous and, he thinks, deleterious influence upon Hinduism Iqbal then compares to the influence of the mystic Ibn Arabi on the world of Islam. Or there is the following footnote in his doctoral dissertation, 'The Development of Metaphysics in Persia', in which the work of the Muslim thinker Jili is thought together with and made inseparable from those of a number of Hindu philosophers:

> This would seem very much like the idea of the phenomenal Brahma of the Vedanta. The Personal Creator or the Prajipati of the Vedanta makes the third step of the Absolute Being or the Noumenal Brahma. Al-Jili seems to admit two kinds of Brahma—with or without qualities like the Samkara and Badarayana. To him the process of creation is essentially a lowering of the Absolute Thought, which is Asat, in so far as it is absolute, and Sat, in so far as it is manifested and hence limited. Notwithstanding this Absolute Monism, he inclines to a view similar to that of Ramanuja. He seems to admit the reality of the individual soul and seems to imply, unlike Samkara, that Iswara and His worship are necessary even after the attainment of the Higher Knowledge.[24]

On the other hand, there are comparisons between Hindu and Muslim thought where the former is seen as being systematic and the latter fragmented. Take the following sentences from Iqbal's introduction to his dissertation:

> The most remarkable feature of the character of the Persian people is their love of Metaphysical speculation. Yet the inquirer who approaches the extant literature of Persia expecting to find any comprehensive systems of thought, like those of Kapila or Kant, will have to turn back disappointed ... In fact the Persian is only half-conscious of Metaphysics as a *system* of thought; his Brahman brother, on the other hand, is fully alive to the need of presenting his theory in the form of a thoroughly reasoned out system. And the result of this mental difference between the two nations is clear. In the one case we have only partially worked out systems of thought: in the other case, the awful sublimity of the searching Vedanta.[25]

Iqbal's task, then, is to translate Muslim thought into modern language in a systematic way, as he claims in the introduction to his dissertation: 'I have endeavoured to trace the logical continuity of Persian thought, which I have tried to interpret in the language of modern Philosophy. This, as far as I know, has not yet been done.'[26]

And so Muslim thought is modelled upon Hindu thought, although not without a certain rivalry, as in the following passage from an essay of 1900, 'The Doctrine of Absolute Unity as Expounded by Abdul Karim al-Jilani', published in the *Indian Antiquary*:

> While European scholars have investigated ancient Hindu philosophy with an unflagging enthusiasm, they have, as a rule, looked upon Muslim Philosophy as only an unprogressive repetition of Aristotle and Plato ... This comparatively indifferent attitude towards Arabic philosophy has been evident, perhaps, ever since the discovery of Sanskrit literature. We admit the superiority of the Hindu in point of

philosophical acumen, yet this admission need not lead us to ignore the intellectual independence of Muslim thinkers.[27]

Yet Iqbal, as we might expect, was no lover of the universality of fully worked out systems, which he frequently criticised, especially with regard to Indian thought, as being inhuman and uninspiring: 'Semitic religion is a code of strict rules of conduct; the Indian Vedanta, on the other hand, is a cold system of thought.'[28]

In his essay on Jili, Iqbal tells us why the system as a form of the universal is necessarily abstract and life-denying:

> We know much in theory and our belief in this kind of knowledge depends on the force of the number of arguments advanced in its support. The detection of some logical flaw in our argument, or the force of the arguments in favour of the opposite view, may at once induce us to abandon our theory, but if the ego has 'realized' the theory, if the theory in question has been a spiritual experience on our part, no argument, however forcible, no logical flaw, can dispose us to abandon our position.[29]

So we come back to what Iqbal elsewhere calls the ideal, conviction or faith; something that, while it is very real indeed, cannot be represented in terms of the universal and the particular. In philosophical language, such conviction occurs as incomplete or unsystematic thought, and in political language it occurs as a prejudice or stereotype, neither being dependent on any worked-out logic. Iqbal tried to explore this conviction both philosophically and politically, because he thought that it alone made a purely human and egalitarian existence possible as something both singular and common, phenomenally real and intellectually fragmentary. One of the ways Iqbal conducted his exploration was by translating the terms Hindu and Muslim philosophically and looking at the way in which they entered into a conversation. In this case, the invisible, unrepresented particularity of Muslim conviction was to be made systematically visible on the universal model of Hindu philosophy, with which it in fact changed places. Yet this immediately put the Hindu in the position of the Muslim, since it was Indian thought that then became invisible in Iqbal's work. Here, in other words, we have a classic form of Hegelian reversal, with the universal and the particular, or in Iqbal's language the visible and the invisible, coming to mediate or rather convert each other, so that Islam becomes the secret of Hinduism and Hinduism of Islam, without either being made equivalent to or a substitute for the other, both having being robbed of all sociological particularity and rendered into metaphysical categories.

The Hindu–Muslim dyad we have been looking at is in fact only one of a series of couplings, all illustrative of the relations between the visible and invisible, universal and particular. The most important of these pairs in Iqbal's work are those formed between men and women, reason and passion, the material and the spiritual. Given the stylised nature of these dyads (derived possibly from Nietzsche's coupling of Apollonian and Dionysian in *The Birth of Tragedy*, though the influence of Persian and Urdu poetics should not be underestimated either), it is obvious that they have no sociological reality because they have been translated completely into thought. The artifice of representation, therefore, has been as effectively exposed here as it was in Iqbal's satirical verse, since these pairs drift one into the other without being mutually substitutable. As with Hinduism and Islam, then, Iqbal works with everyday prejudices and stereotypes to build a relationship between the units of each pair. So women, passion and the spiritual constitute the invisible, unrepresented or fragmentary parts of social relations whose systematic portions are defined by men, reason and the material world. And it is because the units of these pairs are not set up as alternatives to one another but are related as a series of translations that Iqbal can move from one to the other in an apparently contradictory fashion. He famously pours scorn upon the mysteries of Sufism, for instance, accusing it of a retreat from material existence, yet he continues to use its concepts and language, not least those of secrecy and mystery. Iqbal similarly criticises the vulgar representation of history in what, after Henri Bergson, he calls serial time but writes great narrative poems in which Muslim history is plotted precisely in serial time, for example the celebrated *Shikwa* (Complaint) and *Jawab-e Shikwa* (The complaint's answer).

The most common way in which scholars have dealt with these apparent contradictions in Iqbal's thought is by positing strict divisions between its early and later periods. So we are told that Iqbal's early period was characterised by an infatuation with Sufism and Indian nationalism, while his later period tended to be dominated by an anti-mystical and even pan-Islamist religiosity. My own position is that, while there is, of course, development in Iqbal's thinking, its continuities are far more remarkable. The strict division of Iqbal's early and later periods is everywhere belied by his writing, so that in a late work like the *Javid Nama* we see the very Hindu, Indian and Sufi themes that were present in an early one like the doctoral dissertation. Moreover, Iqbal never omitted even his early Indian nationalist poems like 'Naya Shivalay' from the later editions of his work, though he was not averse to expunging other verses from them.

The appearance of contradiction in Iqbal's thought is due to the complicated politics of translation he sets up between Hindus and Muslims, men and women, in which no term can be reduced to another, and where each is translated into a thought well beyond the historical or sociological status of liberal interest, thus becoming philosophically kin to the other. Is it possible that this arcane theory of social relations, as well as its literary practice in Iqbal's poetry, actually reflected in some way the realities of everyday life in British India? It might prove instructive in this respect to study the way in which popular prejudices, then as much as now, also move beyond the historical and sociological terms of liberal interest to operate at least in part amid another politics of social difference: a politics in which the inevitably fragmentary nature of prejudice cannot represent either itself or its object as an interest. Perhaps it is only when such prejudices come systematically to represent both themselves and their objects as interests that they become politically instrumental, which is the same thing as saying that they become liberal.

Like his contemporary, Gandhi, Iqbal concerned himself with social relations that seemed to exist beyond the procedural language of liberalism, which was made up of terms like interest, representation and contract. While these relations, and especially religious ones, were seen by nationalists as much as by imperialists to pose a threat to liberal politics (justifying for the latter at least the temporary withholding of political responsibility from Indians), neither Iqbal nor Gandhi saw religious or non-liberal social relations primarily as threats of this kind. On the contrary, such relations were for them not only inevitable but also valuable because they prevented the complete dominance of liberal principles, which both men saw as posing a far greater threat to humanity than these prejudices. In his own way, then, each man tried to develop those social relations that liberalism had confined to the realm of stereotype into a kind of ethical criticism of liberal politics. And given the nature of religious relations in India, ethical criticism here could by no means be defined in anaemic European terms as a despairing or nostalgic and in any case politically inconsequential practice. Indeed, for Iqbal as much as for Gandhi, the very problem that religion posed for liberalism in India constituted the latter's greatest contribution to ethical and political thought.

The subject of representation

In an essay of 1909 titled 'Islam as a Moral and Political Ideal', and published in the *Hindustan Review*, Iqbal wrote the following:

> The central proposition which regulates the structure of Islam ... is that there is fear in nature, and the object of Islam is to free man from fear. This view of the

universe indicates also the Islamic view of the metaphysical nature of man. If fear is the force which dominates man and counteracts his ethical progress, man must be regarded as a unit of force, an energy, a will, a germ of infinite power, the gradual unfoldment of which must be the object of all human activity. The essential nature of man, then, consists in will, not intellect and understanding ... Give man a keen sense of respect for his own personality, let him move fearless and free in the immensity of God's earth, and he will respect the personalities of others and become perfectly virtuous.[30]

With this quotation, we come back to Iqbal's criticism of intellect and understanding, which is so frequently juxtaposed to what he calls faith, conviction or idealism. The fear that for Iqbal results in unethical or violent action is, he suggests, fostered rather than denied by intellect or understanding, whose uses of representation, whether political or epistemological, end up strengthening divisions between the human and the non-human, as well as between human beings themselves. Representation, in other words, depends upon the epistemological separation of subject and object together with the political separation of public and private, both of which it intensifies by limiting the bounds of individual and other human action to the purely instrumental. And these sets of limits, argues Iqbal, rather than confining the destructive potential of human action, actually expand it by making human beings prey to fear, especially the fear of what lies outside one's own place, on the other side of liberalism's various separations. Such limits and the fear that attends them can only be surmounted by removing human action from the operations of representation that characterise intellect and understanding, both of which Iqbal thought had adopted a fundamentally passive attitude towards reality seen in purely external terms.

In trying to exit the language of separations and limits that characterised a liberal order of representation, epistemological as much as political, Iqbal had recourse to the notion of will, for which he famously used the abstract Persian noun *khudi* (instead of *iradah*, more commonly used for will, but only as a quality). Of course, *khudi*, which had the virtue of doing away with notions of agency relying upon intellect or understanding, could not itself constitute some substance that might be represented, as Iqbal explained in an essay explicating his use of the term and distinguishing it from Nietzsche's:

According to Nietzsche the 'I' is a fiction. It is true that looked at from a purely intellectual point of view this conclusion is inevitable ... There is, however, another point of view, that is to say the point of view of inner experience. From this point of view the 'I' is an indubitable fact ... which stares us in the face in spite of our intellectual analysis of it.[31]

By settling upon a phenomenological definition of will as something insubstantial and even fictive, Iqbal returns to his old concerns with the superiority, or at least intractability, of what he variously calls faith, conviction or the ideal to the intellect's order or representation. Indeed, as the core of individual selfhood, will in this sense is only the miniaturisation of the Muslim's collective selfhood, whose strength as much as fragility was premised upon its immateriality. And will as he defines it here has more in common with the popular prejudice and feeling that exists somewhere below the liberal order of representation than it does with the latter's politics of interest, not to mention its epistemological concept of a subject. That Iqbal was very clear about the fictive and insubstantial nature of the will made possible by faith, conviction or idealism is evident from the notes he collected under the title *Stray Reflections*, of which the following piece of irony is characteristic: 'Belief is a great power. When I see that a proposition of mine is believed by another mind, my own conviction of its truth is thereby immensely increased.'[32]

Returning to his explication of the term *khudi*, it is evident that Iqbal's notion of will can be represented neither as subject nor as interest, but occurs (rather than exists) in a sort of eternal becoming:

> The question, therefore, which should be raised in regard to the human 'I' is not whether it is a substance or not. This question was raised by our theologians, whose philosophical discussion achieved nothing. The question which ought to be raised in my opinion is whether this weak, created and dependent ego or 'I' can be made to survive the shock of death and thus become a permanent element in the constitution of the universe.[33]

> Thus metaphysically the word 'khudi' is used in the sense of that indescribable feeling of 'I' which forms the basis of the uniqueness of each individual.[34]

It should be obvious that the universality of liberal representation, which would make all particulars equivalent and substitutable with each other either as subjects or as interests is being subverted in the quotation above by a singular infinity. An expansively horizontal concept of universality, we might say, is being displaced by an intensively vertical notion of infinity: one with no links to representation, whether political or epistemological. Having (at least in his work) extracted Indians from a liberal order in which they existed as subjects by being represented as equivalent and substitutable particularities, Iqbal is here extracting them from another form of this order, where the subject represents others in the same way as it is represented. And it is to will or *khudi* that this work of extraction is entrusted.

Iqbal's life work may well be seen as an effort to think outside or at the edges of liberal categories like interest, contract and representation, not necessarily in order to destroy their malign visibility but to take into account the invisible social relations that these left out. I have argued here that Iqbal tried to move beyond such categories by rethinking relations among Indians (I have focused in this essay on Hindus and Muslims) in terms that were simultaneously philosophical and popular, these terms being linked, I am suggesting, to prejudice and stereotype as intractable and finally ethical qualities. Not only did Iqbal move away from conceiving of India's religious groups as sociological particularities and therefore as interests; he distanced himself from liberal ideas of the epistemological and political subject as well, by rethinking the notion of will phenomenologically, as an occurrence without substance, *khudi*, which he also linked to the realities of everyday life.

Just as Hindus and Muslims are transformed by Iqbal into metaphysical rather than sociological categories, relating to one another in metaphors of translation instead of representation, so the Indian subject is transformed by him into a phenomenological will, which acts by breaching all the separations and limits of a liberal order based on intellect or understanding. Indeed, it is this will that performs the final ceremonies of translation as a social practice, its task being not to observe limits and respect differences, but to destroy their externality in translation as an act of creative absorption, for as Iqbal puts it:

> To permit the visible to shape the invisible to seek what is scientifically called adjustment with nature is to recognize her mastery over the spirit of man. Power comes from resisting her stimuli, and not from exposing ourselves to their action. Resistance of what is with a view to create what ought to be, is health and life. All else is decay and death. Both God and man live by perpetual creation.[35]

Iqbal comes back in this passage to the visible and invisible relations of social life, recommending the destruction of external reality by its translation into the inner life of the will. The close similarity this idea bears to that celebrated section in Hegel's *Phenomenology* on the dialectic of master and bondsman is probably not accidental, and Iqbal discusses its implications over and over again. So he decries the master's merely ideal command over external objects through the instrumental action of his bondsman and glorifies the latter's manipulation and ultimate destruction of all externality including that of the master. Iqbal calls this external world that must be destroyed an idol, thus making use of a Muslim stereotype to indicate the fetishistic quality that externality assumes in everyday life. As in Hegel's dialectic, the negation of such externality then makes it a part of inner life, which is where it partakes of the will as faith, conviction or belief, no longer having any connection to intellect and understanding as forms of representation. In this sense, idol-breaking as a quintessentially Muslim way of relating to the Hindu ends up lodging the idol and idolatry at the very heart of Islam. Of this no better example can be given than the pride of place the idol enjoys in Persian and Urdu literature, very often standing in for God himself. It is this quality of negation, then, that makes Islam into what Iqbal repeatedly calls a synthetic religion, allowing Muslims to recognise the apparently alien as part of their own inner selves, but as faith, conviction or the ideal rather than as something merely represented.

Iqbal's lauding of what I have been calling negation, destruction or translation by no means indicates his advocacy of violence. On the contrary, he is simply pointing out that even a metaphysics of conflict or annihilation is capable of approaching difference in a far more hopeful and proximate way than the instrumental logic of representational thought. In the case of Hindus and Muslims, Iqbal seems to be suggesting that precisely the invisible relations between the two, tied to popular prejudices and not to liberal categories like representation, contract and interest, make a genuine and productive co-existence possible. In other words, the very fact that everyday relations among Hindus and Muslims cannot be entirely mediated by liberal categories but exist in the realm of prejudice and stereotype, allows them to be rendered into forms of thought and thus assimilated beyond the facts of sociology. It is at this point, then, that it becomes possible for such groups to enter into relationships not reduced to those of a liberal order of representation, making each available to the other metaphysically in a translation that retains all the fire of faith, conviction and idealism.

DEBATES

4

POSTCOLONIAL PROPHETS

ISLAM IN THE LIBERAL ACADEMY

Neguin Yavari

In the popular telling, Islam is a chimera with a broad array of convoluted representations through its long history.[1] In the medieval Christian views, it was frequently branded as a heretical abomination. In the early modern period, derogatory depictions of Muhammad provided an exemplum, 'a dark double of Christianity', against which European religio-political identity was honed.[2] The professionalisation of religious studies in the nineteenth-century academy produced a range of lexical novelties to encapsulate all that separated Islam from more malleable, reason-abiding religions (i.e. those able to accommodate the modern condition, which was in turn equated with liberal democracy). Islam has been described variably as 'a way of life', a religion of orthopraxy rather than orthodoxy, an ideology, a religion in search of its own Martin Luther, and, in the twenty-first century, as a religion prone to excess, violence, discrimination and abuse.[3] These definitions do not add up to a clear picture. We do not seem to know how to identify and place Islam: whether it is a religion, a culture, a polity, a moral code, an ideology or a blueprint for a state.[4] Moreover, the various interpretations of Islam have helped create a sense of fear and danger, engendering an irresolvable *cultural* conflict—a conflict as amorphous as culture itself.

The predicament outlined above is fed by a confluence of factors and currents, some more political than others, and still others that are more ideological than contextual. The focus in this chapter is on the apparent inefficiency of the academic knowledge industry in crafting a more palatable image of Islam in the eyes of the public. The academy's failure to maintain a genuinely political position[5]—one that treats political problems politically, not morally—has undermined its efforts to augment Islam's public standing. A cursory glance at the literature on the Islamic world produced in the Western academy will point to one—perhaps a singular—consensus among experts, namely that there is a forgotten and suppressed kernel, a dormant salience to Islam that is spiritually inclined, open-minded, liberal and tolerant, and which must be recovered before Islam can be normalised in the public arena. Interestingly, the governments of many Western nations subscribe to the same view. The irony of recovering true Islam not just from outside but also *despite* the Islamic world is all but lost on the academy.

Islam's greatest enemy: history

Past greatness in contrast with a diminished present is the unwritten and unspoken meta-history of most histories of the Islamic world.[6] Conventional wisdom in the post-Second World War period held Islam responsible for many of the ills that plagued Muslim-majority societies. The first wave of responses to that simplistic narrative came from Muslim intelligentsia living in the Middle East and North Africa. Writing in the 1960s, Malcolm Kerr, a former professor at UCLA and president of the American University of Beirut, noted that Muslim reformists 'are overly preoccupied with defending Islam against European criticism'.[7] Kerr's warning fell on deaf ears, and Western academics soon joined the chorus. Some sought to dampen European triumphalism by pointing to various lingering problems in those societies, and others blamed these problems on the long-term ramifications of colonial rule.

A number of scholars sought to demystify Islam and tidy up its entanglements with law and with politics by introducing neologisms. Marshall Hodgson's 'Islamicate' was among the most influential.[8] As well as a means of labelling the 'anatomy' of a culture, 'Islamicate' also sought to sever the cultural achievements of Islam from its more religious, and often maligned, features. According to Bruce Lawrence, the term was coined 'to pluralize identities and collapse borders'.[9] Christopher Bayly describes Hodgson's approach as marked by a redemptive turn of mind, and tinged with religious sentiments.[10] According to Bayly, Hodgson believed that the contemporary humiliations of the Islamic world could be redeemed by finding and emphasising those aspects of its religion and culture that had once put it at the pole of human achievement. Fiercely opposed to the Eurocentrism that prevailed in the mid-twentieth-century academy, Hodgson sought to valorise the Islamic world by amplifying its past accomplishments. To further undermine the triumphalist European narrative of progress and growth, Hodgson accused the West of having fallen victim to 'technicalism', and, at least implicitly, prescribed as its antidote 'spiritual fulfilment' (in abundance in Sufi circles, for instance).

Such scholarship aims to reveal the hidden agendas and conceptual pitfalls in arguments put forth by Islam's detractors. Their differences notwithstanding, neither the apologists nor the detractors have moved beyond what is in essence a culturalist explanation that rests on capturing the conceptual ambit of Islam. Hence, a methodologically rigorous explanation for the 'rise' of Europe or the 'fall' of the Islamic remains a desideratum, and the stubborn lingering of that elephant in the room continues to undergird every theoretical foray into modern Islamic history.[11] Before further exploring the impermeability of Islam—epistemologically as well as politically—and the scholarship defending Islam, a brief history is in order.

Scholars, spies, social sciences, and area studies

Although Western academic study of Islam is several centuries old, the field was redefined in the 1950s with the emergence of area studies centres, departments and institutes.[12] Despite a significant increase in resources—such centres were primarily underwritten by various agencies of the US government— regional institutes and area studies departments have largely failed in the task of developing an intellectual vision, methodologically rigorous scholarship, and in influencing public opinion and policy debates on the Islamic world. In a well-known article entitled 'The Study of Middle East Politics 1946–1996: A Stocktaking', James Bill delivered a bleak verdict: 'we have learned disturbingly little after fifty years of heavy exertion'.[13]

Timothy Mitchell has similarly addressed the failure of area studies to advance learning.[14] Against the conventional history, which places the formation of area studies programmes in American universities in the context of Cold War politics, and the security and intelligence interests of the Western world,[15] Mitchell argues that the genesis of regional institutes and culture-specific knowledge lies in the rise of the social sciences in the post-World War II academy, and their claim to the scientific study of society, culture, politics, thought and economics, applicable without restriction. Area studies was necessary to complement the disciplinary-based knowledge industry, and 'integral to the larger attempt to create a sovereign structure of universal knowledge—itself part of the project of a globalized American modernity to which the Cold War also belonged'.[16] Not limited to preparing specialists for intelligence and diplomatic needs, area studies also served to compensate for the parochialism that the division of the social sciences into disciplines entailed. It was only through area studies that social science could become universal.[17]

The lack of disciplinary depth in area studies programmes is the main culprit in their unravelling, Richard Bulliet has argued:

> Area studies centers were mandated with the mission to raise broad-spectrum foreign area specialists possessing competence in language, culture, and modern affairs for their respective areas. The curricular demands of such programs, leaving aside the question of their intellectual validity, caused most Middle East specialists to devote the vast preponderance of their post-graduate education to area-defined courses taught by marginally qualified faculty.[18]

The problem of poorly trained faculty members in area studies programmes that carried little weight in their nominal social science disciplines, Bulliet contends, was compounded by the limited appeal of such programmes to a student body who accepted the national interest agenda embodied in the area studies concept.

The relationship between area studies and the national interests and security objectives of liberal Western states is not restricted to funding from murky sources or intelligence agencies. In her biography of Raymond Carr, the long-time warden of St Antony's College, Oxford, María González Hernández charts the influence of America's strategic interests in encouraging area studies and shaping the college's academic mission. In the 1960s, St Antony's—dubbed 'the CIA's Oxford Annexe'—received large donations from American foundations including Rockefeller, encouraged by the CIA, and many of its fellows and private donors enjoyed connections with the British and American intelligence services.[19] Carr was, famously, a committed Zionist who converted to the cause under the influence of Isaiah Berlin, among others. In the words of William Roger Louis, 'Carr believed that the United States, Britain, and the United Nations—in other words, the countries responsible for the creation of the new Jewish state plus the collective international community—had an obligation to ensure its survival.'[20]

In the United States, ideological screening and funding from sources with non-academic interests kept the lid on academic criticism of Israel and US policy in the Middle East in the 1950s and the 1960s. Over the years the US government, in addition to numerous other soft-intervention projects, has funded a slew of propaganda outlets to craft a receptive audience for Western policy objectives, affects, styles and cultural products.[21] Most of these were authorised and undertaken in secret. Tawfiq Sayyigh's *Al-Hiwar* journal, published in Beirut, ceased publication in 1967,[22] after CIA funding of the Congress for Cultural Freedom (established by the CIA in Paris, which also funded the British magazine *Encounter*, founded in 1953 by Stephen Spender and Irving Kristol) was revealed. In addition to winning the academy's silence on the Arab–Israeli conflict, encouraging the study of minorities—religious, ethnic and racial—was another objective dictated by government monies. CIA funding for *Encounter*, for example, 'carried with it one stipulation: that the journal publish articles dealing with the position of Muslim communities in the Soviet Union.'[23]

Public lectures that raise awareness of human rights violations, as well as oppressive and discriminatory practices towards religious, ethnic and gender groups, are a regular occurrence in such programmes.[24] More recently, it was thanks to Wikileaks that US government efforts to undermine political stability in Iran and elsewhere in the Middle East were publicised. The revelations were particularly damaging to the University of Durham, whose exchange programmes were exposed as a cover for attracting Iranian graduate students, researchers and faculty members out of Iran.[25] Ironically, Durham had also been implicated, just a few years earlier, in another funding scandal, on that occasion involving funding from hard-line and staunchly reactionary clerics and research institutes in Iran.[26]

In the post-Said academy, however, a general shift in political proclivity away from government interests is palpable, especially in area studies programmes.[27] This shift is most pronounced in current research on Israel, if not on the study of repressed populations. But the failure of the academy to have influenced public debate or policymaking runs deeper than the divergence between the worldviews and inclination of politicians, and those upheld by the professoriate.

'Unpolitical' Islam in the 'unpolitically' liberal academy

The remarks above suggest that the study of Islam in the liberal academy is mired in unresolved contradictions and paradoxes because it brings to the fore fissures in the liberal world order, and by extension, in the academy itself. The academy can do no more than point to the ideological biases that prevail in its immediate political context.[28] But it is unable to extricate itself from that liberal order; here liberalism is considered in a rather pedestrian manner, as the constitutive ideology of the West.[29] The act of highlighting the gap between claims and practices of empires professing a civilising mission is at least a few centuries old. The Melians protesting Athenian imperial ambitions by pointing to the discrepancy between what the Athenians saw fit for themselves and what they did to nations in Thucydides' *The History of the Peloponnesian War* is a well-known example, as is the case presented by Bartolomé de las Casas, a Dominican friar in the service of the Spanish crown. Penned in the mid-sixteenth century, de las Casas's painstaking account of the contradictions between the words and deeds of Spanish officials in the Americas, could, with nominal modification, be resurrected to indict the conquest of Iraq by the US-led coalition in the first decade of the twenty-first century. The Spanish crown claimed to propagate civilisation and Christian ethics. Coalition forces evangelised democracy and human rights.

None of this is new. The role of liberalism as the ideology of European empires has been recognised for the past half-century at least,[30] and as the ideology of capitalism a little more recently. As pointed out by Thucydides in the fifth century BCE and de las Casas in the mid-sixteenth, a hallmark of imperial history is the discrepancy between words and actions. Dipesh Chakrabarty, for example, has noted that in the nineteenth century, Europe simultaneously preached its Enlightenment humanism to the colonised and denied its practice.[31] Critics of the imperialist project, however, adopted that same array of Enlightenment values. That contradiction is difficult to overcome, he adds, 'because there is no easy way of dispensing with these values in the condition of political modernity. Without them, there would be no social science that addresses issues of modern social justice.'[32] Similarly, Abdelfattah Kilito's thoughtful *L'auteur et ses doubles*, published in 1985, questioned the promise of translation and other modes of transcultural exchange.[33] And in the same vein, Zaheer Kazmi has pointed to the failure of advocates of Muslim liberalism 'to exit its language or categories', irrespective of whether they 'seek to synthesize, adapt to, or critique Western liberalism.'[34]

Western theory is also manifestly present in Edward Said's indictment of orientalism, the fallout from which deserves further examination. While it is true that refutations of the Saidian thesis share a veiled, but still salient, racist undercurrent, as well as an explicit political agenda, it is also the case that *Orientalism* failed to generate a disciplinary or methodological overhaul.[35] It was an occidental critique, one that gave rise to postcolonial theory, more visible in South Asian studies, which in Mitchell's view, 'offered the possibility of a form of area studies that did not treat the region as "a thing that exists" but explored in the representation of the non-West fundamental questions about Western ways of knowing and the project of a general social science'.[36] The postcolonial approach has occasioned fresh insight into the workings of empire and, most interestingly, on exploring the structural limitations imposed by the centre–periphery divide. Critics point, however, to its abject failure in giving voice to the voiceless. It has remained a critique of power. Said himself was sceptical about postmodernism and postcolonialism, as Robert J.C. Young has demonstrated.[37]

The travails of postcolonial theory and the mixed reception it has received in the academy is also emblematic of political dissonance on another plane.[38] The Second World War and the dismantling of the colonial order redefined nations and states in significant ways. While international orders of governance were introduced, physical borders between states were strengthened for a variety of purposes, including curbing immigration to the West.[39] That the promise of liberalism is neither international nor universal was quickly evident, as was the undeniable monopoly of Western educational institutions on the production of knowledge. Accordingly, the critique of American imperialism and Western prejudice shifted from the third world to the heart of the Western world itself, and subsequently subsumed the quintessential taxonomy of liberalism, that is, identity politics, especially focused on the issue of gender.[40] Whereas, towards the end of the nineteenth century, the concept of a universal West unbound to categories of race or religion, as well as historical context, was dominant in Asia, out of which anti-Western visions of world order were born in the early twentieth century, as Cemil Aydin has documented,[41] the past few decades have hardly seen an intellectual or discursive tradition of anti-Westernism arise among the non-Western secular intelligentsia.[42] That too must be a part of the 'universalisation' of knowledge—and of power—that Mitchell wrote about. This spatial turn is striking in the case of Middle East and Islamic studies. While the writings of Jalal Al Ahmad,[43] Hicham Djait,[44] Abdullah 'Arawi,[45] Samir Amin,[46] and Frantz Fanon were the primary sources listed in anti-imperialist bibliographies throughout the 1960s and 1970s,[47] in the discourse of the early twenty-first century, such literature is regularly forthcoming from diasporic intellectuals. A vast preponderance of that output is occupied with varying shades of liberal Islam, true Islam, true shari'a, or woman-friendly Islam. The search for 'authentic' Islam—framed in the West for a Western audience—is both viral and virtual—its most vocal participants exist outside borders, disciplines, methodologies and relationships of power. They live in the West, not as immigrants, not as global citizens, but beyond nations, states and bordered selves.[48] The political fallout from this unanchored position is multivalent.

In 1992, Rosalind O'Hanlon and David Washbrook argued against Gyan Prakash's exhortation to emancipate subaltern history from the ravages of foundationalism that

> these approaches prescribe remedies which actually create new and in many cases much more serious difficulties of their own, in part because they have, of course, as much to do with arguments about the politics of representation in Western intellectual and academic circles, as they do with imposing that manner of representation on the third world's history.[49]

The incongruence between the political context of the Western intellectual and that of the third world subject is among the more serious limitations of knowledge produced on the non-Western world. Peter Gran has shown, for instance, that the politics of subaltern studies in India are diametrically opposed to that of its practitioners in the West. 'In India, Subaltern Studies is read against liberalism, Marxism and "religious fascism," whereas in the US, its "principal novelty" is its ability to represent India by being read into ideologies of difference and otherness.'[50] While scholars in area studies centres and departments claim to serve as a bridge between East and West, refashioned inevitably in newly minted nomenclature, such as the claim to the simultaneous representation of both East and West,[51] they are hemmed in not by the difficulties germane to the subject matter but rather by their political dissonance. For what exactly does it mean to produce knowledge about the Islamic world that speaks to the West?

One attempt to answer that question is found in Wael Hallaq's *The Impossible State* (2012),[52] which attempts a resolution of contemporary sociopolitical ills in the Western and the Islamic worlds, as well as reconciliation between them. The monograph deserves an in-depth treatment as it exemplifies several of the themes visited so far in this chapter.

Of wishful thinking and dialogue

Dialogue and conviviality between East and West is a central theme in *The Impossible State*. Published more than half a century after Hodgson's works, it amplifies his attempt to absolve the Islamic world from accusations of backwardness by pointing to the moral desertification of Western societies; the culprit in this case, however, is the post-Enlightenment state rather than technology. Hallaq's prescription for his Western audience includes undoing the ravages of the modern state, which has, so he claims, brought incremental solitude, alienation, suffering, environmental degradation and violence to its inhabitants.

Islamists, on the other hand, are plagued by a hopeless quest for an Islamic avatar of this very modern state, which, 'by any standard definition of what the modern state represents, is both an impossibility and a contradiction in terms'.[53] The modern state is an affront to Muslim morality, because it

> represents a process of becoming, the unfolding of a novel and particular political and politicocultural arrangement that is distinctly European in origin ... Europe, defined in geographical and human terms, was the near exclusive laboratory in which the state was first created and later developed, and Euro-America remains until today the location of the paradigmatic state.[54]

On that basis, Hallaq issues to the Muslims a call to revive the true shari'a, the pure, unadulterated shari'a of precolonial times, the sine qua non of which is abandoning the 200-year-old quest for an Islamic state. Pointing to the distorted shari'a that is on parade in the contemporary Islamic world, Hallaq suggests that we 'overlook the modern Islamic experience with the Sharī'a', and focus instead on 'what the Sharī'a meant for Muslims throughout the twelve centuries before the colonialist [*sic*] period, when it existed as a paradigmatic phenomenon'.[55] The technicalities involved in understanding what the shari'a signified to the millions of Muslims of the past notwithstanding, the shari'a that Hallaq upholds was, of course, never the ethos of governance in the Islamic world. Where the shari'a prevailed, as a metaphysical entity with material efficacy, is, to Hallaq, outside of history. It was a 'hegemonic moral system' that 'did its best to address the mess of social reality'.[56] As a paradigm, 'like its particular and technical legal rules', it 'always strove toward the realization of this moral end, sometimes failing but most often succeeding, which is precisely what made it a paradigm'.[57] As proof for the validity of his assertion that history can have a lingering presence without necessitating a return to the past, Hallaq maintains that, if Westerners can invoke Aristotle, Aquinas and

Kant to mobilise an ethos of progress, then the paradigm of Islamic govern-ance may be legitimately invoked to catalyse a modern revival.[58]

It is Western theory—as Chakrabarty had delineated—that defines the parameters of Hallaq's Western gaze, whereas, when eyeing the East, it is the East itself, its very history that is the target of annihilation. Hallaq's mono-graph pits two Middle Eastern thinkers—himself and al-Ghazzali (d.1111)—against a veritable pantheon of theorists of European intellectual history.[59] His oversimplified conception of history is, to use present-day rhetoric, an aca-demic exercise in 'degrade and destroy'.

Meanwhile, back in the Islamic world ...

Paradoxically, in the Islamic world—where it matters most—a defence of Islam was abandoned in the 1970s,[60] almost coevally with the spatial shift outlined above. The case of Iran and the ideological shift imposed by the exi-gencies of the war with Iraq provides a particularly telling example. In his attempt to forge a collective identity that secured Iran against Iraqi aggression but, at the same time, eschewed secular nationalism, rather than advocating ecumenical or tolerant values, or refuting the views held by his political foes by demonstrating how progressive or humanist Islam could be, Khomeini absolved what he called 'true Islam' from such a characterisation. He insisted that there was no separation of religion and state in Islam, and, furthermore, that depoliticised Islam was in fact a political view promoted and nurtured by the imperialist world order. Khomeini's stance was, however, purely rhetorical, for throughout his tenure as an opposition leader as well as the nation's supreme leader, he did not hesitate to separate church from state when expedi-ent, as in the constitutional division of powers.[61]

Reinhard Schulze takes the point further. Just as Islamic ideologies were asserting themselves, 'their disintegration was already being planned and par-tially discussed'.[62] Islamic ideologies gained traction in the Islamic world in the eighteenth and the nineteenth centuries, before taking hold in the twentieth. They 'aimed at the utopian perfection of human existence in this world through the recognition of axioms and norms which were accepted as estab-lished, unquestionable principles of social development'. By the late 1980s, however, a new mythical collective identity, which did not seek a utopia, but a common origin, was gaining ground. It was a new nationalism 'with more pronounced ethnic characteristics', in which Islam provided 'a mythical foun-dation for the specific ethnicity of the nation state'. This new context, Schulze contends, calls for the meaning ascribed to religion to be revisited. In fact, the tortuous relationship between religion and ideology—which marks a vast swath of the academy's quest for an authentic and useful description of Islam—'may be obsolete, and even irrelevant'. For it is possible to consider both religion and ideology 'as suspended by myth operating in the intellectual and political sphere'.[63] But the fascination with the moderate Muslim, the liberal Muslim, the rational Muslim and the democratic Muslim proceeds unabated.[64] In this vein, as well, is best explained the politics of the generous funding of centres charged with propagating true Islam and promoting Muslim–Christian understanding in various Western universities by a number of Saudi donors, in whose own backyard, Christians, as well as all non-Sunnis, are branded as heterodox and considered barely human.[65]

The Islamic political

Politics is organised on a wholly different grid in the Islamic world itself. The political purchase of Khomeini's frontal attack on the separation of public and private in post-revolutionary Iran becomes apparent when it is considered as part of a larger project fostering political community, and of a collective ethos that is neither sectarian nor Western.[66] In the early 1980s, when Iran was losing a substantial number of its scientists, professionals and academics to emigration, the government decided against closing the borders. The departure of a good portion of its disgruntled, vocal elite helped in withstanding Saddam Hussein's military attack, funded by the Saudis and supplied by Western powers including the Soviet Union. By making participation in the Islamic public contingent upon lifestyle, Khomeini strove to erase that very hybridity that Edward Said so embraced and fixed at the heart of the secular critique. When asked about a fresh-from-Harvard PhD as someone to head the Ministry of Economics in the early days of the revolution, Khomeini is famously reported to have said, 'Economics is for donkeys. Give me a pious performer of the *namaz* [ritual prayers].'[67] That distinction was essential to the forging of a new nationalism and a new politics. That point, too, was lost on his erstwhile interlopers in the West.

The fallout from a conflicted notion of the political is also germane to the failure of area studies to advance knowledge of the Islamic world. In the first instance, the ideological stance of a sizeable share of scholars who study the modern Islamic world remains 'crypto-normative', to use Peter Gordon's ascription.[68] Amr Hamzawy has shown that a good number of studies produced on the subject share an anti-Islamist sentiment and present a caricature of Islamism as anti-modernist and as disruptive of societal progress.[69] The study of Islam and of Islamic history also suffers from the short-termism that has engulfed the humanities since the 1960s, as Jo Guldi and David Armitage have argued:

> The triumph of the short durée was brought about by the combination of archival mastery, micro-history, and an emphasis on contingency and context, powered by a suspicion of grand narratives, a hostility to whiggish teleologies, and an ever-advancing anti-essentialism that determined an increasing focus on the synchronic and the short-term across wide swathes of the historical profession.[70]

Short-termism is rife in Middle Eastern and Islamic studies, whose gaze—measured in courses taught, faculty appointments, graduate student training, publications, conferences and sources of funding—is increasingly fixed on the modern period.[71] Consider, as an example of what is on offer from a long-term account, a 1994 study by Richard Bulliet, which traces the history of Islamic societies from the medieval to the modern period, to answer this question: 'How have religious political ideals that have lain unexpressed for a generation regained their potency at the end of the twentieth century?' Part of Bulliet's answer is that 'the eleventh century is as, if not more, important for understanding the origin of today's political and social forces than the nineteenth'.[72] The nature of Islamic religious authority, he contends,

> and the source of its profound impact upon the lives of Muslims—the Muslims of yesterday, today and tomorrow—cannot be grasped without comprehending the social evolution of Islamic society. Nor can such a comprehension be gained from a cursory perusal of the central narrative of Islam. The view from the edge is needed, because in truth, the edge ultimately creates the center.[73]

Time and again, events and currents in the Islamic world have been misinterpreted. The failure of the Iranian Revolution to establish a liberal democracy, for instance, generated volumes on the end of Islamism, or better still, post-Islamism. In the wake of that declaration, Islamist currents dominated what was optimistically dubbed the 'Arab Spring'.[74] Its infelicitous outcome should also be a cause for concern, as should the billions that governments have spent on fighting terrorists and refuting their ideology. Terrorism is, of course, not an ideology, which in Walter Benn Michael's apt characterisation, 'puts both terrorism and the war against it on firm and familiar postmodernist ground'.[75]

In 2012, as professors, politicians and publics in the West waxed lyrical on street protests, youth movements, liberal masses and well-socialised dissenters in the Arab world, a mullah, on vacation in Tehran from Najaf, offered an alternative reading of the tea leaves. In an interview in July 2012, when the 'insurgency' in Syria was almost a year old, the mullah prophesised that, should Bashar Assad stay in power for another six months, he would stay there for good.[76] How much did 'we' expend to learn that? Ali Akbar Mohtashamipur, among Khomeini's closest allies, and Iran's ambassador to Syria in the 1980s, who has taken up residence in Najaf after the election crisis in 2009, neither condones nor condemns Assad's regime; nor does he claim to have a resolution for Syria's ills. It is a simple political understanding: the Ikhwan in Syria, and elsewhere in the Arab world, he begins, resemble al-Qaeda: they are radical, dogmatic and Salafi in their views. Even Ayman al-Zawahiri appears as more temperate. Further, the Syrian opposition is desperately fractured, and the strongest bloc, the Ikhwan, is mistrusted by the Americans.[77] Simply put, the coalition against Assad is not a political force. Muhtashimipur's analysis also explains the genesis of al-Da'ish (ISIS) as a splinter group within the so-called Syrian insurgency that broke away in 2013. The allegedly 'popular uprising' in Syria began in March 2011. Three years on at the time of writing, with an insurgency forged and funded by Turkey, Saudi Arabia, UAE and cheered on especially by the French, the former colonial masters of al-Sham, one wonders if the 'popular' in 'popular Syrian uprising' is appropriate at all, outside the imagination of so-called freedom lovers worldwide.

I would like to end with a suggestion: the end of liberal Islam came from the Islamic world itself. And there will be no return to a Mu'tazili paradise, as Van Ess has argued,[78] or to the mystical shar'ism of Ghazzali as Hallaq has claimed. Like ideologies of all stripes, Islam has and will continue to evolve conceptually, as it will in taking the experts by 'surprise'. As long as 'we' refuse to deign Islam worthy of a political reading, 'we' will not understand the context that generates and is shaped by those conceptual evolutions.

5

A NEW DEAL BETWEEN MANKIND
AND ITS GODS

HOW TO THINK IN THE POST-RELIGIOUS ERA
ACCORDING TO MUHAMMAD IQBAL

Abdennour Bidar

This chapter argues that a new spiritual era, beyond the conventional forms of established religion, is upon us. While such an era exists as a yet unmapped consequence of modernity, it also moves us beyond the widely held belief that the Islamic world faces a 'liberal' political challenge. In fact, the contours of this new era and the challenges that define it are less political than metaphysical. After two centuries centred on Western-led calls for greater 'secularism', a new, post-religious era is beginning that is equally as concerned with progress in the fields of justice, peace and equality. However, this era is marked not by the questions of liberal political philosophy that have increasingly underpinned critical debate on the nature of contemporary Islam, but by a far deeper question facing mankind—its spiritual and historical destiny.

* * *

A powerful argument about the 'exit from religion' concerns 'the death of God' as prophesised by Friedrich Nietzsche. Another was developed in the work of the celebrated Indian poet and philosopher Muhammad Iqbal who considered his work as a response to Nietzsche. Following Iqbal's line of thought, my own work has moved in the direction of a 'de-Westernisation' of the theory of an 'exit from religion'. In so doing, I have sought to depart from Western liberalism, a philosophy based on the Enlightenment premise that human beings are able to build political societies and a moral order solely on the basis of natural reason and thus without any supernatural inspiration. The Nietzschean idea of the 'death of God' is the most symbolic expression of this ontological and existential claim, namely that humanity considers itself to have been liberated from the control and help of gods. However, in Iqbal's view, liberation from the guardianship of God does not mean there is no longer any relationship between god and humanity. Contrary to Ludwig Feuerbach (*The Essence of Christianity*, 1841), who claims that the religious have projected their fantasies of immortality, wisdom, omnipotence and omniscience on to gods, Iqbal argues that these supposed fantasies are in fact an anticipation of our future condition. Gods are not formed from our fantasies but from our own future. Thus, when Iqbal talks about a 'metaphysical liberalism', he is referring to the intuition of the future, characterised by the next step in our spiritual evolution: a step where the human species is liberated from the vision of a divine form as something different from itself, and has instead liberated itself in this divine form. In this sense, the 'exit from religion' is not the end of the complex and mysterious relationship between humanity and its gods, but the beginning of a dialectical process of integrating God into humanity. Accordingly, Iqbal's ideas have the potential to serve as a crucial tool for understanding liberalism and secularisation not only as a political process but also as a spiritual re-birth for humankind.

Iqbal's approach situates humankind's engagement with modernity beyond a Western secular framework, instead defining this engagement as a spiritual event that I call 'a new deal between mankind and its Gods'. This idea is based on Iqbal's works, for whom the 'exit from religion' is the moment in history when man becomes 'the heir of God'; in other words, it signals the moment when humanity expresses a degree of creative power similar or even equal to that which religions had attributed to their gods. Thus if something like the exit from religion must take place for humanity, it will not be by way of 'the death of God' but via inheriting divinity.

Humanity is now in a state of crisis because it is all-powerful. Since the end of the nineteenth century, the human species has amassed a colossal amount of power in its hands. Nature and life itself are increasingly at the mercy of our new technical and scientific powers. This is the true dimension of what we call 'liberalism': it is not only about democracy, political rights and freedom of expression but also the accumulation of technical and scientific power. And for so long as this continues to go unrecognised, the liberalism of the West will continue to exist in a state of ignorance with regard to its true nature, and its expansion to other civilisations will remain problematic, particularly so in the case of Islam, which, as Iqbal claims, is based on the belief that man has to become the heir of God. As such, there will not be an Islamic liberalism until humanity becomes aware of God's inheritance. Viewed in this way, the problem of liberalism in Islam is not principally about the separation between state and religion or secularisation: whereas Christianity, with its theory of two kingdoms—'my kingdom is not of this world' (John 18:36)—helped to establish the basis of liberalism's claim to liberate humanity from the control of gods, the contribution of Islam to liberalism will come on another level: the revelation or the awareness of divine power as the final destination of humanity.

But how will this work in practice? Can the possession of divine power be used for anything other than destructive ends? Civilisation itself is currently facing a vast range of threats, from rising social inequality to environmental degradation because of the scientific and technical power we have accrued, which has become destructive because we have been unable to control it. In Islamic theology, Allah is called the Creator (*hāliq*), the one who gives life (*muhī*) and gives death (*mumīt*) as he is a merciful (*rahmān*) and fair (*'adl*) god. When Allah gives death, it is not the consequence of an uncontrolled power. At present, we resemble young gods, drunk on our immense power. This is why we need a new anthropology—a new anthropology for a new era in which we have accrued immense power—one that can be symbolically expressed by the idea of a new deal between mankind and its gods: we should turn to these divinities one last time, no longer to bow to them but to ask how to express this level of power creatively. How, then, are we to become their worthy heirs?

Can humanity end its course of individuation[1] to self-knowledge and self-realisation by the ultimate experience of oneself as a creator at the level of activity and power contained in the concept of God? Iqbal was the first Islamic thinker to accept the Western proposition that something essential has changed in the relationship between mankind and its gods—other Muslim thinkers preferring to hold to the conventional view that 'god is God' and 'man is a creature of God'—but he was also one of the only Islamic thinkers to have criticised the Western interpretation of this changing relationship. This constitutes the heart, the principal motive, of his critique of Western modernity. It is impossible to describe his thought as either 'oriental' or 'occidental' because he tried to understand the retraction of God against the 'oriental' persistent conviction that god(s) will always remain above humankind in a position of ontological superiority. What the West has tended to view as the end of human spiritual 'dreams' or 'illusions' was in fact the unveiling of our real spiritual and historical destiny—the 'emergence in man' of a creative and powerful nature—the art and mystery of which has been preserved in the concept of God.

The Western exit from religion has failed to conceptualise the emergence of man at a superior level of existence who accrues powers traditionally reserved to God. For many thinkers in the West, the retreat of God signifies the end of all hope of 'transcendence'. Gianni Vattimo is explicit on the collateral damage caused by the death of God for humankind, emphasising that 'humanism is at a critical stage because God is dead: that is to say that the very substance of the humanist crisis, is this death of God, as announced in a non fortuitous way by Nietzsche, who is also the first radical non humanist thinker of our time'.[2] His argument, as applied to Martin Heidegger, runs as follows:

> the writing which inaugurated the contemporary conscience to the humanist crisis, namely the letter of Heidegger *Über den Humanismus* (1946), describes humanism in completely other terms, and highlights his very close connection to onto-theology which characterises the whole of Western metaphysics. Here, humanism is very precisely synonymous with metaphysics: in the sense that it is only in the perspective of a metaphysician (as a general theory of Being being something) that man may find a definition on which it may be possible for him to construct himself, educate himself.[3]

The humanist theme of the fulfilment of man is thus destroyed by the death of God. Yet, at the same time, the negation of the divine as an illusion denies the greatness of man fashioned on the greatness of God. When the model of divinity collapses, the whole ladder of ontological and existential progress also crumbles.

By allowing us to imagine the retreat of God in a sense other than a death, Iqbal saves the possibility of humanism. He saves the oldest intuition of mankind about itself: the ability to transcend its condition on earth as represented by the ontological status of a creature. God does not die; he comes towards man, he becomes man.

Such an approach also has consequences outside of Islam, for it puts Iqbal and Islamic thought at the centre of a debate between interpretations of what has happened—and will happen—to our gods and religions. According to Vattimo, the meaning of the death of God can be interpreted in two, opposed ways. It may signify the end of the illusion of man exceeding his limits; the death of God thus signifying the death of humanism, since this would give to man a greatness that could transcend this world. Or it may signify, as in the case of Iqbal, humanity's realisation of its infinite potential. However, according to Vattimo, modern thought does not see the death of God in terms of the revelation of the essence of humanity:

> the difference between contemporary atheism and that which finds its classic form in Ludwig Feuerbach is contained clearly in the macroscopic fact that the negation of God, the statement or taking note of his death may not today give rise to any 're-appropriation' by man of his alienated essence in the worship of the divine, and 'contemporary atheism' may no longer be a 're-appropriative' kind of atheism.[4]

Iqbal's contribution resides in his viewing the death of God as a metamorphosis rather than as a synonym of death: the era opened by modernity was the starting point in the migration of the divine into the human individual. In the case of Iqbal, this metamorphosis is also a human metamorphosis, because humankind is raised to a new threshold of self-understanding, of being capable of the kinds of creative activities previously attributed to divinities.

The birth of the god-man

Are we, however, concerned here with a predetermined finality, towards which humanity will be driven by nature in a Kantian sense? Or will this ultimate stage of the god-man, again paraphrasing Kant, serve as a regulative idea? Should we act as if we deify ourselves? Put differently, ought one to construct or reconstruct human civilisation according to a plan that would result in the emergence of a 'god-man'? Iqbal's philosophy of history invites us to pose anew not only the question of the ultimate possibilities of the human ego but to ask ourselves at the axiological level about the value, or rather the necessity, to act as if man has a divine destiny and as if humanity ought to aim at what is called 'the birth of the god-man'.[5]

This is one of the major themes in Iqbal's work. But is it in the interest of human beings to deify themselves? The concept of deification itself calls for caution because 'the divine', during more religious periods, may have been used solely as the name for the final character of man. Since the birth of religion, the intuition emerged that, through the divine, humankind is able to make something grow and to cultivate its real identity.

Of Allah, Iqbal writes that 'in order to emphasise the individuality of the Ultimate Ego [that is, God] the Koran gives Him the name of Allah'.[6] From Iqbal's perspective, it would be more correct to say that humankind ought to aim at 'the individuality of the Ultimate Ego' than to say that it should aim at its 'divinisation' or 'deification'.

This leads us to a better understanding of the hypothesis underlying Iqbal's philosophy of history, because the individuation of man is expressed not only as the spiritual itinerary of certain people—the mystics or Sufis to whom he is referring—but in the broader meaning of humanity's possible and desirable destiny. Here, Iqbal comes very close to the ideas of Henri Bergson, who does not speak of human beings as a set of individual atoms, nor of the human condition as having an immutable nature, but registers the individual into society.[7] According to Bergson, the itinerary of each individual is set within the course of a humanity that always progresses towards greater creative freedom: all of 'humanity, in space and in time, is an immense army which gallops at the side of each one of us, ahead of and behind us, within a moving charge/ mass capable of knocking over all resistance and to overcome all obstacles, perhaps even death'.[8] Iqbal represents history in a similar way: man ought to believe in history as a process of the progressive auto-revelation of potentially infinite and invulnerable human power. We should thus see history, and aim to live in it personally and collectively, as the realisation of the potential gestating in our human ego—and hence to arrive at the conclusion that 'Heaven and Hell are states, not places/localities.'[9]

Iqbal's ideas disrupt traditional religious eschatology: he effects a true delocalisation of hell and paradise, of the metaphysical sky as opposed to the fragile world, and a true transfer of the theme of the posthumous transformation of being to the concrete temporality of the past, the present and the future. He makes hell the symbol of all those lives in which man had not kept any conscious relationship with his final destiny as a creative power. Hell is not other people, nor a cursed beyond, but the here and now when the 'I' does not find in the human world any support for individuation[10] to render it more creative. According to Iqbal, contemporary man's ego lives in an infernal world because it is enclosed within the narrowest limits of its basic individuality—without 'reliance' on or 'alliance' with the deeper dimensions of his 'self', and so without any chance to attain the salvation resulting from a work of superior individuation. Iqbal refers to this existential descent into the most inferior and narrow basis of the 'self' as 'the painful realisation of one's failure as a man'.[11] Conversely, 'Heaven is the joy of triumph over the forces of disintegration.'[12]

Iqbal Singh underscores Iqbal's metaphysical revolution when writing that 'this process of the perfection and development of the ego has to take place not outside of time and space, or of the disembodied universe of thought detached from life and matter, but through struggle and striving in the world of time and space'.[13] He goes on to quote Iqbal directly: 'Its [life's] essence is the continual creation of desires and ideals, and for the purpose of its preservation and expansion it has invented or developed out of itself certain instruments, for example, senses, intellect, etc., which help to assimilate obstructions.'[14]

This is an expression of the non-metaphysical nature of Islam as Iqbal interpreted it. This religion could consequently be understood as proposing a rehabilitation of the sensible world—no longer disregarded as a lowly site of ignorance inferior to any 'Beyond' that might exist, but as the best place for the 'process of the perfection and development of the ego', on the scale of universal life and each individual existence. But what in effect remains of religion without metaphysics? Is the 'naturalism' of the Qur'an, with its constant exhortation to admire the wonders of the universe, not the sign of a new spiritual era that looks for itself in mankind's historical existence and evolution, and no longer wants, or needs, to put our consciousness in contact with the superior dimension of reality? Singh insists on the same Islamic singularity as that in Iqbal's works:

> In his attitude to time, too, Iqbal took a position completely contradictory to the Platonic, Sufi and Vedantist views. The world of time is not to be regarded as a world of shadows, a play of illusion on the edge of a void as the Hindu mystagogues had preached. Time is real and time is important.[15]

The singularity and insularity of Islam, therefore, means that it provides a vision of the world with a special status to the exterior limit of the metaphysical sphere of the religious era. Thus, when Iqbal writes of hell, of paradise, of God, he nevertheless disassociates himself from these concepts. According to Singh, Iqbal's rehabilitation of the sensible world—time, space, nature—is not the only way in which he re-registers and circumscribes the spiritual life of the human being in the limits of this world; he also rehabilitates the ego. Iqbal proposes that we view the ontological dignity of the sensible world as possibly the matrix of the ego's spiritual potentialities—the place of an ego-development, an ego-genesis, from a very low level of egoity towards the Ultimate Ego (Pure Creative Self).

In Iqbal's thought, Islam is the spiritual/historical vision of the world that invents the future as a new figure of the beyond, or, more precisely, as the site of man's true spiritual realisation—which, by consequence, the traditional beyond imagined by the religious no longer needs to exist. The human ego arrives at this point in its own spiritual growth because it does not have any need to imagine a metaphysical beyond. The genius of Iqbal vis-à-vis modern Western thinkers is that his substitution of the metaphysical beyond does not devalue human ambition. This is the major difference between what Iqbal finds in Islam and 'Western modernity', some of whose major thinkers (notably Marx, Nietzsche and Freud, the three famous *maîtres du soupçon*) have denounced religious experience as an illusion, and denied what they consider the illusion of man exceeding his (earthly) condition. Man without the beyond is not reduced to his ordinary 'me' or 'self'; quite the opposite, for he will find a spiritual ecosystem in the sensible universe that ought to allow him to exceed his ancient limits naturally. Is Islam, then, a kind of post-religion proposing the first spiritual way to worldly salvation?

According to Iqbal, the Qur'an regards as sacred that which has always been considered as profane: the here below (*dounia*), and the destiny of man. The religious beyond could thus have been a mere primitive allegory of our worldly and spiritual evolution. Religions and myths have furnished us with many descriptions of a metaphysical beyond that can be seen as a series of preparatory images with the aim of impelling us towards what we will one day be able to envisage directly as the sensible, historical future of a superior individuation. In other words, these images have acted as imaginary anticipations of our future. They were true or efficient as erotic stimuli (because they are desirable) or as conscious intuitions produced by what Carl Gustav Jung called the collective unconscious (Iqbal was a great reader of Jung).

The progress of universal life

Man's ontological progress towards his proper Creative Self must take place in this world because the ascendant evolution of the 'I' towards the Ultimate Creative Self is the cardinal expression of the general movement of life. What we call 'liberalism' is only one of the stages on the path to this liberation of the Ultimate Creative Self. According to Iqbal, the ascension of man towards the summit of his actualisation is incorporated in the heart of the ascension of the entire universe towards the production of this Ultimate Ego. The result of humanity's creativity will thus be the crowning of the ascending and creative process that will animate the entirety of being, in which Iqbal sees the 'law of the universe'. According to this view, man fulfils the perfection of the universe; humankind directs and completes the universe's itinerary. As stated, for example, by Teilhard de Chardin in *Le Phénomène humain*,[16] it is through human conscience that the universe clearly perceives its own ascending movement towards its limits. Iqbal writes: 'The law of the universe is an ascending perfection of elemental matter, passing continually from lower to higher forms determined by the kind of food which the fundamental units assimilate.'[17]

Modern science claims that this perspective is metaphysical, and so indemonstrable—making it, therefore, non-scientific. In a text entitled *This is Biology: The Science of the Living World*, Ernst Mayr writes that 'In the history of life, nothing indicates either the least general tendency of evolutionary progress, nor the existence of a mechanism capable of engendering it.'[18] This raises a contradiction from a biological standpoint: Mayr, an eminent biologist, refuses to accept the hypothesis of the progress of life, even if biological discoveries have consistently pointed to the journey of living things as a series of perfections and paths towards the constitution of beings in which individuality is always more distinct, active and powerful because of its capacity to 'evolve', 'believe and differentiate itself', 'metabolise' and 'auto-regulate'.[19]

Is it possible to dissociate, without contradiction, the infinitely superior complexity of organisms appearing last in the course of evolution (animal and human kingdoms) from the idea of the progress of life? In his book, *A History of the Concept of Life*, French philosopher André Pichot uses a range of texts to highlight this contradiction, which also appears in Charles Darwin himself, who didn't appear to see evolution as a finalised progress towards an increasing complexity of the living:

> this classification [of species, the idea of which he takes back to Lamarck] has already been designed in its time, and it discovers a certain order, especially that of a progressive complexity. Darwin obviously does not succeed in integrating all these factors (yet it is more or less possible to do so) and therefore his thesis becomes one of enormous confusion. One enters here on one of the most curious and most difficult to comprehend aspects of *On the Origin of Species*. It is a question on which Darwin accumulated the most sophistry, paralogisms and tautologies in trying to maintain his paradoxical position.[20]

It is here, in the refusal of science to recognise that life is in a state of progress, that a kind of historical difficulty could now be overcome. Indeed, modern science first had to rid itself of any residue of religious belief, probably because of the need to affirm its authority and jurisdiction in the face of religion during the nineteenth and twentieth centuries. Modern thinking has sought to avoid adopting the Christian idea of a *parousia*—literally the second coming of Christ, which could symbolise the final fulfilment of the universe. But is it still necessary to do so today? After all, there does not seem to be any reason why science should avoid recognising the universal progress of life, given humanity's knowledge of the complexity of the most highly evolved organisms. In the words of Emmanuel Kant, science could at least act *as if* (heuristic principle) universal life was attracted by and aiming for its own completion.

Progress does not signify teleology; it does not imply that there is any divine intention or intelligent design in the march of history.[21] It is possible to consider with Iqbal that something like the thought 'I am' has been searching for itself since the beginning of the universe, but first in an unconscious and blind fashion, then groping and uncertain, eventually more and more efficient, until becoming the consciousness of man. There was no conscious intention, therefore, at the beginning of universal progress, nor during the millions of years preceding the appearance of humanity as a species. It was only with the appearance of humankind that this teleological dimension of universal progress would emerge—with the birth of the human species, the improvement of the universe towards the production of an ever-stronger individuality would assume the nature of a project. As Bergson states, 'one will be wrong to consider humanity as we see it now, as pre-programmed in the evolutionary movement'; however, at the same time, 'we consider humanity as [the] reason (raison d'être) of evolution'[22] because evolution finds in man the consciousness of a self that was lacking before. As a result, it is from this human adventure that evolution acquires a retrospective intelligibility, a coherent direction in which it appears to progress. It is from the human being's point of view, Bergson continues, that 'the entire organised world becomes like the humus on which either man or a being which resembles him morally, ought to grow'.[23]

Has science spent a sufficient amount of time reflecting on the difference between these two postulates, of one finality that has been present from the beginning of evolution, and Iqbal's conception of a finality that appears in man and is the product of his orderly understanding of reality? As Bergson writes, 'Everything happens *as if*[24] an indecisive and vague and undecided being, which one could call, as one likes, man or superman, has striven to realise/accomplish himself.'[25] Thus, in this Kantian sense of 'as if', at least, there does not seem to be any reason why evolution cannot be understood as progress.

The Iqbalian sphinx

The universal progress of life serves as the background against which the career of the human ego unfolds. The spiritual future of man is not played out in heaven, but on earth. Iqbal thus turns the future into a new dimension of humanity's transcendental hopes, since he awaits in the future the answers to prayers or answers that our ancestors awaited beyond the limits of this world. But the fundamental difference between Iqbal and modern Western thinkers who conjugate faith in the future and resignation in finiteness (finitude)—like Albert Camus who said that 'the future is the only transcendence of man without God'[26]—is his vision of this future as a place where man will find a kind of infiniteness (infinitude) and be joyful in full expression of himself, of his possibilities and highest aspirations.

But, then, who was Iqbal if not some kind of sphinx? The metaphor of an Iqbalian sphinx is founded on a double analogy with the fabulous animal that Oedipus came across:[27] on the one hand, the Sphinx questions Oedipus on man; on the other, Oedipus will be allowed to follow his path on condition that he can answer his question—in other words, he symbolises those questions that man (and mankind) tries to unravel on the crossroads of existence. This Greek Sphinx is the mythological being who poses a riddle to such a man about man as such—and the answer has the potential to open the doors to the future. Such is the case with Iqbal: not only does he interrogate us, we the sons of the moderns, on the supreme vocation of man, but his interrogation reminds us that our future depends on whether our answer is right or wrong—given that the civilisation we are constructing will be determined in our image of ourselves. Indeed, like all human civilisations, our civilisation ought to be founded on the humanist vision of man and for man—in other words, civilisation should be founded on a philosophy of existence with a spiritual dimension.[28]

One of the virtues of Iqbal's work is that it invites us to pose the question of the superior image of man that ought to be at the heart of all civilisations. What kind of human being do we wish to construct? It is not enough to declare an 'era of the individual' and to place this individual at the centre of the world simply to allow them to better accomplish their desires, or to receive social and political rights. This form of materialist and sociopolitical liberalism is insufficient. The humanism of Western modernity does not go far enough to be a complete humanism—which Christian thinker Jacques Maritain rightly calls an 'integral humanism',[29] a higher form of humanism that enables human beings not only to exist in comfort but also to pursue a spiritual career beyond the limits of their individual egos. Existence is about more than satisfying our ambitions and attaining the rights to exercise our individuality. While we have aspirations for our present ego, we also have aspirations for the Creative Self that sleeps in us, awaiting the means to reveal itself: whereas the former only concerns the level of individuation at which we find ourselves, the second, which our present human civilisation almost completely ignores, concerns a later stage of individuation. In Iqbal's perspective, there is even a third possibility, namely the aspirations of the revealed Ultimate Ego, relative to his (super)nature as a Creative Self, and of which a distant intuition is carried by the aspirations for the present 'I' or 'self'.

The trivialities of our present times too often lead us to forget that we can have aspirations for the 'I' beyond the present 'I'. Societies have fixed their eyes exclusively on aspirations of profit and consumption. Modern societies are based on a certain form of economic organisation, in which human behaviour is understood via a purely instrumental rationality (based on expectations of behaviour). But as Iqbal reminds us, there is also the concomitant necessity of an axiological rationality (based on the idea of a behaviour's inherent value), which leads us towards existential purposes of a most elevated degree. In proposing that this subject aims at the Ultimate Ego/Creative Self, the most troubling factor of our time is the grave error of believing that humanity can be directed purely by economists, capitalists and technocrats, or by political and atheistic humanist views that completely ignore the idea that the dignity of humanity is not founded on the rights of our ordinary ego but on the higher rights of our spiritual ego—the rights of the Ultimate Ego/Creative Self.

Among Western thinkers, critiques of modernity, and of liberalism by those who promote human rights, remain confined to the political and the economic. Cornelius Castoriadis, for example, has argued that the major illusion of contemporary civilisation is its pretence 'that the technical-economical categories were always determining ... but buried under mystifying appearances—political, religious or other—and that capitalism, by de-mystifying or by disenchanting the world, allowed us to see the real significances'.[30] Marshall Sahlins is clear in this regard that the two major ideologies of the contemporary world—Marxism and liberalism—are guilty of the same error in postulating that man is above all a *homo economicus*.[31] But 'the productive forces' of property (riches and tools) to which this *homo economicus* dedicates himself are not 'the fundamental motivations of man ... in all societies'.[32] There are also what may be called the productive forces of 'humanisation', that is to say energies and aims dedicated to man's development of the highest abilities of human nature.

As Castoriadis points out, this process of humaniation concerns the role of 'productive or creative imagination', or of 'radical imagination',[33] whereby a human group gives unto itself the fundamental representation of an existential vocation. But do we know which humanity we want to become? Which great human figure do we want to promote? East and West are both silent on this matter. It is this silence that explains what is today called the 'return of religion', as well as the devastation unfettered capitalism has caused to societies and the planet:

> The spiritual nature of man has a horror of emptiness, and if we, all humans together of all civilisations, are unable to find anything new with which to be replenish this void, it will tomorrow replenish itself by destructive political ideologies and by religions more and more maladjusted to present times—and these obsolete forms of spirituality will produce monsters.[34]

It is to this emptiness that the Iqbalian Sphinx's questions would help us respond in an illuminated way. Is it possible to hope that we are able to evolve towards a more profound expression of the possibilities of our humanity? Is there a sense of our 'I' that we do not yet know, which we have not yet experienced? And what is the potential of this 'I'?

Which evolutionary reserves do we have at our disposal?

The most common prejudice of our era is that humanity is already complete—a prejudice shared by believers and unbelievers alike. As soon as this prejudice emerged, the idea of an enquiry into humanity's superior possibilities seemed redundant. Similarly, the menace of 'post-humanism', which claims that humankind is the past and that we should prepare for the advent of 'cyborgs' or 'augmented humans', suggests that there is little point in thinking of humanity beyond its present limits. Yet these fantasies about replacing humanity with something else can be revealed for what they are by a renewed spiritual reflection on the 'evolutionary reserves' and abilities that man may have in himself. This raises a real ethical imperative because it involves our existence as a species. To discover or conceptualise a later stage of humanisation—of which Iqbal hands us the image with his pedagogy of individuation towards a Creative Self—will thus provide a way to oppose the arguments of those who invoke the idea of post-humanity: if we show that we are not an outdated species, but constantly evolving and therefore capable of crossing thresholds in the realisation of ourselves, the discourse of our replacement by the post-human may be seen as detrimental to our dignity on the grounds that it threatens to interrupt our development.

Have we attained the summit of our evolution biologically and spiritually? This type of question is almost totally absent in French philosophical discussions, doubtless because of the spectre of eugenics, for one does not want to see the effect of a will to power giving way to the morally inadmissible temptation of wanting to create a 'race of super men'. However, it is vital that we reflect on humankind's future, given that we live in a world dominated by a techno-science that is already beginning to conceive the man–machine coupling in such a way that there is an after-man that seems to await us. Thus, unless we are able to conceive of a future humanity that uses these scientific and technical developments to augment the nature of humankind, these new additions will work against us.

The vast literature based on the post-human paradigm, particularly in the United States, poses an unprecedented challenge for humanist thought.[35] Without going so far as to talk about a programme of 'defending man', it is vital that we invoke thinkers like Iqbal in order to resume the effort to determine the future direction of humanity. But a simple reminder of the dignity and grandeur of our human condition is not sufficient to save us.

It is necessary to do more, to think far beyond. That is the possibility offered by the riddle of the Sphinx. It first obstructs the way ahead, but as soon as the enigma has been resolved, it immediately opens a new path forward. As it happens, and for all the reasons mentioned above, human civilisation will not escape this question of the Iqbalian Sphinx on the future of man.

The Ultimate Ego as Creative Self

As is the case with the Oedipal Sphinx, the way in which Iqbal formulates his question contains the necessary clues to reply to it. However, his theory of the ego—the nature and process of individuation—requires more explanation. Singh speaks of it as a 'philosophy of Egohood', a 'philosophy of egoity'.[36] Iqbal believes that both our historical and our present degree of individuation amounts to a very incomplete experience, knowledge and enjoyment of our ego—because for him, there is a very important step between what we call (and live as) ego and the true Ego—the human/divine experience of the Creative Self. Our present 'ego' is only—like in Plato's cavern—the shadow of the full 'I-amness' (égoïté in French). What we experience as our 'I' is only a primitive, partial, superficial experience of the 'I': the ego that we are, which we perceive and conceptualise, is not the complete ego or our total individuality, but only the embryo. It is important to use this image of the embryo, and to extend the metaphor to its gestation, if we wish to understand the direction of this individuation: it is by reflection upon that which already characterises us, and in learning to consider it as the pre-formation of that which we may become, that we can determine the nature of our final individuality. From this point of view, Iqbalian thinking has the same naturalistic characteristics as those Iqbal attributes to the Qur'an. He leans towards observation instead of abstract speculation. The final self-realisation of ego is the complete actualisation of three dimensions of our present ego: his being as creator, self-awareness as a creative source or cause of reality, self-enjoyment as a source of existence and mercy for all beings.[37] The common ego has many wombs, inside which it is wrapped and inside which it grows: the body, family, society, nature and the universe. The great Ego *is* the womb of universes.

Iqbal's thought demands, therefore, that man's ontological and existential identity be seen in the full development of our actual faculties. So what do these actual faculties teach us about ourselves? When considered synthetically, it is possible to regroup these faculties by saying that they all stem from our 'creative power'. Such is their common denominator: tools, instruments, weapons, systems, theories, myths, works of art. Man is the being who adds something to the field of the real, the species who broadens the scope of what is possible, and for whom the border between the real and the imaginary is constantly moving in a multitude of directions for the benefit of the real. Liberalism (democracy, political rights, freedom to engage in business) is only one of the fields of this creative expression. As Bergson claims, man is thus *Homo faber* or *Homo habilis*:

> During thousands of years, when the retreat of the past leaves nothing more to see but the outlines, our wars and our revolutions will count for very little, supposing we still remember them; but of the steam engine, with inventions of all kinds which makes up the procession, we will speak of perhaps as we talk of bronze or stone cutting; it will serve to define an age. If we can strip ourselves of all pride, if, to define our species, we keep strictly to that which history and pre-history presents to us as the constant characteristic of man and of intelligence, we might perhaps not say *Homo sapiens*, but *Homo faber*. In the end, intelligence, as considered in those in whom it appears to be the original impulse, is the faculty to manufacture artificial objects, in particular tools to make tools, and to indefinitely vary the manufacture of them.[38]

On this point, there is clearly a remarkable degree of affinity between Iqbal and Bergson. The human being is a creator—all that humankind has created can be gathered under the concept of the tool, including humanity's intellectual work, because like material tools they ensure that we have the best 'take' and 'hold' on the world. Our systems of thinking are nothing other than machines. Like those of a material technique, in fact, they contribute to imposing our thinking on the real—to branding Being with the seal of our interiority, as Georg W.F. Hegel claimed.[39] This identity of vocation and capacity between the symbolic machine and the physical machine is expressed in the double meaning of the French verb 'saisir', which means to understand and to take hold of, to grab. 'Saisir' corresponds to the actualisation of power in order to define the being of something, either in deciding its sense, or in deciding its use. Whatever he thinks or whatever he does, it is man who by thought, language and hands takes command of Being, and then creates the world as representation, meaning and use, who creates the symbolic and physical tools by which he recreated or remade the world in increasingly radical proportions over thousands of years. This last point also seems to lend reason to Iqbal's thinking: for if we may consider the extension of our 'creative I' as the most plausible future of our individuation, it is not only because this creative faculty already characterised us but equally because, in an observable fashion, it has historically become ever more powerful—and never exhausted.

It is, of course, not necessarily the case that the civilisations that lived in harmony with nature[40] were inferior to our modern and contemporary society; they could even be viewed as superior, depending on how much importance we place on valuing, respecting and conserving nature. As Claude Levi-Strauss points out, it is impossible to progress on all levels at the same time: 'That which we win in one, we are always open to lose in another.'[41] This is also true of the progress of human civilisation, as demonstrated by the fact that human creativity exploded during the period when we ravaged nature for our own needs.

From the point of view of humanity's history, it is clear that this increase in creative power is the zenith of our process of individuation. Iqbal presents the progress of creative capacity as the less speculative direction of our evolution because it will be in continuity with that which has always characterised us: 'In his intimate being, man, as conceived in the Qur'an, is a creative activity, a spirit that ascends and, in its march forward, elevates itself from one state to another.'[42] I call this the Iqbalian cogito: not 'I think, therefore I am' (as René Descartes said) but 'I create therefore I am'—the strength/reality of my 'Iamness' depends on the strength and reality of my creative power. Here, Iqbal quotes the Qur'an: 'It is useless that I assess by the redness of the setting sun and by the night which envelops it, and by the moon when it is full *that you will definitely be transferred from one state to another* [my emphasis].' Here is the clue that gives us the Iqbalian Sphinx: if there is an individuality beyond the actual mode in which we are experiencing it, then we should seek to attain this via developing of the power of this creative resource; that is why Iqbal names 'the Ultimate Ego' as 'the Creative Self'.

The Iqbalian concept of the ego

The concept of the ego has traditionally possessed a negative connotation, but Iqbal employs it indiscriminately, as well as synonymously in English with the notion of self, as well as with that of the Persian *hūdī*. Javed Majeed explains this notion as follows:

> The transgressive nature of Iqbal's notion of *hūdī* is signalled by the term itself. Annemarie Schimmel has stressed that the word has high connotations in Persian, implying selfishness and egotism. The standard Persian–English dictionary by Steingass defines the term as meaning 'selfishness, conceit, egotism'. The term thus carries a transgressive charge, which is maintained by Iqbal in his English prose works. Throughout *The Reconstruction of Religious Thought in Islam*, Iqbal uses the term 'ego' to render the Persian term *hūdī*. Reinterpreting the Qur'an, Iqbal argues that 'it is with the irreplaceable singleness of his individuality that the finite ego will approach the infinite ego ...'

As can be seen from this quotation, Iqbal applies his master language of individual selfhood to God, who is also described variously as an 'ego', so that the transgressive charge of the word *hūdī* is in play in his conception of God as well.[43] Schimmel wrote in this sense that the book:

> *Asrāri hūdī* [Secrets of the self, 1915] were a shock therapy for almost all of Iqbal's friends and admirers. One must think of the highly negative significance in Persian of the word Khûdî, Self, with its implications of selfishness, egotism and similar objectionable meanings. Iqbal gives this word a new meaning as Self, Personality, Ego in an absolutely positive meaning. But still, deepest dismay was caused by his new ideas; brought up since centuries with the idea of seeing in the Self something which has to be annihilated in the Divine Essence, the mystically inclined Indian Muslims could not easily accept a philosophy that taught them to watch over the growth of their personality, to strengthen it, instead of melting away in the highest bliss of union with the Only.[44]

Iqbal, who created or re-created the concept of ego, is thus a philosopher, in the same sense as understood by Gilles Deleuze and Nietzsche before him: philosophy is not simply about contemplating the world, but engaging in a creative activity. More precisely, 'philosophy is the art of shaping, of inventing, of manufacturing objects ... the "substance" of Aristotle, "cogito" of Descartes, "monad" of Leibniz, "condition" of Kant, "power" of Schelling'[45] and therefore the 'Ego' or more exactly 'Creative Self' of Iqbal. On this subject, Deleuze quotes Nietzsche: 'The philosophers ought no longer to be content to accept the concepts which we give them to merely clean them and to make them shine, but they must start to manufacture them, create them, present them and persuade man to resort to them.' Such an explication of the specific role and capacity of the philosopher is particularly important in the case of Iqbal. There are two reasons for this. First, because it is the expression of Creative Self that allows philosophy to create new concepts—to philosophise is to be on the march towards the Ultimate Ego and to be in a situation to receive him as a creative inspiration. More generally, anyone who creates something begins to express the Creative Self in themselves. To create is to offer new births to life, to open in front of it new fields of expression: the creative process starts with dreams of new horizons, or by writing a poem or educating a child. Creation is, in this sense, very close to love—when we love, we try to (or should be able to) consecrate all of our creative energy to our beloved, or to our passions.

Secondly, if it is up to the philosopher to 'persuade men' to 'resort' to new concepts, this is only possible if they correspond to the new needs of civilisation. This is exactly the fertility of the Iqbalian concept of Creative Self. Not only, as Schimmel says, has he come to regenerate the mystic culture of the Sufis by enunciating it with the modern concern with the promotion of the ego, but he can be particularly useful to us today, in a global civilisation that is not able to find any essential vocation for the human ego. There is a tragic vocational crisis for the promotion of ego in the contemporary world: many men manage to give sense to their lives, social, professional, political, intellectual, but few can exalt this life in a spiritual quest with the depth and elevation of the old religions and metaphysics. There remain horizontal significations (material goals) for existence, but no more vertical (metaphysical) goals, which make man see the possibility of transcending his condition. Can this 'verticalisation' of life to the beyond, traditionally proposed by religions, be reinvested in new directions? What would replace the metaphysical beyond that could lead humanity to the same altitude? This raises what can be called the problem of the spiritual subtraction: when one subtracts the metaphysical transcendence of religion from the human aspiration to transcend his condition, what does that leave? For a humanity such as ours, which has made the choice of scientific rationality and political salvation against the religious dreams of another world, does the possibility remain of radically transcending our condition?

The Iqbalian invention/intuition of the Creative Self helps us to answer this type of question because it gives human life a horizon of natural, worldly transcendence—it gives a spiritual meaning and direction to the process of liberalisation. My own books about Islam are motivated by the same quest.[46] Contrary to traditional Sufi culture, Iqbal does not suggest the imaginary or symbolic solution of escaping the limits of this world 'to be annihilated in the Divine Essence', but to deepen the rapport that we have with our own 'I' and to begin to think of giving it a dimension or ontological density unheard of until now. This is the 'shock therapy' that the philosophical creation of the concept of the Creative Self is able to inflict: Iqbal's hypothesis forces us to take another look at our most deeply anchored mental habits. Each one of us is culturally convinced that our identity consists entirely of what we have defined as our condition of 'weakness and misery'. But what if we learn to consider this existential *habitus* as only the most ancient prejudice of the human species, inherent to a primary stage of our development or of our evolution? In this regard, Iqbal's 'philosophy of Egohood'—which I call his pedagogy of individuation—prepares or predisposes man to understand himself in a radically new fashion.

In recreating the concept of the ego, Iqbal aimed to produce a state of perplexity in his reader and have them search for their own human identity beyond all that they had previously experienced and conceived. He leads us down the same path of self-enquiry that Socrates prompted Alcibiades to follow by asking him, 'Whatever, then, is man?'[47] Iqbal and Socrates actually ask the very same question: if we want to improve ourselves, cultivate ourselves, ought we not to know who we can hope to become? 'So what? The art that improves us, can we know it if we ignore the direction for our self-improvement?'[48] The interest of this Platonic *gnôthi sauton* (know thyself) in relation to Iqbal is that, contrary to almost all previous occidental philosophy, he does not look for knowledge of the self in an exploration of our actual condition or of our already shaped ego, but as a conquest of a superior dimension of ourselves. The sense of exploration has been substituted by that of conquest. The exercise of self-reflection has replaced the work of self-creation or re-creation. The counting of the dimensions of the ordinary ego has monopolised thinking and culture, causing a diversion towards the intuition and actualisation/constitution of an extraordinary ego.

Marx and Nietzsche, and Spinoza before them, didn't have sufficient influence on the course of Western civilisation to orient it towards the project of increasing the ego's power to act, nor to create a new man. Why are we never surprised that our view rests entirely circumscribed to the analysis of the ego which we already are, rather than undertaking the creation of an ego of a higher existential and ontological level? Is it not this that Nietzsche has designated 'erroneous dogmatism on the subject of the ego?'[49] Is it not this sense of the conquest/formation of an ulterior level of egoisation for which he tried to retrieve inspiration in *Thus Spoke Zarathustra*, across the process of the 'three metamorphoses'? 'It is the three metamorphoses of the spirit that I name for you: how does the spirit become a camel, and the lion the camel and, to finish, the baby the lion?'[50]

The Iqbalian proposal of a Creative Self wants to warn our critical mind against this assimilation of the 'I' of the spontaneous experience of the self into the totality of the experience of the Ego. When he met one of his spiritual models, the Sufi Ḥallāǧ during the celestial voyage he imagines in the *Javid Namah* (The book of eternity), he presents him as an individual in whom the infinite Creative Self is awakened and describes him as saying 'I have lit the fire of life and the mysteries of life in myself!' The 'Creative Self' and the 'Ultimate Ego': Iqbal continually returns to one or the other of these expressions in *The Reconstruction of Religious Thought in Islam*: 'We may easily grant that the ego, in its finitude, is imperfect as a unity of life. Indeed, its nature is wholly aspiration after a unity more inclusive, more effective, more balanced, and unique.'[51]

The human ego is driven by a fundamental desire to free or open up its deepest being. In his poetic work *The Secrets of Self*, Iqbal writes the following about the Ultimate Ego or Creative Self, which he here calls *Khûdi* in Persian and which is the term for the process of liberation/accomplishment of ourselves:

> The shape of existence is an effect of the Self/All that you see is an effect of the Self ... /It is imagined as other to itself/It creates, from within itself, the shapes of others ... /The immensity of Time is its arena/The sky (Heaven) is a wave of dust along his route ... /The night is born in his sleep, the day flies out in his awakening ...[52]

We should try to understand how Iqbal understands this wonderful existence, so creatively powerful, of the 'Creative Self' or of the Creative Man—and emphasise with Denis Matringe that for Iqbal the Prophet Muhammad is the model of this Creative Man, 'the consummate example of a man having deployed the full range of his possibilities'.[53] What exactly is it that such a concept as *Creative Man* can signify? Where can it lead our vision or understanding of ourselves?

6

THE DISSONANT POLITICS OF RELIGION, CIRCULATION AND CIVILITY IN THE SOCIOLOGY OF ISLAM

Armando Salvatore

Introduction: liberal modernity and Islam

One of the most resistant threads of liberal Islamic thought has been its limited capacity to emancipate itself from the European political mythology and theology that has set the benchmarks for the notions of statehood and citizenship in Westphalian and post-Westphalian colonial and postcolonial nation-states. I am not concerned here with the intellectual limitations of individual thinkers, opting instead to re-examine the categories of Western sociological reflection as they deal with the political concerns of postcolonial reconstruction. The re-imagination of Islam as religion and/or civilisation has played a role in this process, with Muslim reformers (liberal or otherwise) often squeezed between a hegemonic European discourse and the imperatives of anti-colonial struggles. These struggles have often worked to provide reductive renderings of the plurality, complexity and richness of Islamic traditions.

Modernisation theories, so vituperated in recent decades, originated during a high point for the social sciences in the 1950s and 1960s and were path-breaking at the time for laying out an evolutionary pattern of convergence of political (largely in synchrony with economic) development, in ways that did not discriminate against Islamic religious and political traditions. The weight of such traditions was not ignored, but they were expected to converge in the long term on a homogeneous path defined by the erosion of traditional authority, allegedly opening the way to the empowerment of modern citizens and social actors.[1] While this approach was, in its theoretical dullness, representative of the limited set of options open to postcolonial states, the crisis of modernisation theory, which began in the 1970s, was in fact proclaimed in response to events, by none other than Henry Kissinger, during the eruption (and twisted outcome) of the revolution in Iran at the end of the decade. The subsequent talk of re-Islamisation or Islamic revival (along with their academic magnification through the resurrection of several orientalist stereotypes) has prevented scholars, critics and intellectuals from discussing the extent to which membership in a postcolonial polity could also be truly post-Westphalian. By post-Westphalian I mean an idea of statehood and citizenship not bound to a centralised and absolute sovereignty legitimised by the global diffusion of the nation-state form, most notably after the Second World War through the United Nations and affiliated and parallel organisations.

This is where the idea of a sociology of Islam comes in. Its birth might be traced to the publication of *Weber and Islam* by Bryan Turner in 1974,[2] in the middle of the decade that saw the crisis of modernisation theory, the perception of a re-Islamisation process (via the rise of Islamist movements, and culminating in the Iranian revolution) and the global critique of orientalism (which in the 1960s had been restricted to intellectual interventions framed within the anti-colonial and liberation discourse). It is the sociology of Islam that gradually formulated the issue of an Islamic modernity in increasingly explicit terms, in an intermittent relation with both the (rather inconclusive) critique of orientalism and the mostly circular arguments about re-Islamisation. These arguments were circular to the extent they resulted in self-enclosed hermeneutic circles that articulated the purported relation between Islam and politics largely by bracketing out a discussion of modernity's workings and underpinnings.[3]

An increasing part of Turner's work on the sociology of Islam dealt with this conundrum in Weberian terms. From the beginning, however, the idea was not so much to apply Weberian categories to Islam, but rather to redress them (or their trivialisation via 'Weberist' orthodoxies) by studying the complexities of Islam as a religion, civilisation and more. Within this trajectory,

Turner also published, in the same year as Edward Said's *Orientalism*,[4] the often neglected book *Marx and the End of Orientalism* (1978).[5] Through these two volumes from the 1970s he showed how a more attentive consideration of the Marxian heritage in Max Weber, who is otherwise considered a liberal thinker, might have bypassed the limitations of the critique of orientalism and of the re-Islamisation paradigm. I rephrase the question here as one concerning the extent to which an Islamic modernity (including capitalism) might have emerged apart from both the anti-colonial wave of critique and from the culturalist, largely puritan reflex of Muslim reformers' mimicking Weber's famous (or infamous) Protestant ethic thesis.[6] This argues that the origins of European capitalism resulted from Calvinists' turning the theological tenets of predestination into incentives for a life under the aegis of an innerwordly type of asceticism favouring a strongly profit-oriented type of capitalistic entrepreneurship. One would misunderstand Weber's thesis, however, if we did not connect it to his wider argument on the genesis of modernity, which he identified with a process of rationalisation of sheer power, becoming autonomous from religious and cultural traditions.

While building his critically neo-Weberian argument on modernity, Turner stressed the interesting fact that modern Muslim reformers espoused a flat reading of the Protestant Ethic Thesis, linking religious reform with modernisation, and in this way disproved the complexity of Weber's argument on the relation between religious traditions and modern rationality that cannot be easily caged within a liberal view. Indeed, many contemporary Muslim reformers (often celebrated in the West for their 'liberal' outlook) cannot exit such a Weberist straitjacket. Turner's preliminary work on the sociology of Islam acquired a strong relevance throughout the 1980s, a decade that witnessed serious interpretive contentions (often through the opaque prism of re-Islamisation) on the nature of the relations between religion, society and politics in Muslim contexts. The dissertation I started in 1990 that led to the publication of my *Islam and the Political Discourse of Modernity* in 1997 also originated from those contentions.[7]

This was also when I began to explore the notion of the public sphere as potentially less contentious and more accommodative of the conceptual indeterminacies left behind by the academic fashions of the 1990s, which witnessed a revival of 'civil society'. The notion of the public sphere, despite the hegemony of its liberal Habermasian form,[8] is more easily contestable and adaptable than the rigid conceptual apparatus of modernisation theory, the simplified toolkit of re-Islamisation, and the dogmatic certainties of civil society as a liberal arena of democratisation. It can therefore add complexity to the study of modernity and better account for the tensions between its singularity and multiplicity. This strand of reflection was developed in my later work, where I tried to show that the public sphere of liberal modernity twists earlier trajectories, conceptions and practices of the ethos of public life at work both within Western Christendom and the Islamic ecumene, and therefore cannot be considered universally normative. Earlier, premodern trajectories both within Europe and the Muslim world did determine a wider spectrum of options on social and political participation and communication. These options did not ipso facto evaporate with the formation of modern capitalism and the rise of Westphalian, later colonial states.[9]

Instead of focusing on such longer-term trajectories of publicness that cannot be reduced to a single model, contemporary debates on Islam in/and modernity particularly as manifest through the working of public spheres have often been distracted and attracted by two seemingly opposed, but in fact mutually mirroring options having in common the pretension to sideline the liberal (Weberian and Habermasian) understandings of modernity without taking charge of them and their critique, as the sociology of Islam has started to do. The first option consists in framing mutating Islamic ways of political participation and subjectivities within a horizon open to the type of 'difference' purportedly promoted by the modernity of the public sphere (at least at its 'interstices') and incarnate in a politics of visibilities. The second option trashes this idea of difference as part of an identity politics of gestures and visibilities providing a (multi)cultural fig leaf to a neoliberal order that should be tackled in much more activist ways.[10]

The two options mirror each other because seeing Islamic public expressions, via discourses or symbols, as inexorably exposed to a self-referential discourse by and about the liberal subject is not incompatible with the postmodern privileging of fragmented subjectivities and their self-positioning within social and cultural worlds deemed as being devoid of intrinsic norms. In this context, even the potential adoption of supposedly critical notions of the public sphere (let us say of a Foucaultian, Derridean or Deleuzian type) does not escape the looming risk of a one-sided culturalisation of Islam. The consequence is that the debate, as also reflected in this book, risks laying too much emphasis on the limits of Islamic voices that devise ways to co-choreograph the dance of repositioning a largely reified Islamic 'heritage' or a fragile Islamic subjectivity towards paradigms of world order and sovereignty ultimately originating from Western hegemony (however faded it may be). As an alternative to this emphasis, and as a way to feed into a more sustained analysis of the presuppositions and consequences of liberal modernity, I would like to focus on key intersections between two strands of enquiry and theoretical reconstruction: a historical sociology that focuses on the long-term trajectory of the social nexus associated with Islam as a moral and spiritual idiom (what Marshall Hodgson called 'Islamdom'), on one hand;[11] and the somewhat a-moral and also less-than-spiritual, yet largely holistic cement of how individual self-formation fits into the social bond and generates it, on the other— what Norbert Elias called the manners and codes originating from the self-restraint of the 'civilising process'. This process resonates interestingly, albeit sometimes oddly, with Islamic notions about the cultivation of personality and character formation.[12]

While the latter factors are usually attributed to a machine of self-reconstruction associated with the modern state, modern capitalism, and, at the intersection of both, modern liberal civil society, Islamic trajectories, as evidenced by historical sociology, appear, as I will try to show, as the providers of elements of circulation of social forms and normative codes that cannot be easily squeezed into those modern formations, while not constituting their negation either. These Islamic norms and codes interfaced with other realms and cultures, and often provided a source of socio-political constellations that at times were beneficial to developing original forms of personal and collective autonomy. This is clearly apparent in the Islam–Islamdom doublet proposed by Hodgson, and which we will revisit, whereby Islam represented the engine of inner piety and Islamdom its social nexus. This scheme visibly contrasts with the systematic sacredness of Western modern institutions (as reflected in the corporate armature of the Leviathan) for being both unfitting to modern Weberian rationality and potentially ahead of it in a world prefiguring patterns of circulation of ideas and images transcending national borders.

In my argument, I will comment upon Hodgson's approach to the history of Islam by reference to the emerging field of the sociology of Islam (which, by necessity, is largely a historical sociology, at least at its inception), and connect it to notions of civility originating from a critical reassessment of the Eliasian heritage. I will also enrich this double thinking by reference to a more general idea of circulation as originating from the historical study of the interaction among religious and civilisational traditions in a wider Asian realm than the one directly invested by Islam's expansion in history.

Western hegemony and the sociology of religion

Seen from western Europe and its final colonial and imperial triumph during the nineteenth century, the Islamic ecumene had for long represented a more advanced civilisational realm. In the early modern era, this ecumene was still perceived in Europe as a threatening enemy, most immediately in the shape of the Ottoman Empire. During the seventeenth and eighteenth centuries, as Western Europe, but also Russia, gradually managed to gain the upper hand against the Islamic ecumene, the West also came into closer contact with India and China. Such encounters posed new challenges in terms of cultural comparison and civilisational interaction than the relation to the Islamic ecumene had ever been capable of raising. In Hegel's philosophy of history, China and India took the place of distinctive and necessary stages on the road to a full accomplishment of the triumph of reason in human history. As a result, and despite the attention given to Islam by other thinkers of the Enlightenment and Romanticism, Islamic civilisation started to look more like an anomalous sideshow, the outcome of an accumulation of deficits and delays in the road of human civilisation.

What does sociology have to do with these developments? One key trait of sociology is its rise, particularly at the turn of the twentieth century, as a scholarly reflection on modernity and its processes, and therefore as the discipline not only enquiring into, but also reflecting upon modern society and its genesis, which clearly included a colonial dimension. While sociology is characterised by such a focus on modernity, often bordering on a self-referential obsession, it also entails, in its more reflective mode, a questioning of the Western monopoly on the definition of modernity. Here, Islam plays a quite crucial, though often understated role, for representing motives and features of alterity vis-à-vis Western modernity, which can play out both positively and negatively. This occurred, for instance, within the German political-intellectual scene on the axis linking the philosopher Nietzsche and the sociologist Weber at a particularly crucial stage in the intellectual genesis of Western sociology.[13] While Nietzsche radically denied the possibility of an objective reality independent from the knowing subject's perspective, Weber translated this painful intuition into potential parameters to measure the Western man's universal ambitions against the backdrop of a much larger universe, indeed a multiverse, of religious and civilisational trajectories. Therefore, the fact that a peculiar combination of religious and civilisational essentialism, functionalism and reductionism became so central to Western postulates of modernity throughout the genesis of the social sciences in the longer nineteenth century was undermined from within almost from the beginning. The development and institutionalisation of the academic study of Islam and the rise of Islamic studies throughout Europe were integral to this ambivalent development.[14]

Thus, social scientists who were leading their fields between the second half of the nineteenth and the first half of the twentieth century, like Émile Durkheim, Max Weber, Georg Simmel and Marcel Mauss (and, we might add, going further back, Karl Marx, though he was not a sociologist in a conventional sense), passionately engaged with religion. They located religion both at the beginning and at the end of human development, through a wide bow stretching from ancient cosmological cultures and communal life to secular civic life and the modern social division of labour. There was a wider consensus that, far from erasing religion, the need of modern societies for organic solidarity and charismatic leadership facilitated appropriations of the force of religion in new forms. Particularly appealing was the form that has been often defined as 'civil religion', having its origin in the thought of the eighteenth-century philosopher Jean-Jacques Rousseau. The modern fate of religion appeared to be less its disappearance than its metamorphosis into a key ingredient of civility or, in Durkheimian vocabulary, 'civic morals'. The quintessentially secular, modern manifestation of religion is accordingly less its disappearance than its capacity to nurture civility.

Within this background, Islam has constituted, since the rise of sociology, a powerful counter-model representing a potential of resistance, both in history and the present, to this Western matrix of modernity that postulates an increasingly differentiated role for religion as a provider of sense and moral cohesion. Islam featured centrally in this trajectory due to its purported unsuitability for being incorporated in a comparative scheme of 'world religions' on a par with Christianity and Buddhism. In her masterly book, entitled *The Invention of World Religions* (2005), Tomoko Masuzawa shows the role that the conceptualisations of Buddhism and Islam, respectively, had in this construction of the very idea of 'world religion'.[15] She prefaces her investigation by remarking that the suppression of the feeling of uneasiness and unsettledness that still affected the European educated classes of the seventeenth and eighteenth centuries when they looked at Asia needed to be tamed and normalised during the nineteenth century in order to allow Europe to exercise its full colonial hegemony and make this appear as natural and necessary (that is, embedded in the course of history), and even providential. There was, however, one basic difference in the outlook of Islam and Buddhism that crystallised in the course of the century. Islam was constructed as consistently monolithic, without easily passing the test of being a 'world religion', the category that happened to define the emerging academic field of comparative religious studies. Buddhism was also conceived, like Islam, as a religion with a clear-cut name and precise doctrinal boundaries, something that neither European scholars in earlier epochs nor practitioners over the ages had ever dared to do.

This approach responded to an essentialist attitude developed over the nineteenth century not just by the scholars of religion, but by the educated classes themselves, and that neatly reflected the European colonial experience, which required conceiving of religions and civilisations in terms of larger and essentially coherent units. Here, essentialism is on the side of the cultivated and the refined. Yet while Islam was not a big puzzle to European learned men and societies, Buddhism largely was, so that the essentialisation of Buddhism became an even more sophisticated enterprise than that of Islam. Most strikingly, the origin of 'true' Buddhism was considered the preserve of scholars, while its historical and contemporary ramifications were downgraded to a matter of interest for missionaries, travellers and casual observers. This development led some scholars to discover a deep, essential affinity between purportedly true Buddhism and allegedly true Christianity, via an emphasis on the cultivation of the inner self. This development reflected the fact that the benchmark of true religion was Protestant Christianity, and was based on the idea of the primacy of the charisma of the founder of a religion and and/or of its sacred texts ('scriptures'). Buddhism thus earned the mark of a world religion. Its alleged universality resided in it having redressed and reformed what European orientalists saw as the ethnically and nationally, but also priestly and hierarchically oriented Hinduism, and by strengthening the emphasis on the centrality of the individual.

While Buddhism was thus accepted as a world religion on a par with Christianity, this was considered problematic for Islam, which was seen as particularistic and ethnic. This outcome was part of the rising anti-Semitic and pro-Aryan bias of the era, something that was to have a devastating impact on Europe going into the twentieth century, and is still reflected in contemporary perceptions of Islam. This lopsided judgement gained currency despite the historical evidence of the transnational and even transcivilisational import of Islam over longer time spans and regions. Clearly, this differentiated view of Buddhism and Islam was also a reflex of the need to reposition both Christianity and secularism in the context of the modern, global and colonial hegemony of Europe.

A key character in this downgrading of Islam to a backward Semitic religion was the French historian and philosopher Ernest Renan (1823–92), who became an ideologue of the secular nation-state. He wrote extensively about Islam and even engaged in a direct debate with the famous Muslim reformer Jamal al Din al-Afghani. Renan's critique had much to do with the view of Islam as a premodern religion and the idea of the secular nation-state as the highest stage of societal development. He attacked Islam and the Arabs for being innately incapable of engaging in philosophical thought and scientific work.[16] This onslaught was the result of his general typology of religion and provoked a number of responses by Muslim intellectuals, including Namik Kemal, the famous Ottoman writer, poet and activist. Both Kemal and al-Afghani stressed, against Renan, that Islamic traditions did possess the resources to reform both the self and the collectivity, but the imprint of Renan's view of Islam remained deeply stamped on Western perceptions.[17] It instituted the conceptual benchmark for determining, measuring and devaluing the rationalising capacity of Islam's juridical, theological and philosophical traditions to justify the collective pursuit of the common good via adequate means of collective organisation—primarily in the form of modern statehood, but also under the assumption that a modern state could not exist without adequate cultural institutions for educating its citizens, inculcating them with a normative sense of commitment to common welfare, and finally encouraging their attachment to the nation.

The case of Kemal and al-Afghani responding to Renan was not an isolated one in showing an intellectual resistance to a diminishment of the modern value of a non-Western cultural heritage, while accepting the categories through which the Western judgement was pronounced. In the colonial and postcolonial era, students, intellectuals and professionals from various parts of Asia who studied in the West or were significantly exposed to Western ideas absorbed and re-circulated, via their emerging public spheres, ideas of religion that had been preventively rigidified, confessionalised and often nationalised in Europe. Paradoxically, however, such categories were not only subject to ever denser circulation; they also provided resources to anti-colonial campaigns based on the need to pinpoint anti-Western, yet modern identities. This is true of China, where a new type of reformist or 'redemptive' association catered to such needs and linked modern notions of religion to popular ethics and identity. Both China and Japan witnessed the flourishing of large numbers of such groups, simply described as 'new religions'. While such redemptive associations stressed universalism and moral self-transformation, they often retained traditionally popular gods and spirit-medium practices. They became important agents of both cosmological syntheses and social integration by envisioning a connective justice across barriers separating communities, cultures, classes and genders, and often contributed to empowering women in public spaces of voluntarism and activism, frequently emphasising bodily techniques, including breathing.[18]

A similar process occurred in India, where in the early modern period the Advaita (non-dualism) school became the main umbrella of Hinduism and contributed to a pluralism in which many views were allowed to co-exist in acknowledgement of their common aspirations. As highlighted by Prasenjit Duara, this school solidified its dominance in the early twentieth century with transnationally operating masters like Swami Vivekananda (1863–1902) or Sri Aurobindo (1872–1950) proposing a reformed version of Hindu teachings, matching the focus on the inner self highlighted by Masuzawa. This was a key condition for gaining the modern mark of a 'world religion', which facilitated a global recognition for emerging forms of Hindu nationalism.[19] Yet while early modern Sufi and Bhakti (Hindu devotional) works and practices had developed in a mutual dialogue over several centuries before European colonialism and did not represent fixed religious texts or precepts, with the communalisation of these works in the colonial public sphere—considerably aided by the rapid circulation of print media—they rapidly became banners of closed religious communities. Nile Green has observed deep transformations of Sufi and Yogi techniques of bodily and spiritual cultivation from face-to-face, living and shifting forms of practice and instruction to their authentication as emblems of communal identities through the colonial public sphere.[20]

Yet the foremost case of such dynamics among faith traditions within colonial public spheres played out in the entanglement between Europe and the Muslim world. Significant attempts to reconstruct viable Islamic traditions had been carried forward during the seventeenth, eighteenth and early nineteenth centuries by a host of variously motivated Muslim leaders before the rooting of an Islamic reform discourse within the emerging public spheres of mostly colonial states. The activities of these early modern personalities span a variety of regions variably affected by Western colonial expansion. The emerging public spheres of the 1870s and 1880s, from the Maghreb and the Ottoman Empire through Central Asia and India to South East Asia, provided the communicative stage for the formulation of normative claims affecting the idea of *islah*. This keyword means 'redressing' and making wholesome, more than 'reform'. It targets both individual Muslim subjects and the *umma* as a whole. Hereby, the word *umma* itself became at the same time increasingly flexible, often designating the national community, and increasingly reified, no longer denoting a transterritorial 'ecumene' as in the pre-colonial period. We should bear in mind that by the time the Muslim reformist discourse started to be formulated by personalities who were often both thinkers and activists, the Western diagnosis of the inherent deficits of Islamic traditions was already gaining currency.

Muslim reformers faced the arduous task of constructing a shared cultural perspective and promoting a self-sustaining political determination adequate to challenge their Western colonialist counterparts on their own terrain, while relying on what they saw as key elements of strength preserved from their own intellectual traditions and institutional legacies. Yet at the same time, they forcefully inherited, through an increasingly colonial dependence, the European dichotomy of religion and civilisation and the European tension of inner versus public religion. Apart from the crude realities of colonial, political and economic dependence, this reformist path never gained the recognition of the West, not even by scholars—until the irresistible ascent of a Muslim Western discourse of participation and citizenship after 9/11, epitomised by the trajectory of the global public intellectual Tariq Ramadan.[21]

After the turn to the twentieth century, two world wars, the slow agony of direct colonialism and the new transatlantic efflorescence of the social sciences, most notably sociology and anthropology (starting this time from the shores of the new global hegemon, the United States), a new attempt was made to normalise religion's role in the public sphere on a global scale. Particularly important within this trajectory was the work of a leading Austrian sociologist who migrated to the United States after the Second World War, Peter Berger, who, building on phenomenology, theorised the importance of religion for keeping together and providing meaning for a subject immersed in the life world. Ultimately, the civil significance of religion originates in its role as a subjective search for meaning moderately exposed to intersubjective understanding and communication.[22]

Yet Berger—here followed by Thomas Luckmann[23]—constructed an anachronism in providing a transhistorical definition of religion largely stemming from a remoulded use of the word, which crystallised in the 1950s and early 1960s, in particular in the United States, during a period of breath-taking modernisation and intense cultural change increasingly conducted under the banner of individualisation. Overall, if the triumphant notion of religion worked in a highly functionalist way, its yoking to civility ended up sanitising it on a socio-political level and opening the debate on allegedly improper, instrumental uses of religion. The purported role of a civil religion within modernity gained further prominence in the latter third of the twentieth century by securing a cultural capital capable of providing social cohesion and solidarity and so reconciling tradition and modernity.[24]

The common denominator of this type of definition is the ability of religion to support a softly functional search for meaning that stabilises individual and collective life and so has the potential to support civility. While the importance of civil religion was propagated on a global scale by sociologists like Robert Bellah (most notably through studying both America and East Asia, and with an intermezzo dedicated to the study of the Middle East and Islam) and Jeffrey Alexander, it was also represented, though in original ways, in the work of the anthropologist Clifford Geertz, who looked at both North Africa and South East Asia. For Geertz, religion functioned as a source of holistic meaning that stabilises both the life world and social relationships. Yet, according to him, religion plays such a role not only in the most modern among Western societies—especially in those with a strong Protestant background, characterised by an increasing individualist ethos—but also in the new non-Western postcolonial nations—including several Muslim-majority societies. Here, the cultural function of religion as a provider of collective identity is subject to intense reconstruction. Most notably, Geertz saw instances of a religion conceived as a cultural system subject to change, at work in various forms of Islam in such distant places as Morocco and Indonesia, the two main cases he examined. As a 'cultural system', religion is shaped in different ways if we shift the attention from one to the other cultural world, but its function remains identical.[25]

Yet without looking more deeply into history, Geertz's attempt to normalise the modern role of religion in postcolonial Muslim societies remained abortive and largely unconvincing. What appears as a soft attempt to universalise and globalise the relation between religion and civility is less innocent of prior distortions than appears at first sight. The ghost of Western essentialism pushed out of the door, comes back through the window when it is now assumed that a secular subjectivity aligned with the Western model of the nation-state is surrogated within Muslim societies by hybrid formations favouring a basically authoritarian construction of a developmental ethos, as was the case in Morocco and Indonesia. In either case, a conveniently reduced type of Islam, reformatted into a public ideology or at least into a public ethos, symbolically reflecting more popular forms of 'religiosity', remains a key ingredient of collective identity.

The relentless critique performed by another anthropologist, Talal Asad, targeting a wide range of Western social science scholarship stretching from Durkheim to Geertz, presents evidence of a vicious circle more than sheer contradiction. It is characterised by the relation between the affirmation of a secular subjectivity as the banner of Western culture, and the reiteration of an essentialist knowledge of the West's other, best incarnated in Islam. Western norms of modern governance remain, both in the former metropoles and in the former colonies, intimately connected to ideas of individual autonomy rooted in a secular subjectivity. Thus, according to Asad, the 'secular' should not be equated with a rejection of 'religion', as it presupposes an essentialised, reformed religion as the necessary condition for the formation of self-governing agents. Asad sees a reiteration of this circular logic across various stages of world politics (from the colonial to the postcolonial).[26]

Islam's investment into transcendence and circulation

The approach of Marshall Hodgson, who in his career interacted closely with scholars of world history and modernisation theory, is particularly valuable when seeking to subvert and revise teleological assumptions about why Islamic civilisation finally succumbed to the hegemonic power of the West. He looked through a theoretically informed prism at the distinctively Islamic approach to building patterns of life conduct and sociability in connection with highly variable and often flexible institutions of governance. Hodgson suggested ways in which these institutions needed to be analysed as articulating, in original and malleable ways, the civilisational equation of knowledge and power via interactions not only between various sectors of the elite but also between 'commoners' and elites across urban, agrarian and nomadic milieus.[27]

Long before Edward Said, Hodgson was keen to show the extent to which the scholarly categorisations related to Islam came to depend upon the conceptual hegemony of Western modernity. In this sense, he contributed to showing, without indulging in any deconstructionist and anti-essentialist zeal, how even the apparently innocent categories of 'religion' and 'civilisation' required re-examination. Moreover, he recognised that the Islamic ecumene was clearly not an example of a neatly overlapping macro-region and civilisation, like Western Europe/Christendom, China or India. Islam was not imposed on the Nile-to-Oxus region by conquerors coming in from the regional periphery, but was the outcome of complex developments and innovations converging in an original synthesis. Before the advent of Islam, the region was a configuration of heterogeneous religions and cultures with a long history of interaction and conflict. Nonetheless, several key aspects of the new developmental pattern that culminated in the rise of Islam had been in the making over several centuries. The Nile-to-Oxus area was the birthplace of the most important archaic civilisations, whose succession and overlapping did not, however, crystallise into a pattern of regional homogeneity and transregional diffusion.

Yet alongside imperial formations, the region had witnessed the rise of monotheistic traditions—in different Semitic and Iranic shapes—as well as the growing strength of urban, mercantile classes, and the egalitarian social ethics that drew support from both of these trends. Therefore, Hodgson could argue that it was the Islamicate civilisation that for the first time achieved the cultural unification of that part of the world, and it did so through a new elaboration of the monotheistic themes inherited from Iranic and Semitic sources. It provided them with a new trans-civilisational reach by investing its expansive orientation into the depths of the Afro-Eurasian hemisphere or 'the Old World'. Islamdom (a term popularised by Hodgson) quickly became the hub of a composite ecumene that reached its zenith of power and knowledge at the end of the epoch that Hodgson called the 'Middle Periods' (tenth to fifteenth centuries), which orientalists before (but partly also after) Hodgson have mainly depicted as a phase of decadence and lack of creativity following the 'golden age' of the Umayyad and Abbasid caliphates.

Hodgson was quite straightforward in seeing the combined heritage gathered and valorised by Islam as centred on an 'egalitarian cosmopolitanism': or, if this sounds too idealistic, on an appropriate combination of largely egalitarian contractualism and a fairly high degree of social mobility, especially if compared with the bordering civilisations of Western Europe, China and India. The incomplete transformation of the Nile-to-Oxus region into something that looks like a clear-cut civilisation provides the background to Hodgson's interpretation of Islam as doubling up into a highly translocal and transregional Islamdom. The civilisational patterns that served to integrate the region (legal, artistic, multilingual, intellectual and 'spiritual') also manifested a hemisphere-wide, both expansive and integrative, to some extent even entropic dynamics that has no parallel in premodern history. Islam is a notable exception for not configuring a civilisational block marked by solid continuities of lettered and religious traditions since after the Axial Age, the formative era that constituted the onset of transcendence-based teachings around the middle of the first millennium BCE.[28] Islam rather represents a discontinuous and open civilisational pattern or process that, by virtue exactly of this higher degree of openness, produced the only civilisation with a global reach, and as such a civilisation sui generis, something more like a trans-civilisational ecumene.[29]

One of Islam's most striking features over the longer term was its integrative engagement with a variety of local cultural forms and religious cults, an integration performed through the working of two types of high culture, a shari'a-based culture and knowledge of the jurists (*'ilm*) and an *adab*-oriented court culture. Hodgson describes the shari'a-based culture as 'piety-minded', yet suitable to regulate multiple aspects of social life and also to aid in the reconstitution of various types of popular religiosity and integrate them within a coherent institutional framework. Similarly, the cosmopolitan courtly culture (*adab*), which was originally reconstructed at the centre of the Abbasid Empire on the basis of the Persian Sasanian model, fostered literary culture and ideals of all-round cultivation. *Adab* provided a civilisational complement more than a counterweight to the patterns that coalesced around *hadith* (the certified sayings of Muhammad), *fiqh* (jurisprudence) and Qur'anic scholarship, since *adab* often also drew on them.

According to Hodgson, the only possible way to understand Islam is from the standpoint of world history. One should indeed take charge of what is specific to Islam and Muslim actors vis-à-vis the parameters of Western-centred modernity without preventively seeking shelter behind an anti-essentialist shield. If pushed too hard, anti-essentialism brings us back to square one: an absolutisation of stale Western parameters of political, economic and cultural modernity. Therefore, a sociology of Islam treasuring Hodgson's teachings cannot limit itself to looking at modern and contemporary developments, but should also pay attention to the memory of how Islam reassembled and gave an unprecedented impetus to the heritage of a number of civilisational components. Hodgson's approach is important for the sociology of Islam since it entails a sustained criticism of the provincialism of Western orientalist views. These views have historically privileged Islam's Arabian origin and often its Mediterranean significance, to the detriment of the intense and multileveled cross-cultural borrowings with other civilisational realms on the Afro-Eurasian map.

Hodgson knew Weber all too well, including the fact that Weber, in his rather thin dealing with Islam, had not only got basic facts about its origin and development wrong but that he had also raised lopsided questions about it, since Islam and Islamdom did not fit his approach to contrasting Western rational puritan asceticism with purportedly Eastern mystical paths.[30] Bryan Turner first criticised Hodgson for reducing Islam to inner faith and conscience. Yet, in more recent writings, the British sociologist has rehabilitated Hodgson for having been able to show, for the first time and in vivid terms, Islam's original cosmopolitan imagination as rooted not in military imperialism but in an inclusive and socially constructive type of piety. In this way, Hodgson, a committed Quaker, exposed, in the name of a pacifist ethics, the admixture of Western historic provincialism and colonial arrogance in missing the way in which Islam (supposedly a 'religion') smoothly turned into Islamdom, a social nexus and civilisational matrix manifest in networks of local and translocal connectedness and their attendant normative patterns.[31]

For Hodgson, Islam was an excellent example for the wider argument that a civilisational process originating from a prophetic call needs a cumulative religious tradition on which to rely. This is necessary to promote specific ideals of life conduct and ensure that the 'high', lettered traditions of cultural elites are not disconnected from more popular practices. We can see such ideals at work in the type of urban piety that characterised the broader Irano-Semitic civilisational area. This was the cradle of an urban egalitarian social ethics that also worked as a platform of societal self-regulation and organisation (including trans-tribal arrangements). Hodgson was keen to demonstrate, contra Weber, that Islam's expansion, particularly during the half millennium that Hodgson called the Middle Periods, was not only just partly related to military conquest but was also the outcome of a highly original process of transformation. Sufi brotherhoods epitomised Islam's networking momentum, and propelled the underlying, inertial force of social self-organisation well served by locally adapted shariʿa practices. This process helped create enduring patterns of group cohesion and intergroup connectedness that were never completely eclipsed and are reflected in the way Sufism is globally deployed (also through labour-related migration) in the contemporary world. This circulatory momentum comes close to representing the quintessentially social characteristics of the long-term expansiveness of patterns of life conduct inspired by Islam's combination of a moral idiom with spiritual paths and patterns of sociability. The emergent type of civility not exclusively centred on city life, as it occurred in the Late Middle Ages within Western Christendom, was most famously evidenced, once more, by Weber's theorisation of the unique nature of European urban associations and municipal institutions.[32]

In referring to Islam as a circulation-based transcivilisational ecumene and global multiverse rather than as a self-centred universal challenger of Western

Christendom, we need to stress the evanescence of a supposedly Islamic civilisational core (both in political and cultural terms). This gesture pulls the rug from under the feet of modern and contemporary orientalists and Muslim reformers alike, whose converging, relentless efforts insist on the importance of establishing Islam's authentic origin. I am also arguing for the impossibility of a one-to-one relationship between the Muslim allegiance of faith, its traditions and institutions, on the one hand, and the prestige and attractiveness of the wider normative frameworks accompanying Islam's expansion on the other: Islamic civilisation being wrongly seen, by both orientalists and Muslim reformers, as the smooth and natural terrain of convergence of both. Nonetheless, what is most promising in the idea of a transcivilisational ecumene as an inflationary multiverse, substituting for the metaphor of a self-contained civilisational universe or galaxy, could also be linked to an altered notion of 'Islam's core'. Once this core is identified with key traits and components of early Islam, rooted in the wider Irano-Semitic realm, it should then be seen not as a self-same star or constellation, representing a defined cultural identity, but rather as a supermassive black hole favouring absorption, amalgamation, and also the occultation of surrounding cultural factors along with their multiple 'origins'. The civilisational originality of Islam's 'origin' should then be seen in the intrinsic evanescence of any purportedly exclusive authenticity, pace the views of all cultural warriors including neo-orientalists and Salafis (and, with them, a good chunk of public opinion located mainly in the West but also present, by inevitable circulatory reflex, in the Muslim world, often supported by the discourse of Muslim reformers).

Islam's exposure to European Leviathans

European modernity, in its new transatlantic pivoting that spurned overseas colonialism on an unprecedented scale, irreparably discontinued the hemisphere-wide, premodern nexus between circulation and transcendence. Of course, the dialogic resources of transcendence-based teachings and practices had been subject to erosion before the start of modernity. This erosion was largely due to the imperatives of the canonisation of faith traditions and the formation and hierarchisation of their personnel, from which Islam itself, despite its predominantly horizontal authority structure, was far from immune.[33] Yet, it was the modern European, Westphalian state with its top-down and increasingly capillary organisation of social power that created an entirely new environment that placed various restrictions on circulatory dynamics. At the same time, this new type of state imposed on them the circulation of the prestige of its own model (most notably during the colonial and postcolonial eras), whose embracement became the condition, for postcolonial states, for becoming part of the international system—the 'international' being at large a surrogate of the circulatory. Such modern frameworks favoured—also but not only in the case of Islam (as famously propounded by Ernest Gellner, who also intended to contribute to an interdisciplinary-oriented sociology of Islam, interfacing with anthropology and history)[34]—the mobilisation of traditional types of virtuosos or, more often, of specific groups claiming a pure interpretation of a faith tradition, often also by virtue of their not belonging to the religious establishment. This phenomenon is usually understood and categorised as the dynamics of modern 'fundamentalism', but is also, and quite inevitably, an essential part of the genealogy of modern Muslim reform, as suggested above.[35] These were common tendencies in several parts of the early modern world well beyond Europe, including the centralising Muslim empires (the Ottoman, the Safavid and the Mughal). However, it cannot be denied that Reformation and post-Reformation Europe effected an unprecedented hardening of the notion of religion itself as a confined field of human behaviour out of the inherent richness (and, to some extent, messiness) of the deployment of transcendence-based traditions of pious conduct and compassion that originated from the Axial Age onwards.

It was through the upheavals of the sixteenth and seventeenth centuries (up to the European Wars of Religion) that religion became a sphere increasingly differentiated from the realm of public order presided over by the sovereign ruler. The main agent of this traumatic development, the Westphalian state (the Leviathan), attempted to subdue the radicalism of the early modern (often puritan, proto-fundamentalist) religious movements and put an end to the unstable late-medieval balance of spiritual and temporal powers. In this Westphalian regime, which the entire global modern world has inherited in various ways, religion is well circumscribed, controlled by the sovereign, and its function can be flexibly shifted back and forth between the religion of the ruler and the religion of the subject, between the public realm and the inner sphere.

Religious enthusiasm and creativity resurfaced in ever new forms in the eighteenth and nineteenth centuries, especially outside Europe, most notably within European settler colonies. On the other hand, also thanks to the emergence of a print-based public sphere almost everywhere by the nineteenth century, the unity of faith, now commonly standardised as 'belief', was often accompanied by the matching standardisation of the vernacular. Starting with

England, where after all the idea of the Leviathan had first been shaped, the use of English as the liturgical language played an important role in the creation of a confessional identity. Such passions were directed equally against religious minorities within as against enemies outside the state. But the importance of such modern European developments should not distract us from emphasising the deep changes taking place elsewhere, precisely at the time when European societies were encountering the outside world in an unprecedented way through colonial enterprises. The consequence of the process was to set the patterns of circulation among faith traditions on largely new rails, and most notably to standardise the limits of circulation due to the self-entrenchment of national states. In other words, the standardisation of 'religion' based on individual belief was on a par with the subordination of circulation to the power politics of colonial states and their attendant notions of sovereignty.[36]

While these developments did not suddenly discontinue the dynamics of Islam–Islamdom and their potential for social reconstruction and civilisational expansion (or entropy), they certainly determined the orientalisation and, we should add, de-sociologisation of Islam. The big problem with the rise of European sociology itself has been its initial, and to a large extent enduring dependence on orientalist knowledge, which resulted in its incorporation of a conveniently distorted view, of which the Weberian caricature of Islam as a 'warrior religion' and 'monotheism with a tribal face' was just the bluntest version.[37] The result of this de-sociologisation and de-civilisation of Islam is the view of a cultural self-limitation inherent in the allegedly totalising religious orientation of Islamic civilisation. This is seen in turn as working against the presuppositions of capitalist growth and incremental liberalisation and democratisation that enlivened the early modern socio-political formations of Western Europe. Accepting this approach, the Western colonial encroachment upon Muslim lands that unfolded particularly through the eighteenth and nineteenth centuries is interpreted as a necessary consequence (almost a deserved outcome) of a culturally determined imbalance of power between the Western and the Islamic civilisations.[38]

The way forward for the sociology of Islam starts by questioning the hegemonic discourse that propounds a standard, package-like, teleological model of socio-economic and political modernity modelled on a supposed Western prototype of rights, participation and citizenship that never existed anywhere in a pure form. In this sense, the project challenges the idea itself of a compact civilisation, be it Western or Islamic, and focuses on mutual, yet also inner entanglements of knowledge, culture and power. As stressed by Asad, this shift of perspective should not be guided by the old motive of anti-Western resistance, but rather by the analysis of 'new institutional and discursive spaces (themselves not immutably fixed) that make different kinds of knowledge, action, and desire possible'.[39] As argued by him, one should not remain caught in the polarisation between two standard ways of accounting for the emergence of such new spaces, namely 'either ... as evidence of "a failure to modernize properly," or ... as expressions of different experiences rooted in part in traditions other than those to which the European-inspired reforms belonged, and in part in contradictory European representations of European modernity'.[40]

My approach links Asad's sensible recommendations to a re-evaluation of Elias's theory of the civilising process, which has had the merit of condensing several research questions originating from philosophy (Nietzsche), psychoanalysis (Freud) and sociology (Weber) in the framework of a reflexive historical sociology.[41] Elias conceived the civilising process as a largely self-propelling cycle of taming violence and increasing coordination among individual subjects via a cumulative dynamics of self-restraint reflected in etiquette, manners and codes of conduct (including graceful behaviour and a sense for 'taste' and beauty) more than in ethics proper. Elias's approach was far from immune to Eurocentric pitfalls. Additionally, it has been criticised for neglecting the civilising role of religion. Nonetheless, an approach capable of remedying both deficits is possible.

By reinterpreting Elias and some of his commentators and critics, we can see in the civilising process the broader socio-anthropological work of reconstructing the outer conditions for civic life and social cohesion, with a modicum of help from explicit inner conditions. These inner conditions might be based on moral and at root religious orientations, like, for example, through the Islamic parameter of *ihsan*, often translated as the imperative 'to do what is beautiful'. However, for the civilising process to work, they should be subdued (yet not necessarily erased) as far as their public expression is concerned. This is what we might call the 'secular turn' of religion, which is neither its disappearance nor its thorough privatisation (both of which are socially and cultural implausible). Yet the modes of such a civilising process are far from being contained within a narrow, straight path since they respond to a wide spectrum of cultural and religious variables, many of which, most notably in the Islamic case, have an organisational and institutional underpinning rather than a merely ideological distinctiveness or identitarian assertiveness.

This view dovetails nicely with Hodgson's vision, where we see a more sophisticated game of mutual reflection, rather than a sharp separation and an invariant relationship between religious commitments and civilisational processes. Religious commitments tend to figure prominently among the formative ideals and factors that constitute a civilisational pattern, but according to him some religions have a stronger civilisational impact than others, while some civilisations allow for more space to piety (and, we should add, grace) as a formative factor. This intense dynamic between religion and civilisation in Islam creates a distance with both Christianity and Buddhism, since Hodgson did not see a comparable pan-Christian or pan-Buddhist civilisation. The uniqueness of Islam stands as the only global religion literally embodied in an innerly diverse civilisational process. The challenge consists exactly in taking into account more strongly than Hodgson did the inner-civilisational variance, yet originality, of the institutional dimension of the doublet Islam–Islamdom, while he seemed at times to relegate this dimension to the most externalised and routinised, and therefore dependent, crust of the civilisational process.

Thus, a revised Eliasian approach allows us to go beyond Hodgson's own sociological limitations. Instead of postulating a unique case of an almost one-to-one relation between a religion and a civilisation, what looks like a certain uniqueness of Islam should prompt a critical revision of the concepts themselves of religion and civilisation and their stale binary articulation, on which much liberal discourse has been parasitic. This binary conceptualisation does not work well in the case of Islam exactly because of the rather entropic character of its expansion and institutional nesting in a variety of civilisational contexts, most notably across conventional civilisational borders. These borders are such only if we consider them hardened by the strength and singularity of lettered traditions originating in the Axial Age and that nineteenth-century scholars of comparative religion first conceptualised as their 'scriptures'. The inner key but also the outer symptom for this expansive adaptability that makes Islam capable of breaking through these borders and becoming a transcivilisational ecumene, more than a self-contained civilisational monolith, lies in the open and semi-formal approach to the institutional consecration of connective bonds and collective identities. This approach was favoured by a particularly open recombination of religious and civic forms. This is evident in the flexible institutional forms represented by the college (the madrasa), the pious foundation (the *waqf*), and the Sufi order (the *tariqa*). These forms were shaped over time and were decisively influenced by Islam's interfacing with other traditions (see, for example, the hypothesis that the madrasa system, originating in the eastern regions of the

Islamic ecumene, might have been influenced by the monastery schools of Tibetan Buddhism).[42] These institutional patterns, more than hardened models, reflected the contractual patterns of the underlying, enabling norms and a corresponding immunisation against consecrating an institution in the form of a corporation (no caste, no estate, no municipality and not even a corporate guild—especially no church; the *umma* being not an *ekklesia*, a consecrated gathering of the faithful, but a rather inchoate and anorganic ecumene or body).

This re-evaluation of civility in a comparative perspective has been supported by Johann Arnason's sustained effort to make Elias's theory of the civilising process less parochial and evolutionistic and more open to cross-civilisational comparison and resulting reformulations of the dynamic balance (or lack thereof) between knowledge and power mediated by culture.[43] A more plastic notion of civility will also help us gain a better understanding of the factors that allow for spinning wider trans-local, even trans-social types of connectedness (that is, those crossing conventional national and societal borders). In this sense, civility is an obvious key to overcoming a socio-centric approach strictly modelled on the nation-state and fully appreciating civilisational, trans-civilisational and transcultural dynamics. Civilisations are accordingly understood as wider, shifting clusters than either local communities or national societies and therefore also as other than territorially bound regional or transregional monoliths.[44] Civilisations are nothing else than ongoing social and cultural processes. This is also the key to appreciate the social and cultural originality of early modern state-formations within the Islamic ecumene (most notably the Mughal, the Safavid, and the Ottomans' transitioning into a mature stage of statehood) without needing to read them in terms of deficits in comparison with their European and modern Leviathans. Studying a different kind of individual–state–society relationship and attendant patterns of civility is the indispensable key to assess 'what went wrong' not with Islam or Islamdom but with Muslim modernists' arbitrarily selective approach to Islamic traditions.

Conclusion: the sociology of Islam after liberal modernity

The analysis I have offered in this chapter is far from feeding into a delusional backward-looking perspective, like saying 'Islam has been modern before modernity' (as perceived by a liberal Muslim intellectual of the calibre of 'Abduh al-Filali al-Ansari).[45] That might have been the delusion of many

Muslim reformers, compensating for their wilful acceptance of a reductionist appreciation of the dynamism of Islam/Islamdom in history. The perspective I have proposed is rooted in a diagnosis of the present supported by the ongoing project of a sociology of Islam. One can describe the most recent waves of globalisation as pushing towards a lower level of sacralisation of the collective bond defined through the nation-state, despite the enduring power of the latter. While globalisation does not erode state power per se, it contributes to deconstructing the political myth of the Leviathan and the attendant political theologies, including those that have nourished sociology's 'methodological nationalism'. This is why the sociology of Islam is innovative within sociology itself. Retrieving the view of an Islamic civilising process—more than of the conceptual short-circuit of an Islamic modernity—unfolding from the time before colonialism, and discontinued yet not entirely neutralised by it, is not an apology of the past but a contribution to assessing the vulnerabilities of the present global condition. According to this view, more fluid relations can emerge within patterns of mutual support and solidarity (as happens in migration contexts in the West) than the modern state can legitimise in terms of the principle of subsidiary functions. The inoculation against a too high degree of formalisation of law and institutional centralisation might have, again, some comparable advantages: as Hodgson wrote with regard to the Middle Periods, 'the high degree of decentralization in every social institution seems to have favored a ready expansion of these institutions wherever an opportunity presented, whatever the apparent political situation'.[46]

So, what went wrong? Nothing went inherently wrong from a historical viewpoint. However, during the colonial epoch, Islamdom was subject to an erosion that put an increasing and unprecedented strain on Muslim colonial elites and induced Muslim reformers to focus on Islam by neglecting Islamdom, thus contributing to reify the former. By the inter-war period, when the pan-Islamist agitator and intellectual Shakib Arslan launched his dramatic call to Muslims to reflect upon the causes of Islamic 'backwardness' and the urgency of overcoming them, Weber had just formulated his ideas concerning the failure of Islamic civilisation to attain political achievements like municipal autonomy, a discourse of rights, or the organisational and symbolic power of the modern state. While the Weberian catalogue might appear parochial and its underlying reasoning biased and in need of critique and revision, an even narrower Weberist problematic of civilisational comparison for the sake of measuring up the suitability of emerging nations to survive and thrive in the race for progress seems to have penetrated the consciousness and also affected the conceptual dictionary of Muslim reformers.

The cure is not forgetting about sociology, but to deepen its post-Weberian implications. The emergence of cultural, even more strongly than political, patterns of non-Western modernity does not express a wave of anti-universalism, but a distancing from a defective and hegemonically exhausted universalism in favour of its reconstruction on the basis of multiple, overlapping civilisational visions and patterns of imagination. The result seems to be that even those civilisational visions that rely on images that, from a Western universal viewpoint, appear as particularistic and exclusive (as in Western perceptions—or fears—of the Islamic *umma*), in fact provide global interconnectedness in non-linear ways. These modalities of reconstructing transversal, transborder forms of civility are largely alternative to modernist parameters of incorporation embedded in the state–society complex—and in this sense might well herald yet inchoate post-liberal forms of political modernity that the sociology of Islam might help to decipher.

7

ISLAMIC DEMOCRACY BY NUMBERS

Zaheer Kazmi

Returning from his historic visit to Turkey in November 2014, Pope Francis joined in the now ritualistic chorus of calls for Muslims to condemn terrorism in the name of Islam.[1] Turkey was once the heart of Orthodox Byzantine Christianity, until the sacking of Constantinople in 1453. It later became one of the great centres of Muslim civilisation under the Ottoman Caliphate, which was replaced by a secular Turkish state in 1923. Unlike his more abrasive predecessor, Pope Benedict, who, in a 2006 lecture at the University of Regensburg, quoted a fourteenth-century Byzantine emperor who called Islam 'evil', Francis's words were chosen more carefully.[2] Appealing to interfaith values, he mostly avoided treading too firmly on what could have been a diplomatic minefield—from the Ottoman slaughter of Armenians, which he has called genocide, to Turkey's ambiguous relations with jihadis entering Syria, and what some regard as President Erdogan's creeping domestic Islamisation.

By drawing attention to what Rupert Shortt has identified as a growing and virulent strain of religious intolerance in his book *Christianophobia* (2012), Pope Francis's appeal for Muslims to condemn terrorism was, in essence, an appeal for tolerance towards minorities, especially Christians.[3] Prominent

Christians are increasingly shedding light on the dangers of what they see as a rise in the 'mainstreaming' of minority persecution in the Muslim world, graphically depicted by the atrocities meted out by Islamic State (ISIS) jihadists in Syria and Iraq and evident also in the killing of Copts in Egypt.[4] Muslim opponents of ISIS often interpret such acts as being either religious aberrations driven by a fanatical fringe, or symptomatic of the 'blowback' from Western colonial legacies and neo-imperial ventures. In this way, a popular response has been to place faith in the idea that Islam and the majority of Muslims are moderate.

Even Pope Francis seems to be in agreement on this point, having previously stated in a Ramadan message to the Muslim world that the true or 'authentic Islam' of most Muslims is 'opposed to every form of violence'.[5] This only highlights how Muslim 'moderates' are increasingly replicating the majoritarian toleration of Western liberals by, like them, making 'extremists' of outliers in their own societies. By adopting Western practices in this way, such 'moderation' suggests an absence of authentic thinking and the curious futility of exhorting Muslims to be more liberal and democratic than they, in fact, already are. Indeed, projects for moderate Islamic theology—epitomised in the influential Sunni *al-wasatiyyah*, or 'middle way', agenda today—can be used against minorities, including within Islam, precisely because they seek to identify with the West by 'orientalising' others. One of the underlying tensions in the middle-way agenda is that it seeks to define itself as representative of a legitimate majority against an illegitimate minority of Muslims, but that it lacks the concomitant ideological tools to deal with the rights of minorities, Muslims or otherwise. This can lead to slippage between its approach to Muslim 'minorities' and 'extremists', who are equally conceived in religious terms as being 'heretical' or 'heterodox'. Conflating the practices of a denominational majority with timeless authenticity, middle-way moderation also depends upon, and takes its strength from, the brute force of numbers as much as any theology.[6]

This chapter focuses on one aspect of the contemporary deployment of the idea of *al-wasatiyyah*, which has emerged as an important global discourse since 9/11—the ideological use of the concept of the 'middle path' by prominent contemporary Sunni scholars engaged principally in countering Sunni Islamist extremism or jihadism. In particular, I focus on the ways in which, through the idea of the 'middle way', a particular theology combines with a particular narrative of Islamic history, politics and civilisation—based on majoritarianism—to produce a potent synthetic ideology with ambivalent tendencies. This trend has gained a degree of popular support, including in Western policy circles, mainly as an intra-Sunni theological strategy for countering Salafi-jihadism. Its role in countering extremism, however, has tended to obscure its own internal exclusivist and anathematising logic. This has been especially evident in the position of many of its leading lights on Shi'ism (as distinctions are seldom made by them, if at all, this applies to Twelver, Ismaili and, to some extent, Zaydi Shi'a also), as well as towards faiths outside Islam.

Addressing the majoritarian dimension of *al-wasatiyyah* today allows us to explore the ways in which traditional Islamic concepts can be adapted to serve contemporary ideological purposes not only in seeking a synthesis between Islamic and Western values in the face of extremism but in wider intra-Muslim contests over religious legitimacy. While assimilating ideas of the popular will and majoritarianism in Western liberal democratic thought, the simultaneous deployment of *al-wasatiyyah* in anathematising others has also meant that, as a strategy of moderation, it has, paradoxically, lacked the ideological resources for dealing with minority dissent.

The ideology of al-wasatiyyah

The resort to 'moderate' Islam in the face of the rise of global forms of Islamist violence has in many ways become synonymous with efforts to reassert the 'classical' Islam of the four canonical legal schools of the majority Sunni Muslim sect. This religious impulse has been directed principally at the Salafi-Wahhabi ideas—and their rejection of the primacy of the authority of the four canonical schools of Sunni law—seen to be associated with the theology of the Sunni jihadism of organisations such as al-Qaeda and, latterly, ISIS.[7] The impulse has also been tied to a dominant narrative of Islamic history steeped, via a 'Golden Age', in the grandeur and civilisational achievements of successive Muslim empires, from the Umayyads and Abbasids through to the Ottomans. The four schools, named after the medieval Muslim scholars who founded them (Hanafi, Maliki, Shafi'i and Hanbali), are regarded as authoritative by the vast majority of Sunni Muslims, who adhere to one or another of them. For these followers, they are seen as the theological bedrock of Islamic civilisation. These 'madhabs', as they are more commonly known, were largely formalised by the tenth century, at the height of Sunni imperial history, in order to cement an ideal of orthodoxy against heresy. 'Moderate' Islam today sees the Muslim world's current woes as a direct consequence of departing from its true nature and heritage, grounded in this particular reading of Islamic theology and history.

Since 9/11 in particular, this impulse has also been tied to a revival of the concept of the middle way—a rough translation of the term *al-wasatiyyah*, in its original Arabic—as the antithesis of religious extremism. With its symbolic appeal to 'moderation' and 'balance', the middle way—mentioned in the Qur'an—has come to be appropriated by a host of influential scholars and transformed into a global project. Among its most notable proponents are Yusuf al-Qaradawi in the Arab world, Tahir ul-Qadri in Pakistan and Canada, Hamza Yusuf in the United States, and Timothy Winter (Abdal Hakim Murad) in the UK. All are active in debates on Islam in the media and public arena, and each has sought to cultivate his own personal following. These self-styled Muslim moderates have positioned themselves as the authentic expression of Islamic orthodoxy against religious 'extremism', while invoking the compatibility of classical Sunnism, as the majoritarian view in Islam, with liberal democratic norms. The latter has been used as a means of implying that this manifestation of Islam is not only the authentic version but that it is also inherently pluralistic and tolerant.

In a well-known verse, the Qur'an refers to the *ummat al-wasatiyyah* as a way of describing the Muslim community.[8] While the term itself has no precise definition in translation, it has generally come to denote moderation and the idea of a people who follow a 'middle', 'balanced', 'just', 'fair' or 'best' path, which represents the hallmark of the Muslim *umma*. *Al-wasatiyyah* is, on this view, the via media between extreme interpretations of the faith—and other systems of belief—which lie beyond Islam's periphery. In centring Islam as a median way of life, *al-wasatiyyah* is also tied intimately to constructions of Islamic 'orthodoxy'. In other words, the middle way is normative Islam and is seen as fundamentally moderate because this not only ought to be the case, according to Qur'anic precepts, but *is*, in fact, true as it is borne out by the beliefs and practices of a Muslim majority.

As a Qur'anic injunction that is meant to inform the believer's everyday life by guarding against zealotry, *al-wasatiyyah* has been deployed by both Sunni and Shi'a scholars. To some extent, it has underpinned ecumenical initiatives aimed at intra-Muslim unity and moderation, such as the Amman Message.[9] This ecumenical tendency is also evident in a major study on *al-wasatiyyah* by Mohammad Hashim Kamali and, more generally, in the work of Tariq Ramadan (who wrote the preface to Kamali's book).[10] While Kamali and Ramadan tend to include Shi'ism within their conceptions of what constitutes normative Islam, they are, arguably, a minority in asserting this firmly and explicitly. As a prominent contemporary Shi'i scholar in the West, this explicit focus on the centrality of the traditional Sunni and Shi'i madhabs, and the importance of Sunni–Shi'a understanding for defining the normative centre of Islam, is also mirrored in the work of Seyyed Hossein Nasr.[11]

At the same time, however, owing to the nature of Shi'i theology, law and history, which is absent of any concept of Islamic legitimacy based on majority rule or majoritarian consensus, al-wasatiyyah in this sense has had only a limited application.[12] It is perhaps no surprise, then, that the concept of the middle way has tended to loom largest in Sunni Islam, which has been historically preoccupied from its outset with propagating the 'orthodoxy' of the majority—via the institution and ideal of the Caliphate, imagined or otherwise—against 'heterodox' and 'heretical' minorities. This has often been tied to the primacy of Ash'arite (and, to some extent, Maturidite) theology as representing official Islamic doctrinal orthodoxy against the 'extremes' of the Mu'tazilites (associated with the 'rationalism' of the Shi'a), the 'violence' of the historical Kharijites, and the Atharites (most often associated today with the 'literalism' of Salafi-Wahabbism) on a variety of theological issues including the place of reason, anthropomorphism and the createdness of the Qur'an.[13] A kind of 'neo-Ash'arite' position—in which its theology is tied explicitly to the idea of the 'middle path' against extremes—is evident today in the thought of Qaradawi, Winter and Yusuf. Al-wasatiyyah has thus also come to embody a discourse of power that aims to establish the content and parameters of Islamic orthodoxy in a milieu of contending interpretations of the faith. In this way, it can act as a rhetorical device that signals the unique religious legitimacy of those who expound its virtues and anathematises others outside its fold.

Since 9/11, this ideological function has become increasingly explicit among prominent Sunni scholars and activists, particularly those who champion the primacy of the four canonical schools of Sunni jurisprudence, or madhabs. Here, the concept is often interpolated into wider arguments aimed at countering the rise of global Sunni Islamist militancy, on the one hand, and debates about Islam's compatibility with liberal democracy on the other. In this context, it has taken on its most explicit political and institutional form in recent high-profile initiatives sponsored by the Malaysian government, notably the Wasatiyyah Institute Malaysia, which aim to combat religious extremism. The assimilation of the concept to liberal democracy has also been evident in the so-called 'wasatiyyah' trend in Islamist movements such as the Muslim Brotherhood in the Middle East.[14]

Under the banner of the middle way, marginalising or denigrating other forms of Islam and other faith traditions causes tensions with wider liberal commitments to freedom of expression while closing down the space for representative legitimacy in Islam. Religious movements of all kinds will, of course, always make claims about their own rightful legitimacy. What is significant here is how, in order to identify classical Sunnism with authentic Islam, middle-way moderates draw on modern ideas of majoritarian representation and legitimacy. In this way, the idea of the middle way can function less as a theological imperative than a proxy for majority rule. Ironically, this colonisation of the middle ground can provide succour to the intolerance these figures ostensibly seek to contest. This is illustrated by the way Qaradawi, Qadri, Yusuf and Winter are all influential figures at the forefront of a global Muslim 'moderation' agenda, but have, at times, equivocated on issues of religious tolerance. That they all self-identify with Sufism, which has become a kind of shorthand in the West for Muslim compassion, has done little to mitigate this behaviour.

One of the striking things about middle-way intolerance is that it is aired so openly—a far cry from the xenophobic accusations of duplicity that Islamophobes peddle. From the rarefied arena of theological polemics to the more populist pronouncements on Islamic moderation, the upsurge in sectarian violence in the Muslim world has only heightened and widened the scope of this rhetoric. Provocative language that contributes to conflict has emanated from Muslims of all persuasions. Having promoted themselves as the bona fide voices of reason and moderation in the battle against Islamist extremism on the basis of a particular theology, however, one might expect middle-way moderates to display a consistent degree of religious tolerance. But if this is not always the case, and apart from the paranoid imaginings of Islamophobes who, in any case, see all 'moderates' as 'duplicitous', how can we make sense of it?

The polemics of moderation

Timothy Winter (also known as Abdal Hakim Murad), a Cambridge University academic and Sufi shaykh, has been celebrated as the world's most influential British Muslim by the Royal Islamic Strategic Studies Centre in Amman in its popular yearly publication, *The 500 Most Influential Muslims*.[15] As a convert, he is often invoked as a paragon of Muslim virtue and erudition and makes public pronouncements on the inherently moderate nature of Islam and its hijacking by fanatics. Winter is among the most uncompromising proponents of middle-way Sunnism and sees deviation from its four legal schools as the fundamental problem with the current direction of the Muslim world—a strain of thought evident in his many sermons and publications. In common with his fellow 'classical' Muslims, however, this has led him to preach religious tolerance while practising religious anathematisation.

In Winter's case, this excommunication is today focused mainly on the 'deviations' of Salafi-Wahhabis, on the one hand (despite himself having spent time in Saudi Arabia learning from Saudi-based clerics), and the Shi'a, on the other. This allows him to construct the idea of an authentic Islam as a 'middle path' between two heretical 'extremes'. Indeed, in perhaps his most widely read apologetic work, *Understanding the Four Madhabs* (1999), he states that 'Sunni Islam' occupies 'the middle ground between the two extremes of egalitarian Kharijism and hierarchical Shi'ism': Kharijism, in its initial violent iteration as an early denomination in Islam, is today often invoked as a way of describing al-Qaeda's theology.[16]

As an ideological manoeuvre, the strategy of positioning oneself as the voice of reason between extremes has been increasingly common among representatives of classical Islam. In 2008, for example, it was illustrated in the controversial Channel 4 television documentary in the UK, *The Qur'an*, which was even criticised by Muhammad Abdul Bari, the then secretary general of the Muslim Council of Britain (MCB), the UK's largest, predominantly Sunni, umbrella organisation, as having the potential to incite sectarianism.[17] The documentary's principal Muslim advisor, Ajmal Masroor, an imam and MCB member, has frequently appeared on 'middle-way' platforms and in 2010 launched an unsuccessful attempt to be elected as a UK member of parliament for the Liberal Democrats.

As in the documentary—which implicitly asserted a link between the 'deviation' from authentic Islam of Wahhabism and Shi'ism, on the one hand, and Islamist militancy on the other—these forms of purported 'heresy' are, for Winter, inextricably impelled towards extremism and violence by virtue of their deviance. This leaves classical Sunnism as the only panacea, harking back to a supposed pacific and enlightened past and, in the process, burying the reality of its own sometimes brutal history and mixed record of tolerating religious dissent. In the post-9/11 climate, where Muslims are frequently pressed into declaring they are on the right side of a battle against extremism, Winter and Masroor are, of course, well aware of the rhetorical power and uses of labelling a particular theology 'extreme'.

During the rising sectarian violence in Syria in 2012, Winter published his *Commentary on the Eleventh Contentions*, a book in the genre of aphorisms encapsulating his views on pressing contemporary issues.[18] Buried in his oblique philosophical ruminations, and speaking as a self-appointed Sufi sage, he turns his attention in parts of the book to what he condescendingly terms 'the febrile fringes outside the Four Schools'.[19] While he tends to reserve his ire primarily for the Ismaili Shi'a, his rigid stance on the four schools leads to a degree of slippage in the object of his criticism, which includes the Twelver Shi'a.[20] In parts of the work, he refers to Shi'a Muslims in pejorative terms, including as 'Rafidites (Rejectors)', a widely recognised historical term of abuse denoting heresy and most often used today by Salafi-Wahhabi and jihadi clerics.[21] Lumping them with equal disdain alongside the historical Kharijites, in a passage about the Persian Shi'a Safavids he chooses to focus on the Qizilbash or 'red caps', a heterodox Shi'a formation. Here, he summons up an age-old blood libel—not unlike those about Jewish cannibalism among Western anti-Semites—exhorting that they too 'must be called to account for their actions' as they 'would eat their Sunni enemies alive'.[22] Winter could not have known that only a few months later a video of a Sunni Syrian fighter eating an Alawite soldier's heart or lung would emerge and be broadcast around the world.[23]

Given both today's intra-Muslim violence and his preoccupation with pointing out the inferior Islamic scholarship of others, one wonders why Winter chooses to invoke such selective and provocative versions of Islamic history (especially as the latest high-profile project he is involved in, 'Curriculum for Cohesion', includes among its aims the proper teaching of Islamic history in the UK).[24] Online, several of his other 'Contentions' can also be found in such statements as 'Shi'ism is a schism lacking the sea of Mercy' and 'Sunnism is built on *manaqib* (virtues); Shi'ism is built on *math-alib* (vices)'.[25] These polemical attacks on other Muslims are a far cry from his good-humoured cameo appearance in the recent pop parody video by Muslims of Pharrell Williams's 'Happy', or his interfaith activity and leadership of the Cambridge Muslim College, which project an image of conviviality. While Winter has also played a part in combating extremism and there is some wisdom in his warnings against excess, it is hard to see how such sectarian sentiments aimed at his followers will help quell violence in the Muslim world, much of it fuelled by the view that the Shi'a are heretics and, therefore, not worthy even of life. Nor can one see much to distinguish Winter's position from—on his own reckoning—the 'extremist' Salafi-Wahhabi position that pits Sunni against Shi'a.

Defeating deviants

The idea of the Muslim middle way is perhaps most commonly associated today with the Qatari-based Egyptian scholar Yusuf Qaradawi. He is one of the most influential Sunni scholars in the world—and probably the most high-profile one in the Middle East—and has a vast online and satellite TV presence and following. This has included his own regular primetime programme on Al Jazeera with a weekly audience of millions and his chief advisory role to the prominent website 'IslamOnline' through which many of his fatwas are issued globally. Qaradawi's propagation of the concept of *al-wasatiyyah*, for which he is widely known, is an attempt at normalising classical Sunnism, particularly in Islam's Arab heartlands but also beyond.

For Qaradawi and his followers, *al-wasatiyyah* is the normative expression of Islam and the only solution to the conflict within which the Muslim world has become mired. Given the vast historical and interpretative pluralism of Muslim thought and practice, however, it is a discourse that can only be sustained through a logic of anathematisation even as it preaches tolerance towards others. Given its associations with ideas of reasonableness, balance and common sense, the concept of a middle way also maps conveniently on to notions of liberal rationality and conventional, majoritarian and, therefore, representative viewpoints: opposing views within Islam are thus, by extension, seen as irrational, undemocratic or non-representative. It is little wonder, then, that like Winter, Qaradawi's espousal of such orthodoxy in an era of rising sectarian violence has led, perhaps inevitably, towards labelling other Muslims as heretics. This despite his previously prominent global role in initiatives aimed at Sunni–Shi'a understanding. Indeed, it is the apparent ease with which Qaradawi's rhetoric has slipped so readily from rapprochement to anathematisation that reveals the ideological malleability and volatility of *al-wasatiyyah*.

Like Winter, Qaradawi's position on the Shi'a echoes that of Salafi-Wahhabism, though he has been more explicit in commending Saudi clerics on their disavowal of Shi'ism as heresy, lamenting that they were 'more mature and far sighted' on the issue than he had previously been.[26] This resort to 'heresy' is, of course, also driven by a wider geopolitical fear—especially on the part of Gulf monarchies who have their own restive Shi'a populations—of growing Iranian regional hegemony in Iraq, Syria, Lebanon and beyond. Paradoxically, it is, in part, precisely because the official ideology of the Islamic Republic of Iran has tended to be ecumenical rather than sectarian in reaching out to Sunni Muslims, that the fear of a so-called 'Shi'i crescent' has been fuelled. This is most often rendered in the common refrain that they are proselytising among Sunnis, couched in the subversive language of 'infiltration' and 'invasion'—an accusation taken up vigorously by Qaradawi about Egypt where, however, the Shi'a presence is negligible.

Catalysed by President Bashar al-Assad's repression of his own citizens in Syria, and the long-standing political alliance of Syria and Iran, Qaradawi has been instrumental in fostering the idea among his Sunni followers that such acts, along with those of Iran and Hezbollah in the current conflict, are principally driven by the innate impulses of an age-old heretical and extreme theology, rather than the more prosaic political concerns and interests of states and communities. That sectarianism has played a part on all sides of the conflict, not least among so-called Shi'a death squads in Iraq, is not in doubt; but for a 'moderate' scholar to insist that Shi'a heresy is the cause of the conflagration is another order of claim entirely.

Since making his remarks, Qaradawi has sought to clarify that he did not intend to assert that Shi'ism is a heresy, although his statement on this matter is replete with accusations of Shi'i innovation (*bida*) and polytheism (*shirk*).[27] Qaradawi's position echoes deep traditions of heresiography in Sunni theological polemics.[28] This literature views 'fifth column' minority Shi'ism as harbouring the potential to subvert the 'integrity' of the Muslim *umma*—the true community of believers—at any moment. Not by coincidence, these traditions also function very much like forms of anti-Semitism in the West, with which they bear a striking resemblance, directed as they are at a visible minority and often drawing on the fabrication of ancient libels about Shi'a practices. Oddly, in this way, middle-way moderates today assimilate latent Western anxieties about subversion by minorities—minorities of which Muslims themselves are now also a significant part—in the culture of Western modernity they sometimes contest. It is not difficult to see how such attitudes towards minorities can also colour wider perceptions of tacit legitimacy of the jihadi terrorism of ISIS in Syria and Iraq.

The politics of blasphemy

Theological distinctions are, of course, important and legitimate undertakings in their own way, not least as they demonstrate the pluralism inherent in different approaches to revelation. But nobody really expects the principles of a religious movement to be liberal, only that their practices should be tolerant: else there would be nothing distinctive about religion separate from a secular liberal order. Perhaps this is why in trying to meet the expectations of Western models of toleration by aping them, middle-way moderates can find issues around comparative legal principles among the most thorny to reconcile. The harder they try to justify their moderation through the shari'a—as embodying the fundamental principles of Islam—the more awkward their own strategies of toleration become. This is because, as religious directives, there can be no easy fit or correspondence between such demands, which rest on the theological legitimacy of a denominational majority, and the precepts of a secular state. This is nowhere more apparent than on issues of blasphemy.

In contrast to Winter and Qaradawi, the Pakistani scholar and Sufi shaykh, Tahir ul-Qadri, has been at the forefront of vocally condemning the vicious sectarianism that has so marred Pakistani society. Qadri is a dual Canadian and Pakistani national whose global organisation, Minhaj-ul-Qur'an, was founded in Lahore in 1981. He is probably the most widely known religious figure in Pakistan today—rarely out of the media spotlight—presiding over a global network of members and affiliates worldwide, especially among the South Asian diaspora in the UK and North America. While he has recently forged a political alliance with former global celebrity Imran Khan's Tehreek-e-Insaaf party—which has sometimes courted the anti-Western, pro-Taliban vote in its stronghold of Khyber Pakhtunkhwa province—he is often regarded as a religious moderate who preaches tolerance and peace within and among all faiths. His 600-page *Fatwa on Terrorism and Suicide Bombings* (2011), which was translated into English, was widely lauded with high-profile launches in the West.[29]

Despite his belief in the superiority of classical Sunnism and his sometimes ambiguous pronouncements on the status of Shi'i jurisprudence, what is perhaps more notable in the context of Pakistani politics are Qadri's positions on the so-called Hudood Ordinances and the blasphemy law, particularly as they apply to Christians and minority Ahmadis (who, by law, are considered non-Muslims in Pakistan). Faced with accusations from both religious and political opponents, Qadri has denied condoning the killing of non-Muslims for blaspheming the Prophet, and has said that he is, in fact, critical of the way blasphemy is legally instituted in Pakistan.[30] He has also denied his role in the strengthening of such laws while he was a prominent religious leader during President Zia ul-Haq's further Islamisation of the Pakistani state in the 1980s.

While Qadri's protestations, based on distinctions he makes between substantive and procedural law, appear credible to a degree, he nonetheless insists on the necessity for blasphemy to be punished, appealing to its firm grounding in all Abrahamic faiths. And while he may remain equivocal about the need for the death penalty for such a transgression, including for non-Muslims, it is fair to say that Qadri's position is a commonly held Islamic opinion among Sunni and Shi'a clerics in Pakistan and elsewhere. The specific problem this presents for dealing with religious minorities, however, is that it can serve to fuel a constant fear of trumped-up allegations and, in some cases, vigilante justice against them. This was illustrated in the burning alive of a Christian couple in November 2014 by a mob in a Punjabi village.[31]

Like his orthodox counterparts, it is difficult for Qadri to remain entirely tolerant when claiming to speak for all Muslims: to retain authenticity as the representative of Islam, compromises must be made in the name of majoritarian assent. In nearby South East Asia, where the 'the middle way' now functions as part of official state ideology in Malaysia, the establishment of the Wasatiyyah Institute Malaysia by the government has also done little to stem the rising tide of religious chauvinism and persecution against Christians and Muslim minorities. The current Malaysian prime minister, Najib Razak—a key figure in the institute's foundation and a vocal proponent of the 'wasatiyyah' agenda—has remained largely silent in the face of recent calls to outlaw the non-Muslim use of the word 'Allah' by Christians, and official moves to restrict the religious activities of the minority Shi'a community. Perhaps most notably, these latter developments predated 9/11 and the more recent rise of sectarianism in the Muslim world in a country often vaunted as a model of progressive Islam.[32] More recently, Nasharudin Mat Isa, chairman of the Global Movement for Moderates (GMM) and former deputy president of the Pan-Malaysian Islamic Party (PAS), stated that Shi'ism should be 'controlled'.[33] Razak was also instrumental in founding the GMM, which espouses an explicitly 'wasatiyyah' agenda in the interests of promoting wider religious moderation.

The ethics of toleration

Despite their significant global reach, Qaradawi and Qadri hail from the more traditional Muslim societies of the Middle East and South Asia. The American Sufi Shaykh Hamza Yusuf—like the British Muslim, Winter, also a Western convert—is, however, based in the United States. Winter and Yusuf are long-standing colleagues who have frequently shared platforms, not least for middle-way initiatives such as the 'Radical Middle Way' organisation in the UK and the Deen Intensive Foundation in the United States. They are also both proponents of conservative scholars in the Arab world, such as the Saudi-based Abdullah Bin Bayyah. More so than Winter, Yusuf has, since 9/11, become the poster boy for the global propagation of the revival of classical Sunni orthodoxy. The Zaytuna College in California, which he co-founded, describes itself as America's first Muslim liberal arts college, and is now probably classical Sunnism's most notable Western outpost.

Yusuf has largely steered clear of the practice of anathematisation that his bedfellows in orthodoxy have found hard to resist. His belief in the identification of an authentic Islam with the tradition of classical Sunnism's four legal schools has not yet impelled him to call all those outside this fold 'heretics'. But representing the one true Islam is a heavy weight on anyone's shoulders. And if that Islam is also the Islam of the many, as classical Sunnism purports to be, it is always pregnant with the power to extinguish outliers whenever it may feel under threat. In the current climate of rising sectarianism and increasing attacks on religious minorities in the Muslim world, including Christians, it is this tendency that has burst forth once again.

Perhaps the greatest irony of the middle way, from the perspective of the West at least, is how its Sufi figures—often regarded as being steeped in human compassion, spiritual mystique and individualistic transcendence—have succumbed so readily to instrumental rationality in a defence of the majority. While Winter and Qaradawi display a hollow kind of tolerance towards those with whom they disagree, the religious politics of Pakistan increasingly trumps Qadri's religious ethics. However, the deeper conundrum to probe is why, from positions of institutional and numerical power, leading figures of moderation still see fit to engage in divisive theological polemics at a time when the Muslim world has descended into ever-deeper forms of appalling violence against minorities in particular. It is difficult to see why equivocation or slander about the validity of another person's private religious beliefs should have any place when its public consequences can prove fatal. Yet it is precisely because the intolerance that some middle-way moderates display is open—but yet curiously unchallenged publicly for the most part—that suggests that it represents something different and more substantial than the crude and misguided accusations about 'doublespeak' often pushed by Islamophobes.

Part of the answer might lie in the kind of Sufism adopted by middle-way moderates, which the stereotypical Western view of Sufism belies. For far from being the symbol of antinomian exoticism in the popular imagination, Sufism has also always had austere antecedents who have had a far greater impact on it. Pivotal figures in the Sufi canon, from Al-Ghazali (d.1111) to Ahmad Sirhindi (d.1624), were concerned with expunging Islamic mysticism of cultural accretions and ensuring that Sufism accorded with the rigid legalistic demands of shariʻa. In this way, one of their aims was to construct a new kind of majoritarian Sunni orthodoxy and the separation of this 'authentic' Islamic spirituality from the 'false' paths of both excessive mysticism and rationalism—elements that Shiʻism in particular was understood to personify and from which they sought to inoculate Islam. While 'orthodox' Sufism has the latent theoretical potential to anathematise in this way, in the varieties of actual orthodox Sufi practice such a preoccupation has rarely been the rule, and even less so as a justification for violence. But it is perhaps no coincidence that the mixed legacy of Al-Ghazali, the towering mediaeval scholar of the Seljuk Empire whose job at one time was to propagate such orthodoxy via the power of the state on the sultan's behalf, looms large in middle-way projections of Islam today.[34]

In the case of Hamza Yusuf, this invocation of Islamic intellectual history has also extended to rehabilitating the legacy of Ibn Taymiyya (d. 1328)—a key figure in Salafi-jihadi thought today—in relation to Islamic moderation: a reading that has not been without its critics, especially with regard to interpretations of his famous Mardin fatwa.[35] In his own time, the Sufism of Ibn Taymiyya, like that of Al-Ghazali before and Sirhindi after him, though from a different theological position, was also intimately concerned with anathematising Shiʻism among other 'deviant' groups. Countless high-profile public statements of Islamic moderation have now been signed by Qaradawi, Qadri, Winter and Yusuf, some intra- and inter-faith focused. But in staking a claim for what Islam and its majority adherents really stand for, recourse to the middle way can easily morph into a discourse of power rather than moderation. As some of the discriminatory policies of former Iraqi Shiʻa Islamist President Nouri al-Maliki have also shown, no religious sect is immune from the powerful seductions of majority rule. On the other hand, it is sometimes argued by middle-way moderates that the lack of a clerical hierarchy in classical Sunnism means it is intrinsically more open to liberal democracy: some of the literature on 'Islamic democracy' has been premised on this assumption. But, as the deployment of *al-wasatiyyah* shows, this is not necessarily the case because of the peculiar way in which this theological concept, associated specifically with moderation, can also be subverted so readily for opposing ends.

Holding firm to a belief in the unique sanctity of a medieval legal order and an account of Islamic imperial history that papers over the legacies of some deep and violent fissures lessens the possibility of 'tolerance', as the rigid assertion of orthodoxy by middle-way moderates today reveals. It may even be more accurate to assert that the creation of a 'democratic' Sunnism today—via the mining of historical concepts such as *shura* (consultation), *ijma* (consensus) and the absence of a priesthood—derives ultimately from Western conceptions of Islam, which have traditionally modelled Sunnism on Protestantism and Shi'ism on Catholicism.[36] This would make the middle way a kind of looking glass Islam that sees itself through a Western gaze, emptied of authenticity and laying bare its underlying polemical and sectarian dimensions. It is no accident that anti-Catholic sentiment lay at the heart of 'toleration' debates in the West's own early modern history.[37] By the same token, until fairly recently, Shi'ism was for the most part viewed by Western orientalists through a Sunni lens, that is, as a marginal and troublesome heterodox or heretical sect.[38]

Along with some of the Muslim democrats with whom they stress their affinity (Qaradawi has been a key spiritual figure for the Muslim Brotherhood in Egypt), middle-way moderates sometimes tend to imbibe the procedures more than the principles of liberal democracy. But this is not because 'Islamic democracy' or 'Muslim liberalism' are chimeras or deceptions, or 'classical Islam' is in some way innately immoderate, as Islamophobic detractors disingenuously argue. Nor are their misplaced and often prejudiced appeals to Muslims to be more truly liberal and democratic the solution—not least as Western democracy has itself become increasingly hollow and procedural, alienating large swathes of its own populations. It is because toleration and authenticity are not the same things.

The search for an ethics of toleration is a different quest from the current march towards a theology of authenticity. That middle-way scholars see it as essentially the same journey is perhaps one of the reasons why—despite the doubtless good intentions of many on this road—it may ultimately prove to be more a religious cul-de-sac than a path to spiritual liberation. At the same time, while it has become a commonplace among liberals to debate the dangerously fluid interpretations of Islamic concepts that legitimise violence, and which, in turn, transform legitimate *jihad* into illegitimate 'jihadism', less attention, if any, has been given to the equally unstable categories associated with antidotes to religious violence. Deploying the majoritarian dimensions of a concept like the 'middle way', leading scholars today expose the multivalent and volatile nature of theological categories associated with countering extremism. Perhaps, most significantly, it points to some of the limits encountered in searching for correspondence between Islam and the West by way of such categories.

THE STATE

8

BOURGEOIS ISLAM AND MUSLIMS WITHOUT MOSQUES

MUSLIM LIBERALISM AND ITS DISCONTENTS IN INDONESIA

Carool Kersten

Indonesia has been affected by successive religious and ideological currents from both the East and the West. These include various currents of liberalism, which were deposited during colonial and postcolonial times in what is now the world's largest Muslim nation-state. As elsewhere in the Muslim world, responses to these influences have varied, ranging from adopting and adapting notions of freedom derived from classical and later also neoliberalism, quarrying the Islamic heritage itself for equivalent concepts, to the rejection of outside influences on grounds of their alien—and therefore 'un-Islamic' origins.

After a brief historical contextualisation and short excursion into the ambiguities of categories such as 'modernist' and 'liberal' in relation to Islam, the present investigation will focus on critiques formulated by Muslim intellectuals in the aftermath of the fall of General Suharto's New Order regime in 1998. Situated between proponents of free market economics who are also sympathetic to other ideological derivatives from Western liberalism, on the one hand, and detractors with more overtly religious agendas from the opposite end of the Muslim spectrum on the other, the intellectuals in question have been highly critical of both these camps. Challenging existing taxonomies of '(neo-)modernist' and 'liberal Islam', some of these intellectuals propose a qualified acceptance of liberal ideas, whether derived and adapted from exogenous sources (that is, Western philosophical, political and social thinking) or from searching for comparable endogenous notions of freedom and liberalisation in the Islamic heritage. Others have formulated more sceptical critiques inspired by Marxism and post-structuralism. These varied responses not only offer counter-discourses to the influence of Western (neo)liberalism but also alternatives that move beyond received notions of 'Islamic neo-Modernism', 'Islamic liberalism' and 'liberal Islam' shaped by the influence of the writings of the Pakistani-born scholar of Islam Fazlur Rahman, and American political scientists Leonard Binder and Charles Kurzman on Indonesian Muslim thinkers.

The historical context of the Indonesian Muslim encounter with liberalism

One of the earliest waves carrying European ideas of liberalism to what were then still the Dutch East Indies can be traced back to the days of high imperialism. After decades of territorial annexation and blatant exploitation of resources, at the very end of the nineteenth century Dutch governance of their South East Asian colonies was redefined as 'Ethische Politiek': a paradoxical mix of continuing subservience to the economic interests of the metropolis through even more invasive administration, but now expanded with a civilising mission inspired by the loftier aspects of liberalism's intellectual heritage. Lasting until the Japanese invasion of 1942, this included greater efforts towards educating selected members of the local population—allegedly to prepare them for home rule, but in actual fact primarily geared towards training a local human resources pool restricted to staffing the lower echelons of the colonial administration.

While only a very small number of Muslims entered a Dutch-language education system, much larger segments of the population went for other options offered by newly established Islamic mass organisations using indigenous and Middle Eastern-inspired Islamic education systems to emancipate their constituencies. Children of rural Muslim traders and pious peasants continued to congregate at *pesantren*, Islamic schools operated by traditionalist religious scholars. In 1926, they had begun to unite in the Nahdlatul Ulama (NU), an organisation founded in response to the formation, in 1912, of the modernist Muhammadiyah by urban Muslims from pious backgrounds who were attracted to the ideas of Muhammad Abduh. In 1923, more rigidly literalist Islamic reformists had established their own Islamic mass organisation called Persatuan Islam. During the Japanese occupation, these organisations merged into the Majelis Syuro Muslimin Indonesia (Masyumi), which, after the war had ended, continued to function as the largest Islamic political party during the subsequent independence struggle and early decades of the Indonesian republic. Although Masyumi campaigned—strenuously but ultimately unsuccessfully—for a reference to shari'a to be inserted into the newly independent country's constitution, its loyalty to Indonesia as a nation-state reflects the implicit acceptance of the eventual 1945 version of the constitution as a key instrument of political modernity.

As Zaheer Kazmi and Wael Hallaq note, this dependency on 'state authority as a critical guarantor' of religious law 'inhibited radical and creative thinking in Islam' and prevented the development of a 'new conception of the law and legal morality, a new legal system, a new legal culture and education, a new economy, and a new moral community', thus binding Islamists and liberal Muslims together in the same constrictive paradigm.[1]

Western-style liberal politics was not very conspicuous during the first two decades of independence as ideological competition was dominated by secular nationalists, socialists and Islamists vying for political supremacy. Economic liberalisation only became more noticeable from the 1970s onwards, when General Suharto's New Order Regime (1965–98) began using it. It did so, first of all, to underpin the economic development plans defined by US-trained economic policy-makers, known as the 'Berkeley mafia', which were primarily geared towards lifting Indonesia out of the economic quagmire caused by the disastrous left-leaning and authoritarian 'Guided Democracy' (1959–65) of the country's first president, Sukarno. Secondly, it was also employed to vindicate Indonesia's security alliance with the West, cementing in particular relations with the United States and positioning the country as a South East Asian bulwark against the spread of communism.

Compatible political attitudes were also adopted by certain Muslim intellectuals who developed a kind of symbiotic relationship with the New Order; looking for a role for Muslim technocrats, professionals and academics in the government's development policies while simultaneously agreeing to being co-opted by the regime as a counterforce to leftist influences. Although the

Indonesian Communist Party (PKI) had been largely destroyed during the mass-killings and arrests of PKI members and alleged sympathisers in wake of the 1965 military coup that had brought General Suharto to power, the spectre of communism and resurgent support for the political left remained one of the new regime's main concerns. Liberal- or, perhaps more accurately, liberty-minded Muslims were also considered useful for weaning Indonesia's Muslims from Islamist ideas and deflecting any attempts to re-establish the Islamic Masyumi party or prevent a turn to more reactionary revivalist and Islamist organisations such as the puritanical Persatuan Islam (Persis) and the renegade Darul Islam (DI).[2]

In part motivated by their own anti-communist sentiments, and partly driven by the ambition to make the Muslim community stakeholders in the government's development policies, in 1970 a group of young intellectuals dominated by Nurcholish Madjid, then leader of Indonesia's largest Muslim student organisation, rallied around the idea of a 'Movement for the Renewal of Islamic Thinking' (Gerakan Pembaruan Pemikiran Islam). While remaining institutionally amorphous, on the level of ideas the movement was influenced by the secularisation thesis developed by sociologists of religion and theologians such as Peter Berger, Robert Bellah and Harvey Cox. These developments further fragmented the Muslim community beyond the traditionalist–modernist divide of the early twentieth century. Initially, Madjid had been hailed as the political heir to former Masyumi leader Mohammad Natsir, but after arguing that there was no need for an Islamic party, he was disowned by a substantial segment of Indonesia's Muslim constituency, including the former Masyumi establishment, Muhammadiyah puritans, and other Islamic revivalists.[3]

Further intellectual influence was exercised by Leonard Binder and Fazlur Rahman, who visited Indonesia in the early 1970s to scout for potential participants in their 'Islam and Social Change' programme at the University of Chicago. They recruited a number of prominent figures of that generation of budding Muslim intellectuals and upcoming religious leaders for postgraduate studies in Chicago. Aside from Madjid, these also included two future and successive chairmen of the Muhammadiyah: Amien Rais and Ahmad Syafii Maarif. These intellectual encounters led to a new influx of ideas and concomitant—but somewhat cavalier—conflations of Islam with not always clearly defined notions of modernism and liberalism. Since the resulting ambiguities form a central part of the critiques discussed below, it is important to dwell on the influence of these developments on present-day Muslim thinking in Indonesia.

*The problem of taxonomies and categories: Islamic neo-modernism,
Islamic liberalism and liberal Islam*

After moving from Pakistan's Central Institute for Islamic Research to the
University of Chicago in the late 1960s, Rahman had begun developing a new
research agenda and methodology for what he had initially called Islamic 'neo-
modernism', but later mainly referred to as 'contemporary' or 'postcolonial
modernism'.[4] He used these classifications to distinguish this type of new Islamic
thinking from what he called 'classical' Islamic modernism represented by earlier
figures such as Sayyid Ahmed Khan and Muhammad Abduh, but also in contradistinction to the paralleling evolution of Islamic revivalism initiated by the
eighteenth-century Arabian reformer Muhammad ibn Abd al-Wahhab into the
neo-revivalism of twentieth-century movements, including Rahman's own nem-
esis: the Jamaat-e Islami. At the same time, Rahman's neo-modernism contained
a re-appreciation of Ibn Taymiyya, who is generally associated with (neo-)reviv-
alist thinking. It is this association that would become a focal point for the critiques examined in this chapter. Rahman considered the Islamic neo-modernism
he had formulated as a 'prerequisite of Islamic renaissance'.[5] Through his men-
torship of figures such as Madjid, Rais and Maarif, this terminology began entering the Indonesian Islamic vocabulary.

While other contributions to the present volume evince the breadth and
variety of notions of Muslim liberalism, within the context of the present
examination the associations of Islam with liberal or liberalism is confined to
the influence of publications by two American political scientists specialising
in the study of the Muslim world. Appearing exactly ten years apart and coinciding with a crucial decade in Indonesia's political and cultural-religious history, Leonard Binder's *Islamic Liberalism* (1988) and Charles Kurzman's
Liberal Islam (1998) have exercised considerable influence on debates among
Indonesian Muslims.[6] As will be discussed in greater detail, Binder's mono-
graph, which carried the subtitle 'A Critique of Development Theories', was
generally met with greater approval as it also paid attention to the critics and
detractors of free-market economics, and Western trajectories of modernisation, including Sayyid Qutb, Samir Amin and Mohammed Arkoun. The
anthology compiled by Charles Kurzman, however, was subjected to more
severe criticism because it vindicated the inclusion of very different types of
Muslim thinkers as long as they could be classified under the contentious and
rather peculiar categories of 'liberal', 'silent' and 'interpreted' shari'a.[7] Thus the
volume presents figures such as Muhammad Iqbal, Fazlur Rahman,
Mohammed Arkoun and Abdullahi Ahmed al-Na'im alongside Yusuf al-

Qaradhawi and Rachid Ghannouchi. From Indonesia itself, it includes Mohammad Natsir and Madjid, but ignores Abdurrahman Wahid. With thinkers representing such divergent ideas, the category of 'liberal' is emptied of any concrete and substantial content.

'Islamic references' during the late New Order and early Reformasi years

Upon his return from the United States in 1984, Madjid established a Muslim think tank called Paramadina, which also offers 'self-improvement' seminars in five-star hotels for social climbers among Indonesia's increasingly affluent Muslim urban middle class. He began moving closer to the New Order establishment, and eventually even the regime's top echelons began attending Paramadina workshops as part of a rediscovery of their own Islamic roots.[8] This orientation took Madjid in a different direction from former collaborators in the Renewal Movement, such as economist and Muhammadiyah activist M. Dawam Rahardjo and the new NU leader Abdurrahman Wahid (popularly known as Gus Dur), who both opted for grass root-level education and development projects inspired by left-leaning Arab *turāthiyyūn*, or heritage thinkers, and Latin American liberation theologians.

The opening up of the public sphere during the *Reformasi* period that followed the 1998–9 regime change witnessed unprecedented press freedom, the establishment of new Islamic political parties and the emergence of a wide array of NGO and other civil society initiatives, while the leaders of the NU and Muhammadiyah took control of the two highest political offices in the land: with Gus Dur becoming the first freely elected president of the republic and Amien Rais taking the position of speaker of the Consultative Assembly. The early chaotic years of the post-Suharto era also saw the rise of Muslim militias and vigilante organisations, as well as yet another influx of liberal ideas. After 9/11, these torrents grew stronger when Indonesia was the first Muslim country to join America's 'War on Terror', becoming an even more crucial South East Asian partner after the country was confronted with bombings in Bali and Jakarta by local Muslim extremists. This resulted in increased US support for organisations like the Liberal Islam Network (Jaringan Islam Liberal, JIL) and for new initiatives, such as the establishment of the Freedom Institute and the LibforAll Foundation. These platforms functioned not only as Muslim-led outlets for liberal thinking, often in a neoconservative guise. In close association with the administrations of President Susilo Bambang Yudhoyono (2004–14) and his Democrat Party (Partai Demokrat, PD), they also became launching pads for the political careers of some of their founders, although these have since collapsed amid allegations of corruption, disputes with the presidential clan or scepticism on the part of their target constituencies.[9]

Displaying the same bravado and using an equally confrontational rhetoric as their Islamist adversaries, JIL profiled itself as the key Muslim advocacy group of liberal democracy in post-Suharto Indonesia. At the same time, JIL's reliance on foreign financial aid and support from Western NGOs had become a liability. The 'professionalized form of activism' that tends to be the outcome of such relationships brings with it 'a gradual reduction of "civil society" to the realm of bureaucratic NGOs and formalized "grassroots" institutions', which in turn undermines the credibility of platforms like JIL as genuine manifestations of a vibrant civil society.[10] After 2009, the Obama administration and funding bodies such as the Asia Foundation recognised these risks and scaled down support for organisations such as JIL, because it was considered as too much of an intrusion into intra-Muslim debates.[11]

Framing critiques of Muslim liberalism in Indonesia

In Indonesia, too, such associations between Islam and liberalism elicit the same generic objections from opponents and sceptics as elsewhere in the Muslim world. Because of its foreign philosophical and ideological roots, such influences are often termed as a *ghazwul fikri* or 'intellectual invasion'.[12] Muslims watch with trepidation and suspicion the post-Cold War victory of free-market economics promoted by a liberal ideology dressed up in the garb of democratisation and human rights, but in effect pushing a Western neo-conservative agenda riding on a wave of worldwide commercialisation and globalising consumerism. Muslim critics of this type of liberalism are not only found in Islamist organisations such as the puritanical Dewan Dakwah Islamiyah Indonesia (DDII) but also in the NU and Muhammadiyah.[13]

Younger cadres from both organisations share a suspicion of free-market economics and what they perceive as a collusion between Madjid's later interpretation of Islamic renewal thinking and what in Indonesian is referred to as *Islam Murni*, that is, allegedly 'pure' or 'unadulterated' Islam. These critics seek to bridge or overcome the conventional division of Indonesia's Muslim landscape into traditionalist and modernist camps by formulating new Islamic discourses that differ not only from those of the preceding New Order period but which also provide alternatives to the looming spectre of Islamism represented by newly formed Islamic political parties and Muslim vigilante organisations, such as Laskar Jihad and the Islamic Defenders Front (Front Pembela Islam, FPI), which appeared amid the breakdown of law and order in the immediate aftermath of the 1998 regime change. In view of these suspicions towards the term 'liberal', I suggest using the term progressive as an alternative designation for intellectuals whose writings must not only be read as meta-critiques of liberal and neoliberal tendencies in Islamic thinking, which rose to dominance during New Order and which remain prominent in the post-Suharto era, but also as counter-discourses opposing the various strands of Islamism that emerged in the 1980s and 1990s.

Islamic post-traditionalism as a method of discourse critique

Some of the most incisive critiques of the liberal ideas and political tendencies exhibited by Indonesian Muslims are articulated by young cadres of the NU known as Anak Muda NU. A self-described culturally hybrid community of activist-intellectuals operating on the interstices of different Islamic currents, they have formulated an alternative discourse that they call 'Islamic post-tra-ditionalism' or 'postra' for short.[14] Islamic post-traditionalism is neither a disa-vowal of the achievements of the Islamic tradition nor an outright rejection of the principles of liberalism. While the political-intellectual climate created by Madjid, and sustained by his intellectual disciples at Jakarta's State Islamic University clustered in the so-called Mazhab Ciputat ('Ciputat School'— named after the district where the university is located), have helped shape this new discursive formation, the criticisms of Madjid emanating from this 'postra community' show that it is inaccurate to lump him together with their intellectual mentor Abdurrahman Wahid under the single header of Rahman's Islamic 'neo-modernism'.[15]

Instead, postra's intellectual genealogy fits in the lineage of Wahid's ideas. Aside from the latter's promotion of an 'indigenisation of Islam' (*pribumisasi Islam*), it also draws inspiration from Latin American liberation theology and Hasan Hanafi's manifesto of the 'Islamic Left' (*al-Yasār al-Islāmī*), which Wahid helped introduce in the 1980s.[16] This in turn formed part of a major recalibration of NU activities in 1984 when Wahid took charge of the organisation's executive board and became one of the most adamant advo-cates of abandoning party politics altogether and returning instead to the NU's original objectives as an emancipatory Muslim mass organisation as laid down in its founding document of 1926.[17] Also featuring in the pedigree of the Anak Muda NU are members of a new generation of senior NU leaders, including its current Chairman Said Aqil Siradj and Masdar F. Mas'udi, the former head of NU 'think tank' P3M.[18] In the mid-1990s, they were responsible for introducing their younger peers to the writings of another Arab philosopher: the Moroccan Muhammad 'Abid al-Jabri.[19] Like Hanafi, he belongs to the so-called *turathiyyun* or 'heritage thinkers' who emerged in the 1970s and 1980s, proposing that Islam is not understood only in conventional terms as a religion consisting of certain doctrinal tenants and theological concepts but taken as a 'civilisation' with much wider cultural and intellectual manifestations.

The postra community's understanding of tradition is broad and pluralist rather than inclusivist—a crucial differentiation because it is at the core of some of the critiques of Madjid that will be discussed below. Islamic post-traditionalism embraces the same catholicity as the Arab heritage thinkers: a historical but non-teleological understanding of the *turāth*, or what Hamid Dabashi, an Iranian-born historian of Islam and cultural critic based at Columbia University, calls '*sans* historicism'.[20] However, in contrast to Dabashi, the Anak Muda NU is comfortable with simultaneously accommodating scholasticism and humanism. Rethinking the role and relevance of Imam al-Shāfiʿī's *usūl al-fiqh* (Islamic jurisprudence), Ash'arī and Matūridī and al-Ghazālī's Sufism in contemporary Muslim contexts,[21] they turn the notion of *Ahl al-Sunna wa'l-Jamāʿa* ('those who adhere to the Traditions of the Prophet and are loyal to the community', self-identifying as 'orthodox Sunni Muslims') from an identifiable school of thought (*madhhab*) into a methodology (*manhaj*) for present-day Muslims. This resonates with another proposition by Dabashi: to regard tradition as '*a genealogy of here and now* rather than an *archaeology of then and there*'.[22] Retaining an appreciation for localised religious practices that are characteristic of the traditional Muslim cultures in maritime South East Asia, Islamic post-traditionalism stands in marked contrast to (neo-)modernist and revivalist tendencies that reduce Islam to an abstraction, empty of any cultural particularities.[23] This betrays not only a further affinity with Dabashi's depiction of peripheral, vernacular—that is, non-Arabic—Muslim literary humanisms as by definition 'multi-cultural and polyvocal'; Islamic post-traditionalism can also be read as an attempt to build an alternative moral community along the lines suggested by historian of Islamic law Wael Hallaq.[24] In many respects, then, the resulting alternative discourse of Islamic post-traditionalism presents a more radical rethinking of the role of Islam in contemporary Indonesian society than has emerged in modernist Islamic circles.

Islamic post-traditionalism as liberal Islam 'plus'

After Wahid's impeachment in 2001, the postra community took over as the torchbearers for this alternative discourse, which is in clear defiance of the kind of liberal Islam that unabashedly champions capitalist neoliberalism.[25] Ahmad Rumadi, research director of the Jakarta-based Wahid Institute, highlights the difference between such an understanding of liberal Islam and Islamic post-traditionalism: presenting the latter as a more progressive and sophisticated strand of contemporary Muslim thinking in Indonesia. He challenges its cynical rejection as just a form of mimicry employed to reaffirm a group identity grounded in cultural affiliations with the NU, insisting that Islamic post-traditionalism has more serious epistemological ambitions than can be delivered by the proponents of the type of liberal Islam it seeks to criticise:

> Even if the paradigm of liberal Islam stresses the 'authenticity', 'originality' and the 'purity' of Islam, postra is doing better in all these respects because of its familiarity with modern Arab thinkers like Abu Zayd, Shahrur, al-Jabiri, and others whose ideas often function as epistemological references. It is therefore no exaggeration to state that postra is 'liberal Islam plus' since it places more value on the local and the marginal. Personally, I hope liberal Islam will accept [the relevance of] locality and situations of marginality as part of their agenda, so that the liberal and postra agendas can come together.[26]

The underlying argument is that by accounting for the local and marginal, Islamic post-traditionalism brings religion closer to human sensibilities. It opens up the possibilities for historicised interpretations of Islam as a living tradition practised in a specific society, at a particular time, and within concrete cultural settings.

The earliest critiques of the twin-concepts of liberal Islam/Islamic liberalism were published in 2000, in a theme issue of what would become the flagship periodical for Islamic post-traditionalism: *Tashwirul Afkar*, a 'journal for reflective thinking about religion and culture'. As one of its editors, Rumadi problematised this association between Islam and liberalism: presenting the combination as a contradiction in terms, because it seeks to bring together a religion based on revelation—which is axiomatic and transcendental, demanding absolute surrender and obedience—with a secular and anti-axiomatic philosophy based on deconstruction, the rejection of absolute truths and certainties, and a demand for absolute freedom of thought. Aside from being a revealed religion, Islam is also a historical religion, conceived and practised by a community in a particular historical setting. All considered, the question remains whether, as a historical religion, Islam can accommodate any other predicate such as liberal.

Referring to the earlier mentioned books of Kurzman and Binder, Rumadi insists on making a clear distinction between *Islamic liberalism* and *liberal Islam*, explaining that in the latter case liberal is a subset of Islam, while in the former it is the other way around. More important to Rumadi is that in liberal Islam the historical dimension prevails, whereas Islamic liberalism is overlaid with a stronger normative aspect.[27] Rumadi is especially critical of Kurzman's understanding of liberal Islam. The latter's definition of this category as covering the whole domain that does not deal with the explicitly personal dimensions of religiosity introduces a very minimalist standard. Moreover, in choosing texts for his anthology, Kurzman's selection was entirely content-driven—an ahistorical approach at odds with Rumadi's historicised interpretation of liberal Islam. While it may be so that, when Islam appeared on the stage of history, it was suffused with the spirit of freedom, with the establishment of orthodoxy that free-spirited élan was lost. Replacing freedom with a restrained and discriminatory sense of justice, Islam went from a dynamic to a static religion, from pro-change to pro-status quo. Therefore, Rumadi suggests that modern liberal Islam must again become a counter-discourse, opposing orthodox hegemonic religious thinking that sides with those in power at the expense of the oppressed and minority groups: 'In its essence, Liberal Islam wants to bring back that revolutionary religious spirit, a religious spirit that is rational and free. Moreover, Liberal Islam—according to the writer—forms [at one and the same time] an extension (continuity) and a modification (change) of traditional Islam or Islamic traditionalism.'[28]

It is this appreciation for continuity in Islamic religious thought that makes terms like liberal and liberalism inappropriate, and it is for that reason that the group of intellectuals to which Rumadi also belongs prefers the designation Islamic post-traditionalism. Even if its epistemological foundations may not yet be entirely clear, it is regarded as more neutral and less ideology-laden. Rumadi underscores how Islamic post-traditionalism 'bolts' and 'leaps forward from a tradition' (*lompat tradisi*; *loncatan tradisi*) that provides continuity, while articulating a new, liberating way of thinking that is distinct from traditionalism, modernism or neo-modernism.[29]

This is why Rumadi also believes that Australian political scientist Greg Barton is mistaken in seeing NU figures such as Wahid and Masdar F. Mas'udi as neo-modernists of a similar signature as Madjid. For the latter, the point of departure is modernity, whereas the other two—although not opposed to modernisation—remain sceptical of the modernist trajectory. This shapes the thinking of the young NU cadres, in the sense that they are very much aware that Islamic liberalism did not appear all of a sudden, 'nor is it—to borrow from Hegelian logic—the antithesis of traditionalism'.[30] This last point is very important to Rumadi because all too often traditional and modern Islam are seen as standing in a dialectical or binary relation to each other, the assumption being that one is better than the other. The problem with such interpretations is not just that they lead to the repression of opposing viewpoints; they also cloud a proper understanding of the relation between tradition and modernity in the context of Indonesian Islam. Too often, these two are seen as diametrically opposed to one another: the first being rejected as conservative and irrational, the other embraced as dynamic and reasonable. The danger of such dichotomies is the loss of valuable aspects of Islam's heritage, which can be avoided by adopting American scholar of Islam John Voll's interpretation of Islamic reform as a process of 'continuity and change', in which he criticises the idea of complete ruptures between one historical period and another, or—for that matter—between one discourse and another. No movement of thought emerges out of nothing. Some earlier elements continue to exercise influence, while others are indeed transformed or abandoned. For Rumadi, that is reason to see tradition—in the sense of an enlightened tradition—as the right starting point for an alternative formulation of liberal Islam. The core question is how to read this expression, liberal Islam, and 'what parameter is to be used to measure liberal thinking within an Islamic "framework"'.[31]

Within the discourse of Islamic post-traditionalism, tradition is understood as both a way of experiencing religiosity and an epistemological method for creative engagement and measured appreciation of the Islamic heritage. The burden of history must be thrown off to the extent that it prevents Muslims from realising they are a part of universal humankind, while retaining the awareness that Indonesian Muslims are embedded in a specific tradition and localised culture, alongside their participation, *qua* Muslims, in a generic pluralist and egalitarian Islamic culture free from hegemonic tendencies.

Battling Islamic and liberal fundamentalism

Another prominent member of the postra community, Ahmad Baso, underscores the role Islamic post-traditionalism plays as a contrapuntal discourse to the multiple ways in which the term liberal Islam is used. Like Rumadi, he characterises it as an alternative discourse that 'moves beyond' (*melampaui*) not just liberal Islam but also neo-modernism and Wahhabism.[32] He too challenges the way in which liberal Islam is interpreted in Kurzman's *Liberal Islam* and Barton's *The Idea of Liberal Islam in Indonesia*, criticising both not only for their failure to substantially engage with Wahid's thinking about secularism, the 'cultural localisation of Islam' (*pribumisasi Islam*) and social ethics. Whereas Kurzman does not even mention Wahid, Barton is taken to task for lumping him together with Madjid and for implying that the labels liberal and neo-modernist are identical. According to Baso, Barton's inability to see that the thought of these two intellectuals developed each in their own specific setting and epistemological framework reflects a theoretical and methodological shortcoming. In comparison with Kurzman and Barton, Binder's *Islamic Liberalism* is rated higher, because it is conceived as an open dialogue between Western and Arab-Islamic thinking. This way, liberalism is not just traced back to its Western roots, but conceived as 'a process of give and take', in which both Islam and the West give substance to the idea of liberalism by engaging dialectically with questions of modernity, social transformation and local tradition. In his search for the roots of liberal Islam, Kurzman, on the contrary, only looks within Islam itself, ignoring the West as an influential factor in the way liberalism and freethinking in general manifest themselves in the Muslim world and disregarding it as a *mitra dialog*, or 'partner in dialogue', for the emergence of liberal Islamic tendencies.[33] Another problem with using only an endogenous Islamic categorisation of liberal is Kurzman's clustering of very different thinkers, which stand in sharp contrast to the individuals featured in Binder's *Islamic Liberalism*, and their critical and dialectical engagement with Western liberal thought, socialism, Marxism and postmodernism.

Baso's criticism zeroes in on Madjid's mentor and supervisor during his postgraduate studies in Chicago, Fazlur Rahman, alleging that the two regarded the likes of Ibn Taymiyya and Muhammad ibn Abd al-Wahhab as reformists whose ideas can be interpreted as an indigenous Islamic discourse of liberation—rather than liberalism. Notwithstanding Rahman's awareness of the shortcomings of Salafi thinking and despite the fact that he also does not go along with their reactionary anti-Western attitudes and fundamentalist tendencies, Baso maintains that the neo-modernism advocated by Rahman is a closed way of thinking not far removed from literalist understandings of the Qur'an and exhibiting a degree of anti-rationalism, while being supportive of reasoning by analogy and partial to orthodox theology. In the political domain, he accuses neo-modernist Muslims of having 'inherited a mentality that "conflates religion and state" and not foreclosing the possibility of collusion with the military for the sake of obtaining recognition for their reform movement'.[34] This leads Baso to the allegation that, in terms of politics, Madjid's neo-modernism is not all that different from the Wahhabi movement, and also to the conclusion that Islamic neo-modernism is very different from the ideas developed by Wahid, which prefigure those of Islamic post-traditionalism.[35]

To further tease out these contrasts and differences, Baso takes up al-Jabri's 'Critique of Arab Reason', presenting it as an exercise in deconstructing the Arab-Islamic legacy both in terms of its epistemology and politics.[36] Subscribing to interpretations of tradition as something that is invented and constructed, Islamic post-traditionalism operates as a 'hermeneutics of suspicion'—sceptical of the assumption that knowledge production can be neutral, and an integral and substantialist whole. In the case of the Muslim world, the foundations for such projections were laid in what al-Jabri calls the *'Aṣr al-Tadwīn* or 'Age of Recording'—that is to say, the supposedly 'true' or 'pure Islam' defined as early as the second century of the Islamic calendar.[37] However, for Baso, deconstructing a tradition is futile if it is not combined with an effort towards reconstruction. He stresses that, in this respect, Islamic post-traditionalism contrasts most emphatically with Islamic neo-modernism, because the envisaged intellectual and social transformation is grounded in tradition and suffused with what al-Jabri calls the 'spirit of Averroism': offering the germinations of secularisation, democracy and the protection of basic human rights.[38] In the field of Islamic legal thinking, the same ethos animated the criticism of Imam al-Shāfiʿī's text-based paradigm of analogic reasoning by Ibn Hazm and al-Shāṭibī, leading them to adopt alternative approaches using the notion of the 'public good' (*maṣlaḥa*), and the integration of the 'higher objectives of law' (*maqāṣid al-sharīʿa*) into the domain of the 'foundations of faith' (*uṣūl al-dīn*).[39] In Baso's view, Wahid's thinking reflects a similar attitude in present-day Indonesia. In contrast to the religious symbolism that characterises Islamic neo-modernism and literalist-reformist Islam, Gus Dur was of the opinion that—in the case of Islam—upholding the formal aspects of a religion is not enough: it must be an effort of mankind as a whole to liberate the oppressed.[40] With this, Baso makes the liberating function of Islamic post-traditionalism more articulate and explicit than Rumadi, offering a clear contradistinction with the liberalisation politics of the Liberal Islam Network and the Freedom Institute.

Bourgeois versus proletarian Islam

A different way of interrogating liberal Muslim modernity is found in Nur Khalid Ridwan's *Bourgeois Pluralism: A Critique of Cak Nur's Pluralist Reason* (2002) and in his *Bourgeois Religion: A Critique of Puritan Islamic Reason* (2004).[41] Reading these two books together offers not only a dual *Kritik der Vernunft* (Critique of Reason), along the lines of Kant, but also a double Marxian *Ideologiekritik* of liberal and literalist-reformist Islam as two sides of the same coin, pointing up the intellectual closure and institutional constraints that form the limits imposed by liberal modernity.[42] In comparison with other members of the postra community, who work by way of a detour via Arab heritage thinkers, Ridwan also draws directly on the arsenal of postmodern French discourse analysis. Both books are informed by Roland Barthes's 'death of the author' and Foucauldian archaeologies of the nexus between knowledge and power.[43] Ridwan's Marxian orientation shines through in his observation that *epistemes* are not sterile or autonomous, but reflect the social interests of those articulating the discursive formations in question. Consequently, his writings also chime with other forms of poststructuralism, in particular Louis Althusser's theory of ideology and Michel Pêcheux's engagement with the role of class struggle.[44] Ridwan's critiques are comprised by a semiotic analysis of the 'surface narrations' and an investigation into the class interests hidden behind the texts.[45] From these analyses, he derives a binary typology of what he calls bourgeois and liberation religiosity respectively that can be applied to both liberal and puritan Islam on the levels of mind set, conceptualisation, and how the resulting sets of ideas are translated into social practice.[46]

In *Bourgeois Pluralism*, Ridwan argues that Madjid's understanding of the modernisation and liberation of Islamic thinking is shaped by his belonging to a rural but well-educated pious Muslim family from East Java, as well as by his subsequent interaction with the Masyumi establishment and his continued association with the Muslim upper middle class in Jakarta where his ideas came to fruition and gained the greatest acceptance. This prominence translated into a high public profile, which eventually gave him access to New Order's political and economic elite. In contrast to the young firebrand student leader of the sixties and seventies, the appreciation for the Islamic tradition that the mature Madjid gained while studying in Chicago with Rahman resulted in a transformation of his thinking about religious diversity from true religious pluralism along the lines of theorists such as John Hicks and Paul Knitter towards an understanding that privileges not just Islam but also particular dominant discourses within Islamic thinking that have exercised a hegemonic exclusivity by suppressing alternative readings.

In order to establish the bourgeois roots of puritan Islam, Ridwan also draws on W.F. Wertheim, a Dutch sociologist who did extensive research on Indonesia, and the French *Annales* school historian and South East Asianist Denys Lombard. Tracing its origins not only to the Dutch *Ethische Politiek*, Ridwan also maps the connections between individual puritan Muslims and representative bodies and other segments of Indonesian society, including remnants of the once-powerful *priyayi* or indigenous court circles; emancipated members of the nominally Muslim peasantry, referred to as *abangan*; and migrant Chinese, all of whom benefited from the educational and economic opportunities offered in the late colonial era.[47] According to Ridwan, the links that were forged at the time continue to influence the relations between the upper middle classes even when they subscribe to different ideological currents. These also include Islamist dealings with political parties such as the Nationalist PDI-P, and the PPP as the only tolerated Islamic party during the New Order years, as well as non-partisan heirs of the Masyumi legacy, such as the DDII and various vigilante organisations.[48]

Ridwan concludes that the mind set of both the kind of liberal Islam represented by Madjid and puritan Islam are geared towards defending the interests of the establishment. Whereas puritans rely on the authority of texts grounded in a literal interpretation of scripture, liberal Muslims do this by social-theoretic theorising based on the dominant historiographies, as if these constitute the sole narrations of the Islamic past.[49] Although Madjid stresses the importance of intellectual creativity and the dialogical relationship between religion and history, he tends to rely on iconic figures such as al-Shāfiʿī, al-Ghazālī, Ibn Rushd, Ibn Taymiyya and Ibn Khaldūn.[50] The prominence of Madjid's public persona and his idolisation by younger generations of Muslim intellectuals exacerbate the effects of his bourgeois interpretations of Islamic history and religious pluralism. Ridwan points to the irony of the way in which Madjid's initially subversive way of thinking has itself become the dominant discourse, narrowing his brand of Islamic neo-modernism to a single point of reference.

On the conceptual level, bourgeois thinking is elitist and not involved in any drastic or structural activity towards emancipating the powerless, with both puritan and liberal Islamic trajectories being geared towards establishment ideas. While the literalist puritans are preoccupied with religious symbolism, supposedly liberal Muslims focus on a strand of liberalism that has nothing to do with the liberation of the disenfranchised. By contrast, the function of the ideas underlying liberation thinking is to strengthen these notions that contribute to the liberation of the oppressed and powerless or what in Javanese are called the *wong cilik*.[51] While noting that Madjid follows a 'intertextual–semantic–syntagmatic' mode of semiotics coloured by a humanist and socio-historical orientation and vertical, sequential and linear interpretations of religious symbolism, Ridwan understands language on a horizontal level—accounting for a 'zigzag line' of associative relations that produce a plurality of meanings.[52]

In terms of praxis, Madjid's mode of thinking dovetailed nicely with that of the New Order regime, and Ridwan alleges that Madjid's earliest ideas on modernisation and secularisation were therefore received with sympathy, and that his subsequent rejection of Islamic party politics even led to a further 'symbiosis' with the regime.[53] Thus, as he became part of the establishment, liberation and freethinking were side-lined. In relation to religious pluralism, Ridwan argues that Madjid's notion of *Ahl al-Kitab* only applies to religions that are formally recognised under Indonesia's national 'Doctrine of Five Principles' or Pancasila and that he never mentioned indigenous religious traditions or practices.[54] Moreover, he only talks about *Ahl al-Kitab* in general terms without addressing the legal consequences of extending the concept beyond Jews and Christians, nor does he recognise a need to distinguish between oppressed religious groups and religious oppressors.[55] Equating Pancasila as Indonesia's definitive national ideology in both a legal and consti-tutional sense with the Qur'anic notion of the 'common word' (*kalimatun sawa'*) creates a problem for those groups that are not formally recognised.[56] These include the communists and Baha'is, and—after the 2005 fatwas against religious pluralism issued by the Indonesian Council of Religious Scholars (MUI)—also Ahmadis and Shi'is. This precarious situation is further aggra-vated by Madjid's understanding of communists as immoral people who do not believe. Ridwan counters that Indonesian reality shows there are Muslim communists, but that Madjid fails to see this because his use of the notion of pluralism does not explicitly account for oppressed segments of the popula-tion. Moreover, since it applies only to those leading what are in his view 'respectable lives', Madjid's understanding of plurality is subjective, and at best a form of qualified inclusivism rather than truly pluralist.[57]

Thus, when it comes to translating thinking into action, in both its literalist and liberal manifestations bourgeois thinking works towards protecting the position of the establishment.

Inversely, the interconnections between mind set, ideas and interests in liberation thinking is such that those from oppressed backgrounds cannot produce concepts that maintain the status quo, but only notions that help the weak, while its social practices are 'non-elitist and down-to-earth' for the sake of improving the fate of the *wong cilik*.[58] With this contextual reading, Ridwan wants to show that concepts and modes of thinking are not self-sustaining. In order to defend the poor and oppressed, liberation thinking defies any single literal truth claim of religious texts, which must clearly be deconstructed as pointing towards a plurality, whereas its social-theoretical framing differs from bourgeois thinking in terms of defining interests, social status and class struggle.[59]

Although in *Bourgeois Pluralism* Ridwan still entertains a simplified and rather reductionist understanding of class, *Bourgeois Religion* evinces a more sophisticated understanding. Initially, he generalised that—historically—modernist and reformist Muslim organisations such as the Muhammadiyah and Persis are rooted in the Muslim upper middle class, whereas the NU—after its secession from the Masyumi party in 1952—continues as the sole representative of the Muslim proletariat.[60] However, the exalted status of 'ulamā' among the Javanese peasantry milieu evinces the existence of an Islamic aristocracy, which also tends to monopolise the core positions in the traditionalist NU, and thus a direct contravention to this self-proclaimed proletarian representation. At the same time, a strand of proletarian thinking can also be discerned within the Muhammadiyah. Ridwan also includes the caveat that on the level of individual awareness or consciousness it is possible to take a standpoint that is different from one's social background: someone from a bourgeois background can adopt a consciousness geared towards liberation, just as someone from a proletarian background can develop a bourgeois attitude.[61]

Muslims without mosques: between prophetic social science and transformative Islam

The closest counterpart to the Anak Muda NU on the modernist side of Indonesia's Muslim spectrum is a group of activists and academics who call themselves the 'Network of Young Muhammadiyah Intellectuals' (Jaringan Intelektual Muhammadiyah Muda, JIMM). Their inspiration comes primarily from two intellectuals loosely associated with both the traditionalist and modernist Islamic milieus Kuntowijoyo and Moeslim Abdurrahman.

The scholar and man of letters Kuntowijoyo was born into a traditional Javanese family of shadow puppeteers and copyists of Qur'an manuscripts. During his student years in Yogyakarta and postgraduate studies at Columbia University, he dabbled in a variety of cultural activities, publishing a number of novels and collections of poetry. These creative proclivities also carried over into his academic work as a social historian who combined social scientific approaches and an understanding of Islam as a civilisation by developing concepts such as 'prophetic social science' and 'cultural Islam'. These ideas were elaborated in essay collections with titles such as *The Paradigm of Islam* (1991) and *Muslims without Mosques* (2001).[62] In these writings, Kuntowijoyo attempted to bridge the gap between Islam as an ideal type and the social reality of Muslim communities by using social theory. Inspired by Thomas Kuhn's notion of the paradigm shift, and with further bows to Marx and Wittgenstein, he asserted that the potential of religion as a transformative force is socially, ideologically and linguistically determined.[63] Because the development of an endogenous Islamic social theory is still in its infancy, Kuntowijoyo felt vindicated to quarry Western social theories, 'pedagogies of the oppressed', and theologies developed by Marx, Max Weber, Émile Durkheim, Paulo Freire and Latin American liberation theologians in order to use them as building blocks for transforming Islamic normativity into a method of social enquiry combined with an engaged concern for what the Qur'an calls the *dhu'afa* and *mustadha'ifin*—the 'weak and downtrodden'.[64] This is not the only resonance with Ridwan's typology of the liberation approach to religiosity; he actually explicitly mentions Kuntowijoyo's observation that it is entirely appropriate to use the notion of bourgeoisie in Muslim contexts.[65]

Unlike many of his peers in the Muhammadiyah, anthropologist Moeslim Abdurrahman (1948–2012) spent time in traditional Islamic *pesantrens* before attending universities in Indonesia and the United States. This enabled him to establish a rapport with NU leader Abdurrahman Wahid; a relationship that was also based on their joint appreciation of Hanafi's manifesto for an Islamic Left. Working as a university lecturer and NGO activist, Abdurrahman wrote a book called *Transformative Islam* (1995), in which he too argued for a 'transformative social science' and a cultural role for religion.[66] After Muhammadiyah Chairman Ahmad Syafii Maarif recruited him in 2003 to help develop a cultural Islam by putting him in charge of the Maarif Institute for Culture and Humanity, Abdurrahman's book *Transformative Islam* became a foundational text for JIMM. While his ideas about the cultural role of religion are closely linked to those of Kuntowijoyo, they have a firmer social-scientific underpinning.[67]

Meanwhile, proponents of transformative Islam, such as economists Dawam Rahardjo and Adi Sasono, accuse Kuntowijoyo and Abdurrahman of intellectual elitism, claiming their theories are still too acclimatised to hegemonic discourses of Sunni orthodoxy and Islamic rationality, which historically sided with those holding political power. While Sasono is unapologetic about his Marxist leanings, Rahardjo refused to become a 'vulgar follower' of either Marxism of Weberian dependency theory.[68]

These different strands of modernist Islamic thinking come together in JIMM, combining segments of the Muhammadiyah from traditionalist NU backgrounds and representatives of a 'proletarian Muhammadiyah', which historian Munir Mulkhan refers to as *Munu* and *Marhaenis Muhammadiyah* (*Marmuh*) respectively.[69] JIMM was established in 2004 with institutional support from Muhammadiyah's central board, including Chairman Syafii Maarif, Munir Mulkhan, and the rector of the State Islamic University in Yogyakarta, Amin Abdullah. This political backing was short-lived because the trio—disparagingly referred to by its puritan adversaries as *Paman Sam* or 'Uncle Sam' (in reference to their first names)—were ousted in a conservative take-over of the organisation's central board in 2005. Despite losing this top-level support, the network continues to present itself as the 'Second Muhammadiyah', in the sense that it wants to 're-intellectualise' the Muhammadiyah through an agenda founded on 'three pillars'.[70] First of all, the Muhammadiyah should explicitly self-identify as a social movement; secondly, using structural hermeneutics and social theorising, they envisage a more multi-vocal organisation; and finally, intellectuals must become actual agents of social change.[71] For this transformation of intellectuals as mediators of ideas into activists on the basis of their knowledge and personal conduct, JIMM members evoke the Qur'anic notion of the *ulū'l-bāb*, or 'wise ones'.[72]

Unlike the postra community, JIMM co-founder Zuly Qodir subscribes to the view presented by Greg Barton that Madjid and Wahid can both be considered Islamic neo-modernists. At the same time, he stresses that JIMM's transformative Islam is not a sub-category of this Islamic neo-modernism of the 1980s and 1990s, but a separate discursive formation branching off from Cak Nur's earlier renewal thinking of the 1970s.[73] In contrast to the 'first Muhammadiyah's' internal debates on the theological aspects of Islamic renewal thinking or its preoccupation with traditionalist 'deviancies' captured in the terms *takhayyul*, *bid'a* and *churafat* (deviancies, unlawful innovations and superstition, or TBC), the new generation is more concerned with political and social praxis, which need to be actualised within a plural society.[74] JIMM also condones the accommodative-conformist disposition of its intellectual and political mentors towards the regime during the New Order years. Seeing no conflict between Pancasila and Islam, and thus no need for an Islamic state, the network also agrees with intellectual benefactors that 'the essence for political parties should be a political ethics', and that the basis for party-political struggles should be value-driven, not whether a party is Islamic or secular-nationalist.[75]

Conclusion

Although they build on the same ideas about the role of religion in Indonesian society as their intellectual predecessors of the 1970s and 1980s, many of the intellectuals who came of age in the 1990s are more focused on applied thinking and the dissemination and interpretation of universal themes such as democracy, justice, community development and battling corruption. The sweeping ideas introduced by the likes of Madjid and Wahid may have caused Indonesian Muslim intellectualism to run out of steam, but their successors are aware that these grand narratives need to be transformed into concrete intellectual projects, translating ideas into plans of action for the betterment of Indonesian society.

Observed from the perspective of the sociology of knowledge, the political regime changes that affected Indonesia in 1998 and the Arab world in 2011 also represent significant epistemic shifts. However, whether the discourse critiques produced in the early 2000s by Indonesia's new Muslim intelligentsia reflect Mohammed Bamyeh's suggestion that there is something called an 'anarchist gnosis' remains a question.[76] In the end—like their predecessors—neither the Anak Muda NU nor JIMM appear to dispute the value of the Pancasila doctrine for Indonesia as a multi-ethnic and religiously plural country. They have not fundamentally questioned functionalist and rationalised understandings of religion, or—for that matter—the existence of the nation-state. Despite their incisive critiques of Islamism and Muslim liberalism, the Anak Muda NU and JIMM also find it difficult to escape from Weber's 'iron cage'.

9

ISLAMIC SECULARISM AND THE QUESTION OF FREEDOM

Arshin Adib-Moghaddam

It is impossible to unravel the meaning of 'freedom' in Iran from an 'Islamic' perspective. At the same time, liberal concepts and the idea of freedom itself have repeatedly figured prominently in the writings of leading Islamic theoreticians and philosophers in the country. In order to give a brief overview of these ideas and the debates they have provoked, this chapter is divided into three parts. It begins by demonstrating that the idea of freedom has been at the heart of politics in modern Iran via a discussion of some of the major political upheavals in the country, with a particular emphasis on the events surrounding the revolution of 1979. The chapter then examines the relationship between Islam and liberal ideas in the political philosophy of major contemporary Iranian thinkers, before outlining some of their flaws. The chapter does not adopt a strict definitional yardstick to measure complex concepts such as liberalism, democracy or freedom. Instead, it aims to show how these concepts are handled within an Iranian and Islamic framework, while acknowledging that they are defined by context and historical circumstances. To that end, I am refraining from starting with an *a priori* definition of freedom, democracy or liberalism, so that the sites of the chapter's analysis can speak for themselves.

Of imperialism and resistance

What makes the Iranian case so pertinent is that the Islamic revolution of 1979 is an ongoing process. Beyond the pragmatism that the humdrum affairs of governance demand, there is no consensus in Iran about the core tenets of the revolution, neither within the state nor society.[1] The issue of freedom is particularly contested. Consequently, what has happened since the establishment of the Iranian Islamic Republic in 1979 is a struggle to define the revolution and its place within Iranian history. The polity that emerged has been contested by a wide range of intellectuals, students, workers, women's rights activists and members of the Iranian state itself. Hence the recurrent spells of upheaval, the discourse of reform, and recurrent mass demonstrations in favour of change.[2] What we have witnessed, in short, is a struggle for the meaning of the Islamic revolution, which is framed in terms of a struggle for freedom from the authority of the state on the one side, and from foreign dictates on the other. As such, the revolution is a continuation of Iran's historical quest for representative government and independence.[3]

Islamic symbols, imagery and norms, moulded and reconstructed in accordance with historical necessity and Iran's political culture, were repeatedly employed in order to articulate this quest for freedom. There was certainly no exclusively 'Islamic' narrative to establish a freer society. Islam in Iran (as anywhere else) has been invented and reconstructed in close dialogue with the political, economic, cultural and sociological realities on the ground. True, in the popular imagination in the West, Islam continues to be the antithesis to liberal ideas: if the 'West' represents feminism, democracy, freedom of speech and religious tolerance, the Muslim world is regularly represented as inherently misogynistic, homophobic, authoritarian and antagonistic. But the political thought of the figures I will discuss seems to indicate that Islam could be a blueprint for liberalism, pluralism and democracy as much as a recipe for dictatorship—depending on how the canon is interpreted, Islam can be revolutionary, as in the political thought of Ayatollah Khomeini, or it can be liberal and democratic as in the writings of Abdolkarim Soroush, Mohsen Kadivar, Hasan Eshkevari and others. The truth is that Islam can be turned into a recipe for dictatorship or a philosophy accentuating freedom. Modern

Iranian history is emblematic of this interpretive elasticity that discourses of Islam afford their followers.

A few historical examples will illustrate what I mean by such elasticity. It is generally agreed that the first modern mass upheaval in Iranian history occurred in 1891, when Ayatollah Mirza Hossein Shirazi issued a fatwa (or religious opinion) forbidding his followers to use any tobacco-based products. He did this in response to the concession of exclusive tobacco rights in favour of Major G. Talbot, a British citizen who established the Imperial Tobacco Company in Persia, seen as a Trojan horse for further imperial control of the country.

The role of Ayatollah Shirazi was certainly important, and his activism is analytically pertinent given that it galvanised the clerical strata into a politically active role. But the opposition to the Qajar monarchy at the end of the nineteenth century was expressed by several strata of Iranian society.[4] The revolt was aided and abetted by a range of individuals and movements. The role of Jamaladin al-Afghani (also known as Asadabadi), one of the most prolific and prominent non-clerical pan-Islamists, for instance, has not been explored in the scholarly literature.[5] Yet it was al-Afghani who colluded with leading clerics in the seminaries of Qom and Najaf to galvanise protests against the tobacco concession. This explains the ability of the movement to move beyond and motivate several strata of society.[6] As a result of this resistance to the Qajar monarchy, al-Afghani was exiled to Iraq, from where he continued to agitate against the concession and Iran's dependence on foreign powers. The ensuing revolts that started in Shiraz and moved to Tabriz and from there to Isfahan and elsewhere forced King Nasseredin Shah to revoke the concession.

With the tobacco revolts, we find, for the first time in modern Iranian history, a mass upheaval against the monarchy and in opposition to outside interference in Iranian affairs. With al-Afghani, and later with his Egyptian disciple Muhammad Abduh, an Islam emerged that was geared to themes such as progress and independence. Freedom was not merely sought from oppressive governments but also from imperialism, in this case in its British variant.

Al-Afghani was also a proponent of the constitutional revolution in Iran, which occurred primarily between 1906 and 1907. This upheaval led to the establishment of a constitutional monarchy in Iran and entrenched the vocabulary of liberalism and republicanism in the country. As with the tobacco revolt, freedom was not associated merely with opposition to the Qajar monarchs but also to imperialism. After all, during this period, Iran was divided into so-called spheres of influence, with the north being under Russian supervision and the oil-rich south of the country under British control. In 1906, Iran established a parliament and adopted the country's first modern constitution. But in 1921, Reza Khan took over the state in a coup d'état and established an authoritarian monarchy that lasted until 1941, when he was ousted by the British, who remained the dominant external force in Iranian affairs until 1971, when British forces retreated from the Persian Gulf.

The third example, and perhaps the most consequential for the Islamic revolution in 1979, was the nationalisation of Iran's oil company under the premiership of Dr Mohammad Mossadegh between 1951 and 1953. Mossadegh was Iran's first democratically elected prime minister. When he came to power in 1951, he nationalised the Anglo-Iranian Oil Company (out of which British Petroleum emerged) and endeavoured to establish a viable democratic order in Iran. In 1953, he was ousted by a CIA/MI6 engineered coup d'état, which re-established the dictatorship of Mohammad Reza Pahlavi, who ruled the country as a key Western ally until the Islamic revolution of 1979. In all the examples of modern mass movements in Iran, we find a recurring dialectic: opposition to state authoritarianism on the one hand and opposition to external interference in Iranian affairs on the other. Ultimately, the aim was a freer society, a pluralistic order in terms of governance and independence from external powers. Narratives employing Islamic imagery, symbols and norms were repeatedly used in order to accentuate this quest for a freer polity in Iran. Even nationalists such as Mossadegh had a progressive vision of the role of Islam in Iranian politics. He would have agreed that Islam is not inherently anti-democratic and illiberal, which may explain why figureheads of his party (the National Front) such as Mehdi Bazargan had supported the Islamic revolution in the first place. I will discuss their vision of an Islamic-democratic republic in Iran in the following section.

Of governance and liberty

The two grand ambitions of Iran's modern history, democracy and independence, were also central to the Islamic revolution. The mainstream Iranian revolutionaries imagined an authentic Iranian-Islamic order that would be accountable to the people and independent of the dictates of external powers. Hence the revolutionary slogans *na sharghi na gharbi jomhurye eslami* (neither eastern nor western, only the Islamic republic) or *esteghlal, azadi jomhurye eslami* (independence, freedom, Islamic republic). Iran, even today, is in many ways trying to bridge the tensions between these slogans. Even Ayatollah Khomeini had to engage with these narratives in order to boost his position within the revolutionary struggle. If freedom and democracy were not at the heart of the revolutionaries' demands, Khomeini would not have been forced to refer to the 'God-given right of freedom and liberty' that Islam guarantees, nor to emphasise that 'freedom is the primary right of humans' at the beginning of the revolution, promises he breached rather blatantly once his vision for the Iranian state was institutionalised.[7] Khomeini spoke liberal and acted authoritarian, not least because he was more concerned with solidifying the state's power than the sovereignty of the people. In this sense, Khomeini was a typical modernist—a state-builder par excellence.[8]

Mehdi Bazargan provides an interesting example of how the Islam that was invented in the build up to the Iranian revolution (especially in the 1970s) was amenable to democracy and a liberal order within society, and stood in opposition to a totalitarian interpretation of the state. Bazargan was the first director of the National Iranian Oil Company (NIOC) after its nationalisation during the Mossadegh premiership. In 1961, he founded the Freedom Movement of Iran, which comprised such iconoclastic figures of Iran's intellectual and political scene as Ayatollah Mahmoud Taleghani, Ali Shariati and Yadollah Sahabi, and in 1977 he established Iran's Human Rights Association. For this generation of Iran's political class, Islam was a conduit for instituting pluralism, human rights and democracy. In this vein, the Freedom Movement of Iran's charter declares that the 'servitude of God requires refusal of servitude to any other master. Gratefulness to God is contingent upon gaining freedom and utilising it to attain rights, justice, and service.'[9] For Bazargan himself, 'freedom is God's gift to His steward on earth, humankind. Whoever takes away this freedom is guilty of the greatest treason against humankind.'[10] As such, Bazargan was strongly opposed to the absolutist interpretation of Islam that the Khomeinist forces espoused in their emphasis on the total sovereignty of the Supreme Jurisprudent (*velayat-e faqiye motlaq*) who would be positioned at the helm of the state. 'Islamic government', Bazargan argues 'cannot help but be at once consultative, democratic, and divinely inspired.'[11] It must follow from this that 'in Islamic government the relations among individuals and the administration of society are predicated upon relative shared freedom and mutual responsibility'. In more concrete terms, this means that 'Islam permits difference of opinions even within the realm of the tenets of religion, let alone in administrative and governmental issues. Shi'i theology under the rubric ijtihad [independent reasoning]', Bazargan pointed out, 'has left the gate of such debates open until the end of the time and the coming of the messiah.'[12]

Consequently, the Supreme Jurisprudent or any 'source of imitation' (the highest Shi'i authority) cannot claim to be infallible. Citizens should be free to express their grievances because 'freedom means the freedom to oppose, criticize, and object—even if the criticism is untrue and unjust. Where there is freedom there are opponents and currents that disturb routine stability and normalcy.'[13] In terms of governance, all of this translates into the 'principle of division of powers and their mutual non-interference and orderly checks and balances'. The Islamic corpus, the Qur'an and the Sunnah, according to Bazargan's interpretation, is intrinsically just and partial to freedom of choice: 'God bestows both freedom and guidance concerning the consequences of actions. His mercy is infinite and His vengeance great.' In the end, individuals must choose for themselves: 'Freedom exists, so do responsibility and restraint. The choice is ours.'[14]

This emphasis on freedom and individual choice is shared by Ayatollah Taleghani, perhaps the most prominent clerical ally of Bazargan. Taleghani was one of the co-founders of the Freedom Movement of Iran. His discourse typically blended leftist ideas into his vision of Islam. Prominent among the Iranian intelligentsia and opposed to Khomeini's doctrine of the *velayat-e faqih* (rule of the Supreme Jurisprudent), Taleghani argues that 'government must be like the representative and deputy of individuals and not the representative of a special class ... Its purpose is nothing but the preservation of individual rights and of the collectivity of individuals.'[15] It follows that 'government does not have the right to deprive or limit the freedom and independence of individuals or the rights of some classes for the profit of another class in the name of the higher good of the government'.[16] In the last sermon Taleghani delivered before his death in September 1979, in a period when his opposition to Khomeini had become more explicit, he emphasised that the goal of the Prophet Muhammad himself was to 'free the people, to free them from class oppression, to free them from pagan thoughts which had been imposed upon them, to free them from the ordinances and laws which [were] imposed for the benefit of one group, one class, over others'.[17] According to Taleghani, the 'call of Islam is the call to mercy and freedom'. With reference to the Qur'an, he argues that

> even the sinner who is condemned to death—under Islamic law there is mercy for him too. ... His [the Prophet's] jihad [religious struggle] was mercy, his hijra [migration from Mecca to Medina] was mercy, his laws were mercy, his guidance over principles was mercy—the Islamic order ought to be based on mercy.[18]

These lofty views, couched in notions of freedom of expression, democratic Islamic governance and human rights, were bitterly contradicted by the revolutionary reality on the ground. Iran's anarchic environment did not lend itself to the calm and collected paradigm put forward by Ayatollah Taleghani, Bazargan and others. The daily battles for power and the frantic, utopian hope for a better future for Iranians after the departure of the shah in January 1979 gave impetus to revolutionary radicalism and the politics of antagonism that Bazargan and his allies tried to minimise.[19] The reality was that Bazargan and his cabinet were increasingly powerless and that the hardliner-dominated Revolutionary Council was calling the shots. In March 1979, Bazargan submitted his resignation, but Khomeini rejected his request, not least in order to stabilise the state. A month later, amid increasing revolutionary chaos in Iran, Bazargan and the members of his cabinet escaped an assassination attempt. Frustrated over the hostage taking at the US embassy, Bazargan and his cabinet finally resigned in November 1979. In November 1982, he expressed his criticism of the situation in Iran to the then speaker of parliament, Ali-Akbar Rafsanjani:

> The government has created an atmosphere of terror, fear, revenge and national disintegration. ... What has the ruling elite done in nearly four years, besides bringing death and destruction, packing the prisons and the cemeteries in every city, creating long queues, shortages, high prices, unemployment, poverty, homeless people, repetitious slogans and a dark future?[20]

Bazargan died in 1995, yet the idea that Islam can foster a liberal order continued to be put forward by a range of intellectuals, politicians and reformist clerics. The dual ambition of Iranian contemporary history—to gain independence from foreign dictates and to democratise governance in the country—continues to be expressed to this day.

Of reformed revolutionaries

The revolutionary momentum of 1979 established a central political dynamic in Iran: intellectuals and leaders who were too 'loudly' pro-reformist and too overtly in favour of democracy in Iran were silenced, incarcerated, purged or exiled. Bazargan and Ayatollah Taleghani were among the lucky ones. They escaped assassination attempts and remained in the country without being incarcerated. The 'second' wave of reformists opposed to the authoritarian, post-revolutionary order in Iran was less fortunate. Liberal Islamic thinkers such as Abdolkarim Soroush, Mohsen Kadivar and Hasan Eshkevari have been forced into exile without recourse to any institutional resources in Iran. The trajectory of Soroush's fate is emblematic of these devoured children of the revolution. Soroush was a member of the Cultural Revolution Council, which was responsible for reforming the universities in accordance with new revolutionary realities. In retrospect, he has tried to downplay the role of the council in the purges of scholars, in particular in the humanities and social sciences, and the closure of the universities to those ends. According to him, the 'purges did not start in universities ... nor were they initiated or continued in universities by the Cultural Revolution Institute'.[21] Yet at the same time, he concedes that 'the first things that happened on the morrow of the victory of the revolution [were] purges'. These were not decreed by the Cultural Revolution Institute of which he was a member, he claims, but were primarily political in nature. 'Most of the political groups supported them', Soroush maintains, and

> it was only the Prime Minister [Bazargan] of the provisional government who objected ... And he managed, within the limits of his powers, to reduce the number of purges, although, of course, this earned him some curses from those clerics and political activists who didn't like him and who called him a colluder. As to the expulsion of academics, if the Revolution Council asked the University of Tehran's chancellor to participate in the purges and to expel professors—and he assented—it never put such a request, even implicitly, to the Cultural Revolution Institute and there was no suggestion of it in Imam Khomeini's letter to the institute either.[22]

Soroush is clearly trying to address the allegations that he was part of the problem and that his calls for reforms today are hypocritical. He was certainly not known for opposing the purges when he was a member of the Cultural Revolution Council. At the same time, he was a small cog in a big revolutionary machine and was simply not in a position to decide the fate of others.

Soroush's writing is laden with complex philosophical concepts that are used to put forward an interpretive, hermeneutical approach to the corpus of Islam (i.e. the Qur'an, the Sunnah and the *hadiths*). From his perspective, knowledge about Islam expands and contracts with reference to historical circumstances: 'The theory of the contraction and expansion of religious interpretation', Soroush claims, 'separates religion and religious knowledge, considers the latter as a branch of human knowledge, and regards our understanding of religion as evolving along with other branches of human knowledge'.[23] This distinction merits and requires constant reform and renewal through *ijtihad*. 'To treat religious knowledge, a branch of human knowledge, as incomplete, impure, insufficient, and culture-bound; to try to mend and darn its wears and tears is, in itself, an admirable and hallowed undertaking.'[24] Given that religious knowledge can never really be complete, it cannot be monopolised by one religious leader. 'The acceptance of the sovereignty of religion is far from putting one's own words in the Prophet's mouth and arrogating his seat to oneself.' Rather the contrary. For Soroush, it 'means a sincere attempt to understand his message through repeated consultation with the sacred text and the tradition. Scholars of religion have no other status or service than this.'[25]

Soroush calls for a pluralistic understanding of Islam and a democratic order based on spiritual values. Within such an 'Islamic-democratic' polity, human rights would have to be cultivated and secured, given that 'a religion that is oblivious to human rights (including the need for humanity for freedom and justice) is not tenable in the modern world. In other words, religion needs to be right not only logically but also ethically.'[26] Soroush does not explicitly address the plight of non-believers within such a religiously inspired system, but in his writings and lectures he repeatedly alludes to the freedom of choice that any Islamic government must ensure:

> To be sure, contemporary advocates of human rights can claim no monopoly on truth and justice; nevertheless, religious societies, precisely because of their religious nature, need to seriously engage in discussion of the issues they pose. Not only did our predecessors passionately debate such extrareligious issues as the question of free choice and the question of the limits of God's rights to overburden the faithful with religious obligations, but Islamic society felt a religious obligation to allow such debates to spread and prosper. By the same token, the extrareligious debates of our day, which happen to concern human rights, must be viewed as worthy and useful exchanges of opinions in Islamic society. The partisans in these debates deserve a blessed respect, and the outcome of such discussions should be heeded and implemented by the governments. ... Observing human rights (such as justice, freedom, and so on) guarantees not only the democratic character of a government, but also its religious character.[27]

As indicated, Soroush is rather abstract, metaphysical, almost gnostic in his writings and lectures. Mohsen Kadivar, who emerged as one of the most influential reformist clerics in Iran until he was harassed into exile in the United States in 2008, addresses the themes of democracy and liberalism, including the rights of non-believers, in rather more explicit terms, quite comparable to the affirmation of freedom and democracy by Bazargan and Ayatollah Taleghani. In this vein, Kadivar suggests that 'freedom of religion and belief means an individual's right to freely choose any and all ideologies and religions he likes'.[28] In addition, this refers to the 'freedom and the right to think to have beliefs and values, to express one's religion and opinions, to partake in religious rites and practices ... and to be able to freely critique one's religion.'[29] According to Kadivar, even non-believers (*kaffir*) should not be punished for their beliefs: 'The persecution of a heathen is unjustified in Islam. Through renewed *ijtihad* (independent reasoning), and based on the correct principles of the Qur'an and the *hadith*, freedom of religion and belief can be achieved through Islam.'[30] Comparable to Bazargan, who refers to God-given parameters framing a free society,[31] Kadivar indicates that Islam represents 'the correct and just religion' and warns of 'divine punishment at the end of time',[32] but he maintains that Islam secures the 'right of choice in beliefs and in actions in all areas so long as these beliefs and actions do not deprive others of their rights or do not disturb public peace and order'. While it is legitimate and salutary to invite others to embrace Islam (*dawa*), Kadivar reiterates that the Qur'an explicitly states that there is no compulsion in religion. It must follow quite rationally that

> non-Muslims living inside or outside Muslim lands have peace and security so long as they do not wage war on Islam. Whether or not they believe in one of the sanctioned religions or in falsehood, no Muslim has the right to disrupt their peace simply because their beliefs are different. This assertion is substantiated by the eternally valid verses of the Quran ... To sum up, even though most of the interpretations of Islam that are prevalent today augur poorly for freedom of religion and belief, a more correct interpretation, based on the sacred text and valid traditions, finds Islam highly supportive of freedom of thought and religion and easily in accord with the principles of human rights.[33]

Ways forward: the question of Islamic secularism

The thinkers covered in this chapter have sought to reinvent Islam as a *via media* between the authoritarian status quo in Iran (and the Arab world) and a liberal order that would ensure democracy, freedom of belief and religion, and ultimately a liberated society. Such thinkers have reconceptualised Islam as inherently pluralistic, just, accommodating, non-doctrinal and essentially democratic.[34]

In these theories of Islam, freedom comes first and religious ordinances are relegated to individual choice. Islam, in this hermeneutical re-evaluation, is essentially secularised. At the same time, even this secular Islam retains its identitarian precepts and an underlying sense of superiority. While emphasising the role of Islam in liberating and democratising society, there continues to be a hierarchy, on top of which we find the enlightened Muslim who speaks in an Iranian-Shi'a accent with European undertones. Islam, now cleansed from authoritarianism and reimagined as the reincarnation of liberty, continues to be prioritised and idealised. Despite his emphasis on freedom of choice, Kadivar maintains that Islam is the 'correct and just religion', that there are 'false religious and doctrinal beliefs' and that the Qur'an warns 'those who turn their back on the Just Religion of divine punishment at the end of time'.[35] Soroush shares a similar conviction in the superiority and necessity of an Islamic order when he states that 'democratic religious regimes need not wash their hands of religiosity nor turn their backs on God's approval'.[36] The approval of God continues to be central and 'entails religious awareness that is leavened by a more authentic and humane understanding of religiosity and that endeavours to guide the people in accordance with these ideals'.[37] In this view, the non-religious rest continues to be pasted into a religious core defined by guiding authorities. Bazargan is equally ambiguous when he says that 'God has given us freedom of opinion and action within certain parameters, but He has given us plenty of warning ... that rebellion, *disbelief*, and injustice will have dire results ... both in this life and in the hereafter.'[38] The object continues to be Allah, and the right path continues to be signposted by the Surahs of the Qur'an (and the hadiths): 'God bestows both freedom and guidance concerning the consequences of actions. His mercy is infinite and His vengeance great.'[39] For all these believers, there seems to be a correct worldview, the right choice, an ideal and implicitly Islamic order.

The problem is that these proclamations are made in the name of Islam, not humanity. There remains, then, a problematic, almost patronising aftertaste even in what I have called 'secular Islam', precisely because lofty ideals such as freedom, democracy and so forth are claimed to be the purview of one religious community. There is not enough emphasis on the universality of these norms and the global struggles that brought them about. In essence, we are all humans (*bashar*), as Shariati pointed out in the 1970s in his widely disseminated lectures in opposition to the shah. Becoming human (*insan*) is a universal project shared by humankind, which is why Shariati's prose is repeatedly littered with references to Nietzsche, Sartre, Buddha, Iqbal or the Indian philosopher (and statesman) Sarvepalli Radhakrishnan (1888–1975), and why he stresses that it is science that can help humankind 'to completely free themselves'.[40] Compared with the cosmopolitan style of Shariati, the narratives of the secular Islamists covered in this chapter seem rather provincial, despite nods to Karl Popper (for example, in the writings of Soroush), Rumi and others. At base, secular Islam remains an identitarian project that does not sufficiently connect the Muslim 'self' to the rest of humanity. Bahais, Christians, Jews, Heathens, Hindus, Buddhists, and Zoroastrians continue to linger on the side roads of the Islamic highway. In such an idealised Islamic democratic order, judicial equality could be ensured, but true cultural egalitarianism remains confined. Muslims continue to be imagined at the top of a hierarchy that differentiates between human beings on the basis of their religious convictions. In order to refine the secular Islamic viewpoint, it would have to start with a universal understanding of history, and to be represented from the perspective of minorities within the Islamic realm.

Why is it that Islam has to appear with such vehement force in the first place? The term appears at every twist and turn of the narratives covered in this chapter. It is almost obsessive, certainly repetitive and even redundant. Obviously, it has a lot to do with context. Iran is an Islamic republic with an authoritarian state that rules in the name of Islam. All of the thinkers covered in my analysis are at odds with the state, so they have to address and challenge its 'Islamicity'. However, because of this, a paradox ensues: in order to reinvent a liberal Islam that could do battle with a doctrinaire one, Islam has to be stretched so widely that it remains rather heavy with religion, even after its secular diet. When Glasnost met orthodox Soviet communism, it was still sold as Leninist ideology by Gorbachev. Comparably, secular Islam continues to confine itself within the original revolutionary project, for instance by reimagining Khomeini as a reformer or Muhammad as a democrat. It is preaching to the converted, but its language does not appeal to the nonbeliever who was not part of the Islamic universe in the first place.

In this sense, secular Islam lags behind the thought of classical Muslim philosophers, in particular Ibn Sina (Avicenna), who appears as a reference point in the writings of Soroush and Kadivar but remains insufficiently conceptualised. Indeed, in the writings of these philosophers, the notion of a superior Islamic way is almost entirely absent. Islam emerges as an *a priori* and entirely abstract nodal point that has yet to be conquered intellectually. We must therefore distinguish between this '*a priori* Islam' of the classical philosophers and the rather more 'concrete Islam' of the so-called Islamic revivalists from the nineteenth century onwards. *A priori* Islam dispenses with political utilitarianism and the politics of identity; it cannot afford a fundamentalist or literalist reading of the Qur'an, it is not ideological and it does not Islamise reality. It does not refer to a multiplicity of syntheses, every one of which constitutes an individual discourse articulated towards some concrete notion of the meaning of Islam. Islam is there, a desired object, yet it is *a priori* to our existence, it is not a concrete definition of a place into which we can easily venture. (Islamic ontology, the Islam we think we can see, is not that of a totality, but rather that of an engineered totalisation that changes in accordance with the determinations of history and time. Thus, the ontology of any Islamic field must be entirely dependent on the process of human construction). The classical philosophers were central to illuminating this *a priori* existence of Islam that does not yield a significant boundary between self and other. In their writings, the ontology of Islam is stretched so thin, resembling an infinite horizontal line, that the points of contact with adjacent discursivities are exponentially multiplied.

In Ibn Sina's seminal *Danesh nameha-yealai* (Treatise on knowledge) philosophy takes a progressive, forward-looking view. In his *Uyun al-hikmah* (Eyes on philosophy), Ibn Sina writes that *al-hikmah* (which he uses as being the same as philosophy) is the 'perfection of the human soul through conceptualisation (*tasawwur*) of things and judgement (*tasdiq*) of theoretical and practical realities to the measure of human ability.'[41] He went on in his later writings to distinguish between Peripatetic philosophy and what he called 'Oriental philosophy' (*al-hikmat al-mashriqi'yah*), which was not based on ratiocination alone, but included revealed knowledge (it also set the stage for the influential treatises of Sohravardi, and here especially his *Kitabhikmat al-ishraq*). There is a particularly striking poem by Ibn Sina about the fate of the human soul (note that it is not exclusive to Muslims), which exemplifies this emphasis on congruence between rational analysis and spiritual opportunity that was central to the canons of the classical philosophers of Islam.

> Until when the hour of its homeward flight draws near,
> And 'tis time for it to return to its ampler sphere,
> It carols with joy, for the veil is raised, and it spies
> Such things as cannot be witnessed by waking eyes.
> On a lofty height doth it warble its songs of praise
> (for even the lowliest being doth knowledge raise).
> And so it returneth, aware of all hidden things
> In the universe, while no stain to its garment clings.[42]

The ultimate object here is the perfection of the intellectual faculties of the individual, who does not carry an exclusive identity, who is only presumed in his or her physical constitution. There is no realm of knowledge that is exclusive to Muslims in the writings of Ibn Sina, no discernible schematic dichotomy that permeates his narratives. He searches for a supreme truth, not a supreme civilisation or race. He and many of his contemporaries managed to create the archives of classical philosophy without the emergence of a discourse that would legitimate subjugation of the other, without a call to arms and without proclamations of righteousness. The Islamic secularists share with their ideological, Islamist counterparts the conviction of superiority despite the nascent philosophical and critical content of their ideas. They continue to adhere to the viewpoint that Muslims hold the holy grail of truth and that they are obliged to invite and persuade others to understand it. This is certainly not their ambition, but Islam, even in this liberal garb, could easily be turned into another form of hegemony. In such a dystopian world, war and aggression would not be justified in terms of killing the 'infidels' but civilising them.

10

MILITANCY, MONARCHY AND THE STRUGGLE TO DESACRALISE KINGSHIP IN ARABIA

Ahmed Dailami

Introduction

In the immediate aftermath of ISIS's attacks on Paris in November 2015, when the violence of the Middle East spilled over into metropolitan Europe, pundits repeatedly asked why the West was not tackling the financing and ideological export of jihadism at its root, in Saudi Arabia and the Gulf states. Print media, news anchors and journalists from around the world brandished their outrage at the seeming duplicity of favoured Arab allies. And yet when interviewees and experts were pressed for a response, no unequivocal answers came: only lukewarm statements about working with partners, or the necessity of sharing intelligence. For to admit reliance on the Gulf for energy security, financial stability and the global anti-terrorism effort, would make Western powers appear weak and dependent at a time when the media was called on to demonstrate Parisians' fearlessness. Equally, denying any relationship between contemporary Salafi-Jihadi Islam and its intellectual birthplace in Arabia would seem naïve, or even suspicious. The result was a set of confused responses followed by incoherent, diverting answers. In what follows, I argue that there are good reasons for such uncertainty and that the conventional methods of responding to it, namely more detailed studies of the Gulf's political economy or currents of political Islam, will not dispel it.

Nonetheless, while geo-strategy pundits may be unable to produce ready answers about how religion and politics are related at the supposed source of ISIS's ideology (the Gulf), there are those who have taken it upon themselves to explain just that through a resort to history. At the centre of this new historical consensus lies the point at which the noxious pairing of oil wealth and Islamic fundamentalism supposedly took place, sometime after the Second World War. It is this historical conjuncture to which some observers have pinned their hopes for explaining the rise of ISIS, the Taliban, the wars in Iraq and Afghanistan, and indeed the global popularisation of literalist, or 'Wahhabi' Islam. These new histories, popular as well as professional, have taken up the older argument that Islam lies at the root of the Middle East's political failures, but have now refined it into a newer vintage that simultaneously addresses the failure of secular modernity in the Middle East and the rise of post-war global commodity capitalism.

In these revisionist accounts, an older, monolithic culprit—Islam before multiculturalism—is distilled into its 'bad' version, Wahabbism. Wahhabism's enabling globaliser, 'petrodollars', is also refined and folded into the same explanatory narrative. Rather than simply unearned wealth that accrues to anonymous Arab rulers, the story of oil in the Middle East is presented as the story of post-Bretton Woods, financialised global capitalism. The rise of the World Bank and IMF, and that of al-Qaeda and ISIS are thus linked in a way that merits new attention, by drawing on both contemporary objects of global revulsion: capitalist greed and militant Islamism.

This schematic historical narrative simplifies the causes of contemporary violence in the Middle East in ways that both the left and right can agree on. Both material and ideological, it relies on an ominous pairing of retrograde theological thought and vast quantities of 'unearned' wealth—both of which have no place in the social democratic world of nation states built out of the ruins of the Second World War. So powerfully salient are these twin pillars of the explanation for the rise of the region's violent conflicts that they have usually only required evocation rather than any actual explication. Written in the tenor of an uncovered scandal, they have nothing to say about the institution that they assume, and have regularly claimed, lies at the centre of the oil–Islam pairing: Arabian monarchy. Because the hereditary monarchies in question are regarded as a remnant of tradition or as synonymous with religious fundamentalism, they are assumed to survive only because of their financial good fortune in the world. And so, rather than attending to their complex relationship to religious authority, the very existence of these monarchies is reduced to a historical mistake: a combination of geological fiat and the dull inertia of tradition.

A popular rendering of this historical revision is Adam Curtis's film, *Bitter Lake* (2015). The film takes its name from the saltwater lagoon on the Suez canal where King Abdulaziz of Saudi Arabia and President Roosevelt met to sign the deal that set in motion a series of events, which, according to the film, are ultimately responsible for the violent, politically incomprehensible Middle East of today. It was a deal that traded American silence over the way Saudi Arabia was ruled—and the fundamentalism upon which it relied to survive—for its cheap oil. This was the very oil that fuelled post-war global reconstruction in the 1960s and the subsequent financilalisation of global markets in the 1970s. The pairing of oil money and Wahhabism is not new, nor is the renewed interest in the birth of neoliberalism and the empowerment of the banks in the age of oil. Curtis's film, therefore, does not overturn any preexisting assumptions about the spread of Islamism or the ways in which global capitalism entered new and unprecedented phases of unhindered expansion. It creatively pairs the roots of today's sectarian and religious violence with the overriding explanations for it. Except that it does so with a particular focus on the dynastic state in Arabia as both the agent of this history and its silent beneficiary. It is the unearthed history of a secret deal that enabled the New Deal, at the expense of the world.

Other works of popular history directed at a public increasingly curious about Saudi Arabia and the Gulf have followed suit. These include the popular BBC television series, *Oil Planet: The Treasure That Conquered the World*, presented by Iain Stewart. Another BBC documentary, *Sands of Time: The Rise of the Kingdom*, presented by Tarek Osman, provides a largely similar narrative. At the core of these works is the miraculous rise of the Middle Eastern hydrocarbon industry, the corporations and modern states built around it, and the political consequences of its exploitation. I do not contest the importance or veracity of the post-war historical conjuncture they all indirectly take as their subject—this is, after all, one of the defining moments of the twentieth century. However, I would like to explore the evolving nature of this narrative, and particularly to question why it has prevented deeper thinking into the nature of the nation-states in the Arabian Peninsula that are central to its explanatory thrust. For in such narratives these nation-states do not yet merit attention as political forms beyond their redistributive functions, an oil industry that facilitated state formation, or for the various ways in which such states 'use' particular varieties of Islam.

These revisionist histories, despite their ubiquity, seem curiously incapable of accounting for the remarkably variable attitude of Arabia's monarchies towards militant jihadist Islam, let alone when they make an enemy of it, as they recently have done with increasing vehemence. But perhaps most tellingly, these histories cannot account for the remarkable endurance of both popular and official Americo-European comfort with the status quo in the Gulf, a comfort that possibly stems from unpronounced, resentment-laden beliefs that such states still underwrite much of the West's material security from both economic catastrophe and jihadist onslaught, even when journalists repeatedly attack them for doing just the opposite.

Such discussions often end up in the service of power by reinforcing its claims to authenticity and largess, rather than what they presume to do, which is to subvert it. In that sense, history written in the tenor of the exposé functions like media publicity, it ultimately validates rather than undermines. It does so by giving credence to the notion that the arrangements of power that govern the present are ultimately rooted in rational economic exchange, or that they are the reconciled products of unshakable tradition (as a myth of state-building), rather than the tentative products of clashing political ideas, for which, I shall argue, there has been no clear ideological resolutions. Moreover, it is no longer possible to understand or contribute to the debate about the place of religion in the political order of the Gulf unless it is also seen as a genuine logical, political and historical problem directly linked to the question of sovereignty and statehood there.

Arabia as a political desert

From their founding sometime in the early to mid-twentieth century as modern institutional states, the monarchies of the Arabian Peninsula entered the world as a politically meaningless geographic term: 'the Gulf'. No political categories were deployed to think of the Arabian Peninsula beyond palace intrigue and the ruthless self-preservation of local rulers. As Arabia entered the age of oil, the city-states of the Peninsula, and its preponderant giant in Saudi Arabia, circumvented the historical relationships that defined much of the twentieth-century's political history. These were the relations between labour and industry, and the institutional maturation of popular sovereignty in the form of stable parliaments, preferably as social democratic checks on the forces of the market and on religion. Such items underpinned both post-war European social-democracy and much of the 'third world' nationalism of the 1950s to 1970s. They still, whether explicitly or implicitly, constitute the fundaments of political history as a genre of historical writing. The pursuit of freedom from arbitrary power (be it profane or sacred) is largely considered constitutive of what we mean by history since the Enlightenment.[1]

Yet, because this form of nation-statehood never took root in Arabia, the world was left with no way to think about it politically other than through predetermination by its geological assets and the timeless 'traditions' attached to tribe, sect and kin. In fact, it is the notion that politics is determined by nature or tradition that is at the source of the popular refrain that the Gulf 'has no history'. Yet Arabia was no longer the silent, romantic place traversed by shepherd poets, but a frequently violent one that attracted prospectors, immigrants, armies, rebels and political dreamers of various stripes. The film *Lawrence of Arabia* sits at the artistic apex of thinking about Arabia on the threshold of this transition from romantic pre-modern desert empire to the political ironies of modern statehood. By the Second World War, then, the Arabian Peninsula arguably became a place of great economic and religious influence, but remained undefined in political terms that went beyond descriptions of tribal tradition, religious literalism or pacts between the two sustained by an economic and geological miracle.

Many historians, however, have imagined that the careful study of the past can serve as the antidote to the simplistic schematics described above. In the case of Saudi Arabia, the bedrock of the modern history of the state is the much-vaunted pact between dynastic rulers, and the Wahhabi clerical establishment of Najd that solidified during the early twentieth century.[2] Yet in these attempts at historical nuance, the relationship between palace and mosque is presented either as a contractual exchange of mutual interests, or one that has dissolved entirely so that political and moral authority seem indistinguishable, sedimented deep in some desert tradition of puritanical Islam salient to Arabia. Both perspectives preclude an understanding of such a relationship as a logical problem between ethics and politics, between militant purification of faith and reason of state, let alone one that remains fundamentally unanswered. If anything, using the term 'pact' to make sense of the historical relationship between moral and profane authority in Arabia equally implies an unresolved difference put aside for another time. Yet when history is written in order to identify culprits, as much recent commentary on the Gulf tacitly does, the paradoxes at the heart of the political relationships that define the Gulf, ones that historians have had difficulty identifying as such, are rendered invisible.

The problem with history

The first two decades of the twentieth century saw the expansion of the third Saudi state in a series of conquests that brought most of the Arabian Peninsula under the authority of a single dynasty. For our purposes, the details of this military expansion are not as consequential as the way in which historians have explained how it was possible to sustain and consolidate: a Faustian pact of sorts between the new ruling dynasty and a Wahhabi clerical establishment. Central to this narrative are the marauding Ikhwan, the armed group of Wahhabi warriors who fought for the house of Saud, but also provided the conquests with an ideology: that of the zealous missionary. We have a variety of convincing histories that account for the process by which the pact emerged and was consolidated among a variety of social groups.[3] However, once King Abdulaziz, as head of his dynasty, began to behave like a politician rather than the imam (most prominently, disallowing the Ikhwan to attack British protected territory around the Gulf, Iraq and Jordan), the pact immediately broke down. Abdulaziz, by then king of Nejd and the Hijaz, had to crush a rebellion by the Ikhwan in 1928, temporarily pacifying the militant element within the Wahhabi clerical establishment and their following.

Since then, the Saudi state has drawn limits as to where and how the moral authority of the 'ulamā' or clergy applies, and where it stops, thus allowing historians to speak of a 'clear division of labour' between the political authority of rulers, and the moral authority of clerics in Saudi Arabia.[4] Yet the differentiation between religion and politics that almost all historians of the Saudi Arabian monarcho-religious 'system' cite only accounts for it on the 'diplomatic' level, analytically separating religion from politics on this one count (the historical events of the pact, and subsequent Ikhwan rebellion in 1928) in order to connect the two even more closely on the level of mundane politics and Saudi Arabian state-building (the building of religious schools, the 'ulamā' being on state payrolls, the moral police's relationship with the wider public). In other words, the relationship between political and religious authority becomes an organic historical growth that no longer evokes the problem of sovereignty in trying to identify if and where it resides. In fact, the epistemic thrust and intellectual labour of the bulk of scholarship on Saudi Arabia has been to see the enmeshment, overlap and mutual embeddedness between religion and politics, rather than explore their respective limits. The authority of Wahhabi clerics and that of hereditary rulers, monarchs or otherwise, then, are thought to exist as two sides of the same coin in this historiography and social science literature. And yet this history of how politics and religion are related in Arabia suffers from a conceptual shortcoming: it presupposes the very categories of analysis whose origin it is intended to explain.

It is not that the lines between religion and politics are either clear or blurred in Saudi Arabia, for that is regularly explored in probing new scholarship on the mundane (and sometimes violent) ways in which Wahhabism both survives and is challenged in daily life.[5] What interests me here is the fact that, because of the transcendent element inherent in such fundamentalism, because of its identity as a mission, there always remains an immanent critique of profane power that is characteristic of all literalist fundamentalisms that exceeds the limits drawn for it by sovereign rulers.[6] The adherents of what I shall call jihadi-Salafism, as opposed to their Wahhabi progenitors, and their attitudes towards legitimate violence, exemplify this.[7] Thus for this form of religious fundamentalism to survive in Arabia, and more importantly, for them to be sincere and true to themselves, jihadi-Salafists have always splintered from mainstream, or what some scholars of Saudi Arabia have called 'compromise Wahhabism'.[8] Such deviations from the clerical establishment are almost always the result of different opinions on the legitimate use and targets of violence in the form of jihad. Jihadists accordingly claim and operate in political, social and now even physical territory beyond that allotted to them by the monarchy. In other words, jihadi-Salafism has to constantly recreate the imam and movement its progenitors 'betrayed' in 1928.

Since then, there have been spectacularly violent attempts at such reassertion, like the seizure of the Grand Mosque in Mecca in 1979, or even the events of 9/11. Without such excesses, jihadi-Salafists, or those who are not prepared to live ironically, will find themselves living in anxious contradiction between allegiance to God and an earthly king. Such contradictions are central to what regularly generates the violent phenomena that are then attributed to jihadi-Salafism, such as ISIS. Within Saudi Arabia itself, the historical pattern that resulted was paradoxical: every attempt to heal jihadi-Salafism's relationship with dynastic rulers by means of liberalising reforms or calls for moderation could only make the crisis worse. Such was the state of affairs between 'radical' and 'moderate' Islamists in Saudi Arabia throughout the first decade of the twenty-first century.[9]

Accordingly, the resort to history actually poses more questions than it answers. Having given us an understanding of an initial pact between the house of Saud and Wahhabism, historians have not paid attention to how such an alliance threw modern politics into a crisis ever after because of an unresolved conflict between the ethical imperatives of literalist puritanism and the cold realpolitik of dynastic power. The problem is compounded by the fact that 'while there is an elaborate Wahhabi discourse on Islamic law, creed, worship, and ritual, Wahhabis are not known for creating a political theology. Their views on the rightful Islamic leadership are a reiteration of classical Sunni opinions.'[10] This leaves their own creed open to pietistic reassertion by those interested in maintaining its purity, especially from corruption by politics per se. This results, as Faisal Devji has already suggested, in the constant need to recreate an even purer, legalistic Islamic state with increasing literalism and violence in order to dispose of political authority once and for all. To use the juridical term, this is what jihadi-Salafists justify as *al-khuruj 'ala alhakim*, or to discard the authority of a ruler. In other words, the militant feels increasingly compelled to live a life lived in sincere application of scripture and its laws, free of innovation. And it is precisely because sovereign political authority in the Arabian monarchy lies prior and above the law that makes it susceptible to accusations by fundamentalists as being blasphemously 'god-like'. In a reversal of Carl Schmitt's definition of the sovereign as he who decides on the exception from law, the sovereign here enjoys the exception as the norm. This fact lies at the heart of the political form of the dynastic-states in question, and without it we can only speak of the state's functions, not the locus and character of its sovereignty.

However, unlike European absolutism, this 'god-like' power, uncodified and unbridled by law, has no tradition of divine sanction attached to it, a matter I shall return to in due course. Any religious endorsement monarchs do enjoy comes sporadically (usually in times of crisis) in the form of the religious injunction of *ta'at waliyy al amr* or 'obeying he who is entrusted'. Under its restrictions, interpreted so as to preserve the unity of the realm, a ruler is to be obeyed, no matter how tyrannical, so long as he is deemed (presumably by those seeking divine guidance for their political allegiance) a practising Muslim. This leaves the conditions of obedience notoriously open to interpretation. And so without the possibility of declaring its own authority as one derived entirely from scripture as 'God-given', all the monarchy can do ideologically about jihadi-Salafism exceeding its limits is to call for moderation.

By definition, moderation can only be conceived of as compromise by jihadi-Salafists. More interestingly, because religious moderation is a stance that the Saudi and other Gulf governments strongly advocate precisely as a response to fundamentalist violence, it becomes a category of political calculation rather than moral conviction. In other words, moderation is a result of a sovereign decision, in the strong Schmittian sense: a deviation from jihadi-Salafism's doctrine or laws. In that sense, there is something fundamentally intractable at the core of the political order in Saudi Arabia. Yet such intractability is something that those insisting on separate discussions about Islamic or economic reform and the political form of the state are unwilling or resistant to acknowledge. As much as they may try, there cannot be a clear-cut separation between the norms of a legal system rooted in shari'a and the facts of political power as they stand. Yet this is precisely what liberal Islamist reformers insist on doing.

When the law is not enough: Abdulaziz al-Qasim

A telling illustration of such resistance is the intellectual project of one of the most articulate religious thinkers in Saudi Arabia. Shaykh Abdulaziz al-Qasim is a former Saudi Arabian judge, lawyer, legal adviser and Islamic scholar. His work reflects the evolution of the Wahhabi clerical establishment's search for coherence and consistency with its own doctrine. In doing so, al-Qasim's project seeks to derive an intellectually consistent, modern juridical order from the shari'a while maintaining a rationality and moderation acceptable to modern social life. Unsurprisingly, it was almost immediately after the most violent events of the Arab Spring in the Arabian Peninsula during the summer of 2011 that al-Qasim became an increasingly visible public figure. Of particular note in al-Qasim's thought is that he initiates his intellectual project with the following paraphrased formulation: that 'we' the juridical establishment in Saudi Arabia either endorse those who read scripture and then join al-Qaeda and other violent groups, or we create a less contradictory, oppressive juridical apparatus based on a more coherent and systematised legal reasoning.

This is what separates al-Qasim from most of the clerical establishment: he has recognised and fully acknowledged the intellectual impasse at which even establishment Wahhabism has arrived. In other words, al-Qasim believes it is no longer possible to say that existing literalist interpretations of the Qur'an are correct, and that those who wish to fully apply them (and hence possibly engage in violent jihad) are misguided. He views the recent history of escalating jihadi violence as symptomatic of such a contradiction. Even so, when al-Qasim speaks of these two positions as fundamentally irreconcilable, they remain to him a matter internal to religious debate. In other words, an amendment to the application of religious law alone would suffice, without considering the way in which it relates to matters of sovereignty, or the political form of the state that he calls *nizam al hukm*. Accordingly, al-Qasim wishes to solve the problem of militancy by reducing the scope for arbitrary power to operate through the juridical apparatus of the state. To him, eliminating the legal gaps left open to manipulation, corruption, dishonesty or oppression would not only eliminate the social roots of jihadism but also bring the state into reconciliation with itself, as one imagined to be in consistent application of the shari'a. This renders both the problem of jihadi radicalism and its solution (juridical reform) social matters that stem from the appropriate interpretation of scripture, and its limitation to areas of law in which there is no dispute among scholars.

An example of how this would be achieved is al-Qasim's advocacy of the withdrawal of all legal force from existing laws or legal norms that derive from any human juridical effort: *ijtihad*. Any matters around which there is some disagreement would therefore be left to resolution through private choice. For example, al-Qasim's reformed laws would decouple how individuals comport themselves in public and the state's ability to regulate it, given that much of the regulation of public comportment in Saudi Arabia (dress codes, women's freedom of movement, etc.) is derived from human juridical effort. This would amount to a radical, if not revolutionary disempowerment of the clerical establishment, and a sharp contraction to its sphere of influence. Moreover, when al-Qasim advocates the elimination of *ijtihad* in matters of legislation, he envisions replacing it with a scientific approach to 'public policy'. To link the shari'a (stripped of human deductive efforts) and public policy he advocates the use of post-Aristotelian philosophy and the human and social sciences. For example, economics would replace *ijtihad* on financial matters, and psychology on certain questions of family law. Thus contrary to the Islamic revolution in Iran that placed the jurist at the helm of political power, the liberal or reformists among the Wahhabi establishment are engaged in an intellectual effort to eradicate the place of jurists in favour of laws forged in rational social-scientific thought.

Yet every attempt by a liberal (broadly defined) religious scholar such as al-Qasim to engage in problem-solving of this kind runs aground when defining the mechanism that would engage in such an effort of reform: the state. For al-Qasim, 'the state is not the regime'. His is an attempt to separate the nature of sovereignty in Saudi Arabia (absolute hereditary monarchy) from the institutional-legal apparatus of the state. It is a technocrat's definition of the state born out of a desire to protect it from those who have deemed it an enemy (jihadi-Salafists). Yet in order to sanctify the state as an abstract or neutral *kayan* (entity), as he calls it, al-Qasim ultimately requires a justification for its existence beyond Islam and thus immediately calls on his own political opinion, rather than Islamic legal reasoning to do so. And so he asserts that protecting the nation-state takes precedent over consensus within any such state: *al-muhafadha 'ala al-kayan muqaddam 'ala nshu' jama'a fil kayan'.*[11] This reference to the role of rulers in maintaining the stability of the nation state (*al luhma al wataniyya*) comes from political reasoning that is ontologically distinct from the project of Islamic legal reform internal to the functioning of the state itself. Al-Qasim's reformist thought, then, can only proceed without engaging with the very thing that militants insist on defining for themselves: the sources of political sovereignty.

Al-Qasim's opinions are not particularly ground-breaking. In fact, they owe their origins to an unprecedented attempt in the Gulf to marry technocracy, good governance and legal reform. As a 'third way' between revolution (Iran) or imposed democracy (Iraq) and the status quo, governments throughout the Gulf Cooperation Council (GCC) embarked on reform initiatives almost immediately after the start of the Iraq War of 2003. The motivations for reform were complex, but they can be characterised as an attempt at gradualist improvements to the functioning of the state without major alterations to political structures. These reform initiatives had to be public precisely because they were a response to internal and external pressure for public participation in the business of government. The result was a remarkable set of documents published by almost every Gulf country roughly between 2005 and 2010, which were called 'visions', or 'national strategies'. Neither publicly endorsed, nor secretly hatched, these documents skirted a middle way between a constitution and a manifesto. Al-Qasim and the thought of other liberal Islamists fit precisely within the intellectual paradigm and political spirit that gave birth to such documents and to the popularity of public policy in the Gulf (and globally) as a 'science', an area of acceptable public debate, and even an educational qualification. For a brief period, the scientific character of public policy rendered it non-political on the one hand and non-religious on the other, making it particularly appealing for reformers of a particular stripe to engage with.

Burnt by a bishop or saved by a prince?

Yet the altered priorities that emerged out of a sectarian war in Iraq, and the mass mobilisations of the Arab Spring, made such gradualist visions of social transformation implausible. The post-2011 reversal from liberalising experimentation between 2005 and 2010 was swift and unequivocal. With the rise of the Muslim Brotherhood in Egypt and a sectarian war in Iraq, coupled with a perceived Iranian existential threat, reformist constituencies throughout the Arabian Peninsula rushed back into the protective custody of governments. Yet this reaction to militant and revolutionary violence was only the start of a more forceful reaction against the threat of jihadist violence from ISIS within the GCC itself, and not only in Saudi Arabia.

Thus when a suicide bomber detonated an explosive device in Kuwait's Imam al-Sadiq mosque killing over two dozen civilian worshipers in May 2015, it was the third major attack by ISIS to target the Shi'a living within the borders of the Gulf's monarchies. Two others occurred in Saudi Arabia during 2015 as well. ISIS threatened further attacks on Shi'a worshippers in Bahrain, and then carried out another attack on Sunni Saudi security forces. The latest bombing within the Gulf made it clear that ISIS had not only declared Shi'a Muslims unwelcome in the territory it claimed as the Caliphate, but anyone in direct service of the monarchy as well, the military being at the top of that particular hierarchy of culpability. Even the most vehement critics of governments in the Gulf did not question the state's prerogative to sovereign action when a self-appointed religious authority attempted to redefine the region's polities on its own terms. Obviously ISIS's ideology is not collapsible to that of the Wahhabi clerical establishment, but it does undermine the latter's authority by challenging its deference to the monarchy on its own terms of authenticity, literalism and fidelity to the original mission of Muhammad b. Abd al-Wahhab.

When condemning the attacks, the state in Kuwait, and to some extent in Saudi Arabia, took something of a pluralistic position on the freedom of belief. Without even needing to explicitly defend Shi'ism as a legitimate and recognised Muslim sect, the state proclaimed the lives of Shi'i citizens inviolable as it rounded up those suspected of collaboration with ISIS for the killing of Shi'as. In the event that these actions are a harbinger to a more explicitly liberal language on religion and religious freedom, it will mark an important and perhaps permanent change of political rhetoric within the Gulf. When a non-religious authority in the form of a state, its ruling executives and security apparatus move to protect the lives of subjects regardless of their religious affiliation, it implicitly creates a hierarchy between its own and religious authority. In other words, ISIS may have incited a discourse within the Gulf that can make the hitherto convenient combinations of profane and sacred power—'using Islam'—so to speak, much more difficult than it has been in the past. By joining Iran as a mortal threat to the social and political order, ISIS has begun to shift the terms of debate from one internal to Islam (Shi'a versus Sunni) to one between the realm of puritan ethics and an increasingly autonomous one of politics. Perhaps more precisely, it has pried open the question of allegiance to insist on a choice to obey God or a king.

Yet again, in order to make an enemy of ISIS, the state ultimately resorts to the rhetoric of moderation. And when calls for moderation prove practically insufficient, and the state itself is forced to take violent action to protect itself and its subjects, its rhetoric also makes bold ideological leaps that match its increasingly confident action against militancy. The consequence of this has been that it is not only religious and legal reformers such as al-Qasim who have come to confront the ideological impasse between religious literalists and political sovereigns in the Gulf. Rulers themselves have begun to articulate new visions of political community, something that can be summarised as a leap from mere traditionalism to a more assertive conservatism.

Although extremely recent, such political language makes an enemy not of terrorism, violence or even extremism, but of theocracy itself as the outlandish politicisation of religious belief. Somewhat similar to recent pronouncements of the state in Egypt, such a language does not take order and stability as goods in themselves. The qualitative leap that such a politics had to take in response to jihadist and revolutionary danger was to make twin allies out of both freedom and the calamity of its potential loss. Thus the language on the protection of lives, property and the rule of law is now articulated not merely for its own sake, or even through the particularities of national belonging, but through a new rhetorical commitment, however muted, to freedom.

In late 2014, the crown prince of Bahrain, Shaykh Salman bin Hamad Al-Khalifa gave a speech where he called for an abandonment of the War on Terror, and for its replacement with a war against theocracy. Rhetorically elaborate and suggestive in its historical analogies, Shaykh Salman's speech first clarified the correct space for religion within the polity and as separate from politics:[12] 'It [theocracy] is unfair to those of us who practice our religion responsibly ... and it sullies the name of a great tradition and a great philosophy that is divine and must be above politics ...' He then defines the parameters of enmity explicitly in terms of a battle with theocracy: 'if we are to call ourselves in a war with theocrats, then I believe that we can start to put together the military social and political and maybe even economic policies in a holistic manner to counter this threat, as we did with Communism':

But what do we call it, do we call it theocrism? Do we call it fascist theocracy? We must find a term that we can all share. [This lack of a term] ... allows us to hop blindly and haphazardly from one threat to another, without containing it within a complete paradigm. I'm afraid that the events of 2011 ... and history will judge, whether it was berlin of 1989, or the Bolsheviks in 1917, where state paradigms collapse and into the vacuum comes an extreme ideology ... We will be fighting these theocrats for a very long time, of that I have no doubt ... These are people who try to govern us here on earth and in the hereafter ... These are people who disregard human life, and do not value the social order and the social contracts that we have established among ourselves as societies and peoples, these are people who oppress women and these are people who slaughter anyone who does not condone, or approve of or subscribe to their own twisted ideology.

... And eventually we must use all resources to hold accountable those who place themselves over other ordinary human beings and claim they have a divine right to rule ... [although] faith can certainly be part of any political platform. But what we cannot have is a man, an individual, placed at the top of a religious ideology who has the power by religious edict, to strip someone of either [*sic*] their hereafter, and use that for political gains. [This] Sounds very much like the 17th century to me, and the 17th century, ladies and gentlemen, has no place in our modern 21st. I call on you to discard the term War on Terror and focus instead on the rise of these evil theocracies.

Because the prince's intellectual effort here is to draw clear lines of political enmity, these words are also an act of self-definition. Perhaps the most articulate public repudiation of divinely sanctioned moral authority by a member of ruling dynasty in the Gulf, the prince's speech made an unmistakable gesture towards monarchy as a political form that may enter into a mutual embrace with the liberal creed, together with its pluralism, its talismanic centrepiece that is human rights, but most importantly with the idea of a social contract. This is not only directed at the international audience of statesmen and journalists whom he is addressing but perhaps to other dynasts who may still think of mounting a bold defence of absolute monarchy in 2014. Moreover, the term theocracy equates and then makes an enemy of both ISIS and Iran. Linking these contemporary theocracies of the Middle East and the churches of seventeenth-century Europe may be music to the ears of liberal audiences, yet the comparison is there as much to remind the audience of the Wars of Religion's ultimate victors—European monarchs who eventually faced the spectre of the social contract and popular sovereignty—as it is to discount the moral authority of religious leaders having any serious basis to claim political authority whatsoever.

Political language such as this may be easier to produce in Bahrain than in Saudi Arabia, where the political implications of rearranging the relationship between religion and politics are infinitely more difficult. This is why, although well meaning, the task of the liberal jurist in the figure of Abdulaziz al-Qasim—and his attempts to separate a reformed shari'a from matters of political power—will inevitably be of limited efficacy. In contrast, Shaykh Salman's call for war on theocracy represents the monarchy's early pangs of estrangement from the language of religious sanction in a more malleable political context of the smaller states of the Gulf. For now, the former wields the law, while the latter the rhetoric of reason and reasonability. Both encourage distinctions between private and public; between conscience and politics. Yet their mutual challenge (and particularly for al-Qasim) remains that the political authority of monarchs (as such) in Arabia was never a fully differentiated functional system with its own media, codes, organisations and roles, which was then 'coupled' with some form of Islam, or as in Saudi Arabia, with Wahhabism.[13]

That is why scholars historically only speak of it in terms of the pre-monarchical 'traditional' or 'tribal' authority. In order to be able to speak of fully differentiated political and religious systems (and therefore describe some alliance in which they then entered), there would have to be at least a political code that has been built around the issue of power, and why it should be in the hands of particular individuals, and a religious code dedicated to the issue of morality/transcendence, and so on. The former does not exist as an officially adopted doctrine, nor is monarchism even spoken of as a category of political thought in its own right. Hence, to desacralise kingship here is to engage in an act of political creation, and not merely to fall back on custom. And it is this act that a prince may be more equipped to handle than any jurist unwilling to engage with questions on the sources of sovereignty that lie beyond religious justification.

Conclusion

Corey Robin's 2011 book on conservative political thought defines conservatism at its most abstract as 'a meditation on—and theoretical rendition of—the felt experience of having power, feeling it threatened, and trying to win it back'.[14] This is perhaps why shifts in the language of conservative politics are often, if not always, precipitated by crisis. At any rate, only a crisis worthy of pragmatic change in the face of mortal danger to the status quo has produced any such accelerated periods of political activity among the Gulf's ruling elites. Most notably, the Islamic Revolution, and the fall of the Middle East's most formidable monarchy in 1979, instigated the formation of the GCC as a union of monarchies itself. That was the first formal expression and commitment in the Gulf to itself as a political idea.

Since then, a small army of pundits has made a career out of predicting the fortunes of Saudi Arabia's relationship with Iran. Such commentary, and indeed the majority of work on the Gulf, has now placed sectarian affiliations at the centre of the political debacle that supposedly shapes the political fortunes of the entire region. This is why commentators fixated on the execution of prominent religious scholar and activist Nimr al-Nimr, while largely ignoring the more telling fact that the bulk of those executed were Sunni jihadi Salafists. Yet the rousing of dormant religious minorities in the Gulf, such as its native Shi'as, continues to fascinate those engaged in a politics of prediction in the Gulf, as if only Shi'ism could be the source of political change in a region so dominated by Sunni orthodoxy.

Unlike the aftermath of 1979, however, the Gulf's monarchies are no longer confronted by the spectre of theological revolution elsewhere, but by forces that threaten the political order from within. I have outlined the clash of ideas born out of such threats of violence that has acted like a solvent for political certainties at a time when new political forms have not yet emerged to replace those fatigued by their own indeterminacy. To characterise the interregnum, I have presented voices that attempt to strike a balance between the right and the good, and have hinted at the conceptual limitations that saddle the audible strands of vernacular liberalism in their programmatic language. Cumulatively, these impressions are meant to convey the ways in which older political relationships yield to new ones, and that such a process of ideological transformation is irreducible to matters of political economy or political Islam alone. This is because monarchs, militants and moderates may now have to begin motivating allegiance to conceptions of sovereignty, statehood and citizenship in new ways. None currently enjoy a monopoly on violence and most likely realise that they may never secure one without some attempt at reincarnation.

11

ISLAMOTOPIA

REVIVAL, REFORM, AND AMERICAN EXCEPTIONALISM

Michael Muhammad Knight

> A distinctly American Islam has already begun to take shape.
> Michael Muhammad Knight, *Blue-Eyed Devil*[1]

> The United States of America can save Islam.
> Michael Muhammad Knight, *The Taqwacores*[2]

Introduction

This chapter seeks to problematise a trend in which my own work has participated, and which has in fact been described by one reviewer as my work's 'central argument'.[3] This chapter considers the discourse of 'American Islam': the notion that American Muslims have created, or are in the process of creating, a uniquely American expression of Islam. The concept of 'American Islam' has been employed by a variety of Muslim intellectuals, including Republican activists, promoters of interfaith dialogue, 'Progressive Muslim' leaders, advocates for African American Muslim communities, Salafi revivalists, and scholars engaging American Muslims as an academic subfield. These diverse actors employ 'American Islam' to represent a wide range of ideals. The notion of 'American Islam' also overlaps with the conceptualisation of Islam as a genuinely American religion whose adherents live in complete harmony with ideals of pluralism and liberal democracy. In various imaginaries of American Islam, we additionally find what could be called an 'American Muslim Exceptionalism': the belief that, due to factors such as constitutional separation of religion and state, the diversity of Muslim communities in the United States, and greater opportunities for Muslim women, American Muslims will achieve a more perfect and authentic Islam and then proceed to enlighten the rest of the global *umma*.

When Muslim intellectuals envision 'American Islam', what do they see? My interest lies in the exclusions and marginalisations that 'American Islam' discourse performs. In this chapter, I demonstrate that constructions of 'American Islam' not only treat American-ness and Muslim-ness as measurable quantities, but also tend to merge them into one category, creating a new 'American Muslim' subject for whom being fully 'American' makes one more fully 'Muslim' and vice versa. The term 'American Muslim' itself participates in the construction of a subject who self-identifies chiefly by US citizenship and Muslim religious conviction. In contrast to other hybrid identifications that point to racialised regional or national origins, such as 'African American' or 'Italian American', 'American Muslim' (popularly reversed as 'Muslim American') erases the subject's membership in other communities, naming religion as the primary identity marker.

In these discourses, the idea of an American Islamic tradition operates on particular definitions of 'American' and 'Islamic' and excludes those who fail to qualify for one or both terms. In other words, as the creation of a category constitutes a drawing of boundaries, imaginaries of 'American Islam' must necessarily mark someone as not fully American or sufficiently Muslim. As this 'American Islam' discourse often relies on a binary division between 'indigenous' (typically conflated with African American converts and their descendants) and 'immigrant' Muslims, constructions of American Islam intersect with issues of US race history, citizenship and assimilation. Therefore, to speak of American Islam, as with our attempts to speak of an American anything, means an encounter with white supremacy. In this chapter, I demonstrate that constructions of 'American Islam' have typically served to disqualify African American and immigrant Muslims as American Islam's representatives, pathologising their beliefs, practices, histories and identities.

I also read with attention to an important silence, as these pathologising discourses tend to ignore the question of white converts. I argue that this silence is not reducible to the reality that white converts form a numerically insignificant portion of American Muslim communities; rather, the discourses examined here operate on assumptions that implicitly locate white conversion at American Islam's privileged centre.

Before American Islam: Isma'il al-Faruqi and Islam in America

Palestinian American academic Isma'il Raji al-Faruqi (1921–86), a figure who was enormously influential in the development of American Muslim institutions, imagined Muslim immigrants to the US as coming from dysfunctional homelands. 'In Muslim countries,' he wrote, 'an essential failure was their separation from Islam,' that is, the prevalence in the twentieth century of secular ideologies such as communism and nationalism.[4] North America was also presented as dysfunctional, 'a whole continent giving itself to alcohol and drugs, to sexual promiscuity and exploitation, to family destruction and individualism, to cynicism and pessimism, to racism and discrimination ... to political and economic imperialism against the rest of humanity.'[5] However, in the challenges faced by Muslims coming from one broken culture to another, al-Faruqi found potential for both the diaspora and the adopted homeland to be transformed.

Al-Faruqi first envisioned the United States as an opportunity for international Muslim students to obtain mastery of 'Western' sciences, after which they could return to their countries of origin, and through their newly acquired knowledge, revitalise the global *umma*. When it became clear that most students were choosing to stay in the United States after completing their studies, and that Muslim communities in the country were thus transitioning from visiting students to settled families, al-Faruqi's prescriptions for Muslims in the US underwent significant revision. He found inspiration from encounters in the 1960s with members of the Muslim Students Association (MSA), a newly established national network which—in contrast to Muslim student groups that organised on the basis of ethnicity or national origin—located its identity in shared religious commitment. Re-envisioning Muslims in the US as forming a permanent community, al-Faruqi imagined the United States as a site in which immigrants could transcend their diversity and unite as one exemplary Muslim community. This shedding of cultural distinctions coincided with the Salafi revivalist project. As Muslims united on the basis of

Islam rather than their specific national and cultural heritages, al-Faruqi argued, they would reject the local innovations through which universal Islam had been corrupted, restoring Islam to the purity of its foundational texts.[6]

Al-Faruqi wrote dismissively of Muslims who moved to the West for material benefit, criticising what he called the 'immigrant mentality' as rooted in disgust for the homeland and uncritical admiration for the new home. However, he added that many Muslim immigrants who came for professional advancement also 'awakened' themselves and 'recaptured' their Muslim selfhood while in North America. In al-Faruqi's view, these awakened Muslims could potentially make North America the locus of a new Islamic revival that would transform their host country: al-Faruqi outlined several ways in which 'Islamic consciousness' acted upon the mind of the Muslim immigrant, including Islam's capacity for providing immigrants with 'the deepest love, attachment, and aspiration for a North America reformed and returned to God'.[7] Whereas he had previously emphasised the need for the global Muslim *umma* to retrieve scientific knowledge from the West, he now wrote of North America obtaining 'Islamic vision' to complement its scientific and technological supremacy. What al-Faruqi called 'Islamic vision' would enable North America to 'increase its mastery and use of nature', while disciplining this mastery with a sense of responsibility towards God, humanity and other creatures.[8]

For al-Faruqi, the permanent settling of Muslim immigrants in North America took on religious significance, through which Muslims shared in the foundational mythic history of American origins:

> [America] will not fail to recognize in the person with Islamic vision a true son, though born overseas, whose spirit is nearly identical with that of the early founders of the New World, who ran away from oppression and tyranny seeking a haven where they would remold their lives under God, seek His bounty, and raise high His banner.[9]

While connecting Muslim immigrants to the Anabaptist Pilgrim refugees who first came to America, al-Faruqi also compared Muslim immigration to the United States to the historic seventh-century migration (*hijra*) from Mecca to Medina, through which Muḥammad and his companions established the first Muslim society. The *hijra* comparison positioned transnational Muslims as parallels to the Muhājirūn, the Migrants. In this model, African American Muslim communities would constitute the logical parallel to the Muhājirūn, the Anṣār (Helpers)—those who already lived in Medina and welcomed the Muhājirūn—though al-Faruqi's focus on diasporic Muslim communities does not extend his analogy to consider African Americans.

Presenting his analysis in racially essentialised terms, al-Faruqi wrote of Christianity as having 'no hold on the Afro-American mind ... the Afro-American could hardly understand, and much less digest, the myths of Hellenized Christianity'.[10] Because Christianity 'had never penetrated his mind', the African American was open to Muslim conversion.[11] Additionally, al-Faruqi dismissed Christianity in African American experience with a critique that repeated modern Sunni revivalist critiques of Sufism: Christianity denigrated the flesh, held no interest in worldly affairs or social injustice, and thus left communities vulnerable to oppression from outside. Just as al-Faruqi partly blamed global Muslim decline upon Sufis' supposed lack of interest in worldly matters, he charged that African Americans were enslaved, oppressed and marginalised in American life directly due to 'the irrelevance of social justice to Christianity'.[12] Al-Faruqi argued that African American conversion to Islam was motivated by this social and spiritual condition, rather than 'ancient attachment to a Muslim African identity'. Islam was uniquely qualified to offer a universal message of justice and equality, and it endowed oppressed peoples with 'a new identity as well as a new dignity'.[13] Al-Faruqi credited Nation of Islam (NOI) leader, Elijah Muhammad, for his contribution to Muslim consciousness in the United States, and argued that under Warith Deen Mohammed's reforms, African American Muslims were growing 'in number, in consciousness, in understanding of, and attachment to, the genuine ideals of Islam'.[14]

Al-Faruqi, discussing African American and immigrant Muslims as essentially isolated from one another, treated both communities as works in progress: African American converts and Muslim immigrants had been broken by their respective histories and were gradually repairing themselves through Islamic awakening, but neither had completed the journey. An aspect largely missing from his analysis, however, is the white convert. Though al-Faruqi made brief references to white converts in his discussions of Christianity's failures, he did not suggest that there was anything particular to 'white culture' or the experience of being white in America that informed conversions to Islam. While white converts may also be described as dissatisfied with various elements of 'Western' society, al-Faruqi did not subject them to the psychologising through which he attempted to read the minds of African Americans and immigrants and pathologise their experiences.

Twin pathologies: 'indigenous' and 'immigrant' Muslims

Muslim intellectuals following al-Faruqi would treat the realisation of a genuine 'American Muslim' subject as an attainable future, but one that would require much effort on the part of both African American and transnational Muslims. Pakistani academic Zafar Ishaq Ansari (1932–2016), who held teaching positions in the United States and Canada, writes on African American Muslim communities with attention to their prospects for transcending their own 'religio-cultural milieu' and achieving authentic Islam.[15] In his assessment of the Nation of Islam, Ansari describes the NOI's doctrines as 'crude', 'unsophisticated' and 'unconvincing', but nonetheless grants the NOI a place in American Muslim history. Because it drew not from Islam but rather 'the religious tradition of the Blacks', Ansari writes, the NOI succeeded in 'being not too foreign to its audience' and thus provided an accessible 'stepping-stone' towards Islam.[16]

Ansari's 'Islam among African Americans: An Overview' explicitly lays out the conditions by which not only African American ('indigenous') but also 'immigrant' Muslims are to achieve a cohesive American Muslim community. Ansari observes that what he terms 'immigrant' and 'indigenous' Muslim communities have largely existed 'in separate orbits', but argues that they have gradually moved towards deeper intersection, due to transformations on both sides of the binary. On the immigrant side, Ansari attributes greater Muslim unity to a 'function of Americanization': among the children and grandchildren of Muslim immigrants, English has emerged as a first language, which 'will be instrumental in solidifying Muslim ranks, since it enables them to have effective communication'; and assimilation to the 'American way of life—from such trivialities as Kentucky Fried Chicken and Dunkin' Donuts to the nation's more profound aspects.'[17] Ansari asserts that 'In the melting pot of the United States, the edge of ethnic, linguistic, and cultural particularities of immigrant Muslims has already begun to be blunted', and compares this to the processes by which Jewish and Catholic immigrants from different European nations shed their diverse ethnic origins and became 'simply Jews' and 'simply Catholics'. Indigenous Muslims, in Ansari's treatment, have contributed to greater Muslim unity as a result of 'increased upward mobility' and by discarding the 'vogue of sectarianism and heterodoxy among a section of African Americans' that had previously divided them from immigrant Muslims.[18] In both groups, Ansari finds a lack of qualified Muslim intellectuals to guide their communities. Immigrant communities, he writes, possess great scholars who have made important contributions to the cause of Islam, but lack sufficient fluency in English and cannot effectively communicate with children who have been born and raised in the United States. Additionally, many immigrant scholars bring 'baggage from their home country', which Ansari describes as 'narrow, sectarian', and 'fairly rigid'; they cannot cater to American Muslims' specific needs or serve as representatives of Islam to the broader American public.[19] African American Muslim communities, meanwhile, 'have scarcely brought imams and religious leaders from abroad', but have instead 'appointed local persons from among themselves' who generally lack legitimate Islamic education.[20] Ansari offers a biological determinist argument that African American Muslims are indeed capable of becoming scholars, as 'their forefathers in Africa had made rich scholastic contributions', including works in Islamic sciences.[21]

In Ansari's account, therefore, immigrant Muslims possess authentic Islam, but must become more fully American by jettisoning the markers of their homeland identities; indigenous Muslims are American, but must move up in socioeconomic class and also meet the immigrants' standards of orthodoxy and religious training. A cohesive American Muslim community is thus achieved when both sides de-particularise their communities: immigrants must lose their languages and homeland prejudices in America's melting pot; indigenous Muslims must abandon what Ansari calls their 'Black-centeredness' and embrace 'Islamic universalism', while also moving in from the margins of American life. White converts, who are more privileged as fully American than both groups, while also free from both the immigrants' homeland prejudices and the 'heterodoxy' of African American communities, are not discussed by Ansari as having any obstacles to overcome as contributors to American Islam.

Kenyan American scholar Ali A. Mazrui's (1933–2014) 'Muslims between the Jewish Example and the Black Experience: American Policy Implications' argues that there are actually 'two Islams' in the United States: the 'indigenous' and 'immigrant'. Mazrui defines 'indigenous' as 'people who have been American for at least two centuries'; indigenous American Muslims, therefore, are 'mainly African Americans, with a small percentage of white Americans'. He defines 'immigrant' Americans as 'those who have been part of American society for less than a century'. This category of 'immigrants', therefore, includes the children and grandchildren of immigrants, regardless of where they were born or even whether they had ever been outside the United States. Repeating al-Faruqi, Mazrui describes immigrant Muslims as heirs to the legacy of the Prophet's migration from Mecca to Medina.[22] Like al-Faruqi, Mazrui does not extend the *hijra* analogy to include African American Muslims as heirs to the Anṣār.

Speculating on the future demographics of American Muslims, Mazrui considers that antiterrorist legislation may restrict immigration from Muslim-majority countries, but also suggests that as a result of Republican attacks on welfare and Medicaid, 'More poor Blacks may turn to Islam.'[23] Mazrui asserts that indigenous and immigrant Muslims have started the 'process' of being 'forged' into a singular Muslim community, but that each faces particular challenges. Indigenous Muslims, he writes, are 'new to Islam but old to America ... fully Americanized but not always fully Islamized', while immigrants represent the reverse: 'old to Islam but new to America ... often substantially Islamized but not yet fully Americanized'. They also represent opposites in terms of economics and political engagement: indigenous Muslims suffer from a lower income than the national average, but have 'considerable potential political leverage', while immigrant Muslims are economically strong but politically weak. As a result of their different contexts, these groups express different responses to American mythos: 'Indigenous Muslims (especially African Americans) tend to rebel against the mythology of the American dream', while immigrant Muslims 'seem to be like Jewish Americans' and believe that capitalism offers 'more opportunity than oppression'. As a result, Muslims in the United States are 'caught between the lessons of the Black experience and the power of the Jewish example.'[24] What white Muslim converts (who possess access to both the economic and political resources that Mazrui parses between immigrants and African Americans) bring to this context is not addressed.

The common privileging of immigrant Muslims, being 'old to Islam', as generally representative of a more authentic and authoritative Muslim practice than African American Muslims has met with pushback from important African American Muslim intellectuals. Perhaps the most prominent critique has come from American Islamic studies scholar Sherman Jackson (b.1956) in *Islam and the Blackamerican: Looking Toward the Third Resurrection* (2005), in which he emphasises the need for Blackamerican Muslims to achieve mastery of 'classical Sunni Tradition' in order to become 'self-authenticating subjects rather than dependent objects' in their relationship to that tradition.[25] Jackson writes of an essentialised, capitalised 'Immigrant Islam' that arrived following the 1960s reform of US immigration policy. Held as representative of a universal, dehistoricised, and 'true' Islam, this 'Immigrant Islam' was granted a 'presumed normativeness' that denied Muslim legitimacy to Blackamerican Muslims. Jackson argues against the privileging of immigrant Islam, asserting that 'most immigrant Muslims are themselves only slightly less removed from the classical Tradition than are their Blackamerican counterparts', and that 'Immigrant Islam is not really based on the classical

Tradition.'[26] Nonetheless, he regards Black American Muslims' 'non-mastery' of tradition as '*the* defining feature of Blackamerican Islam by the end of the twentieth century', leaving their self-definition 'practically dysfunctional'.[27] While advocating for Blackamerican Islam against the hegemony of what he has termed immigrant Islam, Jackson upholds the image of Black American Muslims as insufficiently authorised to articulate Islam for themselves. Moreover, he argues, Black American Muslims remain trapped in the heritage of 'Black Religion'; following C. Eric Lincoln, Jackson defines Black Religion as a 'holy protest', 'cosmic "No"', and 'spontaneous folk orientation' that possesses no theology, orthodoxy, institutions, foundational texts or even a specific god.[28] What Black Americans embraced as 'Islam', according to Jackson, was really Black religion at its core, with 'Islam serving as the outer shell'.[29] The leaders of what he calls 'proto-Islamic' movements in the early twentieth century were 'not so much *interpreting* Islam as they were *appropriating* it ... there is little evidence that Noble Drew Ali or Elijah Muhammad knew much at all about Islamic doctrine'.[30]

Jackson regards these 'proto-Islamic' leaders as pioneers of the first resurrection; this phase was eventually succeeded by the second resurrection, the movement of Black American Muslims towards Sunni Islam. Despite its greater claim to 'orthodoxy', the second resurrection retained the first resurrection's reliance on charismatic leadership rather than mastery of tradition. For Jackson, this era has had mixed results. Jackson regards Warith Deen Mohammed, who had called for the development of a uniquely American school of Muslim jurisprudence (*fiqh*), as 'dogged by a perduring authority deficit' that has inhibited his ability to sustain a 'positive expression of American blackness that is recognized as being sufficiently "Islamic"'.[31] As the second resurrection era draws to a close, Jackson foresees the future of Islam in Black America as 'one in which the authenticating agent is almost certain to be the structured discourse of Sunni Tradition'.[32] It is in this third resurrection, Jackson argues, that Black American Muslims will finally achieve their full authenticity as Black, American and Muslim. The third resurrection, in his view, represents the Islam of Malcolm X, if Malcolm had survived into the present: a Malcolm with the scholarly qualifications to articulate his position as an American Muslim, affirming, 'Yes, I am an American' without endangering his Muslim legitimacy, since 'he could now argue and show that such a position was consistent with the best tradition of Sunni Islam'. This Malcolm of an alternate universe would have performed the transition from 'consumer' to 'producer', contributing to a 'properly constituted orthodox Islam in

America' and 'leading the way in the transfer of Islamic religious authority from immigrant to native-born hands'.[33]

Jackson does suggest that he prefers an 'ecumenical American Islam' over 'the proliferation of monadic Blackamerican, white American, and Hispanic Islams', and recognises that white American Muslims 'must also find ways to come to terms with racism and other American realities without exposing themselves to the charge of "cultural or ethnic apostasy"'.[34] White converts and other groups, which could potentially complicate the immigrant/black American binary of Jackson's narrative, do not receive significant discussion in *Islam and the Blackamerican*. Jackson's most salient insights regarding white converts come in his argument against African American studies scholar Molefi Asante's claims in *Afrocentricity* that Blackamerican converts surrender themselves to Arab cultural hegemony. 'One should note that white American Muslims change their names, perform the pilgrimage, turn to prayer, modify their customs, and often replace their dress,' Jackson writes; but Asante does not charge these white converts with submitting to Arab culture or religion. The difference, Jackson observes, is located in power relations: in Asante's experience, 'whites simply do not have culture and religion imposed upon them, certainly not by people of color'.[35]

The notion that labels such as 'American Muslim' or 'Muslim American' can signify a coherent identity faces challenge from American academic Amina Wadud (b.1952) in her essay, 'American Muslim Identity: Race and Ethnicity in Progressive Islam'. Wadud argues that the hyphenated 'Muslim-American' imagines a unity that has not yet been realised, obscuring and erasing 'profound and unreconciled differences ... latent and overt ethnic and cultural prejudices ... and the hegemony of immigrant Muslim leadership and representation in the American Muslim context'.[36] Wadud also critiques the academic study of American Islam for its according priority to immigrants, as evidenced in volumes such as *Muslims on the Americanization Path*. The book's title, she argues, automatically prioritises those for whom being Muslim is presumed and becoming American is a matter of intention, while marginalising African Americans, 'for whom being American is presumed and Islamization is the voluntary and intentional operation'.[37] The chapter entitled 'Americans towards Islamization,' which exclusively discusses African American Muslims, further marks 'Islam' as the domain of immigrants and 'America' as the domain of African Americans.

If both African American and transnational Muslims are discussed as progressing towards an eventual telos of 'American Islam', one might ask how this American Islam is supposed to look. Here, we arrive at the discourse of 'American Islam' as a product that will not only fulfil the unique needs of American Muslims but must urgently be exported to the rest of the 'Muslim world'.

Saving the umma: American exceptionalism and 'true' Islam

As the children and grandchildren of post-1965 immigrants as well as Warith Deen Mohammed's 'second resurrection' came of age, and American Muslims at large experienced unprecedented pressures to defend their Americanness, the imaginary of a unique 'American Islam' flourished in the years following 9/11. Popular Muslim discourses presented the United States as home to a superior Islam, as Muslims were said to have enjoyed greater freedom to rigorously explore their religion in the US than in autocratic regimes or oppressive cultures.[38] Such discourses operated in full harmony with the narrative offered by the Bush administration, which differentiated between 'true' Islam and the 'distorted' version followed by the 9/11 attackers (whom Bush proclaimed 'traitors to their own faith'), defended the US invasion of Afghanistan through a Qur'an-based argument, and utilised the symbol of hijab-wearing Muslim women to demonstrate the acceptance of Muslims in American public space.[39]

Feisal Abdul Rauf (b.1948), Kuwaiti American imam and author of *What's Right with Islam* (later retitled *What's Right with Islam Is What's Right with America*), presents a narrative of the United States as founded upon 'Abrahamic ethics', thereby linking Americans and Islam in a shared heritage. As Rosemary R. Corbett notes, Rauf's idea of American values resonates powerfully with Newt Gingrich's advocacy for 'American Exceptionalism', which Gingrich attributes to its 'Judeo-Christian' origins.[40] Moreover, Corbett writes, Rauf argues that 'U.S. political and economic systems progressively evolved to fulfill Islamic norms.'[41] Rauf thereby presents America as a 'shariah-compliant' state and asserts the validity of Muslims embracing American values and norms.[42] Rauf's wife Daisy Khan, with whom he cofounded the American Society for Muslim Advancement, explains, 'All religions Americanize over time.'[43] Arguing that Americanisation does not compromise one's authenticity as a Muslim, Rauf and Khan name their project as the development of a 'culturally American expression of Islam' and promotion of Islam's 'essentials' that 'cut across cultural boundaries'—arguing for the Islamic authenticity of values such as secular democracy, religious pluralism and gender equality.[44] In turn, they advocate American Muslims promoting and exporting American values to the transnational *umma*.[45]

In the Bush and Obama years, constructions of 'American Islam' have emphasised Islam's compatibility with popular American ideals of desirable religiosity and constructions of gender. Moreover, this American Islam is presented as not only authentic in its religious claims but exceptionally authentic, a more genuine expression of Islam than the entire 'Muslim world' can offer. In the volume of essays entitled *Taking Back Islam: American Muslims Reclaim Their Faith* (2002), for example, we find assertions such as 'Islam in America is probably closer to the true teachings of the Prophet Muhammad than anywhere else at any other time in the last five hundred years.'[46] As American sociologist Mitra Rastegar has observed, such claims draw attention away from US interventions that have devastated Muslim-majority countries, as well as the scrutiny and surveillance to which Muslims are subjected within the United States.[47]

In 'Living on Borderlines: Islam beyond the Clash and Dialogue', American academic M.A. Muqtedar Khan (b.1966) argues that while 'the American Muslim identity has not yet stabilized', but remains highly contested, the experience of being Muslim in America has already 'compelled American Muslims to reimagine America and rethink their conceptions of the self'. Amid this reimagining, Khan argues, some American Muslims have started to develop a 'third identity'. Though accused of 'inventing an American Islam', they are proud to be both American and Muslim. These American Muslims, Khan suggests, are characterised by idealism, respect for human rights, concern for animals and the environment, economic and political liberalism, social conservatism, belief in freedom of religion and equal rights for all religious and ethnic minorities, self-awareness of their 'economic and political privileges', and hope for creating a 'model Muslim community' that would guide both Muslim-majority and Western societies. For the advocates of this third identity, the 'relative opportunity' to practise Islam and establish Muslim institutions within the United States, compared with the 'presently autocratic Muslim world', constitutes the 'most thrilling aspect of American life'. Celebrating this opportunity, Khan argues, American Muslims 'dream of making changes in Muslim attitudes as well as Muslim conditions so that their fellow Muslims can also learn the bliss of practicing Islam by choice and without any fear of the state or a dominant group'.[48]

The idealisation of a uniquely American Muslim identity, tradition and worldview—necessarily seen as impossible within, and liberated from, the outside 'Muslim world'—has appeared frequently in regard to questions of gender and sexuality. Multiple examples can be found in *Living Islam Out Loud* (2005), a collection of essays by American Muslim women under forty. In her introduction to the volume, editor Saleemah Abdul-Ghafur calls attention to the fact that none of the contributors are converts or immigrants: they come from diverse backgrounds, including the daughters of converts and the daughters of immigrants, but cannot 'remember a time when they weren't both American and Muslim'. In contrast to Mazrui's earlier diagnosis of American Muslims as either 'new to America, old to Islam' or 'old to America, new to Islam', Abdul-Ghafur authenticates these women via their equal footing in both categories, noting that they have been initiated in both the *juz 'amma* (the final thirtieth portion of the Qur'an) and Michael Jackson's *Thriller*. Because these women have been both American and Muslim for their entire lives, Abdul-Ghafur explains, they constitute 'the first true generation of American Muslim women'. Privileged as more naturally American than immigrants and more innately Muslim than converts, they represent the harmonisation of two identity markers into a third category, the American Muslim, for whom both US citizenship and Muslim faith are unquestioned birth rights.

Abdul-Ghafur defends the need for an 'American Muslim' construction against those who regard this identity as a departure from an essentialised, unchanging Islam and the guidance of its foundational texts. Not only is the American Muslim context different from the historical settings in which those texts emerged, she argues, but these texts are often offered to American Muslims through the mediation of un-American forces: 'Much of the Islam we American Muslim women know was defined and interpreted abroad, in the larger Muslim world. It is Islam fused with foreign culture.' Just as 'each culture has its own interpretation', she suggests, 'we in the United States are creating a distinctly American Muslim culture. American Muslim women are choosing a path that honors our Islamic faith and our American heritage without apology.' In addition, this new American Muslim tradition can have global impact, she argues, as 'Islam is in the midst of global transformation', which is being achieved 'largely by Muslims in the West', due to their exceptional freedoms that are 'largely unknown in Muslim-majority countries'.[49] While Abdul-Ghafur disparages influence from 'foreign' Muslim cultures as an unwelcome intrusion that American Muslims must overcome, she presents influence that moves in the opposite direction—American Muslims leading Islam's 'global transformation'—as redemptive.

One of the contributors to *Living Islam Out Loud*, Khalida Saed, offers reflections on what she presents as her tripartite identity of queer, American and Muslim. Saed came out to her Iranian immigrant mother at fourteen, and attributed her courage to do so to the 'American' side of her identity: 'I'm not sure I would have had the balls to discuss my sexuality at all, or even consider it, if my American side hadn't told me I had the right.' Saed's experience would alienate her from Islam until she encountered progressive Muslim communities. Saed defines 'Progressive Islam' as rooted in the belief that concern for social justice and opposition to discrimination are core Islamic values, while also naming this formulation as 'the branch of Islam that is distinctly American'. The bridging of her Muslim identity to her American identity simultaneously rescues Islam from her identity as Iranian: 'I realize that a lot of what I had been attributing to Islam is really a byproduct of my own culture. Patriarchy and sexism are not necessarily Islamic traits but are actually cultural traits. Realizing this has allowed me to give religion another chance.'[50]

Saed's differentiation between religion and culture, while resonating with al-Faruqi's vision of the United States as a place where Muslims could become culture-free and purify Islam, can serve to privilege American Muslim perspectives as taking place above and beyond culture. This is exemplified in the work of Republican author and self-identified 'Muslim feminist cowgirl', Asma Gull Hasan (b.1974). A member of the Hasan family that established the 'Muslims for Bush' organisation, Hasan has authored two books, *Why I Am a Muslim* and *American Muslims: the Next Generation*, and worked internationally as a representative of the US State Department. For Hasan, American Islam amounts to a 'new version of Islam' that arises when Muslim immigrants from various cultures 'mix' with American converts.[51] This mixture of cultures, she argues, will produce its own hermeneutic: Hasan defines 'American Islam' specifically as 'a return to the Qur'an without the influence of pre-Islamic Arab culture'.[52] Hasan then expands the problem of 'culture' to include not only pre-Islamic *jahiliyya*, but the diverse national backgrounds of Muslim immigrants. As mosques in the United States are likely to serve diverse populations, Hasan suggests, cultural differences will inevitably be washed away in favour of 'the only guidance they have that is not culturally biased: the Qur'an'.[53] Like al-Faruqi, Hasan marks cultural diversity as an obstacle to achieving scripturally authenticated Islam, and looks to a Muslim melting pot in the United States as the solution: a Muslim community with no culture, only texts. 'As a result,' she writes, 'I believe American Islam is a purer form of Islam than is practiced in some Islamic countries, because of the absence of cultural amplifications.'[54] Unlike al-Faruqi, however, Hasan does uphold 'American culture' as an acceptable influence on this otherwise culture-free Islam, asserting that 'American culture has influenced American Muslims to be better Muslims.'[55] The problem for Hasan, therefore, is not exactly the interference of 'culture', but rather the wrong cultures, those of Muslim-majority societies. In contrast, Hasan presents 'American culture' as an ideal lens through which Muslims can engage the Qur'an: 'American Muslims have reread the Qur'an from an American perspective, paying special attention to passages that emphasize American values—self-respect and gender equality, among others.'[56] For Hasan, the Qur'an must first be rescued from homeland cultures' destructive misreadings, then restored to its pure textual meaning, which means reading through the 'American perspective'. American Islam, which Hasan describes as both culture-less and grounded in American culture, becomes 'Islam's chance to prove its inherent compatibility with the West minus all the cultural baggage.'[57] Similar to Saed, Hasan has defined 'progressive Islam' as 'being Muslim and being American without a contradiction between the two'.[58]

While Hasan's liberal echo of al-Faruqi's 'culture-free' revivalist project resonates with her American exceptionalism, other writers have called for an Islam specifically rooted within 'American culture' as they choose to define it. Ani Zonneveld (b.1962), head of Muslims for Progressive Values (MPV), unapologetically declares, 'It's time for an American Islam.'[59] For Zonneveld, reports that most Muslims in the United States do not actively participate in their local mosque communities serve to demonstrate that these mosques cannot properly fulfil the needs of American Muslims. She locates the problem with immigrants who bring 'the cultural practices of Islam as defined by their "home" country', for such 'cultural practices, judgmental and rigid ... are unwelcoming to many American Muslims'. New converts to Islam, she argues, often grow alienated when they witness a gap between these 'cultural practices' and the 'mercy and kindness' emphasised in the Qur'an, while also facing pressures to 'conform to an Arabic culture' and change their names and clothing. The varying fortunes of the Ahmadiyya, Salafiyya and other international movements and networks among American Muslims are treated by Zonneveld as taking place outside of genuine American history and culture.

The answer to rising numbers of estranged and unmosqued Muslims, Zonneveld suggests, is the production of an 'American Islam—an Islam that fits in neatly into an American glove, to go hand in hand with our American traditions.'[60] The conditions by which this American Islam can be achieved, according to Zonneveld, include prayers in English, abandonment of 'all the foreign garb', the hiring of 'American Imams', and 'musical expressions like choirs that are not Eastern in scale or in language.'[61] In Zonneveld's view, the tragedy of African American Muslims is that they have no Islam of their own: 'I wish African American Muslims created an Islam that reflected their cultural and artistic heritage.' Zonneveld, a Malaysian American pop singer, defines the African American heritage as consisting of musical traditions such as the blues and gospel choirs, along with 'soaring sermons and humor'. African American Muslims who have adopted 'foreign garb' or studied Arabic for religious practice, Zonneveld suggests, have abandoned their distinctive Americanness. Zonneveld's logic of American legitimacy as measurable by clothing and language also disqualifies numerous non-Muslim practitioners, such as khalsa-observant Sikhs who wear turbans and Christian congregations that pray in Spanish, as properly American.

Throughout these discourses, we find that both immigrants and African Americans are problematised as repeatedly failing at both their Muslimness and Americanness. Gender remains significant for these double-pathologisations, as articulations of 'American Islam' frequently present gender equality as both an essential American value and a correct understanding of 'true' Islam. Such discourses tend to assume that a genuinely American Islam will always turn out to be liberal or progressive on questions of gender. To be a Muslim man and sexist, in this imaginary, is to be either foreign or under foreign influence, that is, to have surrendered one's American Islam for Arab or South Asian Islam. Constructions of American Islam often ignore the potential for sexism to be an American value—even an American religious value. The notion of American religiosity as inherently liberatory and inclusive on issues of gender and sexuality, needless to say, only considers a particular version of American religiosity, performing significant exclusions.

This blind spot also fails to consider the historical American intersection of gender and race. Sherman Jackson's argument that notions of Muslim hypermasculinity were in fact popular attractions for African American men to convert, regarding Islam as a 'haven of sorts for black manhood',[62] disrupts progressive Muslim narratives of the United States as an ideal site for the renewal of Islam's 'true spirit' of gender egalitarianism.[63] Constructions of gender found in a variety of American Muslim contexts represent what many would perceive as a less 'American' way of doing gender, despite their deep embeddedness in broader histories of American religion and masculinities, Black and white, Muslim and non-Muslim alike.

Great white Muslim hopes

In contrast to the frequent disqualification of African American and transnational Muslims as representatives of American Islam by their pathologised contexts, the privilege of white people in broader American society as 'non-raced' extends to privilege for white converts within American Muslim communities and discourses.[64] Being non-raced, the white convert is not subjected to the interrogations of background, context, politics, orthodoxy and culture that we have seen in analyses of African American and transnational Muslims: the white convert is widely represented as possessing unique access to Islam *as it is*.

Considering their relatively small numbers, white converts to Islam have been disproportionately visible as public representatives of Muslim communities in the United States. Foremost among them has been Hamza Yusuf, religious scholar and co-founder of Zaytuna College. Born Mark Hanson in 1958, Yusuf converted in 1977, subsequently embarked on a decade of religious study overseas, and returned to the United States in 1988, after which he began a rapid ascent to stardom. He has become famous for his skilful demonstration of 'traditional' Muslim scholarship (including the performance of his mastery of Arabic) and his ability to make Islam relevant and relatable in American contexts, significantly for American Muslim youth.[65] He has also been harshly critical of immigrant Muslims for failing to properly engage what he regards as classical Muslim intellectual tradition, while praising the ways that Muslims are welcomed in the West and maintaining that Islam 'confirms and enhances' the Enlightenment of which he self-identifies as a product.[66]

White advantage marks Yusuf's body as more essentially American than the bodies of Muslim immigrants. After the events of 9/11, Yusuf famously shed his turbans and robes for suits and ties, instantly restoring a body that might have been racially othered back into an invisible white body. Yusuf's post-9/11 rhetoric additionally indulged in xenophobic criticisms of immigrant Muslims; if Muslims wish to 'rant and rave about the west', he argues, 'they should emigrate to a Muslim country'.[67] Meanwhile, through his performance of 'classical' Muslim intellectual traditions, Yusuf marks himself as more authentically Muslim than his transnational admirers, qualified to inform them as to which of their beliefs, perceptions and practices are genuinely from 'Islam' and which ones are merely 'cultural'.

As a British Muslim observer remarked, Yusuf 'inspires confidence that you can build Islam in the west from all the local ingredients. You do not have to include political or theological burdens from traditional parts of the Muslim world.'[68] Yusuf is similarly unhindered by the burdens of American race history. Yusuf's whiteness marks him as more universally or generically American even than African Americans, possessing an Americanness that needs no qualifier.[69] As a non-raced, generic American (and human), Yusuf's journey to Islam does not appear as a response to his particular context as a white American (let alone a white American man, exempted from the 'Islam and gender' question that must be answered in women's conversion narratives). Rather, his conversion narrative unfolds as a seeker's quest for the capitalised 'Truth', inspired by his near-death experience in a car accident, which had led him to read an English translation of the Qur'an along with Shakespeare's *Midsummer's Night Dream*.[70] Whiteness allows Yusuf to dehistoricise and depoliticise his conversion narrative in ways that are not as readily accessible for African American conversion narratives.

Canadian scholar Mahdi Tourage has argued that in the culture of North American Muslim revival conferences, converts become fetishised for their capacity to exteriorise the inner condition of belief: like the object of a sexual fetish activating arousal, the fetishised convert as an object—through the ornamentation of language mastery, 'authentic' clothing and demonstration of classical training—serves to embody faith and thus activate faith in others. In addition, Tourage argues that whiteness itself becomes fetishised, as the white convert in particular achieves a 'hyper-performativity' of faith that makes him or her (especially him) powerful as an activator of audiences' piety.[71] In the case of American Islam as a construct, the white convert not only functions as a potent signifier of Islamic piety, but specifically embodies the possibilities for an American Muslim identity. Anxieties and tensions regarding religious authenticity and authority, orthodoxy, rationality, history, modernity, race, citizenship and Islam's relationship to the liberal Western state are resolved at the intersection of Islamic universalism, US exceptionalism and white invisibility, with a white man's mastery of textual sources as the ultimate personification of what it means to be American and Muslim.

Conclusion

> Islam does not require us to abandon our own culture for an alien culture in order to be Muslim. That is unacceptable cultural hegemony ... 'Islam in America' is its own entity, and it has to emerge as an indigenous cultural phenomenon rooted in the religion's permanent spiritual and ethical realities that are not subject to change, irrespective of time or place.
>
> Hamza Yusuf, Facebook post, 25 April 2014[72]

The above post from Yusuf's public Facebook page expresses a careful negotiation with the idea of 'American Islam'. Yusuf allows the possibility of an Islam that is 'indigenous' to America, in contrast to the demands of an unspecified 'alien culture'. However, Yusuf also insists that the indigenous American Islam must remain in conformity to a timeless, historically consistent Islam that stands beyond human culture. The assertion that true Islam transcends cultural particularities requires that no pre-existing homeland traditions are to be privileged in formulating American Islam. While resisting the 'cultural hegemony' that might be imposed upon American Muslims by 'alien' actors, Yusuf opens American Islam to an alternate hegemony, to be determined by those who hold proper claims on both Americanness and Islam.

Yusuf's oppositions of the indigenous to the alien and the religious to the cultural would resonate with visions of American Islam as offered by a wide spectrum of Muslims, many of whom disagree dramatically with Yusuf as to where these lines are to be drawn. In response to the above Facebook post, Ani Zonneveld posted, 'Nice speech from a man who changed his name, not to mention adopting clothing etc from one of Arab tradition.'[73]

As opposed to the 'alien' practices of immigrant-led communities, Zonneveld insists that a purely American Islam, more firmly grounded in domestic traditions, 'would have easily won over the hearts and minds of the masses'. This means that in Zonneveld's argument, African American Muslim communities ought to have performed the work of Americanising Islam, but have failed to do so. Zonneveld concludes that the necessary Americanisation of Islam only follows precedents found throughout the *umma*, in which every modern state apparently produces its own self-contained and hermetically sealed variant of Islam within its borders: 'There's a Malaysian Islam, a Pakistani Islam and a Chinese Islam,' she argues. 'Why not an American Islam?'[74] The consequences of her argument are (1) that this American Islam will be a singular entity, the discourses, practices and norms of which will be determined primarily by its relationship to the American state; (2) if a unique 'Pakistani Islam' actually exists but American Islam does not, we are to assume that this Pakistani Islam is too inescapably foreign to suffice as American Islam for anyone, including Pakistani American communities; (3) African American Muslim communities and narratives, having been infected with the contagion of Arab influence, are also inadequate.

Reflections upon 'American Islam' as a distinct tradition or possible future, treating both halves of that construction as measurable states of being, have pathologised African American and transnational Muslim communities as lacking authenticity in one category or the other, and often both. These discourses widely represent African American Muslims as struggling to overcome 'heterodox' traditions, lack of qualified religious scholarship, and an anti-Islamic fixation on race to earn recognition as 'real' Muslims, while immigrant Muslims are imagined as gradually assimilating to become 'real' Americans. Simultaneously, however, African American Muslims are often denied the privilege of being fully American, with representations of conversion emphasising social marginalisation, poverty and political radicalism, while their attempts to become legitimate Muslims through Saudi-influenced networks potentially undo their claims to authentic Americanness. Immigrant Muslims are in turn denied credibility as bearers of authentic Islam when homeland practices are perceived as riddled with heretical innovations and 'cultural' interference.[75] They are tasked with assimilating not only to broader American society but also to the diversity and new rules of authenticity in American mosques.

In such treatments, the hypothetical 'American Islam' is presented as attainable only when everyone universalises. For African American Muslims, this means transcending the 'holy protest' of 'Black Religion', leaving behind the legacy of 'proto-Islamic' movements such as the Nation of Islam and Moorish Science Temple, and somehow becoming simultaneously more American and more global. For transnational Muslims, this means abandoning homeland languages, dissolving their national backgrounds within an American Muslim 'melting pot', and rejecting traditional practices that have been marked as un-Islamic, thus arriving at 'pure' and cultureless Islam (as defined in American Muslim institutions). For this ideal of 'American Islam' to be realised, 'black' must become less Black, 'foreign' must become less foreign (or, as Zonneveld's advice to African American Muslims demonstrates, 'Black' and 'foreign' can preserve their uniqueness in ways determined acceptable by outsiders) and everyone must become more authentically 'Muslim'.

Largely absent from these discourses are considerations of white converts. The immediate explanation for this would be that in comparison to African American and immigrant Muslims, white converts lack numerical significance; nor is there a self-evident 'white Muslim community' or network of 'white mosques'. This response is reasonable, and attention to Latino Muslims and other identities becomes even more difficult to find in the 'American Islam' conversation. However, I would suggest that even as white converts have been largely ignored in analyses of American Muslim communities, whiteness remains consistently present in formulations of American Islam in ways that privilege white converts as its most desirable representatives.

White hegemony is so pervasive that it actually renders whiteness invisible, enabling white Americans to escape the mark of race.[76] The Americanness of white people is accepted as generic, simply 'American' and thus privileged over both Muslim immigrants and African Americans. The invisibility of whiteness means that white people, being generic Americans, also have an opportunity to be seen as generically Muslim: as an undifferentiated human, the white convert comes to signify a purely scripturalist Islam that is supposed to transcend all ethnic and tribal divisions. The white convert is assigned no context, no history through which his or her encounter with Islam is mediated. White conversion is not subjected to the acts of mind-reading that we have seen in numerous treatments of African American conversion, in which conversion becomes essentialised as a response to oppression. Without their experiences defined by the specific context of a 'white community' or 'white history', white converts are granted the privilege of being seen as individual subjects engaged in rational searches for truth.[77] Assumed to be cultureless,[78] the white American undergoes re-imagination as the pristine blank slate upon which 'pure' Islam can inscribe itself. Without the respective burdens imposed upon African American and immigrant Muslims, white American Muslims who successfully perform religious authenticity can possess all of the desired universals. White Muslims' comparatively small numbers may in fact help the power that they are granted as Islam's representatives: if the definitive tension in American Muslim communities is that between imagined binaries of 'African American' and 'immigrant' Islams, white Muslims do not constitute a party of their own, and can only occupy a neutral (that is, universal) space. As Amina Wadud notes in regard to Hamza Yusuf, white Muslims have the luxury of representing Islam as 'neither foreign nor black'.[79] To be neither foreign nor Black resonates not only with Islam's claim to transnational, transracial and transcultural universalism but specifically the ways in which particular Muslim identities have been pathologised in the United States, and also the historically dominant image of what it means to be fully American. 'American Islam', as it has been conceptualised over the course of several decades, despite the richness of variegated American Muslim legacies, thus seeks its embodiment chiefly in white bodies.

The prioritisation of white converts as ideal embodiments of American Islam has met resistance. At a Muslim revival conference in the final week of 2016, Hamza Yusuf alienated many Muslims with his dismissal of the Black Lives Matter movement, which he articulated with an array of anti-Black tropes (including references to black-on-black crime, apologetics for the

United States as having 'the best anti-discriminatory laws on the planet,' assertions that 'The police aren't all racist', and the complaint, 'It actually makes me a little sick to my stomach to see all these people rising up about ... white privilege'). Yusuf's remarks provoked an array of responses throughout online Muslim media, including criticisms that he was 'clueless' about systematic racism and functionally a white supremacist himself.[80]

Just a month later, amid mass protests accompanying the presidential inauguration of Donald Trump, artist Shepard Fairey produced and disseminated a new American Muslim icon: a portrait, presented in the style that Fairey made famous with his Obama 'Hope' icon, of a woman of South Asian heritage wearing the United States flag as her hijab. Muslim and American identities now achieve their confluence at the body of a Muslim woman whose hijab and unflinching stare into the camera simultaneously project both a confident expression of her Muslim selfhood and an assertion of her rightful home within the American empire. Fairey's icon of faith and citizenship, based on a 2007 photograph for Muslim magazine *Illume*, reverberates a prominent theme of the 2016 presidential election: the right to full Americanness of an immigrant Muslim family that sacrifices its son to the US military (in turn echoing Colin Powell, who addressed the 'Muslim question' during Obama's 2008 campaign by referring to a Muslim soldier's grave at Arlington National Cemetery). Transforming the material expression of American exceptionalism into gendered Muslim embodiment (and vice versa) presents American Islam as so secure in both its Muslim authenticity and embrace of US nationalism that the two become mutually coherent and inseparable, each serving an operation of the other. With his icon of a brown Muslim woman literally wrapped in pious patriotism, Fairey, a non-Muslim white man, fulfils decades of Muslim discourses that envision the best Muslim as also the truest American.

RESISTANCE

12

PRELIMINARY THOUGHTS ON ART AND SOCIETY

Sadia Abbas

Intimacies

Crisscrossing society, a *na't* (devotional poem), an abstract or a complexly iconographic yet 'realist' and very modern painting, and a contemporary *qawwali* (Sufi devotional musical form) may all be points of departure for the meditation on art and society that I will undertake in the following pages. Existing in unease and tension, open conflict, and happy proximity, these forms and performances invite us to think about society in a manner that does not sacrifice the connections between varieties of action that may appear to be completely disconnected, but which reveal intricate webs of consequence and connectivity. Putting them together in ways that are sometimes obviated by too faithful a following of disciplinary boundaries or artistic genres reveals the possibilities of proximity in our current age. The relationship between society, sociality and aesthesis is one axis of this closeness, an examination of which enables us to recognise the complexity of social constitutions in a variety of Muslim contexts.

Recent discussions of Islam, as manifested in the new anthropology of Islam represented by Talal Asad and Saba Mahmood and in the sociology of Tariq Modood, preclude such thinking, as they seem so antipathetic to aesthetics as to prevent any serious engagement with the subject and are greatly circumscribed by the politics of reception in the West. Overdetermined by a liberalism that such anthropology and sociology routinely critique, these discussions have simplified our understanding of many a Muslim life world. Perhaps because a number of conversations about modern Islam and aesthetics have arisen out of particular confrontations, such as the Rushdie Affair or the controversy surrounding the Danish political cartoons, they have engaged with questions pertaining to art and literature largely by focusing on the problem of free speech and the contradictions of contemporary liberalism.

In a 1990 essay on the Rushdie Affair, for instance, Modood argued that those who tried both to acknowledge racism and support Rushdie simply misunderstood the nature of the injury:

> 'Fight racism not Rushdie': the stickers bearing this slogan were worn by many in 1989 who wanted to be on the same side as the Muslims. It was well-meant but betrayed a poverty of understanding. It is a strange idea that when somebody is shot in the leg one says, 'Never mind, the pain in the elbow is surely worse.' Why should reference to the real problem of racism lessen religious pain?[1]

More than a decade later, Mahmood returned to the concept of religious pain in her discussion of the Danish political cartoons to explicate the confusion of liberals when confronted with moral injury and its consequent pain. Her diagnosis of the perceived stalemate, which may also have been a suggestion for a way out, was that the future of the Muslim minority in Europe depends on a 'transformation of cultural and ethical sensibilities of the Judeo-Christian population that undergird the cultural practices of secular-liberal law'.[2] In so doing, she exacerbated an untenable conceptual division between 'Judeo-Christian' and Muslim.

After the publication of *The Satanic Verses* in 1988 and the events that followed, Asad wrote two essays that manifested a scepticism, bordering on distaste, regarding literature and literary reading. This distaste could be said to have attained full-blown, if not entirely intelligible form in the essay 'Freedom of Speech and Religious Limitations' published almost two decades later in 2011. By the end of the essay—drawing a line from the Enlightenment and Romantic development of the concept of the author and the literary work to the relation of modernist aesthetics with paranoia—which is also for Asad the pathology of Islamophobia—he was able to suggest that modernist aesthetics, or perhaps aesthetics at large, give us Islamophobia. Along the way, Asad wrote passages such as the following:

> Modernism—the aesthetics accompanying modernity—engages with powerful feelings of visceral disgust. And it is in *mimesis* that modernism finds one of the most potent sources of revulsion and of paranoia, revulsion because modernism values only independence of judgment and despises imitation, paranoia because modernism seeks to penetrate disguises that make things (people, action, words) appear normal and innocent and shows them to be really meaningful and hostile.[3]

Although these lines do not indicate any serious engagement with modernism—their ostensible referent—they do work symptomatically to betray (or elicit) an antipathy to aesthetics. It is not possible here to reflect at length on the passage's presentation of modernism, but as a quick example it is worth pointing out that such a description cannot account for T.S. Eliot's notion of tradition in an essay like 'Tradition and the Individual Talent', his fascination with pre-Reformation Christianity as manifested in 'The Metaphysical Poets' or even his Anglo-Catholicism. My point is not to defend a high modernist such as Eliot, but to ask whether such accounts serve any identifiable purpose.[4]

A more explicit antipathy to aesthetics can be found in Mahmood's 2006 essay, 'Secularism, Hermeneutics, Empire: The Politics of Islamic Reformation', in which she argues that the 'hermeneutic of secularism', which is a hermeneutic of empire, is (perhaps fatally) imbricated with an 'aesthetic sensibility' overly reliant on Judeo-Christian poetic resources and fundamentally opposed to religious sensibilities. Mahmood identifies those who have such a sensibility as 'cavorting with empire'.[5]

Discussions such as those of Modood and Asad in the 1980s and 1990s regarding Britain's failure to integrate its Muslim immigrants, and the way in which such failures have revolved around literature and aesthetics, having crossed the Euro-American divide, have expanded and hybridised. What has emerged is a suspicion of aesthetics that can now be located squarely in the US academy in the 2000s. Since the discussions remain framed within a context where majoritarian sentiment is non-Muslim, and, in some cases, explicitly hostile to Islam, 'Muslim' itself seems to have become a category of alterity—seeming, in fact, permanently so. As a result, a Muslim majority, real in many parts of the world, seems inconceivable within the conceptual frames put forward by such writers.

Although it does not engage directly with the history of aesthetics, the new anthropology of Islam relies on critiques of Enlightenment and Romantic thinkers and accepts their claims in its general dismissal of aesthetics.[6] In other words, it accepts an identification of the author and artist with the free and autonomous subject, and of art and aesthetic performance as only constituted by the endless drama of the paradoxes generated by Western conceptions of freedom. At the same time, this new anthropology participates in a conversation in which Islam is construed as a problem for Europe, and is, in the process, turned into a flashpoint for a confrontation with the crisis of the very idea of Europe.

However, the accounts of the arts and literature implicit in such critiques of literature and the 'aesthetic sensibility' are overly focused on, and located within, the realm of Western liberal reception. Moreover, their overreliance, even if only in a negative delineation, on Enlightenment and Romantic notions of aesthetics and the subject has a question-begging quality, seeming to prohibit a more engaged and socially embedded understanding of art, in which art, aesthetics and literature are not simply abstractions to be invoked in the service of liberal and conservative self-congratulation, or left and anti-liberal excoriation, but can instead be seen as complex participants in the production of society.

The performances, poems and paintings referred to here may or may not slot into ongoing meditations on the history of (post-)Enlightenment aesthetics, but making them fit, or conversely, demonstrating their dramatic, contrastive distinctness is not the aim of this essay. To the extent that studies of aesthetics seek to bring all meditation on aesthetic objects and performances into the line of this aesthetic genealogy, they seem primed to become reflections on the crisis of Europe, stuck within a cycle of accusation, defence and even despair; they seem to bring, perhaps inadvertently, every conversation into a referendum on the idea of Europe, which is in turn a reflection on the idea of the integrity and superiority of the idea of Europe, of which the United States, through the notion of 'the West', is an extension.

Yet, when one shifts to the postcolonial context of Pakistan, perhaps the Enlightenment question that obtains most is the problem of the nation-state. Focusing on it as the apparatus for organising society that has tremendous consequences for historic life worlds enables a reorientation of some of the predispositions of current discussions of aesthetics and modern Islam. The performances and art discussed here open up the relationship of art to the state and to society in a way that enables some understanding of the intricate relation between history, aesthetic production and performance, and the apparatus of structures and discourses of power. For, even as certain performances produce communities of affect and socialities structured by a participation in social practices reliant on aesthesis, they can also rupture other collectivities precisely because of their implication in the state project.

Moreover, focusing on examples located within or emanating from Pakistan expands our conception of the realm of reception, which in the discussions I have cited often proceeds as if there is no audience other than a 'Western' one (thus inadvertently certifying certain Euro-American fantasies of centrality). It enables us to imagine artistic production in a way that is not artificially riven by the claims of religious orthodoxy or secular exception. Thinking about devotional aesthetics and secular kinds together provides a more nuanced view of contemporary forms of sociality in disparate Muslim contexts.

Finality

I will begin my readings, not entirely arbitrarily, with a discussion of a *na't*—a genre of Urdu devotional poem celebrating Muhammad, sung in often exquisite acapella rendition.[7] The *na't* is very much a living form, central, one might argue, to South Asian Muslim life worlds, recited publicly by men and women, especially at the occasions of festive piety that commemorate Muhammad's birth. The power and beauty of such recitations rely on complex techniques of harmony and melody that pull the listener into an affective community. The one that interests me particularly here is a version of 'Meri Janib bhi ho ek nigah-e-karam' (Cast a magnanimous glance my way), which is readily available on YouTube, performed by the very accomplished *na't khwan* (performer), Umm-e-Habiba, who is a significant presence in television performances.[8] She has appeared on Pakistan Television, the state channel, and on the popular television show *Aalim Online*, which airs on the private channel, GEO. *Aalim Online* is in turn hosted by the *aalim* (religious scholar) Amir Liaqat.

Prayer and petition, the poem Umm-e-Habiba sings works through a celebratory list of Muhammad's attributes. Part of the beauty of the performance lies in the way that petition, song and celebration are merged—turning performance itself into a form of prayer. In at least one of the performances for PTV, she sits with a deliberately chaste composure—a beautiful woman with a carefully draped *dupatta* covering her head. Her makeup is carefully applied and she presents herself with conscious dignity. The effect is powerful and at the same time purveys a deliberate aesthetics of modesty.

One of the terms used for Muhammad in the poem, and also its haunting refrain, is 'khatim-ul-ambiya'—the man who finishes the line of prophets, in other words, the final prophet, which is also translatable as the seal of the prophets. The refrain formally reinforces this finality as it closes every couplet, ending every new plea or list of attributes. Here are two exemplary couplets from the performance:

> Cast a magnanimous glance my way, O intercessor for humanity, seal of the prophets [the final prophet]
>
> You are the light of eternity, you are the flame of the haram [Kaaba], you are the bright sun, seal of the prophets.

> You wear the crown that God would not have created the world but for you, you alone have the distinction of the *meraj* [the visit to heaven]
>
> Islam's honour is because of you, O prophet Mustafa, seal of the prophets.

Yet strict Sunni Muslims belonging to certain groups (and often called Wahhabis in a general way) consider even such devotional forms *shirk* or idolatry, and such practices, which predominate among another group called the Barelvis, who are particularly associated with devotion to Muhammad, require increasing defence from their adherents.[9] At the same time, this devotional poem foregrounds a different problem, for its celebratory refrain is based on the doctrinal proposition that Muhammad is the last of the prophets, which is now central to the status and persecution of minorities in Pakistan. So, shifting discursive and formal registers somewhat, I quote from the second amendment to the Pakistani Constitution of 1973. As is well known, the amendment specifically targets the Ahmadiyya, whose origins, indigenous to South Asia, lie in nineteenth-century Punjab. The sect considers itself Muslim, but is said not to recognise that Muhammad is the last Prophet:

> A person who does not believe in the absolute and unqualified finality of The Prophethood of Muhammad (Peace be upon him), the last of the Prophets or claims to be a Prophet, in any sense of the word or of any description whatsoever, after Muhammad (Peace be upon him), or recognizes such a claimant as a Prophet or religious reformer, is not a Muslim for the purposes of the Constitution or the law.[10]

With this amendment, it is clear that the objections of Muhammad Iqbal, the 'spiritual father' of Pakistan, to the Ahmadis and his insistence on the finality of prophethood securing the boundaries of Islam have entered into the apparatus of the state, with substantial help from the late head of the Islamist Jamaat-e-Islami party Abul Ala Mawdudi and his followers. As Iqbal puts it, 'the integrity of Muslim society is secured by the Finality of Prophethood alone' and Islam 'cannot reconcile itself with a movement that threatens its present solidarity and promises of further rifts in human society'.[11] The objections Iqbal refined and certified surface in the amendment quoted above, as well as in two amendments of the Pakistan Penal Code and identity card and passport applications, in which Pakistanis are required to sign a statement saying that people who do not believe in the finality of prophethood are not Muslims. The attestation to the proposition is, in other words, a requirement of citizenship.

How this requirement is experienced may be evident in this brief excerpt from a speech delivered by Asiya Nasir, a Christian member of Pakistan's National Assembly, upon the death of Shahbaz Bhatti, the Christian minority affairs minister, murdered in the agitation that followed a bid to repeal Pakistan's blasphemy law: 'We know very well how to respect the final prophet and protect his honour. No minority could even imagine insulting the glory of any prophet.'[12]

Elsewhere in the speech, Nasir asks whether Pakistan is only a country for Muslims, as she says some 'extremist' journalists are suggesting, and whether Christians need to take up residence elsewhere.[13] Muslim notions of respect for the people of the book rely on the narrative that Muhammad completes history and supersedes the prophets who have preceded him—in other words, on the idea that other prophets are part of a prior history conceived as Muslim through an understanding of Islam as their teleological end. That a Christian feels obliged to assert this doctrine of finality in a speech raising the spectre of ethnic or, more precisely, religious cleansing reveals the great proximity and terrible tension in which the *na't*, the speech and the amendments exist.

The beautiful refrain of the poem, powerfully disseminated on the airwaves, is also the frame of a current problem of the state.[14] The state defamiliarises the refrain, revealing the propositional element in its proud celebration, reminding us at the same time of how this veneration of the Prophet can quickly turn into an instrument of the law. As the web of connections and references I have laid out suggests, and as I have argued at some length elsewhere, the doctrine of the finality of prophethood—fully entangled with religious affect and Muhammad devotion—has become a mode of securing the conceptual boundaries of the Pakistani state, as well as being one of the movers of state-regulated persecution and para-state carnage.[15]

Conceptions of an 'aesthetic sensibility' as the putative other of an uncontaminated Islam enable little by way of understanding the combination of devotional aesthetics and practice and affective community, which is also, in the case of Pakistan, the name of a violent fracture. Even as the state enshrines the proposition of finality, derived from habits of religious devotion, in the juridical structure, it cultivates para-state actors who are relentlessly iconoclastic and hostile to many of the manifestations of precisely such devotion, as evinced, for instance, by attacks on Sufi shrines and gatherings.[16]

Folds and borders

A painting such as Unver Shafi's *The Two Souzas* (6′ x 5′, oil on canvas, 2009, fig. 12.1) is hard to assimilate to the problem I have laid out. Yet it inhabits the same society and circulates within the same polity as the *na't*. After all, it is not uncommon for people from the middle and upper middle class to attend a *milad* (a gathering in celebration of the Prophet's birth at which *na'ts* are recited), go to an art gallery or collect such a painting. Moreover, given the success of institutions like the National College of Arts in attracting students from different classes, art is becoming more accessible across class lines, ironically at the same time as it is increasingly imbricated in a global economy of collection.

The Two Souzas is a painting that confronts the viewer with its powerful opacity. Distant from the 'realist' language of pictorial illusionism and representation, the painting does not have a recognisable iconography and seems designed to evade all semiotic stability and thus to be resistant to all discursive structures. The bold forms of the large oil appear to defy origin and be in the process of perpetual transformation; the latent shapes, which are both carefully defined and seem to be collapsing into themselves, appear ready to break out from the under the 'surface' of the deceptively tranquil monochromatic canvas. The blue of the painting invites the viewer to dive in, or refers back to so many blues, Moroccan, Turkish, Persian, implying that even colours are signs, conventional to the core, and that I am wrong to suggest that the painting can indeed evade being understood through discursive structures—even as its suggesting these associations reveals the arbitrariness of such a system, dependent as it is on the viewer's perception and the reliance of such perception on the perceiver's visual knowledge. Such knowledge may not help in reading the yellow-brown version of the same image (*Homage to Souza*, 6′ x 5′, oil on canvas, 2012), for that colour does not appear to have a set of nameable aesthetic associations. This is unsurprising, for Shafi says that he set out to paint a colour that was difficult to place, although he was interested in the khaki he saw in company paintings. When pressed to name the colour, he describes it as a 'grey toned form washed in umber giving the darker parts the greenish tint'.[17]

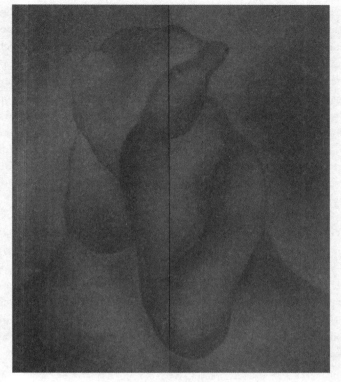

Figure 12.1: The Two Souzas

The problem of affect, citizenship and sociality so evident in the state's defamiliarisation of the *na't*'s refrain is taken up by *The Two Souzas*, which stymies a social and epistemic formation in which the salient language of understanding is the one officially sanctioned by the state. By the very fact of the title's celebratory reference to a Christian painter, the painting engages the state, defying its structure of mandated identities in which some are—in practice and legal effect—lesser citizens than others. It also refuses the erasures in which the historical and cultural affinities and proximities between those on either side of the partitioned border can be conjured away as it reaches across to Francis Newton Souza, who powerfully (re-)imagines crucifixions as inflected with an African imaginary usually associated with 'primitive' alterity in Western art, and whose provocation lies, at least in part, in his works' refusal of the racism of colonial Christianity.[18]

The painting's opacity (the way in which the shape(s) fold over, sinking into and rising out of their own blueness, seeming to militate against any possibility of division as they deny the cleavage of the two panels in the diptych) and its homage to Souza gesture across the border, refusing to let the state project and the violent history of Partition set the parameters of aesthetic community or of perception and affect. Form, reference and homage converge to become border-crossing gestures, aligning a temporal disruption with a spatial one. The division in the diptych plays with the clarity of division and of proposition by drawing a line through the remarkably infolded image. The fundamental formal reference to, in Shafi's own words, 'a common pictorial history', pushes against the violence of the cartography of Partition and the historical finality that borders seek to secure.[19]

The border-crossing gesture, present in both the painting's form and its title, is of a piece with Shafi's work in the *Fabulist* series, painted with acrylics, a series that plays with the idea of the miniature in the scale of the paintings (usually 6″ x 6″ to 18″ x 18″), as compared with the oils, which tend to be quite large, ranging from 3′ x 4′ to 8′ x 7′. At the same time, these paintings push against the state project in a different way, by reaching into regional aesthetics and forms—a pointillism that seems inspired by fabric dying and embroidery methods such as *chunri* and *makaish*, references to Hindu sculpture, a colour palette drawn from the Thar Desert or Rajasthan.

The Proposal (15″ x 15″, acrylic on canvas, 2009, fig. 12.2) and *Desi Wedding* (15″ x 15″, acrylic on canvas, 2012, fig. 12.3) present a dark eroticism and seem more obviously consonant with the hyper-sexualised imagery of Souza's corpus, even though Shafi's emphasis on beauty, and ornament and (complicated) joy in colour is very distinct. 'Complicated' is particularly apt in the context of *Desi Wedding* because, in that painting, colour itself seems complicit in the collapse the image figures, as shapes suggesting tongues and penises seem at the same time merely to be vividly colourful fabric patterns. In its combination of erotic violence and flashy colouring, the painting makes 'desi' weddings themselves seem like intensely coloured and overwrought events of highly metamorphic invasion.

In *The Anecdote of a Cat* (18″ x 18″, acrylic on canvas, 2014, fig. 12.4), these visual elements are brought into play in the service of an almost naïve visual world of children's storytelling and fable—the fish is now part of the cat and visually inseparable from it. Such playfulness is consistent with Shafi's tendency to collapse the borders between shapes and objects in his work, indicating his interest in metamorphosis and transformation, which has a profound

Figure 12.2: The Proposal

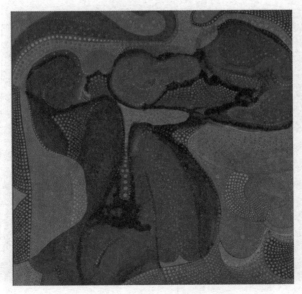

Figure 12.3: Desi Wedding

effect on his formal habits and affinities. At the same time, it is a reminder that a space like Pakistan, now entirely constituted by Islam in the Western imagination, in segments of the Pakistani consciousness, and certainly also in the state's conception of its citizenry, has all sorts of activity and interest that have little to do with it, even if such activity and performance can be invisible within current intellectual configurations.

Inverted iconographies

A formally distinct but nonetheless socially related set of aesthetic impulses can be found in the paintings of Komail Aijazuddin, whose work provides an

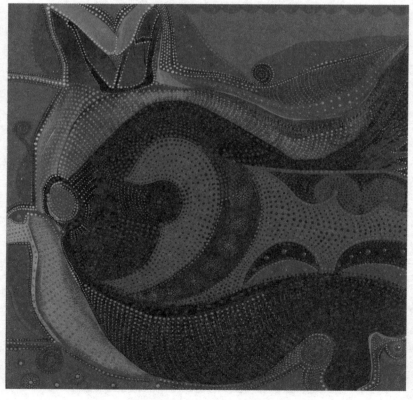

Figure 12.4: Anecdote of the Cat

exemplary instance of the formation I have called Cold War Baroque.[20] Cold War Baroque is an aesthetic formation that emerged in response to the cultivation by American and Saudi Arabian anti-communist and various third-world nationalist and postcolonial praetorian governments of intensely iconoclastic and anti-aesthetic brands of Islam. It is marked by the use of iconic theological ideas and narratives and varieties of profoundly visual iconicism. It is preoccupied with the layering of devotional and theological ideas and of the torn and suffering body and is often characterised by ornateness. The term can apply to the novelist Mohammed Hanif's *Our Lady of Alice Bhatti* and much of Nadeem Aslam's corpus. Here, I will focus on three paintings by Aijazuddin.

Although he is a young painter, Aijazuddin's body of work already provides a remarkably sustained reflection on the very idea of iconography. In some of his earlier paintings, such as the very poignant altarpiece *The First Majlis* (29.9" x 46", acrylic and oil on panel, 2011, fig. 12.5), Aijazuddin blurs the lines between the Abrahamic religions by combining the frame of the altarpiece with visual imaginings of scenes from early Muslim history. The symbolism of various traditions is powerfully juxtaposed, leading to unexpected fusions calling upon Renaissance, Byzantine and a variety of Muslim traditions of design, ornamentation and narrative. *The First Majlis*, for instance, cites the compositions of Renaissance triptychs and the dark colours and exaggerated movement of line in body, fabric and gesture of Baroque and Mannerist painting, painted in a consciously anachronistic manner. Aijazuddin's breadth of pictorial reference, and his deployment of iconographies that are both excessive and inverted, work against a state apparatus characterised by control of iconographies and an attitude towards history that is marked by a profound need to produce a social structure determined by the privative, in which identities and narratives that gesture towards a pre-Partition history are controlled and erased.

Aijazuddin's Zia paintings, a series in each of which Zia-ul-Haq's portrait forms a focal point, might as well be called *Nation and Icon*, for they figure the military dictator Zia-ul-Haq as iconic to some in the country, even as to others he is a reviled figure. More modern in composition than the earliest altarpieces, these six paintings (at least two of which are displayed on his website) present a dark and visually striking vision of power in the nation. Although the execution of the graphite portrait is disembodied and the graphite less emphatic than the red acrylic, in each of the 4-by-4 foot paintings, the much larger than life head of Zia in the background seems powerfully present, an authorising figure dominating, or even haunting, the world of the painting.

Figure 12.5: The First Majlis

Figure 12.6: Flagellation

The red acrylic wash recalls Shakir Ali's work, which Aijazuddin was sur-
rounded by in his youth (since his family owns a number of these paintings)
and, at the same time, makes the paintings seem bathed in blood.

In *Flagellation* (4' x 4', oil and acrylic on canvas, 2011, fig. 12.6), positioned
at an angle in the front right foreground is a man tied to wooden beams that
form a cross, being flogged by a policeman. The two policemen behind are closer
to Zia's face. One seems almost to be carrying a book of laws or rules. It appears
official, and he officious. The three policemen and the man being flogged seem
more embodied as they are painted in oils—almost as if in this blood-bathed
environment only the torturer and the tortured can be given their fully embodied form. The representation of the flogging is based on a photograph taken after
the Hudood Ordinances—in effect, a series of vice laws—were put in place by
Zia-ul-Haq.[21] The painting calls on the feature of icons that relies on the inter-
play between word and image; the name encourages an openness to linguistic
association as well. The opening up of a connection between the Roman
Imperial Guard and the militaristic apparatus—of which Zia was a product and
which he did much to strengthen—is precisely such an association. Though the
word *praetorian* is not used, it is implied by the iconographic tradition made
available by the titular reference to 'flagellation', which simultaneously foregrounds the Christic element and (along with the cross) implicitly connects the
Hudood Ordinances with the 'blasphemy' laws that have come to govern the
life of Pakistan's minorities and particularly its Christians.

State of Affairs (4' x 12', mixed media mounted on antique wooden balcony,
2014, fig. 12.7), painted a few years later, extends the question of nation and
icon in another direction: What happens when one puts the founder next to
an aspect of that which was founded? In the four-panel painting, Aijazuddin
turns his iconographic preoccupations to more overtly parodic use. Jinnah's
almost full-length portrait is placed in the second panel, flanked in the first,
third and fourth by scenes of sex, violence and one floating portrait of a scholarly girl, angled in such a way that that they exude chaos and clutter while at
the same time suggesting the choreography of fashion magazine spreads. The
dress and demeanour of the figures shows them to be upper class. The *alam*,
the hand of Fatima, brandished on a stick like a weapon in a medieval joust,
horizontally cutting across two of the panels, is free of its religious iconic
content, as is the crescent and star, here clearly lifted from the Pakistani flag,
made into context-less signs and visually equivalent to the floating and snaky
showerhead in the fourth panel. The painting combines the melting and dis-
integrating halos (the halo is one of Aijazuddin's favourite visual motifs) with
these excessive and almost violently context-less icons.

Figure 12.7: State of Affairs

Jinnah's portrait is also an icon, bestowing a talismanic, nationalist aura on those sitting below it in countless bureaucratic and political offices, or giving speeches on national television. Here, religious icons and the nationalist one combine to provide a parody of the ubiquitous phrase 'Jinnah's Pakistan'. The phrase can be used by a wide variety of people seeking secular protection or advocating secularism. In this painting, the degradation of a secular vision by the more Westernised and deracinated segments of the elite is ruthlessly satirised. Of course, a figure like Asiya Nasir, far from the social world depicted here, can also invoke Jinnah's Pakistan to claim secular protection. Yet the class to which Aijazuddin himself belongs is mocked for its disconnection from the ethical complexity and, given Jinnah's inconsistency on matters pertaining to religion, ultimate instability of someone like Nasir's invocation of Jinnah.

Devotion

In the very popular *qawwali*, performed by Nusrat Fateh Ali Khan, *Tum Ek Gorakh Dhanda Ho* (You are one tricky business), the breadth of prophetic and religio-poetic reference is large. Prophets from the three Abrahamic faiths and Muhammad's martyred grandson Husain are mentioned; allusions are made to heroic lovers of Sufi significance such as Shams, Sarmad, Qais/Majnun, Ranjha, Sohni, Mahiwal and Sassi.[22] The lyrics are replete with historical paradox and irony, as the poetic lover addresses God in an affectionate intimacy, employing the performative conceit that the intimacy of love gives the speaker/lover the right to marvel ironically at his ways, all combined within the context of a celebration of the wonder of Allah's ineffability ('You are your own veil').

Fundamentally a *hamd* (praise of God), the *qawwali* has elements of *man-qabat* (celebration of revered figures) and contains a reference to Muhammad's *meraj* that could be consonant with the celebration of Muhammad in *na't*.[23] At the same time, the lyrics also reveal an overlap with explicitly Shi'a devotional forms such as the *nauha* and *marsiya*, which commemorate the martyrdom of Hussain at Karbala:

> You sat silently watching in the heavens
> Muhammad's grandson in Karbala's scorching desert
> O how he gave his blood to the cause of fidelity/faithfulness
> Even though he had been thirsty for three days
> After all his enemies were his enemies
> But oh sadness that even you didn't provide any water.[24]

Despite the fissure between and even within sects created by the state's attempt to define the terms of a proper adherence to Islam, and despite its cultivation of para-state actors more influenced by 'Wahabbi' and iconoclastic Salafi ideology, the devotion to Muhammad crosses these genres.[25]

The references to Adam, Jesus, Moses and Jacob alongside Sarmad, Shams, Hallaj, Sassi and Majnun allow for a meditation on all of human history (as understood by the religion and its interpreters) pulled together by the conceit of love for and of Allah. Each example is presented as a puzzle regarding Allah's justice:

> Adam commits the crime and you punish his sons
> What a standard of justice and equity you have maintained.

> The messiah who revived the many dead is the very one you use to decorate the crucifix.

> When a man reaches the destination of spiritual ecstasy
> You make him say 'I am the Truth'
> You have fatwas of apostasy leveled against him
> And then you send Mansur [Hallaj] to the gallows.

The *qawwali* thus provides a meditation on history and justice, always emphasising divine omnipotence, but skirts theodicy by turning the mystery of Allah's ways into an opportunity for the lover to mention the examples of tribulation in a litany of ironically affectionate complaint. That is, a certain eschatological history of prophets preceding Islam and those who might be considered its inheritors is swirled into a love poem meditating on the beloved's mysterious ways. The shift is from an emphasis on the juridical impulse of an eschatological account of history to the paradoxes of history in terms of ineffability and transcendence. The hypnotic, repetitive quality of the *qawwali* performance reinforces the sense of mystery as the repetition allows the need for an answer, which might in narrative terms constitute a resolution, to be replaced by musical call, response and crescendo. The rhetorical device of paradox and the musical structure of the *qawwali* reinforce each other. Eschatology is subordinated to mystery.

Complicity

Despite the rampant circulation of 'liberal', 'elite' and 'secular' as epithets in current discussions of Islam, the divisions that are presumed to undergird 'liberal' thinking on the separation between religious and secular expression on matters such as aesthetics are accepted and reproduced in the use of these epithets and in the conceptualisation of aesthetics in many current discussions. My preliminary questions and juxtapositions are meant as an invitation to imagine different approaches and themes, and to raise some questions about current ways of organising discussions of aesthetics in contexts in which Islam is a significant or dominant element.

Placing these disparate artistic performances in critical proximity sparks some unusual connections. *The First Majlis* shares a certain affinity with the *marsiya*, and one could argue that its combination of altarpiece and *majlis* resonates with the list of God's beloveds who have suffered tribulation in the *qawwali*. The *qawwali*'s folding of a vast history and range of reference speaks in an interesting way to Shafi's completely abstract engagement with Souza on the one hand, and with the *n'at*'s devotion to Muhammad on the other. At the same time, following a thread from the *qawwali* to Shafi, one might remember that he has a painting called *Rumi's Onion* and that he likes to listen to Nusrat Fateh Ali Khan when he paints.[26] One might also be reminded of the further tightening of a world in which the market defines value and enables (and seeks to control) circulation.

If the *n'at* has been pulled into alignment with the state project and circulates within a juridical sphere authorised by the state discourse on the finality of prophethood and thus reveals itself as hegemonic, does it mean, given positions like Mahmood's and Modood's that require the transformation of the religious sensibilities of majority populations in order to accommodate minority ones, that Muslims in Pakistan should give up their devotion to

Muhammad and that, at the very least, this *na't* should be eschewed as a form? Nonetheless, it must be said that despite its imbrication in a very troubling juridical sphere, the *na't* retains its beauty, which is an effect both of its rendition and of the way in which both in the poem and, in such performances as Umm-e-Habiba's, prayer is turned into lyric. Moreover, a gathering such as a *milad* can be characterised by great beauty, festivity and is very much part of Muslim South Asian life worlds. Devotion to Muhammad is, of course, central to their constitution. Yet, such life worlds both overlap and sit in tension with other forms of South Asian and, specifically, Pakistani belonging and sociality. Thus devotion to Muhammad is also complicit with a dark juridical sphere. Does this complicity, then, necessitate that these life worlds be shattered? For how are such sensibilities to be transformed without the breaking of the life worlds they help constitute?

On the other hand, a painting such as Shafi's *Two Souzas* (whose painter manifests an unselfconscious class privilege and has so far demonstrated little interest in overcoming the very intense class hierarchies of Pakistan) is more readily intelligible than the *na't* as 'elite' and as part of a rather protected sphere of cultural activity.[27] It makes its way into the collections of rich people, clearly vigorous beneficiaries of neoliberal economies, but yet has an unstable place in relation to the state project—as do paintings such as *The First Majlis*, *Flagellation* and *State of Affairs*. Despite *State of Affairs* having been purchased by the young political dynast Bilawal Bhutto, the painting and Aijazuddin's corpus in general manifest an unease with the class structures of the nation. The state, on the other hand, is fully implicated in neoliberalism, which continues to consolidate and exacerbate those very structures.

The connections, overlaps and tensions laid out above are complex, yet the performances and objects I have described are neither reducible to their material conditions nor separable from them. They both contribute to the social situation, shaping its materiality, pulling their performers, creators, and audiences into crisscrossing communities, and elude and sometimes resist the structures—including the ones that they themselves might summon into being—that constitute the social situation. At the same time, their intersections and resonances call into question discourses regarding Islam that slice up society along neatly religious and secular lines in order to critique, and perhaps even transcend, a variety of liberal positions. That such discourses unwittingly reproduce the divisions assumed by the very liberal thinking motivating the critique is merely one of the ironies of the current intellectual moment. The sometimes counterintuitive connections that I have sought to make visible in this essay cut against the grain of such a bifurcated way of conceptualising society. Rethinking the relationship between varieties of aesthetic performance along less schematic lines enables a less truncated and more vigorous conception of society—alienating aesthetics from which does little to enable an understanding of society or sociality. Paying closer attention to how aesthetic production constitutes the society may, however, enable a more intricate understanding of the tensions, contradictions and intimacies of the current social situation, whether of Muslim minorities in the 'West' or of the populations in Muslim-majority countries like Pakistan.

13

THE POLITICAL MEANINGS OF ELIJAH MUHAMMAD'S NATION OF ISLAM

Edward E. Curtis IV

Known for its radical resistance to white supremacy, US foreign policy, black Christianity and the liberal dream of racial integration, Elijah Muhammad's Nation of Islam (NOI) was a prime target of US governmental surveillance and repression. Its very presence was perceived as a threat to the ideological foundations of 1960s US liberalism, which rested on anti-communism and the suppression of political dissent both at home and abroad, on the rhetoric of equal rights under the law and sometimes racial integration, and on federal welfare programmes.[1] Instead, the Nation of Islam advocated racial separatism, black capitalism, Afro-Asian solidarity and a cultural and religious identity that revolved around its unique understanding of Islam. Often aligning themselves, like other African American radicals in the 1960s, against US intervention in Africa and Asia, Nation of Islam members imagined themselves in solidarity with non-aligned leaders, especially the Egyptian president, Gamal Abdel Nasser.

The story of this small but important American movement is so 'marginal' to the history of modern Islam that it also exposes the 'vital centre' of Muslim liberalism, which in its anti-communist, nationalist and capitalist orientation shared a great deal in common with and was mutually constitutive of US liberalism during the heyday of the Cold War. The politics of Muslim liberalism were tied in no small part to the development, funding and institutionalisation of a missionary Islam that sought to oppose Nasserism and the non-aligned movement for which Nasserism stood as a symbolic centre.[2] The vesting of Islamic religious authority in revivalist and missionary organisations such as the Egyptian Muslim Brothers and the Pakistani Jamaat-e Islami and in the Saudi-financed Muslim World League became a tool to defeat the idea of non-alignment and neutrality across the Muslim-majority world—one that the US government sometimes supported.[3] The charismatic, prophetic authority of Messenger of Allah Elijah Muhammad may have offended the doctrinal imaginations of many Sunni and Shi'a Muslims around the world, but Muslim opposition to the Messenger was more than a matter of theological dispute. The Nation of Islam's radical politics questioned the very assumptions of the US-dominated world order from which Muslim liberals or those aligned with their interests, including Saudi-funded missionaries, were unable or unwilling diverge.

Despite its radical rejection of the religious authority of Sunni leaders abroad, the Nation of Islam's leadership did not advocate either violent or non-violent African American involvement in freedom struggles abroad (or, for that matter, at home). The Nation of Islam's leadership also appropriated and furthered what were, at the time, several other modes of liberalism: it policed its members' middle-class, straight sexuality; it embraced the dream of black capitalism and encouraged entrepreneurship; it used the US courts to argue for freedom of religion and framed its activities as such; and it forbade its members from engaging in violent revolution or even non-violent political resistance against many of the very liberal institutions that it identified as a religious evil. The presence of these liberalisms within the Nation of Islam renders useless any facile judgements of its radical or conservative nature. Instead, the meaning of liberalism and radicalism in the movement must be understood carefully within the overlapping political, social and cultural contexts within which the group operated. Rather than judging the movement liberal or conservative, this chapter reveals the ways that it preserved certain elements of liberalism while also challenging its multiple foundations—and how its political meaning changed over time.

The radical political challenge of Elijah Muhammad's Nation of Islam

After the Second World War, Elijah Muhammad's Nation of Islam emerged out of a pack of associations and movements founded during the interwar period to become the most popular expression of black American Islam.[4] Like most other African American Muslims groups, whether Sunni, Ahmadi or Moorish in religious orientation, the politics of the Nation of Islam linked the struggle for black dignity, freedom and self-determination in the United States to the struggle of people of colour abroad. The 1955 Afro-Asian Conference in Bandung, Indonesia, was a signal event for the group's most powerful political theorist, Malcolm X. As the chief spokesperson for the movement's prophetic leader, Elijah Muhammad, Malcolm X drew out the radical elements of its theology and doctrine, fusing them with third world non-alignment. He positioned the organisation as the US vanguard of the global movement not only to eschew colonial and neocolonial political control but also to rid people of colour of a colonised consciousness.[5] Unlike many black radicals who saw an alternative in communism, however, Malcolm X and his teacher, Elijah Muhammad, identified Islam as the solution to such problems.

During the 1950s and 1960s, Nation of Islam members would debate, define and engender this revolutionary notion of Islam in different ways. At least some members, especially Malcolm X, identified Gamal Abdel Nasser, the revolutionary leader of the United Arab Republic (the combined state of Egypt and Syria), as a model of Islamic engagement. Like others around the world, many African American Muslims and African American leftists more generally hailed Nasser's weathering of the Suez Crisis in 1956. Some members hung pictures of him in their homes.[6] In 1958, the year in which the UAR was formed and Nasser convened a meeting of the Afro-Asian Conference in Cairo, Elijah Muhammad cabled Nasser to seek his support for the group in the United States. In words that seem to have been crafted by Malcolm X, he urged Nasser to see their movements as branches of the same tree: 'Freedom, justice, and equality for all Africans and Asians is of far-reaching importance, not only to you of the East, but also to over 17,000,000 of your long-lost brothers of African-Asian descent here in the West.' While Nasser may have been seen as a threat to the vision of the political Islam advocated by the Muslim Brothers and eventually the Muslim World League, for some in Nation of Islam he was the perfect embodiment of the politically engaged Muslim.

The symbolic link between the Nation of Islam and Nasser was so strong by the late 1950s that it prompted Thurgood Marshall, counsel for the National Association for the Advancement of Colored People (NAACP) and future

US Supreme Court Justice, to denounce the entire movement in anti-Nasser-ite terms. Speaking at Princeton University in New Jersey, Marshall claimed that the group was 'run by a bunch of thugs organised from prisons and jails, and financed, I am sure, by Nasser or some Arab group'. The association of a domestic black Muslim group with a foreign power, especially with Nasser or 'some Arab group', was a serious threat, according to the US Federal Bureau of Investigation (FBI).[7] Marshall's comment indicated the boundaries of the Cold War-era liberalism that formed the basis of his case for racial equality. When the 'free speech' of the NOI questioned the foundations of the liberal consensus, the NOI could no longer be regarded as just another voice to be engaged in liberal society. Its speech had to be policed.

Indeed, the FBI had been conducting surveillance on black Muslim and other religious groups since the 1930s, and it had sought via legal means to repress African American Muslim identifications and possible cooperation with non-US groups and persons. A secret study called the 'Survey of Racial Conditions in the United States', code-named RACON, conducted from 1942 to 1943, sought to discover what it deemed 'foreign-inspired agitation among the American Negroes'. Its scope was so extensive that it included obvi-ously anti-communist groups such as A. Philip Randolph's March on Washington Movement, which sought to obtain jobs for African Americans in the US defence industry. The point of this investigation was to determine the 'source(s) of the rising tide of black resistance to the wave of racial dis-crimination unleashed by the national defense program', according to histo-rian Robert A. Hill.[8] But RACON also discovered the rising identification of African Americans with the Japanese Empire, a kernel of African American consciousness planted in the Japanese victory over Russia in 1905 that grew as some African Americans saw in the rise of Japan the possibility of their own freedom from white supremacy and domination. Among the various groups that eventually endorsed the war objectives of Japan were Mittie Maud Lena Gordon's Peace Movement of Ethiopia and Holiness pastor David D. Ervin's Triumph the Church of the New Age, both based out of Chicago.[9]

Though Elijah Muhammad may or may not have been associated with these groups, he did oppose African American participation in the Second World War based partly on the claim that the United States was not his nation—the *Nation* of Islam was. Elijah Muhammad refused to register for the military draft and was indicted on federal charges of sedition. Convicted of a lesser charge, the religious leader was imprisoned from 1943 to 1946. It was a pat-tern that the movement's luminaries would repeat over the following decades, as the leader's son, Wallace D. Muhammad, went to prison for refusing the draft in the era of the Korean War and then, most famously, Cassius Marcellus Clay—Muhammad Ali—refused to be inducted during the Vietnam War.[10]

By the 1950s, Elijah Muhammad's Nation of Islam had stood as a symbol of (non-violent) resistance to US militarism for more than a decade. But what started as a relatively small movement, one of many different groups that were cultivating religious, political and cultural identities grounded in alternative notions of black ethnicity, emerged in the postwar period as the most prominent and successful Muslim religious organisation among African Americans. It was becoming what historian Penny Von Eschen calls 'a space—for the most part unthinkable in the Cold War era—for an anti-American critique of the Cold War'.[11]

As a result, the FBI adopted more aggressive counter-intelligence techniques to try to repress the movement. FBI informants were either placed inside of, or recruited from, the ranks of the Nation of Islam. In 1956, J. Edgar Hoover, FBI director, authorised the wire-tapping of Elijah Muhammad's phones. In 1959, the intelligence gathered as a result of all this surveillance was then used in a systematic disinformation campaign against the group. For the next several years, the FBI briefed mainstream media outlets such as *U.S. News and World Report*, *Time* and the *Saturday Evening Post* on its various findings. Eventually, the FBI even turned to writing anonymous letters to Elijah Muhammad's wife about his extra-marital affairs. The point of the activities, according to a declassified FBI memorandum, was to expose the movement as a fraud and to create dissension in the ranks.[12]

But it was not only the FBI that was worried about the Nation of Islam, as Thurgood Marshall's comment in 1959 revealed. In advocating the establishment of racially separate social and cultural institutions and businesses along with a religion that preached black superiority, the Nation of Islam offered an alternative to the postwar liberal vision of a racially integrated country sustained by a strong welfare state. Liberals, both black and white, were deeply disappointed in the weak, watered-down civil rights bill that majority leader and future President Lyndon B. Johnson managed to pass through the Southern-dominated US Senate in 1958. Their top priority was a federalisation of the civil rights campaign, a bill that would provide the federal law enforcement necessary to end Jim Crow segregation in the South. After putting a Northerner in the White House in 1960, liberal hopes were high for more substantive civil rights legislation.[13]

The Nation of Islam was a useful prop in liberal politics at the time, in that it could be cited as the offspring of bad race relations, while also being played up as a threat to social stability. The fact that African American liberals such as Thurgood Marshall, Roy Wilkins and Derrick Bell, all of whom were NAACP officials at the time, so ferociously attacked the Nation of Islam indicates the depth of its challenge. This critique of the group was also adopted by the Rev. Dr Martin Luther King Jr, who named the Nation of Islam as the 'largest' and 'best known' black nationalist movement in the United States in his now-canonical 1963 'Letter from a Birmingham Jail'. King tried to make the threat plain to his white audience by arguing that domestic black nationalism would spill over into violence in the same way that political revolutions were sweeping through the developing world. He said the need for change was urgent. The Nation of Islam was thus appropriated, at times in apocalyptic language, as a symbol of what was to come—'the fire next time'—unless racial equality was achieved.[14]

The passage of civil rights laws in 1964 and 1965 did not, however, quiet the radical voice of opposition to postwar liberalism. In fact, both white and black youth began to amplify the call for greater social and political changes. For most African Americans, the passage of these laws did little to eliminate the presence of de facto racial discrimination—and even in the case of *de jure* discrimination, it would take years before Jim Crow segregation was dismantled through federal law enforcement and the courts. Various advocates of Black Power and eventually Black Consciousness began to adopt and adapt the rhetoric and programmes of the Nation of Islam, advocating black pride, community self-defence, separate schools, racially separate businesses, and perhaps most commonly, an opposition to the Vietnam War. Even as various aspects of the movement were rejected as insufficiently radical, Nation of Islam member Muhammad Ali's willingness to give up the heavyweight boxing crown and then to go to jail rather be inducted into the US Army became a symbol of dissent unmatched in the United States and around the world.[15]

As a result, the FBI still regarded the NOI as a major threat. In 1967, it increased what it described as its 'operational intensity' in counter-intelligence operations—called COINTELPRO—against the NOI. Targeting 'Black Nationalist-Hate Groups', the FBI sought, in Director Hoover's words, 'to expose, disrupt, misdirect, discredit, or otherwise neutralise the activities of black nationalist, hate type organizations'. In addition to relying on the surveillance and disinformation that it had conducted since the 1950s, the Bureau attempted to create dissension among movement members and spark conflict between the Nation of Islam and the Black Panther Party.[16] In some cases, the agency succeeded in eliminating various black activist groups, but the Nation of Islam, having dealt with government repression since the 1930s, was able to withstand the interference. Even after the departure of Malcolm X in 1964, the movement established new mosques, increased the circulation of its weekly newspaper, *Muhammad Speaks*, and expanded its sales of fish and bean pies.

During this era, the Nation of Islam was also a threat to the modern, reformist vision of Islam that many Sunni and Shi'a Muslims were attempting to promulgate in the United States after the Second World War. The dozens of Sunni and Shi'a Muslim American congregations that appeared across the country—from Ross, North Dakota, and Detroit, to New York City and Los Angeles—were eclipsed in the media and often the popular imagination by the Nation of Islam. This was partly a result of the disinformation campaign of the FBI, whose leaks to major media led to national press coverage. In 1959, after CBS News ran a Mike Wallace exposé on the movement called 'The Hate that Hate Produced', what had been a growing consciousness of the movement among African American communities was transformed. With Malcolm X's rise as a media figure in New York, his separation from the Nation of Islam in 1964, and his assassination, the Nation of Islam remained a 'good story'. It would become an even bigger story when US Olympian Cassius Clay won the heavyweight boxing crown and changed his name to Muhammad Ali—and then became perhaps the most prominent face of global protest against US involvement in the Vietnam War. While Muslim groups not associated with the Nation of Islam succeeded at building political ties and social influence at the local level in places such as New York City, Detroit and Toledo—and among the diplomatic corps in Washington, DC—there was little doubt that in the 1960s most Americans who had heard of Muslims equated them with the 'Black Muslims', that is, the Nation of Islam.

There was fascination with and simultaneous repulsion felt by many Sunni and Shi'a Muslim leaders in the United States and abroad with the Nation of Islam's unorthodox teachings, which included a belief in the divinity of Nation of Islam founder W.D. Fard and the prophecy of the Messenger from Georgia, Elijah Muhammad. In addition to foreign leaders such as Gamal Abdel Nasser, some American Muslim leaders were interested in cultivating ties to and making alliances with the Nation of Islam. For some, the NOI represented a business opportunity. Among them was the Pakistani entrepreneur Abdul Basit Naeem, who downplayed the difference between his Sunni Islamic commitments and the theology of the NOI as he used his magazine, *The Moslem World and the U.S.A.*, to 'introduce Muhammad to the "Moslem" world' in the mid-1950s.[17] For others, the NOI represented a popular Muslim movement whose 'heretical' theology must be challenged gently and at times set aside for the sake of Muslim American political unity. In 1972, for example, Muhammad Abdul-Rauf, the director of the Islamic Center in Washington, DC, appeared at an NOI rally against police violence in New York, praising the accomplishments of Elijah Muhammad and stressing the unity of all Muslims abroad with Muslims in the United States.[18]

But for many local leaders of Muslim congregations, especially African American leaders of Ahmadi and Sunni congregations, the success of Nation of Islam as perhaps the best organised, the best funded and the most popular Muslim organisation in the United States was frustrating, even maddening at times. The same was true for American-born and foreign-born missionaries who were associated with the South Asian-based Tablighi Jama'at, the Egyptian-based Muslim Brothers, and the (Saudi-funded) Muslim World League. The Nation of Islam accounted for almost half of all operating Muslim congregations in the United States, and its budget, though secret, was likely in the millions of dollars by the 1960s. Upon Elijah Muhammad's death in 1975, he was estimated to be worth tens of millions. Its weekly newspaper, *Muhammad Speaks*, had a circulation in tens of thousands, if not the hundreds of thousands—making it one of the most read black newspapers in the country. By the 1960s, the Nation of Islam's competitors launched a variety of attacks against the legitimacy of Elijah Muhammad and the Nation of Islam. The intellectual machinery of the Nation of Islam responded with a vigorous defence of the Messenger's Islamic authenticity while also seeking through aggressive street recruiting to maintain a rate of congregational growth that most Muslim American organisations could only envy.[19]

The strong institutional presence of the Nation of Islam translated into a threat for the hegemony of modern, reformist and ultimately liberal visions of Islam. Its very structure, a Muslim organisation based not so much on authoritative readings of the Qur'an and the Sunnah as on the prophetic authority of a man from Georgia who lacked formal education, Arabic literacy and traditional Islamic credentials, was revolutionary. It created a new source of mystical, charismatic Islamic authority during a time in which Islamic reform and renewal groups such as the Muslim Brothers and the Jamaat-e Islami were challenging the legitimacy of such authority. Moreover, the Nation of Islam's interpretation of Islam as a religion of black liberation contradicted the liberal notion, then in its ascendency, that Islam was a religion that eliminated racial prejudice. It is no wonder that liberals and even some leftists, Muslim or not, reacted in an apoplectic manner to the group's teaching. Figures ranging from the nineteenth-century Liberian nationalist Edward Wilmot Blyden and Indian Ahmadi missionary Muhammad Sadiq to historian Arnold Toynbee and Islamic Center of Geneva Director Said Ramadan were agreed: Islam was the most anti-racist religion in the world.[20] The Nation of Islam concurred, but went further, articulating an Islamic theology of black chosen-ness that rejected the desirability of integration. Finally, the Nation of Islam's anti-American critique was a position that, at the time, was undesirable to many doggedly anti-communist reformers. Instead, the Nation of Islam allied itself and its Islamic teachings with third world revolutionaries and the non-aligned movement.[21]

The liberal/conservative side of the NOI

Even as the Nation of Islam challenged a postwar liberal world order linked to US military power, Euro-American proxy wars in the third world, white supremacy and Christian identity, it also advocated and enforced deeply conservative elements of American culture among its membership. In the 1950s and early 1960s, Elijah Muhammad's Victorian and heteronormative approach to human sexuality and gender relations did not distinguish his movement from many other religious groups, whether conservative or liberal. For example, until the late 1960s and the 1970s, the mainstream liberal position in American religious organisations on matters of women's reproduction rights was not very different from the conservative one. At the very least, the gap between liberal and conservative religionists widened as conservatives identified the 1973 *Roe v. Wade* decision, which effectively defined abortion as an individual right of women (during a certain period of time during pregnancy), as a key issue for the practice of Christianity and other religious traditions in the United States.[22]

Throughout this period, young and old leaders of the Nation of Islam remained committed to conservative notions of gender and sexuality. The official gender and sexual ethics of the Nation of Islam were derived from the prophetic pronouncements of Elijah Muhammad, but they were informed by a much older politics of respectability. Ascendant in Elijah Muhammad's youth, the link between respectability and Victorian constructions of the black body responded to the physical and emotional harm that black people in the United States faced during so-called nadir in race relations from 1880 to 1920. Its main idea was to protect the black body from lynching and job discrimination by making it 'respectable'. Also called civilisationism, this important aspect of African American religious and secular culture emphasised the need for the black body to be morally clean, pure, strong, well dressed, disciplined, chaste and industrious. Men and women had distinctly different roles in the ethical system that was anchored in these bourgeois, Victorian assumptions. Appropriating these old values under a new religious teaching called Islam, Elijah Muhammad managed to reinterpret the conservative nature of such ethics for his followers. Clothing these ethics as the embodied aspect of Islam was itself transgressive of the US nationalist and Christian identity to which middle-class black respectability aspired.[23] But it was also conservative. As Darlene Clark Hine points out more generally of Afrocentrism, it 'blurs easy distinctions between conservative and radical because it fosters liberation *and* fuels essentialism, empowers people *and* polices boundaries'.[24]

Both in oral history interviews reflecting back on the late 1960s and the early 1970s and in documents from the time, hundreds of women went on record to say that they liked the conservative ethics of the movement. At the same time that many second-wave feminists criticised the movement as horribly sexist, these women praised multiple aspects of the group's Islamic ethos. Some wanted brother members to protect them from violence. Others sometimes referred to themselves as 'queens', and wrote poems praising the head scarves and flowing gowns that adorned their royal bodies. Male members often made sure that women got home safely from organisation meetings and in some places the threat of male retribution acted as a deterrent against potential sexual and physical abuse. In addition, many women praised how men in the Nation of Islam were held to a high moral standard. Those who had sex outside of marriage were put on trial and shunned. Men were also required to give up alcohol and were told that they had the financial responsibility to support their families. White women were often depicted as temptresses in official Nation of Islam literature—and Malcolm X, who had once dated white women, alluded to black male desire for white female partners as a form of black male psychosis. All of these aspects of Elijah Muhammad's ethics were cited by many black women in the movement in favourable terms. For many female members, such conservative values, when enacted by the men in their lives, often felt liberating.[25]

At the same time, men and women in the movement challenged or subverted some of the conservative rules that they found oppressive. For young male jazz fans in the Nation of Islam, the prohibition against intoxicants did not always apply to the use of marijuana in spaces outside the gaze of local movement leaders. Elijah Muhammad's condemnation of musical performance in the mosque was often ignored, as various mosques had de facto jazz groups and hosted various concerts. By the late 1960s, many younger men and women in the movement were also experimenting with Afrocentric styles of dress, prompting Elijah Muhammad to issue a stern warning to Muslim women wearing dashiki tunics and Afrocentric head wraps (*jejes*).[26]

In addition, some women ignored the prohibition against the use of birth control. Tubal ligations and birth control pills alike were seen by the movement's leadership as existential threats to the black race. Such fears were not irrational. State medical authorities still sterilised significant numbers of black, poor and disabled women without their consent into the 1970s. Like other black activists of the time, Elijah Muhammad saw the spread of widely available birth control as potential racial genocide. Since unmarried men and women in the movement were not supposed to have sex outside of wedlock in any case, various columnists for the movement's newspaper instead offered advice on how to control and channel sexual desire into spiritual activities. If the unmarried member was unsuccessful in so doing, and he or she was caught, prosecution and ostracism would result. Contrariwise, married women were expected to be sexually active with their husbands, but they also often used some form of birth control to control the size of their families. Some said that it was matter of life and death, or that their physicians advised them that having additional children could be dangerous to their health. Women made such decisions on a case-by-case basis, showing that the conservative edicts of their prophet were reinterpreted, transformed or violated in daily life.[27]

Gender and sexuality was not the only area of movement activity that contained such contradictions or complexity. The use of the US legal system to defend the individual rights of members was yet another strategy that contained both liberal and radical elements. The refusal of movement members to be inducted into the US armed forces was radical in that it explicitly challenged US patriotism and the social contract of US citizenship. But when it came time to defend members from prison, the strategies of their lawyers was to make First Amendment claims that their clients were simply practising their freedom of religion. In the case of Muhammad Ali, the argument was that since his religion prohibited participation in offensive war, he should be granted conscientious objector (CO) status. It is worth noting here that the religion to which the lawyers were referring was not Sunni Islam, but the interpretation of Islam revealed by the Messenger Elijah Muhammad—an interpretation of Islam that allowed for only personal self-defence. Their claim to CO status was reasonable, though it was ultimately denied in Ali's case. Ali eventually won his case on appeal, but the 1971 decision was made by the US Supreme Court on technical grounds, avoiding the larger issue of whether Ali was entitled to CO status.[28]

The use of the US state and federal courts to protect the individual rights of Nation of Islam members was not an isolated one. In fact, from the perspective of US legal history, the far more consequential use of the courts in this manner was in the area of prisoners' rights. Muslim prisoners wished to gather for religious meetings, read religious literature, receive visits from Muslim ministers (which is what they were called in the Nation of Islam), eat pork-free food and celebrate religious holidays such as Ramadan (which was celebrated in the Nation of Islam during Yuletide rather than during the Islamic month of Ramadan). Unlike *Clay v. United States*, some of the rulings issued with regard to these issues became precedent-setting, thus influencing the history of US jurisprudence with regard to all prisoners. Among the precedent-setting cases involving members of the Nation of Islam was *Fulwood v. Clemmer*, a case decided by the US District Court for the District of Columbia in 1962, which ruled that prisoners had the right to wear religious medals and attend religious services. That same year, the New York State Court of Appeals said in *Brown v. McGinnis* that members of the Nation of Islam had the right to sue for their religious liberty in state courts. Finally, and most importantly, in 1964 the US Supreme Court ruled in *Cooper v. Pate* that members of the Nation of Islam had 'standing' or the right to sue prison officials in federal courts for religious discrimination. The ruling came as a blow not only to prison officials who hoped to effectively ban the Nation of Islam but also to law enforcement agencies, especially the FBI, which had been arguing since the 1950s that the Nation of Islam was not a legitimate religion, but a political movement. This was also the argument of the State of Illinois, which lost the case. This precedent thus limited, for the time being, the use of the courts in the attempts of both federal and state officials to retard the growth of the Nation of Islam—from now on, the movement would have to be considered a legal religious organisation in any dispute that became a subject of litigation in the US courts.[29]

While such victories by the Nation of Islam increased their standing in the eyes of the law and also among liberals outside the movement, the group's reliance on the discourse of individual rights seemed to be a capitulation to the very nation from which they were seeking a separate identity. Relying on the US legal system lent legitimacy to the state, and perhaps most importantly, led Nation of Islam members to rehearse the social contract of liberalism at the heart of US nationalism. By the 1970s, some Nation of Islam members under the new leadership of W.D. Mohammed would become flag-waving US patriots, and one wonders if the habituation of organisation members in the 1960s into the legal promise of liberalism did not in fact prepare the political ground for the sudden appearance of US nationalism among people who were dissenters in the 1960s. Perhaps, however, the use of the courts was ultimately cynical, a tactic that was appropriated not out of devotion to the individual rights tradition but as a means to strengthen their organisation and protect its members from harm.

While the Nation of Islam's interaction with the US legal system can be interpreted in a variety of ways, there was another component of the Nation of Islam's ideology and practice that seemed unambiguously, even classically liberal—namely its belief in free markets and the encouragement of black capitalism. First, Elijah Muhammad taught that thrift, industriousness, capital investment and accumulation, punctuality—in short, the values of modern industrial capitalism—were part of Islam. Professionals such as the dentist Leo McCallum were lauded for their knowledge and success, while working-class members often aspired to become small business owners. The social networks of members in each city created both a consumer market and an internal sales force for various goods, and the movement became known for its entrepreneurial spirit. Decades after the heyday of the Nation of Islam, the organisation is remembered across urban America for its sales of the bean pie—which allowed women in the Nation of Islam to supplement family incomes by baking pies in their home kitchens and then selling them in or immediately outside the mosque or asking their male relatives to do so on various street corners. In addition, members of the Nation of Islam established bakeries, restaurants, barber shops and other small shops, often in the same neighbourhood or even street on which the mosque was located. Before they achieved success as small business owners or managers, younger men in the movement often spent time selling their quotas of *Muhammad Speaks* newspaper, becoming known in urban black neighbourhoods and along busy streets for their aggressive, but polite salesmanship.[30]

In addition to serving as an incubator of small business, the Nation of Islam itself became big business. Or more accurately, Elijah Muhammad became a big businessman. By the early 1970s, Elijah Muhammad owned a small bank, a dairy, a meat processing plant and farms in Georgia, Michigan and Alabama.

In 1974, the year before his death, he also launched a fish import business, Whiting H and G (headed and gutted). All of these businesses benefited from the internal markets and built-in sales forces for their goods. The fish could be sold by the same young men who hawked the newspaper. Movement members and the general public were encouraged to purchase their groceries and baked goods from Muslim-owned stores that were supplied by Elijah Muhammad's farms, dairy, and meat processing plant.

The focus on foodstuffs in this vertically integrated, multi-million dollar empire reflected Elijah Muhammad's ethical teachings about the black body. The prophetic pronouncements that commanded members to practise values of sexual discipline, healthy eating, good hygiene and respectable dress were joined by demands that one become economically productive, whether at home or in the marketplace. So, in addition to studying the lessons of the Prophet, attending temple meetings and fishing for new members, Nation of Islam families sought to exhibit their commitment to Islam through market-oriented activity. In Elijah Muhammad's view, this productivity and capital accumulation was supposed to lead to some degree of self-determination in a white-dominated marketplace. Elijah Muhammad did not critique the techniques and rules of capitalism; he sought to get his own piece of the pie. In so doing, Elijah Muhammad replicated the capitalist ideologies of past leaders such as Booker T. Washington and Marcus Garvey, who framed black liberation at least partially in terms of black capitalism. As with the Nation of Islam's use of the US legal system, the advocacy on entrepreneurial and petit-bourgeois economic activity no doubt aided some individual members of the organisation and stood as a psychological and symbolic victory over ideas of black inferiority and generational poverty.[31]

Any economic revolution, however, would have to wait in Elijah Muhammad's prophetic worldview for the apocalypse. Elijah Muhammad had taught from the 1940s, if not before, that at the end of the current dispensation of world history a Mothership would appear in the sky and destroy white people or perhaps simply white supremacy. Blacks would become the rulers of the planet, a position they had once held when the Tribe of Shabazz ruled the Holy City of Mecca. Until then, the Messenger taught, Muslims should reform themselves morally, separate from whites, and work for economic success. While such teachings may have helped to redirect any political or economic revolutionary impulses among members of the movement, they did not stand in the way of the movement's focus on worldly success. Elijah Muhammad told his followers to live their lives in the here and now, rather than wait for their reward in Heaven. Heaven and hell, he preached, were states of mind on earth, not separate worlds to which one goes after death.[32]

By the late 1960s, these teachings came under fire from many younger activists in the Black Power movement for its lack of revolutionary ideology and action. While groups such as the Black Panthers Party clearly built on the notions of black identity that the Nation of Islam had popularised, many of its members expressed the same frustration with the organisation that Malcolm X had felt during the early 1960s. Critiques of the Nation of Islam did not focus on its radical symbolic protest of white supremacy, US nationalism, US foreign policy or Christianity—in fact, those critiques would be adopted and adapted by an increasing number of African Americans—but rather on the non-violent, insular and politically quietistic nature of the movement. In addition, Islam itself became an object of scorn by various cultural nationalists or Black Consciousness advocates who cast Islam and Arabs as foreign to the African continent and African people. This was a period of African American history characterised by greater interest in African languages such as Swahili, devotion to African deities such as the Orisha, and in various forms of clothing and food inspired by what were seen as authentic African traditions, sometimes in distinction from Muslim cultural practices. In 1971, Black Panther Party Prime Minister Stokely Carmichael argued, for example, that Islam was barbaric, and that Arab armies had brought it and the slave trade to Africa. That same year, writer Chancellor Williams issued a similar indictment of Islam and Arabs, identifying them as conspirators in his *Destruction of Black Civilization*.[33]

These critiques of the movement help to identify the shifting political ground on which it stood, fairly immoveable, for decades. The movement's teachings, once regarded by large numbers of both black and white Americans as a radical assault on the ideological foundations of American culture during the era of the liberal consensus in the 1950s and 1960s, seemed politically quietistic or insufficiently 'black' by the 1970s. The movement also began to look different to some of the same liberals who in the early 1960s saw it a threat to the promise of civil rights. When Elijah Muhammad died in 1975, for example, a *New York Times* editorial praised the leader for his ability to reform the lives of those whom federal programmes had been unable to help and for his contributions to the black pride movement.[34] By the 1970s, when Alex Haley's *Roots* became a national bestseller, it seems that even the stark black separatism of the Nation of Islam could be viewed as yet another form of ethnic revival and heritage.[35]

The movement would split into two major groups after its Messenger's death. The more popular branch, led by Elijah Muhammad's son, W.D. Muhammad, changed the name of the group to the World Community of al-Islam in the West, and later to the American Muslim Mission and the American Society of Muslims. Muhammad considered himself to be a *mujaddid*, or renewer of the faith, and oversaw a Sunni reformation of the once prophetic movement. He replaced the charismatic authority and revelations of his father with the scriptural authority of the Qur'an, and to a lesser degree, the Sunnah. The new organisation allied itself with Sunni religious authorities across the Muslim world and especially with those associated with the Muslim World League. W.D. Muhammad retained his independence from foreign-born American Muslim leaders and foreign missionaries, but helped to broadcast a liberal version of Islam that was thoroughly in support of US patriotism, global capitalism, and eventually, US involvement in the First Gulf War.[36]

Minister Louis Farrakhan formed the other major branch of the post-Elijah Muhammad Nation of Islam in reaction to these Sunni reforms. Farrakhan announced by 1978 that he would resurrect Elijah Muhammad's teachings. Farrakhan retained all components of the Nation of Islam outlined above, but also incorporated more and more Sunni teachings into his pronouncements. Eventually, some Nation of Islam congregations would perform *salat*, the five daily prayers of Sunni and Shi'a Muslims, and benches would be taken out of some mosques. Farrakhan became arguably more radical than Elijah Muhammad in his association with non-aligned, often explicitly anti-US leaders such as Mu'ammar Qaddafi.[37] Like a notable number of leaders in sub-Saharan Africa, Farrakhan supported Qaddafi until the bitter end. He did not relinquish his focus on black separatism in the United States nor did he soften his critique of anti-black racism; his philosophy of economics was decidedly capitalist.

Conclusion

The changing ways in which the Nation of Islam was viewed, and by whom, offer helpful indices by which the evolving meaning of liberalism in the United States during the twentieth century can be evaluated. The Nation of Islam was regarded as so counter-cultural that it exposed the nature of what historian Arthur Schlesinger Jr in 1949 dubbed the 'vital center', that is, the liberal Western alternative to communism and socialism. Regarded as seditious by the FBI during the Second World War and prosecuted as such, the Nation of Islam became merely subversive, but even more dangerous to law enforcement agencies by the 1950s and 1960s. Though law-abiding and largely non-violent, the Nation of Islam encouraged a moral and political geography among black Americans that denied the legitimacy of claims by both the nation-state and the Christian Church to the loyalty of African Americans. In the United States, black liberals were as likely as white liberals to condemn the racial separatism of the movement, which was seen as a threat to and negation of the dream of a racially integrated society. Foreign Muslim students and many domestic Muslims outside the Nation of Islam criticised the movement as religiously illegitimate. But beyond the borders of the United States, third world revolutionary leaders, including Muslims in Africa and Asia, came to see the Nation of Islam, especially in the persons of Malcolm X and Muhammad Ali, as potential allies in their attempts to throw off a colonised consciousness and oppose US foreign policy in their countries and regions.

While this aspect of Nation of Islam politics remained a radical component of the movement under the leadership of Elijah Muhammad and later Louis Farrakhan, other elements of the movement came to be seen as increasingly conservative by black liberals and radicals in the 1970s. The emphasis on Victorian gender relations was sometimes framed as reactionary, while the endorsement of Islam over African traditional religion was at times seen as a form of black self-hatred. For black socialists, it goes without saying that the Nation of Islam's enthusiastic endorsement of capital accumulation and petit-bourgeois behaviours was anathema. Strangely enough, by the 1970s many American liberals had found something in the movement to respect. The fact that its one-time critics had become at least partial admirers shows how much US politics, both liberal and conservative, had begun to change. In the aftermath of Vietnam and the Watergate scandals, the Nation of Islam's essential distrust of the US government was widely shared by US citizens. More and more mainstream citizens saw their government as hypocritical and became cynical about its prosecution of dissenters. The Nation of Islam may not have been liked much more, but it no longer seemed so dangerous.

The radical critique of white supremacy and the dream of Afro-Asian solidarity once represented by Elijah Muhammad's Nation of Islam were kept alive by Minister Farrakhan, but as in the United States, the shifting political landscape of the Muslim-majority world changed the nature of its impact. Whereas Gamal Abdel Nasser once offered leadership in a non-aligned movement that was seen as an existential threat to the Cold War interests of the United States, the open-door, pro-US stance of his successor, Anwar Sadat, meant that the United States no longer had to fear Egyptian leadership of an anti-colonial alliance. Even though Libya's Mu'ammar Qaddafi attempted to fill Nasser's shoes, and Minister Farrakhan sought a close alliance with him, the impact of this partnership was not the same kind of challenge that the Nation of Islam, Elijah Muhammad, Malcolm X and Muhammad Ali had once represented to Cold War liberalism.

14

POST-ISLAMISM AS NEOLIBERALISATION

NEW SOCIAL MOVEMENTS IN THE MUSLIM WORLD

Peter Mandaville

Introduction

The landscape of Islamist politics has witnessed significant transformation since the first decade of the twenty-first century. This includes, most notably, the phenomenal rise to power through democratic elections of Tunisia's Ennahda and the Egyptian Muslim Brotherhood (followed in the latter case by a dramatic fall in 2013) in the aftermath of popular revolutions in 2010 and 2011. The decision of Islamists to pursue their agendas primarily through the ballot box is of course nothing new and represents a trend that can be identified in several other countries—such as Yemen, Jordan and Kuwait—where Ikhwan-affiliated parties now regularly contest elections. We have also seen the emergence of the 'Justice and Development' phenomenon in Turkey, Morocco, Malaysia and Indonesia.[1] In these countries, political parties claiming an 'Islamic framework of reference' (rather than and in distinct contrast to a totalising legal-political model deriving exclusively from Islam)—but pursuing conventional liberal economic and political agendas—have enjoyed recent electoral success, going so far as to win control of the government in Turkey.

Leading analysts of political Islam have offered up a variety of terms that seek to capture shifts in contemporary political Islam. Vali Nasr speaks of 'Muslim democrats', Ray Baker of 'new Islamism', and Augustus Richard Norton of 'liberal Islamists'.[2] Others have sought to characterise the situation by reference to what they take to be the operative social and political processes. Hence Jillian Schwedler's work on the relationship between political participation and Islamist moderation,[3] or Carrie Rosefsky Wickham's account of 'Islamist auto-reform'.[4] These various depictions of the changing face of political Islam have appeared against the backdrop of another, related—but in some senses more fundamental—debate in the literature about the meaning and nature of 'post-Islamism'. This concept, coined in the 1990s by Asef Bayat to describe the social trends that eventually led to the reformist movement in post-Khomeini Iran, is today most commonly associated with the work of Olivier Roy. In short, Roy's account of post-Islamism argues that Muslims have lost interest in attempts to translate Islam into a systematic ideology and mass political movement à la the Muslim Brotherhood. However, Roy argues that this does not entail a decline in religiosity. Rather, he sees Islamic commitment shifting from the public sphere into the private domain of personal piety. Muslim religiosity may well be on the increase, but we are still witnessing—to invoke the title of Roy's earlier work, the failure of political Islam. But what, we need to ask, does 'political Islam' actually refer to in the social world, and what is at stake in regarding as 'political' only those Muslim social movements that aim to participate in formal, institutionalised politics?

This question is particularly relevant given the scepticism that some analysts have expressed about the extent to which traditional Islamism continues to represent a distinctive ideological project. So while it is impossible to ignore the fact that the Islamists possess the only significant base of organised opposition—witness their strong showing at the ballot box in Tunisia and Egypt—the persuasiveness of their alternative political vision seems in some regards to be in doubt.[5] Again, this does not in any way indicate a decline in religiosity among Egyptians; if anything, the opposite appears to be true if we look at trends over the past decades.[6] As a consequence of this, however, religion has not simply retreated wholly and exclusively into the realm of the private. The failure of political Islam and the individualisation of religion entail neither an end to the social and public functions of religion nor a desire on the part of

Muslims to abandon the collective dimensions of finding social meaning in religion. Movements predicated on a public or social role for Islam continue to be relevant, but the nature, form and vision of Islamic social movements may today be undergoing significant transformation.

In this chapter, I will argue that while Roy's account of post-Islamism provides highly original insights into the relationship between modernity, globalisation and the privatisation of Muslim religiosity, it ultimately suffers from a form of reductionism that defines the political as coterminous with, and limited to, the exercise of state power. By creating, in effect, a binary configuration in which Islam can function only as the organising principle of a political ideology in search of state power, or as the focus of individual piety, Roy neglects important forms of Islamic social mobilisation located between the state and the individual. What follows, however, is not a celebratory account of the transformative potential to be found in civil society or voluntary association. Rather—and seeking to argue for the analytic utility of a somewhat different take on the nature and significance of post-Islamist social movements—I want to suggest that mobilisation for social change organised around and through Islam continues to be of interest to the younger generation today. It does not, however, involve an understanding of transformative politics that sets as its goal the capture of state power. What we are seeing in the Muslim world today is the rise of a number of heterogeneous networks and groups organised loosely and often flexibly around a particular discursive referent ('justice', 'development', 'social change through proper Islamic observance', etc.). These can be seen to share certain characteristics in common with what sociologists have termed 'new social movements', a parallel already drawn by observers of more radical Muslim networks[7] insofar as they are organised primarily around the promotion of particular values, cultures or ethos rather than economic change or public policy. This 'post-materialist'[8] form of Muslim politics represents an alternative to traditional Islamist mobilisation seeking to establish a shari'a-based polity. So while we can point, on the one hand, to the rise of a new generation of Islamist political parties represented by the likes of the AKP in Turkey and the PJD in Morocco, alongside and sometimes in tension with them, we are also seeing efforts by a range of new religious intellectuals, activists and 'everyday social movements' that seek to define the contours of a supposedly transformative Islam beyond the rubric of conventional Ikhwanist politics—hence post-Islamism.[9]

Thus, the main contention of this chapter is that the most interesting story to be told about Islamists and Islamism today is not the story of their recent political victories, but rather the story of how Islamic activism has transformed over the past couple of decades in response to market forces generated by the global neoliberalism whose geopolitical face Islamism opposed for so long.

The meaning and boundaries of political Islam

In their conventional usage within Western social science, the terms 'political Islam' and 'Islamism' have been used more or less interchangeably to refer to actors and groups whose ideological orientation, organisational modes and ultimate agenda revolve around the establishment of a political order based on Islam—usually through the capture of state power and the direct implementation of shari'a law by that state—with the Muslim Brotherhood movement generally serving as the chief exemplar of this approach. Analyses of Islamism and the 'Islamic revival' have pointed out that this kind of activism is primarily a middle-class phenomenon, reflecting the embrace of 'authentic' nativist or local alternatives by educated, newly urbanised segments of Muslim society whose social mobility has been blocked by the authoritarianism of corrupted national-secular or monarchical regimes allied to the West. In other words, and invoking the language of classical social movement theory, political Islam stems from the relative deprivation experienced by new middle classes whose rising expectations of economic success and political participation do not materialise.[10] Since the late 1990s, however, a number of scholars have begun to question some of the conceptual categories and causal logic that underpin this account of Islamism. In his essay 'What Is Political Islam?' anthropologist Charles Hirschkind points out that the very term political Islam seems to imply a preoccupation with the separation of religion and politics that reflects Western secular norms and marks as dangerous (or, at the very least, analytically noteworthy) the encroachment of religion into spaces of politics, while the massive colonisation of religious institutions and social spaces by the modern state in the Muslim world does not seem to have created a similar preoccupation with 'religious statism'.[11]

Two further dimensions of Hirschkind's critique are particularly relevant for our purposes and have been echoed in the work of other scholars studying the sociology of Muslim politics. The first of these, which has already been alluded to above, relates to the over-reliance in much of the literature on structuralist accounts of Islamism. Hirschkind decries what he sees as a 'reduction of [Islamic] movements to an expression of the socio-economic conditions which gave rise to them'.[12] Similarly, others have rejected the reduction of

Islamic activism to the class interests of the relevant actors or the propensity to see Muslim collective action 'primarily as a compensatory reaction to structural changes rather than a potential force for change in itself'.[13] Hirschkind's essay also makes the point that not all forms of Islamic activism have as their goal the capture of state power, but that we should nevertheless understand what they do to be deeply political in nature.[14] Enquiring into the nature of Islamism and its contemporary social location, Bayat similarly invites us to consider various forms of Islamic activism that do not correspond to the classic model of political Islam. Among these he includes the recent conservative upsurge in the Egyptian courts, media, and universities, the expansion of local Islamic reading circles, and a number of public religious figures—among them Selim al-Awwa and Mustafa Mahmoud—whose identities do not fit easily into the categories of religious scholar (*'alim*) or Islamist,[15] but who can still be thought of as exponents of the 'Islamic movement'. Moreover, he suggests that we may be seeing in countries such as Egypt a downturn in support for Islamic activism oriented towards formal political power precisely because Islamisation at the societal level seems to have been so successful.[16] In other words, if there is no need for top-down Islamisation by the state due to the prevalence of effective Islamising forces within society, then the Muslim Brotherhood as a formal political project has put itself out of business. Going on to chastise social movement theory for conceptualising political impact exclusively in terms of official power, Bayat suggests that 'social movements may also succeed in terms of changing civil societies, behavior, attitudes, cultural symbols and value systems which, in the long run, may confront political power'.[17] This slippage at the end, however, leaves us wondering whether even Bayat, while championing the transformative capacity of social movements whose immediate object is not state power, might still see much of their effectiveness as linked to an eventual impact on formal politics. So how can we conceptualise and think about social movements such that their political significance exists in something other than an interest in capturing—or, at some point in the future, having an impact on—state power?

Everyday movements and the heterogeneity of social power

Scholars of 'new social movements' have emphasised that these projects are different in type from the traditional model of social movement found in the nineteenth and early twentieth century, which tended to focus on material conditions, class interests and achieving changes in the prevailing political or economic order.[18] Rather, new social movements demonstrate their 'post-material' character through grounding themselves in values, cultural systems and identity politics (for example, human rights, ecological thought, queer identities). This does not mean that such movements have no interest in changing the material conditions of the world—obviously this is a major priority for, say, the green movement—but rather that the basis of the social solidarity that defines them as a movement lies less in their co-location within structures of production and exchange (for example, membership of the working class), and more in terms of shared values or cultural systems. Likewise, the individualisation of Islamic belief and action (of which more below) that scholars such as Roy have identified as part of the turn to post-Islamism does not entail a wholesale abandonment by Muslims of the realm of the public. Dale Eickelman, Jon Anderson and Armando Salvatore, for example, invite us to consider the emergence and growing relevance of new and functionally differentiated Muslim public spheres.[19] Yet we are still left with the conceptual challenge of reconciling the shift towards individualisation that Roy correctly identifies, and the continued relevance of socially engaged activism by Muslims. For this we turn to the work of Italian sociologist Alberto Melucci.

Melucci's approach to understanding social movements is premised on a particular conception of the nature of contemporary social power and the processes through which social action accrues meaning in the world.[20] This is a methodology that shifts our emphasis away from the state and from 'top-down' models of delivering social power—but which does not simply go on to replace the state with an argument for greater emphasis on the grassroots, or on 'bottom-up' conceptions of social agency. Rather, Melucci—along with other social theorists such as Henri Lefebvre and Michel de Certeau[21]—invites us to consider the realm of the everyday as an arena in which the social movement is embedded. In Melucci's schema, processes of producing and organising social meaning transcend the predominance of hierarchical, material power (for example, labour, bureaucratic governance) in favour of heterogeneous relations of power. Key to this insight is Melucci's argument that not only are we accustomed to recognising a very limited range of institutional spaces as properly political (for example, elections, governmental policymaking) but that we also associate the political exclusively with visible speech and practice in the public sphere. By shifting our attention to the realm of the everyday (and to everyday public spheres—of which more below), Melucci would suggest, we can identify idioms of social movement, which, while seemingly 'invisible' in terms of their absence from those spaces conventionally marked as public (civil society, media, etc.), nonetheless must be recognised as forms of collective mobilisation towards shared norms and worldly aspirations. This mode of social movement adopts a sceptical view of the instrumentalism of state power, seeing its concerns as immune to being effectively addressed by instruments of official bureaucracy or large-scale social organisation.[22] Melucci's evocative formulation of contemporary social movements as 'nomads of the present' points to the essentially 'homeless' nature of such activism (in terms of its alienation from conventional spaces of public and political life), and its embrace of 'temporary public spaces and bio-degradable forms of representation'.[23]

Part of what Melucci tries to argue relates to the notion that involvement with such movements becomes an *end in itself*, without any aspiration to translating this mobilisation into formal political activism. An alternative vision of the good life is seen to lie precisely in the expression of movement norms through daily life activities:

> Participation within movements is considered a goal in itself because, paradoxically, actors self-consciously practice in the present the future social changes they seek ... They are no longer driven by an all-encompassing vision of some future order. They focus on the present, and consequently their goals are temporary and replaceable, and their organizational means are valued as ends in themselves.[24]

It is through this kind of insight that we might begin to understand the characteristics of contemporary Islamic activism commonly—though amorphously—described in terms of 'pragmatism'. This is not, however, a pragmatism defined in terms of short-term tactical compromise, a willingness to negotiate on strategy and a privileging of practical outcomes over theory, ideology and even principle—but rather a notion of the pragmatic that derives from the more literal roots of *pragma* as 'deed'. In other words, a movement premised on the idea that social vision is expressed through the everyday activities that characterise a particular way of 'being in the world', rather than through external organisation towards the achievement of political power.

While such a conception of social movement succeeds in drawing our attention to aspects of collective action and forms of 'heterogeneous and fragile' mobilisation that might otherwise remain invisible to our political radars,[25] we need to keep in perspective the continued relevance of formal, institutionalised political power and—particularly under globalisation—the role of large-scale cultural and economic enterprises. So this cannot simply be a story about the triumph of everyday sociopolitical activity over the state, but rather an effort to understand the processes through which social normativity, as embedded in quotidian life, interacts with, reconfigures and is in turn itself mediated not only by the abiding structural force of the modern state (and social movement aspirants to the same, such as classic Islamism) but also through more pervasive forms of social power that transcend sovereign territoriality, such as neoliberal economic thought and practice. Indeed, the case studies of new Muslim movements examined below will throw into particular relief the heightened importance of neoliberal norms (such as consumerism) and structures (such as globalised markets) in the negotiation and contestation of Islamic meaning. Neoliberalism, of course, also brings us squarely back to *individualisation*, and it is here that we need to engage in a little more conceptual digging in order to flesh out the dynamics of contemporary Muslim movements.

Individualisation and Islamic social normativity

The individualisation of religious experience and activism is central to Roy's account of what he terms post-Islamism. Dovetailing closely with the aforementioned shift away from totalising Islamist ideologies that seek to remake society through state intervention, post-Islamism entails the pursuit of the Islamic 'good life' through a diverse and disparate range of strategies. 'Contemporary re-Islamization', Roy argues, 'is a cluster of *individual* practices that are used as a means of finding jobs, money, respect and self-esteem, and bargaining with a marginalized state that has played on conservative re-Islamization but been unable to control it.'[26] The privatisation and individualisation of Islam, of course, also relate closely to the idea that this new idiom of Islamic activism is thoroughly compatible with—indeed, that it thrives within—the global free market. Consumption and the neoliberal circulation of capital are crucial vehicles for its growth and spread. Hence Roy's reference to a religious market that is 'globalized, fed by economic liberalization and diaspora connections'.[27] This is an environment conducive not only to the activity of entrepreneurs looking to commodify Islam (for example, Islamic fashion, Islamic music, Islamic travel, Islamic soft drinks) but also to the rising influence of conservative business figures whose commercial concerns do not involve the production of religious goods or services, but who privilege and seek to espouse Islamic norms in the conduct of their professional activities. It is here that we begin to see the relevance for post-Islamism of Melucci's emphasis on everyday social movements. Rather than viewing the Islamisation of society as a project engaged through membership and participation in politically organised movements separate from the realms of everyday life (home, work, education, shopping), the pursuit of Islamic normativity becomes ingrained within the pragmatic spaces of quotidian activity. Islam is not rendered as an external ideology, but instead is *lived*.

While our discussion of post-Islamism as involving the privatisation of religion in contexts of heterogeneous social power and proliferating Muslim public spheres is helpful in understanding some of the key dynamics behind the emergence of new forms of religious authority and social movements in the Muslim world, a piece of the conceptual puzzle still seems to be missing. If, as Roy and others have argued, Muslim politics today is about the individualisation of religious belief and practice, in what sense can we appropriately speak of these actors as constituting a *movement*? How can we discern in this trend any meaningful sense of collective action, the standard indicator of a social movement? Are we dealing with anything more than new intellectuals and popular preachers speaking to atomised believers who interpret and act on their ideas and teachings in the context of their individual daily lives? As Bayat poses the question, 'what makes them a movement defined as co-operative unit [sic], in terms of the collective activities of many people to bring about social change? After all unity of purpose and action is the hallmark, indeed a defining feature, of a social movement.'[28]

Bayat addresses this question by arguing that we must disabuse ourselves of the idea that new social movements can always be thought of as being defined by a precise set of concrete aspirations and goals, universally accepted within the movement. What he suggests instead—particularly with regard to the 'non-Western' (that is, politically illiberal) world, where opportunities for unfettered social mobilisation and strategic communication by opposition movements and civil society actors are limited—is that movements come to be built around a loosely shared normative core and a movement 'frame'[29] that thematises, but does not concretely specify, the purposes of collective action. Just as the anti-globalisation movement today contains within it many diverse and at times competing conceptions of justice, so do contemporary Islamist and Islamic movements contend with multiple visions of what the social realisation of Islam might look like. Likewise, and recalling Melucci's idiom of movements for social change as constituted through everyday life rather than through dedicated social organisations and mobilisation, it becomes possible to see the contours of new Islamic movements in the 'imagined solidarities'[30] created through mediated communication. In other words, Muslims work in their individual capacities for social change while simultaneously embodying the ethics of a shared conception of the good life. Their communion exists not through common membership in tight, hierarchical social movement organisations but rather through shared patterns of consumption (listening, reading, shopping) and forms of everyday life. Contrast this with, for example, the relatively rigid array of hierarchical 'family' (*usra*) units that constitutes the classic organisational model of the Muslim Brotherhood, itself drawing heavily on Leninist precepts. These are above all everyday life forms associated with neoliberal forms of subjectivity.

Amr Khaled and neoliberal Islamic activism

The case of Amr Khaled (b.1967), an Egyptian accountant turned television preacher and social entrepreneur, and the vast network of socially engaged young 'consumer-activists' he created, serves to illustrate some of the broader points made above about new social movements of the everyday based in neoliberal norms and practices. The case of Amr Khaled is by no means unique, and it is possible to identify cognate figures and movements in a number of other Muslim countries today such as Turkey and Indonesia.

Khaled was raised in an upper middle-class family in Cairo. After receiving a university education, he entered the private sector as an accountant, handling the Egyptian portfolios of companies such as Pepsi and Colgate.[31] In his early thirties, he began to give informal inspirational talks in private homes and local neighbourhood clubs in affluent areas of Cairo, quickly gaining a reputation as a skilled and engaging speaker. Khaled was soon approached by a television producer friend who invited him to serve as the on-screen face of a new style of religious programming he was trying to develop. This first show, *Word from the Heart*, which aired in 2001, borrowed stylistic elements from Christian programming on US television, seeking to articulate religion in terms of everyday experience and life issues. The approach employed here was in distinct contrast to the traditional idiom of religious programming on Egyptian television. Audiences had become accustomed to Islam on TV in the form of traditional Qur'anic recitation, or a religious scholar seated against the austere backdrop of a mosque intoning 'disciplinary' lessons about right and wrong, the permitted and the forbidden, and the respective pathways to heaven and hellfire. Indeed, in reaction to this kind of programming, Khaled has described his own approach as an attempt to get people to 'love Islam rather than to fear it'. It seems to have worked, as his first programme was a phenomenal success, leading to a contract with the Saudi-owned religious satellite channel Iqra TV. From this followed two further programmes, *Beloved Companions*, based on stories from the life of the Prophet Muhammad, and *Until They Change Themselves*, a series whose main thrust was the idea that the problems of the Muslim community would only be solved once Muslims began to improve themselves. With an audience initially confined to Egypt, Khaled has developed an extremely large and devoted following throughout the Arabic-speaking world. In the mid-2000s, public opinion surveys in the Middle East suggested that he was among the figures that Arabs trust most—second, in fact, only to the Prophet Muhammad.[32]

This 'self-help' ethos is a defining feature of the Amr Khaled discourse. Working in the mode of a *da'i*, that is, someone who engages in *da'wa* to 'call' people (Muslim and non-Muslim alike) to religion, Khaled focuses on ideas of self-improvement, the need to have initiative and ambition, and the virtues of a strong work ethic. A great fan of the classic twelve-step self-help programme, Khaled takes this model and imbues it with an Islamic flavour by explaining each of its elements in terms of religious values. Cribbing the title of Mormon author Steven Covey's US bestseller, we might think of Khaled as articulating something like the 'seven habits of highly effective Muslims'.[33] His audience is exhorted to work hard, study hard, eat well, exercise, all of which are seen to be virtues encouraged by Islam. In terms of religion, Khaled balances the mufti's focus on discipline, punishment and the potentially fiery hereafter (elements of which—it should be said—are present in Khaled's teaching) with a discourse that emphasises God's love, tolerance and forgiveness. He figures Islam as a resource for the spirit when morale is low, something to turn to—and here riffing from Houston-based preacher Joel Osteen—when the complexities of modern life get to be too much. It should be emphasised, however, that Khaled is not in any sense engaged in a project of Islamic reform. He is not producing a new form of 'Islamic liberalism', nor departing in any significant way from the teachings of Sunni orthodoxy. Indeed, lying behind a project that essentially seeks to deploy religion towards new ends in terms of individual and social development is a set of relatively conservative values. While he would never say so in doctrinaire or chastising terms, Khaled does, for example, teach that women should wear headscarves. One area in which he is relatively progressive is interfaith relations, often going out of his way to emphasise points of commonality between Islam and Christianity and to focus on the universalist dimensions of his work by involving people of other faiths in his charitable and social development work.

Khaled's aesthetics and style also deserve some attention as they relate in important ways to the question of his target audience. We have already mentioned that Khaled's approach to religious programming differs significantly from the standard idiom of Islam on television. Where the latter identifies Islam with traditional spaces and figures such as the mosque and the mufti, Khaled's programming can be understood as an attempt to bring Islam into the realm of the popular. The style and format of his shows borrows considerably from American daytime talk shows. This Islam is upbeat, glitzy and participatory. Video montages are interspersed with pop music by modern devotional singers such as Sami Yusuf. Khaled himself wears the best suits, speaks in colloquial Egyptian Arabic, jokes and uses slang. He shares his microphone with members of the audience who ask questions, share their feelings or report on changes in their lives. The shifting cadences of Khaled's speaking are an important feature, one moment jovial, the next slightly sombre—he might seem close to tears recounting a story from the life of the Prophet Muhammad or discussing the ill effects of drugs on society—but then right back to ecstatic and enthusiastic. Performance and emotion are integral to the form. He draws on a highly eclectic range of sources and examples to make his points, ranging from Thomas Edison, to Mahatma Gandhi, to Hamas founder Shaykh Ahmad Yassin. He cites the post-Second World War reconstruction of Japan and Europe as evidence that it is possible for defeated and damaged societies to re-emerge in prosperity.[34] Clearly present within the codes and styles of his teaching is an appeal to middle- and upper middle-class viewers. This segment of Arab society does indeed represent his core demographic, with young women featuring particularly prominently among his fans. The middle-class nature of his religious discourse is evident in the way he speaks and the pop cultural symbols to which he refers. His is a message about the symbiotic relationship between religion and personal success. Not only is making and having money to be encouraged under Islam, but being visibly wealthy and successful, while simultaneously religious, he suggests, will encourage other people to be better Muslims. Seeking prosperity and consumption are refigured as forms of *da'wa* in their own right. This is a message with an enormous appeal to the consuming middle classes of Egypt, allowing them to feel that religion is still an important part of their lives. Khaled, it should be noted, is not the only player in this arena, although his involves the broadest portfolio of spinoff activities and products. Other popular television preachers in Egypt include Moez Masoud, Khaled El-Genndy and Mona Abdul-Ghani.

Lest we dismiss Khaled, as many of his critics do, as an elite apologist who couches excessive middle-class consumption in the guise of religion, there are other dimensions to this phenomenon that need to be considered—and which will also allow us to begin teasing out of his work the contours of something like a neoliberal social movement. Whereas the first phase of his work (1998–2004) was concerned primarily with introducing and 'mainstreaming' his new style of preaching, Khaled's work in the last few years has had a far more explicit focus on issues of social development, charity and dialogue between Islam and the West. Here, he begins to transform his audience from 'passive viewers' into active agents of social change.[35] This shift began with the airing of his programme *Suna'a al-Hayah* (Lifemakers) in 2004–5. Here Khaled began to develop a more explicit focus on grassroots social change. He urged his viewers to translate Islamic virtues (such as 'enjoining good and preventing vice') into practical programmes of social change in their communities. The idea was to encourage young people to establish grassroots charitable organisations that could then undertake a wide range of activities from collecting litter to clothes drives and—tellingly—microfinance projects. He urged them to phone in, e-mail, and send videos of their work so that they could be shown on his programme, with the aim of creating an 'imagined community'[36] of Lifemakers engaged in a common effort of faith-based social development. As Sara Lei Sparre and Marie Juul Petersen put it:

> The movement has inspired young people all over Egypt to establish their own organizations, and it also had an influence on some already existing organizations. In line with Amr Khaled and similar lay preachers, the young people in these organizations believe in making Islam a natural part of their and their target groups' daily lives. Introducing a new approach of Islam and voluntarism, the organizations combine conventional social welfare activities with a human development approach, as well activities associated with advocacy and awareness-raising aimed at mobilizing young people to participate in civil society.[37]

Khaled's goal with this initiative was to foster a collective sense of people's ability to bring about change and to plant the idea that societal transformation begins with the actions of individuals and small groups. By 2008, Khaled claimed that some 1.5 million people worldwide were involved in Lifemakers-inspired organisations, some 500,000 of them in Egypt.[38]

How did other Muslim leaders and groups react to the rise of the Amr Khaled phenomenon? Many from among Egypt's intellectual elite have tended to regard Khaled with distaste or suspicion. Some dismiss his media-savvy popular Islam as superficial and intellectually vacuous, while others—particularly secular figures—take issue with what they perceive as an attempt to re-Islamise Egyptian society via clever marketing ploys. In this, they see him

as simply a 'politician in disguise'.[39] Religious scholars such as Yusuf al-Qaradawi emphasise that Khaled has no formal religious qualifications and therefore
possesses no authority as a religious leader. To be fair, Khaled himself has
never claimed for himself the status of a religious scholar or mufti, emphasising that he is a religious educator and social entrepreneur. Another common
reaction, often to be found among Islamists, is to dismiss Khaled for not being
more politically engaged—that is, an accusation that he preaches an 'air-conditioned Islam'[40] that fails to address what they regard as the overriding issues
of the day (for example, lack of government accountability, the war in Iraq, the
Israel–Palestine conflict). No less a figure than Tariq Ramadan has criticised
Khaled as the purveyor of 'lite Islam', in which religion is reduced to simplistic
formulations and aphorisms. Khaled, of course, would argue that it is precisely
this approach that has enabled a mass audience to relate Islam to their daily
lives. But what of the charges that Khaled either avoids politics, or, conversely,
that he harbours a clandestine political agenda?

Khaled's relationship to politics is a complex issue. While he is clearly not
an Islamist in the conventional sense of the term, there is no doubt that his
work brings religion into the public sphere and leads people to associate Islam
with social change and solutions to societal problems. Furthermore, the fact
that his religious discourse differs significantly from both that of the official
religious establishment as represented by Al-Azhar, and classic political Islam
in the form of the Muslim Brotherhood, leaves the government feeling uneasy.
The fact that he has gained a significant following among even some of the
country's secular-national elite compounds the issue even further, prompting
government fears, as Lindsay Wise argues, of

> Islamizing from within [its own ranks], a process that promotes the resocialization
> of Islam instead of outright, political maneuvering or radical revolutionary activi-
> ties. Such overt political Islam can be thwarted by well-worn tactics of force and
> coercion, but Khaled's deft manipulation of Islamic symbols enables him to strad-
> dle spheres of popular culture and religious tradition, refusing to fit neatly into
> conventional categories, and enabling him to reach social circles previously
> untouched by Islamism.[41]

At a very fundamental level, the government is also concerned simply by
the extent of his popularity, fearing any social force outside its control—
Islamist or otherwise—that seems to wield considerable influence over society.
The fact that Islam is involved adds fuel to the fire and, in the eyes of the
government, makes some of his activities (for example, the organisation of
youth camps and neighbourhood groups) look very similar to the Muslim

Brotherhood in its early days. This likely helps to explain why, at the height of his popularity, the Egyptian government banned Khaled from speaking publicly in Egypt—a move that prompted him to relocate his entire operation to the United Kingdom. After the 25 January 2011 revolution, Khaled returned to Egypt and founded a political party, Hizb Misr (Egypt party). He has generally kept a low profile and sought—with some success—to avoid being caught up in the intense polarisation that has characterised Egyptian politics in recent years.

Aside from whatever political plans he may have, we also need to remember that Amr Khaled is also—perhaps even first and foremost—a marketing phenomenon and a 'brand name'. Approaching him this way also helps us to work our way back towards thinking about what he might represent in terms of a social movement of the everyday. Unlike a rigid and hierarchical social movement organisation, the power of a brand name lies precisely in its ability to build community through practices that bridge individual and collective consumption. There are of course limitations to this kind of movement, not least of which is to be found in their rather diffuse nature, making it difficult for the movement as a whole to be mobilised towards a particular goal.[42] Also, consumers are fickle and brand names consequently volatile. In order to be transformed into something approaching a sustainable mass social movement, the brand name must manage not only to become a constitutive element of social identity, but also to develop a concrete manifestation in social reality—hence Khaled's shift with Lifemakers towards an implementation of his teaching at the level of society. We have already noted, however, that his target demographic has certain boundaries. While Khaled markets certain versions of his products to those consuming at a lower price point—such as audio cassettes, glossy books and leaflets summarising his lessons—the substance of his social activism lies in his ability to get people out into society to foment change, and the capacity to do this is limited to those who have time and resources on hand.

Post-Islamism and neoliberalism revisited

It is clear from the discussion above that Muslim groups today are developing a new 'repertoire of collective action', to use political sociologist Charles Tilly's terms.[43] Movements constituted by the loose (and often diffuse) coordination of aggregated individual everyday practices seem to be gaining momentum as an alternative to classic Islamism. Conventional social movement organisations in the mould of the Muslim Brotherhood will certainly continue to represent an important political force in the Muslim world, alongside the emerging 'new Islamist' parties (such as AKP in Turkey and PJD in Morocco). But these two formations do not constitute the totality of Muslim politics, and the success or failure of Islamism cannot be determined simply by how well such groups fare at the ballot box. Rather, we need to consider the possibility that the nature of Islamic activism may be changing in significant ways. Likewise, what it means to belong to an Islamic movement and the modalities through which such affiliation occurs are similarly in transformation today. As was argued above using the case of Amr Khaled, young people today seem to be drawn towards an approach to the Islamisation of society that operates through the spaces and meanings of everyday life rather than through formal membership in organised opposition groups. The reasons for this are varied. One can point, on the one hand, to explanations that emphasise the failure of existing Islamist groups and parties to achieve their political goals. The relative success of such groups at the societal level, ironically, might damage their political fortunes insofar as it leads people to wonder whether Islam actually needs to be in power in order for society to become more Islamic. In other cases, it appears that people are shying away from conventional Islamist movements not only because of the latter's lack of political success but because they have a very different conception of what Islamic social activism means and how it is to be carried out.

This last point leads requires considering the possibility that contemporary cleavages in political Islam might be best captured through an examination of differential experiences of neoliberalism, globalisation and unequal development in Muslim societies. The vision contained in the work of Khaled, as well as the pro-West, pro-business orientation of new Islamists such as the AKP in Turkey, is decidedly friendly towards globalisation—at least in its economic dimensions. Unsurprisingly, the demographics of their core audiences reflect high levels of education and participation in global markets and media consumption. The new middle classes, and socially mobile aspirants to this status, compose the bulk of their constituencies. But this cannot simply be dismissed as the comfortable Islam of the privileged. Khaled and his ilk are popular in part because, in distinct contrast to the Islamists, they embody success and offer a concrete and tangible pathway to social mobility. This insight also suggests that the shift to post-Islamism represents something more than the rise of value-based new social movements premised on a post-materialist vision. Rather, people opt pragmatically for a vision of societal Islamisation that resonates with dominant neoliberal norms.

Pushing one aspect of the argument even further, we can also speculate about how the primacy of consumption practices within certain segments of Muslim societies is having an impact on how people think about what it means to engage with social and political issues from an Islamic perspective. This is where Melucci's conception of social movements of the everyday becomes relevant, particularly those aspects of his work that focus on conceptions of social change premised on the lived embodiment of movement norms within daily individual conduct. Bringing in the ubiquity of neoliberal norms and media saturation among Muslims in the West and middle-class settings in the Muslim-majority world, this approach transposes the location of Islamic activism from revolutionary movements to spaces and practices of consumption. As Amel Boubekeur puts it:

> The traditional intra-Islamic modes of action and mobilization, such as aggressive street demonstrations and political militancy, make less sense. The new Islamic elites reinterpret their relations ... in terms of networks and partnerships. Notions of partnership will develop according to standards of competence and competitiveness ... Where the traditional Islamic [activism] was heavy, expensive, and very framed, the Islamic identity suggested by this new culture sets of mobilizations, identifications, modes of actions, and participation that is less expensive, less stigmatizing. The classical notions of Islamism, such as the sacrifice for the cause and the suffering, weak, and dominated disappear. What is proposed is the revalorization of the personal pleasure of consumption, success, and competitiveness.[44]

Given this characterisation, it is not surprising that some of the more traditional Islamist actors have dismissed this new consumer-oriented trend as superficial and disengaged from the hard questions of 'real' politics. At the same time, however, the Islamists—like the state—are in two minds about these new movements. They are a growing force, and since they are premised on Islam they threaten the Islamists' turf and threaten to poach away their constituents. The Islamists and the state are both concerned about the amorphous and diffuse nature of these new actors. The state because they locate themselves in spaces and practices less easily regulated through traditional instruments of power. Moreover, the state finds itself in something of a dilemma since these new movements are to be found in specific domains (such as private enterprise and small-to-medium business growth) that the state is actually trying to encourage in the name of national development. Some Islamists also worry about the inability of the state to check the rapid growth of neoliberal Islamisation. Locked for decades in a tense struggle with the state that often saw their advances blocked, these Islamists worry about the impact on their fortunes of a rapidly proliferating rival that appears largely immune to the same tactics: precisely because it articulates the promise of an Islamism (of sorts) offering the semblance of alternative normativity while simultaneously embodying a familiar and comfortable neoliberalism.

NOTES

INTRODUCTION

1. See Joseph Massad's recent book, *Islam in Liberalism*, Chicago: University of Chicago Press, 2015.
2. For the invention of religion as a universal category, see Tomoko Masuzawa, *The Invention of World Religions: Or, How European Universalism Was Preserved in the Language of Pluralism*, Chicago: University of Chicago Press, 2005.
3. See Wilfred Cantwell Smith, 'The Historical Development in Islam of the Concept of Islam as an Historical Development', in *On Understanding Islam: Selected Studies*, The Hague: Mouton Publishers, 1981, pp. 41–77. See also Shahab Ahmad, *What Is Islam? The Importance of Being Islamic*, Princeton: Princeton University Press, 2015.
4. Muhammad Iqbal, 'Reply to Questions Raised by Pandit Jawahar Lal Nehru', in Syed Abdul Vahid (ed.), *Thoughts and Reflections of Iqbal*, Lahore: Sh. Muhammad Ashraf, 1992, p. 271. The chapters by Faisal Devji and Abdennour Bidar in this volume engage with the thought and influence of Iqbal.
5. For reappraisals of the nineteenth-century Arab 'renaissance', see the chapters by Hussein Omar and Nadia Bou Ali in this volume.
6. See Uday Singh Mehta, *Liberalism and Empire: A Study in Nineteenth-Century British Liberal Thought*, Chicago: University of Chicago Press, 1999. For the contested nature of liberalism, including within this period, see Duncan Bell, 'What is Liberalism?', *Political Theory*, 42, 6 (2014), pp. 682–715.
7. See Mark Mazower, *No Enchanted Palace: The End of Empire and the Ideological Origins of the United Nations*, Princeton: Princeton University Press, 2009.
8. For a discussion of the making of non-Western liberalism as an autonomous and creative rather than merely derivative phenomenon, see C.A. Bayly, *Recovering Liberties: Indian Thought in the Age of Liberalism and Empire*, Cambridge: Cambridge University Press, 2012.

9. Ayman al-Zawahiri, 'Selected Questions and Answers from Dr. Ayman al-Zawahiri: Part 2 Released on April 17, 2008', Nefa Foundation, p. 8 (http://www.actforamericaeducation.com/downloads/All_Files_by_Type/nefazawahiri0508–2.pdf).

10. For imperial liberalism, see Thomas R. Metcalf, *Ideologies of the Raj*, Cambridge: Cambridge University Press, 1997.

11. See the chapters by Neguin Yavari and Arshin Adib-Moghaddam in this volume.

12. For the 'culture talk' that often defines Islam, see Mahmoud Mamdani, *Good Muslim, Bad Muslim: America, the Cold War and the Roots of Terror*, New York: Pantheon, 2004.

13. See Armando Salvatore's chapter in this volume for the bad faith of the 'debate' on Muslim liberalism.

14. See Chibli Mallat, *The Renewal of Islamic Law: Muhammad Baqer as-Sadr, Najaf and the Shi'i International*, Cambridge: Cambridge University Press, 1993. See also Arshin Adib-Moghaddam's chapter in this volume.

15. See Faisal Devji, 'Islamism as Anti-politics', Political Theology blog, 2 August 2013 (http://www.politicaltheology.com/blog/ political-theology-and-islamic-studies-symposium-islamism-as-anti-politics/).

16. For an example of such an anti-liberal stance, see Faisal Devji's chapter on Muhammad Iqbal in this volume.

17. For the recent emergence of new political narratives in the Gulf, see Ahmed Dailami's chapter in this volume.

18. For the persistence of race in contemporary constructions of Islam, see the chapters on US Islam by Michael Muhammad Knight and Edward E. Curtis IV in this volume.

19. Leonard Binder, *Islamic Liberalism: A Critique of Development Ideologies*, Chicago: Chicago University Press 1988; Albert Hourani, *Arabic Thought in the Liberal Age 1798–1939*, Cambridge: Cambridge University Press 1983.

20. This has included engagement by prominent Western political philosophers such as Charles Taylor and Jurgen Habermas on wider issues relating to religion and the public sphere. See Eduardo Mendieta and Jonathan Antwerpen (eds), *The Power of Religion in the Public Sphere*, New York: Columbia University Press, 2011.

21. For a Rawlsian approach, see Andrew March, *Islam and Liberal Citizenship: The Search for an Overlapping Consensus*, New York: Oxford University Press, 2009.

22. For contemporary intellectual developments in Indonesia in this regard, see Carool Kersten's chapter in this volume.

23. Evident, for example, in Abdennour Bidar's exposition of Muhammad Iqbal in this volume.

24. Wael Hallaq, *The Impossible State: Islam, Politics and Modernity's Moral Predicament*, New York: Columbia University Press, 2013. On Hallaq, see also Neguin Yavari's chapter in this volume.

25. See, for example, the work of Mohammed Bamyeh and Michael Muhammad Knight. See also Zaheer Kazmi, 'Automatic Islam: Divine Anarchy and the Machines of God', *Modern Intellectual History*, 12, 1 (2015), pp. 33–64.

26. See Zaheer Kazmi, 'The United Kingdom's Extreme Anti-extremism Policy', ForeignAffairs.com, 5 August 2015 (https://www.foreignaffairs.com/articles/united-kingdom/2015–08–05/united-kingdoms-extreme-anti-extremism-policy).

27. See Sadia Abbas's chapter on art and protest in this volume. On Muslim social movements and the limits of the 'political' as a category of analysis, see also Peter Mandaville's chapter.

28. For a paradigmatic example of this method, see Mustafa Akyol, *Islam Without Extremes: A Muslim Case for Liberty*, New York: W.W. Norton, 2011.

29. For the ideological uses of the Islamic concept of *al-wasatiyya* in the context of current debates on Islamic moderation, see Zaheer Kazmi's chapter in this volume.

30. See, for example, Edward Curtis's chapter on the Nation of Islam's strategic use of liberalism in this volume.

31. These areas of academic enquiry are contested and not yet well established but there has been a growing interest and intellectual output in recent years regarding questions of comparison in political thought and the neglect of non-Western approaches to the study of history and politics wherein the role and nature of liberalism has also loomed large. See, among others, Michael Freeden and Andrew Vincent (eds), *Comparative Political Thought: Theorizing Practices*, Abingdon: Routledge 2013, and Bayly, *Recovering Liberties*.

1. ARABIC THOUGHT IN THE LIBERAL CAGE

1. Albert Hourani, *Arabic Thought in the Liberal Age*, London: Oxford University Press, 1962.

2. Israel Gershoni, 'The Theory of Crisis', in Israel Gershoni, Amy Singer and Hakan Erdem (eds), *Middle East Historiographies: Narrating the Twentieth Century*, Seattle: University of Washington Press, 2006, p. 158.

3. See Marilyn Booth, 'Before Qasim Amin: Writing Histories of Gender Politics in 1890s Egypt', in Marilyn Booth and Anthony Gorman (eds), *The Long 1890s in Egypt: Colonial Quiescence, Subterranean Resistance*, Edinburgh: Edinburgh University Press, 2014; and 'Women in Islam: Men and the "Women's Press" in Turn-of-the-20th-Century Egypt', *International Journal of Middle East Studies*, 33, 2 (2001), pp. 171–201.

4. Evelyn Baring, *Modern Egypt*, London: Macmillan, 1908, p. 180.

5. Cromer, despatch no. 105 (6 June 1899), Foreign Office 78/5023.

6. Ibid.

7. The one exception is Zachary Lockman, 'Exploring the Field: Lost Voices and Emerging Practices, 1882–1914', in Israel Gershoni et al. (eds), *Histories of the Modern Middle East: New Directions*, Boulder: Lynne Rienner, 2002, pp. 137–54.

8. See Leila Ahmed, *Women and Gender in Islam*, New Haven: Yale University Press, 1993, pp. 144–69.

9. Eric Davis, *Challenging Colonialism: Bank Misr and Egyptian Industrialization, 1920–1941*, Princeton: Princeton University Press, 1983.

10. This approach is best encapsulated in the seminal article by Walid Kazziha, 'The Ummah–Jarīdah Group and Egyptian Politics', *Middle Eastern Studies*, 13, 3 (1997), p. 376.

11. Kazziha, 'Jarīdah–Ummah Group', is a paradigmatic example.

12. Reinhard Schulze, 'Mass Culture and Islamic Cultural Production in 19th Century Middle East', in Georg Strauth and Sami Zubaida (eds), *Mass Culture, Popular Culture and Social Life in the Middle East*, Boulder: Westview Press, 1987, pp. 189–222.

13. Abdeslam Maghraoui in *Liberalism Without Democracy: Nationhood and Citizenship in Egypt, 1922–1936*, Durham: Duke University Press, 2006.

14. Noting the mass proliferation of the term 'liberal' both within and outside of the academy, Duncan Bell rejects an essentialised and transhistorical understanding of liberalism. Bell argued that the invention of liberalism as a deep (and exclusively) European essence was the legacy of the Cold War. See Duncan Bell, 'What Is Liberalism?', *Political Theory*, 42, 6 (2014), pp. 1–34.

15. Ibid., p. 6.

16. Ibid., p. 10.

17. Ibid., p. 6.

18. Saba Mahmood, *Politics of Piety: The Islamic Revival and the Feminist Subject*, Princeton: Princeton University Press, 2011, p. 11.

19. Michael Gasper, *The Politics of Representation: Publics, Peasants, and Islam in Egypt*, Stanford: Stanford University Press, 2008, p. 223.

20. It is no coincide that the only Egyptian party of the early years, the Egyptian Liberal Party, was developed to stymie the growing nationalism and to defend the necessity of the British Empire.

21. See FO 78/4763, which describes a 'very moderate newspaper, which generally supports the cause of the British occupation'.

22. PRO 30/29/160, 'Malet to Granville', 18 September 1882.

23. Baring, *Modern Egypt*, p. 225.

24. The term 'machine' is used with great frequency to describe the colonial administration of Egypt. See ibid., p. 234, for but one example.

25. Ibid., p. 194.

26. Ibid., 234.

27. Aaron Jakes, 'State of the Field: Agrarian Transformation, Colonial Rule and the Politics of Material Wealth in Egypt, 1882–1914', PhD diss., New York University, 2014, p. 5.

28. Ahmad Lutfi al-Sayyid, *Safahhat Matwiyya min Tarikh al-Haraka al-Istiqlaliya fi Masr: Min Māris sanat 1907 ilá Māris sanat 1909; 'Aṣr al-inqilab al-fikri fi al-siyasa al-wataniya*, Cairo: Maṭbaʿat al-Muqtaṭaf wa-al-Muqaṭṭam, 1946, pp. 121–35.

29. Ibid., pp. 14–15.

30. John Romich Alexander, The Truth About Egypt (London: Cassell and Company Ltd, 1911), p. 95. The Egyptian Liberal Party was known as Hizb al-Ahrar in Arabic but usually went, on accounts of its Anglophilia, by its English name.

31. Ibid.

32. FO 371/249 no. 3058, 12 September 1907.

33. Ibid.

34. Mustafa Kamil, *What the National Party Wants*, Cairo: The Egyptian Standard, 1908, pp. 8–9.

35. Ibid.

36. Ibid., p. 10.

37. Ibid.

38. FO 371/ no. 33861, 12 October 1907.

39. Kamil charged ʿUrabi with incitement to civil strife (*fitna*). See Yuwaqim Rizq Murqus (ed.), *Awraq Mustafa Kamil: Al-Maqalat*, Cairo: al-Hayʾa al-Misriyya al-ʿAmma li-l-Kitab, 1992, p. 273

40. An English translation of the speech delivered on 22 October 1907 at the Zizinia Theatre in Alexandria was published as Mustafa Kamil, *What the National Party Wants* (Cairo: The Egyptian Standard, 1908), p. 31.

41. *Al-Garida*, 3 April 1907.

42. Although the leaders of Hizb al-Umma frequently denounced Pan-Islamism, comparing it unfavourably to socialism—both disregarded national borders—they never accused Kamil's party of espousing the former. See *al-Garida*, 'Nationalism in Egypt', 10 March 1907. By contrast, Jawish spoke favourably of socialism. See ʿAbd al-ʾAziz Jawish, *al-ʿAlam al-Islami*, Istanbul: Dar al-Khilafa al-Islamiyya, 1912, p. 10.

43. Kamil, 'Speech', p. 32.

44. Ibid., pp. 31–2.

45. Hourani, *Arabic Thought*, pp. 208–9.

46. This referred to the Chinese boycott of 1905–6, which was a response to American exclusionary and discriminatory practices toward Chinese immigrants. See Sin-Kiong Wong, 'Die for the Boycott and Nation: Martyrdom and the 1905 Anti-American Movement in China', *Modern Asian Studies*, 35, 3 (July 2001), pp. 565–88. Similarly, the Swadeshi (self-sufficiency) movement was launched in

the same year in 1905 and was aimed at making India economically self-sufficient. This involved the boycott of British goods as the first step toward home-rule.

47. Aaron Jakes, *State of the Field*, p. 554; Jawish, *al-'Alam al-Islami*, pp. 10–15.

48. Kazziha, 'Ummah–Jarīdah Group', pp. 374–78. Ahmad Fathi Zaghlul at first joined the party, but later renounced it.

49. 'Abd al-Khaliq Lashin, *Sa'd Zaghlul Dawruhu fi al-Siyasa al-Misriyya hatta Sanat 1914*, Cairo: Dar al-Ma'arif, 1971, pp. 87–9.

50. See Yaseen Noorani, *Culture and Hegemony in the Colonial Middle East*, New York: Palgrave Macmillan US, 2010, p. 129, for this mistaken view.

51. See *al-Garida*, 26 April 1908. On Amin's refusal to join the party, see 'Abd al-'Azim Ramadan (ed.), *Mudhakkirat Sa'd Zaghlul*, Cairo: al-Hay'a al-'Amma al-Misriyya li-l Kitab, 1982, vol. 1, p. 334.

52. Hourani, *Arabic Thought*, p. 147.

53. Indira Falk Gesink, *Islamic Reform and Conservatism: Al-Azhar and the Evolution of Modern Sunni Islam*, London: IB Tauris, 2009, pp. 163–96.

54. Qasim Amin, *Les Égyptiens: Réponse à M. le Duc d'Harcourt*, Cairo: J. Barbier, 1894.

55. Ibid.

56. Muhammad Talaat Harb, *Tarbiyat al-Mar'a wa-l-Hijab*, Cairo: Maṭba'at al-Ṭaraqī, 1899, p. 3.

57. Ibid., p. 5.

58. Yuwaqim Rizq Murqus (ed.), *Awraq Mustafa Kamil: Al-Maqalat*, Cairo: al-Hay'a al-Misriyya al-'Amma li-l-Kitab, 1992, p. 155.

59. Ibid.

60. Ibid.

61. See in particular the influential essay 'Algeria Unveiled' in Frantz Fanon, *A Dying Colonialism*, New York: Grove Press, 1965, pp. 35–67.

62. Leila Ahmed, *Women and Gender*, pp. 44–69.

63. Ahmed explains her motivations for re-examining Amin's book by pointing to the post-1979 years, for she argues that Hourani's account has failed to explain the Islamic Revival. See Leila Ahmed, *A Quiet Revolution: The Veil's Resurgence, from the Middle East to America*, New Haven: Yale University Press, 2012, pp. 19–46, 305–8.

64. Ahmed, *Women and Gender*, pp. 144–69.

65. Faisal Devji, 'Apologetic Modernity', *Modern Intellectual History*, 4, 1 (2007), p. 62.

66. Ahmed, *Women and Gender*, pp. 148–9.

67. Ibid., pp. 144–69.

68. Partha Chatterjee, *The Nation and Its Fragments: Colonial and Postcolonial Histories*, Princeton: Princeton University Press, 1993, p. 6.

69. On the suppression of slavery, see Gabriel Baer, 'Slavery in Nineteenth Century Egypt', *Journal of African Studies*, 8, 3 (1967), pp. 417–41.

70. Mahmood, *Politics of Piety*, 11.

71. Kamil, *What the National Party Wants*, 32.

72. Ibid.

73. See Anwar Jindi, *'Abd al-'Aziz Jawish min Ruwwad al-Tarbiya wa-al-Sahafah wa-l-Ijtima'*, Cairo: al-Mu'asasa al-Miṣriyya al-'Amma; al-Dar al-Qawmiya li-l-Ṭiba'a wa-al-Nashr, 1965, and Salim Qunaybar, *al-Itijahat al-Siyasiyya wa-l-Fikriyyah wa-l-Ijtima'iyya fi al-Adab al-'Arabi al-Mu'asir: 'Abd al-'Aziz Jawish, 1872–1929*, Benghazi: Dār Maktabat al-Andalus, 1968.

74. 'Abd al-'Aziz Jawish, *Al-Islam: Din al-Fitra wa-l-Hurriyya*, Cairo: Dār al-Hilāl, n.d., p. 10.

75. Jawish, *Al-Islam*, p. 10.

76. Ibid., p. 11.

77. Ibid., p. 10.

78. Ibid., pp. 95–7.

79. Ibid., pp. 97–8.

80. Ibid., pp. 61–2.

81. Ibid., p. 60.

82. Ibid., p. 59.

83. Ibid.

84. 'A Stranger in the Land', *al-Liwa'*, 17 June 1908.

85. 'Innocent Victims', *al-Garida*, 28 June 1908.

86. Ibid.

87. 'Self-Denial', *al-Garida*, 12 January 1909.

88. *Al-Garida*, 26 January 1908.

89. 'Self-Rule', *al-Garida*, 15 September 1907.

90. *Kuttāb:* a small, single-room educational unit for children, attached to a mosque.

91. See *al-Garida*, 17 September 1907.

92. Ibid.

93. 'Independence and Us', *al-Garida*, 11 April 1908.

94. Lutfi al-Sayyid, *Safahhat Matwiyya*, p. 21.

95. 'The English in Egypt, or a Critique of "Modern Egypt"', *al-Garida*, 14 April 1908.

96. Ibid.

97. Ibid.

98. Ibid.

99. Jacques-Bénigne Bossuet, *Politics Drawn from the Very Words of Holy Scripture*, edited by Patrick Riley, Cambridge: Cambridge University Press, 1999.

100. 'English in Egypt'.

101. Ibid.

102. 'Self-Rule', *al-Garida*, 15 September 1907.

103. Ibid. See Aaron Jakes, 'State of the Field: Agrarian Transformation, Colonial Rule, and the Politics of Material Wealth in Egypt, 1882–1914', PhD diss., New York University, 2014.

104. 'English in Egypt'.

105. Samah Selim, *The Novel and the Rural Imaginary in Egypt, 1880–1895*, London: Routledge, 2004, p. 9.

106. 'Self-Denial', *al-Garida*, 12 January 1909.

107. 'Independence and Us', *al-Garida*, 11 April 1908.

108. See *Mudawat al-Nufus wa-Tahdhib al-Akhlaq wa-l-Zuhd fi al-Radha'il*, Cairo: Matba'at al-Nil, 1905.

109. 'Is the Nation a Single Party?', *al-Garida*, 27 October 1907.

110. Ibid.

111. Ibid.

112. *Al-Garida*, 25 April 1908.

113. Arabian poet, died c. 712 CE. Best known for his unrestrained love poetry, of which he was one of the chief innovators.

114. Ibid.

115. See Mahmood, *Politics of Piety*, pp. 26–9.

116. Lutfi al-Sayyid, *Safahhat Matwiyya*, p. 14.

117. Partha Chatterjee, *Nationalist Thought and the Colonial World: A Derivative Discourse*, Minneapolis: University of Minnesota Press, 1993.

118. Timothy Mitchell's *Colonising Egypt*, Berkeley: University of California Press, 1988.

119. Muhammad 'Imara (ed.), *Qasim Amin: al-A'mal al-Kamila*, Cairo: Dār al-Shurūq, 1989, p. 433.

120. Samera Esmeir, *Juridical Humanity: A Colonial History*, Stanford: Stanford University Press, 2012, p. 81.

121. 'Let Us Agree or Disagree', *al-Garida*, 29 September 1907.

122. 'Our Political Situation', *al-Garida*, 23 March 1907.

123. Saba Mahmood, 'Secularism, Hermeneutics, and Empire: The Politics of Islamic Reformation', *Public Culture*, 18, 2 (2006), pp. 323–47. For a critique, see Sadia Abbas, *At Freedom's Limit: Islam and the Postcolonial Predicament*, New York: Fordham University Press, 2014, pp. 56–70. See also Talal Asad, *Formations of the Secular: Christianity, Islam, Modernity*, Stanford: Stanford University Press, 2003; and Uday Mehta, *Liberalism and Empire: A Study in Nineteenth-Century British Liberal Thought*, Chicago: Chicago University Press, 1999.

124. Kamil, *What the National Party Wants*, p. 32.

125. Bell, 'What Is Liberalism?', p. 5.

126. See FO 371/249, no. 33861, 12 October 1907.

127. Marilyn Booth, 'Review of *Formations of the Secular: Christianity, Islam*,

Modernity', *Bryn Mawr Review of Comparative Literature*, 4, 2 (2004); http://www.brynmawr.edu/bmrcl/Summer2004/Asad.html (accessed 20 June 2014).

128. Andrew Sartori, *Liberalism in Empire: An Alternative History*, Berkley: University of California Press, 2014, p. 143.

129. *Al-Ahram*, 4 November 1908.

2. CORRUPTING POLITICS

1. Buṭrus al-Bustānī, *Khutba fī' adāb al-'arab*, Beirut: American University of Beirut, Archives and Special Collections Department, 1859.

2. Andrew Sartori, *Bengal in Global Concept History, Culturalism in the Age of Capital*, Chicago: University of Chicago Press, 2008, p. 27.

3. Ibid., p. 47.

4. Ibid., p. 51.

5. Interpellation in its Althusserian understanding is the process through which subjects are constituted by ideology. Althusser's oft-quoted example to illustrate this is of the hailing of an individual by a police officer, whereby the subject recognizes himself or herself in the other's hail. Mladen Dolar has argued, however, that the Althusserian schema falls short of accounting for the process of misrecognition underpinning interpellation. Dolar proposes, contra the Althusserian reading, that the subject can only emerge from the failures of structure or from misrecognition. Dolar's critique of Althusser allows for an analysis of the moments of breakdown of liberal ideology and culturalism rather than historicizing them as a self-enclosed totality. Refer to Dolar's 'Beyond Interpellation', *Qui Parle*, Vol. 6, No. 2 (Spring/Summer 1993), pp. 75–96.

6. al-Bustānī Buṭrus, *al-Tuhfa l-Bustānīy ya fil-asfār al-kurūziyya* (Bustānī's masterpiece of Crusoe's travels). Beirut: American Missionary Press, 1860. American University of Beirut, Archives and Special Collections Department.

7. Eric Santner, *On the Psycotheology of Everyday Life*, Chicago: University of Chicago Press, 2001, p. 5.

8. Andrew Sartori, 'The Resonance of "Culture": Framing a Problem in Global Concept-History', *Comparative Studies in Society and History*, Vol. 47, No. 4 (Oct. 2005), p. 681.

9. Slavoj Žižek, 'Tolerance as an Ideological Category', *Critical Inquiry* (Autumn 2007).

10. Aḥmad Fāris al-Shidyāq, *Kitāb al-sāq 'ala al-sāq fi ma huwa al-fāryāq: aw ayyām wa-shuhūr wa-a'wām fī 'ajm al-'arab wa-al-a'jām*, Beirut: Dār al-ḥayāt, n.d., p. 82.

11. A form of metaphor that alludes implicitly to the attribute of the described (usually praised) subject without naming it explicitly.

12. Shidyāq, *Al-Sāq*, p. 82.

13. Shidyāq, '*Al-Dhawq*' (On taste), *Mukhtārat*, p. 167.

14. Shidyāq, 'Al-Musīqā' (On music), Mukhtārat, p. 182.

14. Ibid.

15. Al-Shidyāq, Kitāb al-sāq 'ala al-sāq fī ma huwa al-fāryāq, p. 2.

16. In Why Are the Arabs Not Free? The Politics of Writing (Oxford: Wiley-Blackwell, 2007), Moustapha Safouan highlights the impoverished nature of the translation of politics as siyasa whereby the original meaning of politics from polis is replaced by sasa, which means to lead as a horse leads a cart.

17. Buṭrus al-Bustānī, Dāʾirat al-Maʿārif, vols. 1–11, Beirut: Dār al-Maʿrifa, n.d. The dictionary was compiled between 1867 and 1882; ironically, it remained incomplete at the last entry, 'Ottoman'.

18. Dāʾirat al-Maʿārif, vol. 4, p. 466.

19. Ibid.

20. Ibid.

21. Ibid

22. Aḥmad Fāris al-Shidyāq, 'Fi uṣūl al-siyāsa' (On the principles of politics), Mukhtārat Aḥmad Fāris al-Shidyāq, pp. 148–67.

23. Ibid., p. 150.

24. Ibid., p. 148.

25. Ibid., p. 151.

26. Ibid.

27. Eric Santner's reading of the Hobbesian Leviathan or social contract as a prosthetic device, a mutation that grows between nature and culture and for which the preservation of life is intertwined with the possibility of its being taken away by the sovereign who guards it. Santner argues that there is an excess underlying sovereignty, which he defines as a 'bit of flesh,' an element exceeding the immunisation that sovereignty is meant to offer society. This 'bit of flesh' is always there once the signifier of master is contracted by subjects, like a virus, and in which is discerned 'the bareness, nakedness, and vulnerability pertaining to the precariousness of our organic, mortal lives; the bareness, nakedness, and vulnerability pertaining to the fact that the historical forms of life in which we dwell are susceptible to breakdown.' Eric Santner, The Royal Remains: The People's Two Bodies and the Endgames of Sovereignty, Chicago: University of Chicago Press, 2011, p. 18.

28. Al-Shidyāq, 'Fi uṣūl al-siyāsa', p. 151.

29. Lacan's four discourses or structures of social bonds (the master's discourse, the hysteric's discourse, the university discourse, and the discourse of the analysis) consider the social and political as realms organised around a peculiar set of symbolic identifications. In the master's discourse, which best describes pre-capitalist relations, there exists a relation of fetishistic domination between lord and serf, premised on conceiving of the master as being in the position of 'absolute knowledge' or as a 'subject supposed to know.' The master's discourse is an episteme in which the know-how or savoir-faire of the worker is literally abducted from them by the lord.

30. In Lacan's 'university discourse', as opposed to the 'master's discourse', science and knowledge take the master's position in the social bond (see note 30).

31. Santner, *Royal Remains*, p. 12.

32. Ibid.

33. Al-Shidyāq, '*Fi uṣūl al-siyāsa*', p. 157.

34. Aḥmad Fāris Al-Shidyāq, '*al-Insān ashraf al-makhlūqāt*' (On the supposed dignified state of humankind over all other creatures), in Yūsuf Qazma Khūrī (ed.), *Mukhtārat Aḥmad Fāris al-Shidyāq*, Beirut: Al-Mu'asasa al-sharqiyya lil-nashr wa-al-ṭibāʿa, 2001, p. 227.

35. Ibid.

36. Refer to Eric Santner's *My Own Private Germany, Daniel Paul Schreber's Secret History of Modernity*, Princeton: Princeton University Press, 1998.

37. Jacques Lacan, *The Sinthome, The Seminar of Jacques Lacan Book XXIII*, Cambridge: Polity, 2016.

38. Buṭrus al-Bustānī, *Al-Hayʾa al-ijtimāʿiya, w-al-muqābala bayn al-ʿawāʾid al-ʿarabiya w-al-ifranjiya* (On social organisation and the comparison between Arab and European cultures), American University of Beirut Archive and Special Collections, 1849.

39. Nadia Bou Ali, 'Buṭrus al-Bustānī and the Shipwreck of the Nation', *Middle Eastern Literatures*, vol. 16, no. 3 (2013), pp. 266–81.

40. This is a story that Bustani translates into Arabic during the wars of 1860. He refers to the plight of Crusoe who is shipwrecked and isolated when discussing post-war society in the *Nafir Sūriyya* (The clarion of Syria) Pamphlets (1860–1) as well as in his speech on society in 1849.

41. Al-Bustānī, *Al-Hayʾa al-ijtimāʿiya*, p. 17.

42. Al-Bustānī, *Nafir Sūriyya*, Pamphlet 10, 22 February 1861.

43. Al-Bustānī, *Nafir Sūriyya*, Pamphlet 11, 22 April 1861.

44. Aḥmad Fāris al-Shidyāq, '*Fi al-mukhayila aw al-takhayul*' (On imagination and imagining), *Mukhtārat Aḥmad Fāris al-Shidyāq*, pp. 97–100.

45. Al-Bustānī, *Al-Hayʾa al-ijtimāʿiya*, p. 14.

46. Ibid.

47. Santner, *Royal Remains*, p. 6.

48. al-Bustānī, '*Ḥurriya*' (Liberty), *Dāʾirat al-Maʿārif*, vol. 6, p. 2.

49. Ibid.

50. Ibid., p. 3.

51. Ibid.

52. Ibid.

53. Ibid.

54. Suleiman al-Bustānī, '*Al-islāḥ*' (On reform), *al-Jinān*, vol. 5, March 1870, p. 18.

55. Al-Bustānī, *Al-Hayʾa al-ijtimāʿiya*, p. 16.

56. Al-Shidyāq, '*Al-Insān ashraf al-makhlūqāt*', p. 227.

3. ILLIBERAL ISLAM

1. Muhammad Iqbal, *Thoughts and Reflections of Iqbal*, edited with notes by Syed Abdul Vahid, Lahore: Sh. Muhammad Ashraf, 1992, p. 321.
2. Ibid., p. 211.
3. Ibid., pp. 163–4.
4. For this, see especially the sections on capitalism and communism in Iqbal's Persian work of 1932, the *Javid Nama*, in Sir Muhammad Iqbal, *Javid-Nama*, trans. Arthur Arberry, London: George Allen and Unwin Ltd., 1966, pp. 66–71.
5. Muhammad Iqbal, *The Reconstruction of Religious Thought in Islam*, New Delhi: Kitab Bhavan, 1990, p. 179.
6. Muhammad Iqbal, *Thoughts and Reflections of Iqbal*, pp. 373–4.
7. Ibid., p. 168.
8. Ibid., p. 162.
9. Ibid., pp. 248–9.
10. Ibid., pp. 196–7.
11. Ibid., pp. 167–8.
12. Ibid., p. 204.
13. Ibid., p. 173.
14. Ibid., p. 193.
15. Ibid., pp. 212–13.
16. Ibid., p. 190.
17. Ibid., pp. 261–2.
18. Ibid., p. 194.
19. Ibid., p. 197.
20. Ibid., p. 102.
21. Muhammad Iqbal, *The Reconstruction of Religious Thought in Islam*, ch. 4.
22. For an elaboration of this idea along somewhat different lines, see Emmanuel Levinas, 'Language and Proximity', in *Collected Philosophical Papers*, trans, Alphonso Lingis, Dordrecht: Kluwer, 1993.
23. Iqbal, *Thoughts and Reflections of Iqbal*, p. 227.
24. Muhammad Iqbal, *The Development of Metaphysics in Persia: A Contribution to the Study of Muslim Philosophy*, Lahore: Bazm-e Iqbal, 1959, p. 125.
25. Ibid., pp. ix–x.
26. Ibid., p. xi.
27. Iqbal, *Thoughts and Reflections of Iqbal*, p. 3.
28. Iqbal, *Development of Metaphysics in Persia*, p. 83.
29. Iqbal, *Thoughts and Reflections of Iqbal*, pp. 4–5.
30. Ibid., p. 35.
31. Ibid., pp. 239–40.
32. Ibid., p. 90.

33. Ibid., p. 240.
34. Ibid., p. 243.
35. Ibid., p. 145.

4. POSTCOLONIAL PROPHETS: ISLAM IN THE LIBERAL ACADEMY

1. An early treatment is Richard Southern's lectures on Western views of Islam in the Middle Ages, delivered at Harvard University in 1961. The lectures were published in 1978 by Harvard University Press; see also David Runciman, 'Review of *Western Views of Islam in the Middle Ages*', *Speculum*, 38, 3 (1963), pp. 505–6.

2. Particularly pertinent to the present discussion is the argument in Matthew Dimock's *Mythologies of the Prophet Muhammad in Early Modern English Culture*, Cambridge: Cambridge University Press, 2013. Negative portrayals of Muhammad and misconceptions of Islam allowed English thinkers and readers to question and examine their own beliefs, and to frame their own identity, as Protestant, Anglicans, and Englishmen.

3. One recent example is a panel discussion entitled 'Is Islam a Religion? Islamophobia, Public Discourse, and the Idea of Religion', held at the Union Theological Seminary in New York. According to the event website, the forum would 'provide an overview of common patterns in Islamophobic and anti-Muslim discourse. It will then explore this discourse's political underpinnings, its impact on public and academic teaching about Islam, and the challenges it poses to the concept of "religion" itself and the role of religion in public life': http://www.mei.columbia.edu/news-fall-2014/2017/3/31/is-islam-a-religion-islamophobia-public-discourse-and-the-idea-of-religion

4. A recent iteration of the same tired debate is found in *Critical Muslim* 2 (2012), which collects a number of essays on 'The Idea of Islam'.

5. A worldview that is above the dirty world of politics is doomed to political failure. Kari Palonen, 'The History of Concepts as a Style of Political Theorizing: Quentin Skinner's and Reinhart Koselleck's Subversion of Normative Political Theory', *European Journal of Political Theory*, 1, 1 (2002), pp. 91–106, reference is at p. 95; and, as it applies to the clash of civilisations between the Western and Islamic worlds, and the exhortation to free political philosophy and conceptual history from a commitment to Westernisation and modernization, as John Rawls freed it from secularization, see David M. Rasmussen, 'The Emerging Domain of the Political', *Philosophy & Social Criticism*, 38, 4–5 (2012), pp. 457–66.

6. Reinhard Schulze's work is among the most influential exceptions. For his refutation of Hourani's thesis—that the eighteenth century in the Islamic world was characterised by decline because liberalism failed to take hold—see Reinhard Schulze, 'Das islamische achtzehnte Jahrhundert: Versuch einer historiographischen Kritik', *Die Welt des Islams*, 30, 1 (1990), pp. 140–9; and Schulze, 'Was ist die islamische

Aufklärung?', *Die Welt des Islams*, 36, 3 (1996), pp. 317–25 and for an opposing view, Rudolf Peters, 'Reinhard Schulze's Quest for an Islamic Enlightenment', *Die Welt des Islams*, 30, 1 (1990), pp. 160–2; also, a thoughtful commentary by Mehmet Yilmaz Akbulut, 'The Debate on the "Islamic Enlightenment" of the Eighteenth Century' (https://www.academia.edu/8612787/The_Debate_on_the_Islamic_ Enlightenment_of_the_eighteenth_Century).

7. Malcolm Kerr, *Islamic Reform: the Political and Legal Theories of Muhammad Abduh and Rashid Rida*, Berkeley: University of California Press, 1966, as quoted in Abdulkader Tayob, *Religion in Modern Islamic Discourse*, New York: Columbia University Press, 2009, p. 24.

8. See Marshall Hodgson, *The Venture of Islam*, 3 vols., Chicago: University of Chicago Press, 1974; and Bruce Lawrence and David Gilmartin, 'Introduction', in David Gilmartin and Bruce B. Lawrence (eds), *Beyond Turk and Hindu: Rethinking Religious Identity in Islamicate South Asia*, Gainesville: University Press of Florida, 2000, pp. 1–20, at p. 2.

9. Bruce B. Lawrence, 'Genius Denied and Reclaimed: A 40-Year Retrospect on Marshall G. S. Hodgson's *The Venture of Islam*', Marginalia: A Los Angeles Review of Books Channel, 11 November 2014 (http://marginalia.lareviewofbooks.org/ retrospect-hodgson-venture-islam/).

10. Chris Bayly, 'Marshall G.S. Hodgson, Islam and World History', Humanitas Visiting Professorship in Historiography Lecture, University of Oxford, 13 May 2013 (http://oxforddigital.tv/streaming/humanitas-chris-bayly.html).

11. The emerging field of environmental history may furnish a fresh and culture-free approach. Trendsetters in this regard include Rhoads Murphey, 'The Decline of North Africa since the Roman Occupation: Climatic or Human?', *Annals of the Association of American Geographers*, 41 (1951), pp. 116–32. In an article on the ramifications of environmental change for debunking pseudo-explanations for European ascendancy in social, cultural, religious, or political terms, Richard W. Bulliet has argued that cheap animal labour available in the arid zones of the Middle East and North Africa where grazing is abundant and free, in contrast with the relatively high costs of harnessing animal power in cold and forested Europe, where animals must be fed and sheltered, explains the rise of technologies—the water mill in this instance—that led to capital accumulation in Europe around the twelfth century (well before the Renaissance and the Industrial Revolution). This hypothesis, Bulliet writes, is 'crucial to moving the debate over the post-1400 economic disjunction between Europe and the lands of Islam from the realm of culture, religion, and politics to the realm of the economics of natural resource management'. Richard W. Bulliet, 'History and Animal Energy in the Arid Zone', in Alan Mikhail (ed.), *Water on Sand: Environmental Histories of the Middle East and North Africa*, New York: Oxford University Press, 2012, pp. 51–70; reference is at p. 66.

12. Metahistories on the rise of Islamic and Middle Eastern Studies in the Anglo-American academy published after 9/11 must be separated from those authored previously. Examples of these critiques, which see in the study of Islam in the Anglo-American academy a genealogy for Islamophobia and military aggression against Muslim majority nations in the post-9/11 world, are provided in the bibliography.

13. James Bill, 'The Study of Middle East Politics 1946–1996: A Stocktaking', *The Middle East Journal*, 50, 4 (1996), pp. 501–12.

14. Timothy Mitchell, 'The Middle East in the Past and Future of Social Sciences', in David L. Szanton (ed.), *The Politics of Knowledge: Area Studies and the Disciplines*, Berkeley: University of California Press and University of California Area Studies Digital Collection, 2002, pp. 28–60; reference is at p. 8 (HYPERLINK "http://escholarship.org/uc/item/59n2d2n1" \l "page-50" http://escholarship.org/uc/item/59n2d2n1#page-50).

15. See among others, R. Stephen Humphreys, *Tradition and Innovation in the Study of Islamic History* Islamic Area Studies Working Paper Series 1, Tokyo, Islamic Area Studies Project, 1998.

16. Mitchell, 'Middle East in the Past and Future of Social Sciences', p. 9.

17. Ibid., p. 8.

18. Richard Bulliet, 'Pages from a Memoir: The Middle East Studies Association', 1980 (https://www. academia.edu/8302705/pages_from_a_memoir-the_middle_east_studies_association).

19. María Jesús González Hernández, *Raymond Carr: The Curiosity of the Fox*, trans. Nigel Griffin, Eastbourne: Sussex Academic Publications, 2013, pp. 212–35.

20. Ibid., pp. 341–51; and William Roger Louis, 'Review of Raymond Carr, *The Curiosity of the Fox* by María Jesús González Hernández', *English Historical Review*, 129 (October 2014), pp. 1250–2; reference is at p. 1251.

21. The Nadav Safron debacle at Harvard University's Center for Middle Eastern Studies is among the best known, although several other professors, including Samuel Huntington, whose clash of civilisations thesis met an eager audience in the post 9/11 world, had suffered his own CIA-scandal in 1986 (see Michelle M. Hu and Radhika Jain, 'Controversy Erupts Over Professors' Ties to the CIA, *The Harvard Crimson*, 25 May 2011, http://www.thecrimson.com/article/2011/5/25/research-cia-harvard-betts/, last accessed 15 May 2017).

22. Tawfiq Sayyigh (d. 1971) was a celebrated Christian Arab poet and literary critic, see Issa J. Boullata, 'The Beleaguered Unicorn: A Study of Tawfiq Sāyigh', *Journal of Arabic Literature*, 4 (1973), pp. 69–93; and Mitchell, 'The Middle East in the Past and Future of Social Sciences', p. 10.

23. Mitchell, 'The Middle East in the Past and the Future of Social Sciences', p. 12.

24. Literature on the hypocritical stance of human rights advocates, who proclaim a liberal and progressive platform while—even if unwittingly—supporting and pro-

moting Western interests in the third world is gathering steam. See Samuel Moyn, 'Human Rights in Heaven', in Adam Etinson (ed.), *Human Rights: Moral or Political?*, New York: Oxford University Press, 2014; and, Stephen Kinzer, 'Are Today's Human Rights Activists Warmongers?', *Boston Globe*, 25 May 2014 (http://www.bostonglobe.com/opinion/2014/05/24/are-human-rights-activists-today-warmongers/gef04rpPxgEdCEdx4DQ87J/story.html). Against gay rights platforms, see Joseph Massad's *Desiring Arabs*, Chicago: University of Chicago Press, 2007, and contra feminism, see Deepa Kumar, 'Imperialist Feminism and Liberalism', Open Democracy, 6 November 2014 (https://www.opendemocracy.net/deepa-kumar/imperialist-feminism-and-liberalism).

25. Ian Black, 'Wikileaks Reveals Degree of Durham University's Involvement in Iran', *The Guardian*, 10 February 2011 (http://www.theguardian.com/commentisfree/2011/feb/10/wikileaks-durham-university-iran-us-embassy); and Daniel Johnson and Jack Battersby, 'Durham University Engulfed in Wikileaks Allegations', The Palatinate, 8 February 2011 (http://www.palatinate.org.uk/?p=10679).

26. Ian Black, 'Iranian Tensions Shake Durham's Ivory Towers', *The Guardian*, 10 February 2010 (http://www.theguardian.com/uk/2010/feb/10/iranian-funding-durham-university-boycott); and http://www.brotherhoodwatch.co.uk/2013/09/iran-and-syria-durham-universitys-controversial-funding-policies/

27. On this particular tug of war, with shifting opposing sides, see Zachary Lockman, *Contending Visions of the Middle East: The History and Politics of Orientalism*, Cambridge: Cambridge University Press, 2010.

28. Usama Makdisi has written on the dilemmas facing scholars of the Middle East who have ventured into the public realm after 9/11, see Usama Makdisi, 'Once More into the Breach', Merip Interventions, December 2009 (http://www.merip.org/mero/interventions/once-more-breach).

29. On the dynamic landscape of liberalism, and its expansion in the 1950s to mean the ideological superstructure of the Western world, see Duncan Bell, 'What Is Liberalism?', *Political Theory*, 42, 6 (2014), pp. 682–715.

30. Edward Said, *The World, the Text, and the Critic*, Cambridge, MA: Harvard University Press, 1983, pp. 1–30; Duncan Bell, 'Ideologies of Empire', in Michael Freeden and Marc Stears (eds), *The Oxford Handbook of Political Ideologies*, Oxford: Oxford University Press, 2013, pp. 536–61.

31. Dipesh Chakrabarty, *Provincializing Europe: Postcolonial Thought and Historical Difference*, Princeton: Princeton University Press, 2007, p. 4

32. Ibid., p. 5.

33. The French original is translated into English; Abdelfattah Kilito, *The Author and His Doubles: Essays on Classical Arabic Culture*, trans. Michael Cooperson, Syracuse: Syracuse University Press, 2001.

34. Zaheer Kazmi, 'The Limits of Muslim Liberalism', *Los Angeles Review of Books*, 4 April 2014 (https://lareviewofbooks.org/essay/limits-muslim-liberalism/).

35. Bryan S. Turner, 'Re-reading Said: Late Thoughts', Middle East Institute, 20 April 2012 (http://www.mideasti.org/content/re-reading-said-late-thoughts).

36. Mitchell, 'Middle East in the Past and Future of Social Sciences', p. 16.

37. Robert J.C. Young, 'Edward Said: Opponent of Postcolonial Theory', in Tobias Döring and Mark Stein (eds), *Edward Said's Translocations: Essays in Secular Criticism*, New York: Routledge, 2012, pp. 23–43.

38. Samer Frangie, 'On the Broken Conversation between Postcolonialism and Intellectuals in the Periphery', *Studies in Social and Political Thought*, 19 (2011), pp. 41–54, Arif Dirlik emphatically ties the rise of postcolonial theory to 'when Third World intellectuals arrived in the First World academe', see his 'The Postcolonial Aura: Third World Criticism in the Age of Global Capitalism', *Critical Inquiry*, 20, 2 (1994), pp. 328–56, reference is at p. 329; 'Roger Owen, "Edward Said and the Two Critiques of Orientalism"', Middle East Institute, 20 April 2012 (http://www.mideasti.org/content/edward-said-and-two-critiques-orientalism); Lawrence Rosen, 'Orientalism Revisited: Edward Said's Unfinished Critique', *Boston Review*, 1 January 2007 (http://www.bostonreview.net/rosen-orientalism-revisited); and Daniel Martin Varisco, 'Orientalism's Wake: The Ongoing Politics of a Polemic', Middle East Institute, 16 August 2012 (http://www.mideasti.org/content/orientalisms-wake-ongoing-politics-polemic-0); and Jens Hanssen, 'Nietzsche and the 20th-Century Arab Intellectual Tradition (Précis)', Nietzsche 13/13 Seminar, Columbia University, 21 April 2017 (http://blogs.law.columbia.edu/nietzsche1313/jens-hanssen-nietzsche-and-the-20th-century-arab-intellectual-tradition-precis/).

39. Mark Mazower has drawn attention to the chequered history of internationalism and global regimes of governance in *Governing the World: The History of an Idea*, New York: Penguin, 2012.

40. Diversity is the newest iteration of the double-speak at the heart of liberalism; Walter Benn Michaels, 'Let Them Eat Diversity', *Jacobin Magazine*, 1 January 2011 (https://www.jacobinmag.com/2011/01/let-them-eat-diversity/).

41. Cemil Aydin, *The Politics of Anti-Westernism in Asia: Visions of World Order in Pan-Islamic and Pan-Asian Thought*, New York: Columbia University Press, 2007, pp. 191–3.

42. For a fuller articulation of that critical platform, see Richard Bulliet, 'Orientalism and Medieval Islamic Studies', in John Van Engen (ed.), *The Past and Future of Medieval Studies*, Notre Dame: University of Notre Dame Press, 1994, pp. 94–104; and the debate between Richard Bulliet and Hichem Djaït in *Diogenes*, 95 (1976), pp. 93–104.

43. Jalal Al Ahmad, *Plagued by the West, Gharbzadagī*, trans. Paul Sprachman, Delmar, NY: Caravan Books, 1982; and *Dar khidmat va khiyānat-i rawshanfikrān*, Tehran: Ravaq, 1980.

44. Hichem Djait, *La personnalité et le devenir arabo-islamiques*, Paris, Éditions du Seuil, 1974.

45. Abdallah 'Arawi (Abdullah Laroui), *The Crisis of the Arab Intellectual: Traditionalism or Historicism*, Berkeley: University of California Press, 1976.

46. Samir Amin, *The Arab Nation: Nationalism and Class Struggles*, London: Zed Press, 1978; on Samir Amin, see also, Timothy Mitchell, 'The Stage of Modernity', in Timothy Mitchell (ed.), *Questions of Modernity*, Minneapolis: University of Minnesota Press, 2000, pp. 1–34.

47. Frantz Fanon, *Black Skin, White Masks*, New York: Grove Press, 2008.

48. Hybridity as a hallmark of a globalising world order is often assumed to destabilise binaries and 'Western' notions of race and belonging; see Judith Butler and Gayatri Chakravorty-Spivak, *Who Sings the Nation-State? Language, Politics, Belonging*, London: Seagull Books, 2007.

49. Rosalind O'Hanlon and David Washbrook, 'After Orientalism: Culture, Criticism, and Politics in the Third World', *Comparative Studies in Society and History*, 34, 1 (1992), pp. 141–67; reference is at p. 142.

50. Peter Gran, 'Subaltern Studies, Racism, and Class Struggle: Examples from India and the United States', unpublished paper form Working Paper series, Department of Comparative American Cultures, Washington State University, Pullman, WA, 1999, as quoted in David Ludden, *Reading Subaltern Studies: Critical History, Contested Meaning and the Globalization of South Asia*, London: Anthem Press, 2003, p. 4.

51. One example among many is Maya Jasanoff's facile resolution of Edward Said's dilemma, when asked in an interview if he had written *Orientalism* as an oriental or an occidental. 'I really don't know', Said had responded. Dismissing Said's response as hasty, 'the real answer', Jasanoff claims, 'is that he wrote it as both'. See Maya Jasanoff, 'The Book that Shook Us: Orientalism at 30', *The Guardian*, 13 June 2008 (http://www.theguardian.com/commentisfree/2008/jun/13/middleeast.israelandthepalestinians).

52. *The Impossible State: Islam, Politics and Modernity's Moral Predicament*, New York: Columbia University Press, 2012, has received multiple reviews; see Andrew F. March, 'What Can the Islamic Past Teach Us about Secular Modernity?', *Political Theory* (forthcoming). Available at SSRN: http://ssrn.com/abstract=2386075; Lama Abu-Odeh 'Book Review of *The Impossible State* by Wael Hallaq, *International Journal of Middle East Studies* 46 (2014), pp. 216–18; Mark D. Welton, "Review of *The Impossible State*', *Middle East Journal*, 67, 3 (2013), pp. 492–3; Muhammad Hashas, 'Qirā'at fī kitāb al-dawla al-mustaḥīla', 23 January 2014, Mominoun without Borders Foundation for Studies and Research, Religion and Politics Division (www.mominoun.com/arabic/ar-sa/articles/9381); and Hussain Iza, Nathan J. Brown and Neguin Yavari, "Review Symposium: *The Impossible State*', *Perspectives on Politics*, 12, 2 (2014), pp. 461–7.

53. Hallaq, *Impossible State*, p. ix.

54. Ibid., p. 23.

55. Ibid., p. 2.

56. Ibid., p. 11.

57. Ibid.

58. Ibid., pp. 16–18.

59. Hallaq's discussion of the modern paradigmatic state is a namedropping spree. He enlists a motley troop of theorists: from Carl Schmitt to Thomas Kuhn, John Gray, Michel Foucault, Leo Strauss, Charles Larmore and Charles Taylor. Plato, Aristotle, Aquinas, Descartes, Francis Bacon, Voltaire, Hobbes, Rousseau, Hume, Spinoza, Hegel, Kant, Vico, Marx, Nietzsche, Bentham, Mill, Kierkegaard, Rawls, Gramsci and many more; all making cameo appearances. He cites these theorists not to draw them into a conversation. Rather, bits and pieces from each theorist are strewn together to make possible his claim that re-enchantment is in order in the West, or that Ghazzali anticipates Foucault. See Hallaq, *Impossible State*, p. 129.

60. Reinhard Schulze, *A Modern History of the Islamic World*, trans. Azizeh Azodi, New York: New York University Press, 2002, pp. 222–6.

61. Neguin Yavari, '*Tafsīr* and the Mythology of Islamic Fundamentalism', in Andreas Görke and Johanna Pink (eds), *Tafsīr and Islamic Intellectual History: Exploring the Boundaries of a Genre*, Oxford: Oxford University Press, 2014, Chapter 9

62. Schulze, *Modern History of the Islamic World*, p. 247.

63. Ibid., pp. 248–9.

64. See on this Zaheer Kazmi's review of Tariq Ramadan's *The Arab Awakening*; "The Limits of Muslim Liberalism," *Los Angeles Review of Books*, 4 April 2014 (https://lareviewofbooks.org/essay/limits-muslim-liberalism/).

65. Ahmad Ghorab, *Subverting Islam: The Role of Orientalist Centers*, London: Minerva, 1995, is a salacious if lightly sourced account of this relationship. On sectarian politics in several Persian Gulf states, see Toby Matthiesen, *Sectarian Gulf: Bahrain, Saudi Arabia, and the Arab Spring that Wasn't*, Stanford: Stanford University Press, 2013.

66. Muhammad Fikri, 'Harim-i khus--i shahrvandan dar andisha-i Imam Khomeini', *Ittila'at*, 4 February 2012, issue no. 25240, pp. 6–7.

67. Vali Nasr, *Shia Revival: How Conflicts within Islam with Shape the Future*, New York: Norton, 2006, p. 134, as quoted in Wikipedia, 'Ruhollah Khomeini', modified 5 October 2014 (http://en.wikipedia.org/wiki/Ruhollah_Khomeini). See also in this regard, Timothy Mitchell; 'Economists and the Economy in the Twentieth Century', in George Steinmetz (ed.), *The Politics of Method in the Human Sciences: Positivism and Its Epistemological Others*, Durham: Duke University Press, 2005, pp. 126–41; John Markoff and Verónica Montecinos, 'The Ubiquitous Rise of Economists', *Journal of Public Policy*, 13 (1993), pp. 37–68; Marion Fourcade, 'The Construction of a Global Profession: The Transnationalization of Economics', *American Journal of Sociology*, 112 (2006), pp. 145–94.

68. Peter Gordon, 'What Is Intellectual History? A Frankly Partisan Introduction to

a Frequently Misunderstood Field' (2007, revised 2009) (http://history.fas.harvard.edu/people/faculty/documents/pgordon-whatisintellhist.pdf).

69. Amr Hamzawy, 'Arab Writings on Islamist Parties and Movements', *International Journal of Middle East Studies*, 43, 1 (2011), pp. 138–40.

70. Jo Guldi and David Armitage, *The History Manifesto*, Cambridge: Cambridge University Press, 2015, p. 54.

71. In 2016, for example, 342 (32.39%) of the 1056 papers presented at the annual conference of the Middle East Studies Association of North America Boston focused on the 19th-21st centuries; 188 papers had 'modern' in the title; 228 papers were in Political Science/International Affairs, and 419 papers in History. *Issues in Middle East Studies*, 39, 1 (2017), p. 17 (https://mesana.org/mymesa/display_publications.php?f=1373-d645920e395fedad7bbbed0eca3fe2e0).

72. Richard Bulliet, *Islam: The View from the Edge*, New York: Columbia University Press, 1994, p. 3.

73. Ibid., p. 12.

74. For a thorough discussion on the Arab Spring, see 'Reflections Symposium', *Perspectives on Politics*, 12, 2 (2014), pp. 394–419.

75. Walter Benn Michaels, *The Shape of the Signifier*, Princeton: Princeton University Press, 2004, p. 170.

76. Muhtashimipur, among Khomeini's staunchest allies and the architect of Iran's Syria policy in the early days of the revolution, left Iran in protest following the election crisis of 2009. Power cuts in Najaf have forced him to spend the summers in Tehran. Sayyid 'Ali Akbar Muhtashimipur, 'Payam-i Imam bi Hafiz Assad', *Asiman*, n.s. 31 (1991), pp. 16–20; and Muhtashimipur, 'Bashshar Assad bi in rahati-ha raftani nist', Khabar Online, 22 July 2012 (1 Mordad 1391); http://khabaronline.ir/detail/229669/Politics/diplomacy

77. Muhtashimipur, 'Payam-i Imam bi Hafiz Assad', p. 20.

78. Many influential scholars have espoused a revival of Mu'tazili teachings (those of the 'Muslim rationalists' that flourished in the ninth century) to counter contemporary extremism; see Josef Van Ess, *The Flowering of Muslim Theology*, trans. Jane Marie Todd, Cambridge, MA: Harvard University Press, 2006; and my review of Van Ess in *The American Historical Review*, 112, 2 (2007), pp. 623–4.

5. A NEW DEAL BETWEEEN MANKIND AND ITS GODS: HOW TO THINK IN THE POST-RELIGIOUS ERA ACCORDING TO MUHAMMAD IQBAL

1. Individuation means the path to become oneself, as a real singular or single person, by expression of one's deepest self. My doctoral thesis (viva voce 2013, University Paris Diderot) is entitled 'Muhammad Iqbal, a Pedagogy of Individuation'. Not yet translated in English. On this theme of individualisation in Iqbal's thought, I have

published *L'islam face à la mort de Dieu* (Bourin Editeur, Paris, 2010) and *L'islam spirituel de Mohammed Iqbal* (Albin Michel, Paris, 2007)

2. Gianni Vattimo, *La fin de la modernité, nihilisme et herméneutique dans la culture post-moderne* (The end of modernity, Nihilism and hermeneutics in the postmodern culture), trans. Charles Alunni, Paris: Seuil, 1987 [1985], pp. 35–6.

3. Ibid., p. 36.

4. Ibid., p. 35.

5. Muhammad Iqbal, *The Development of Metaphysics in Persia*, East Lansing, MI: H-Bahai, 2001 [1908]. English translation by Eva de Vitray-Meyerovitch, Paris: Sindbad, 1st edn 1980, p. 115.

6. Muhammad Iqbal, *Reconstruire la pensée religieuse de l'islam* (Six lectures on the reconstruction of religious thought in Islam), London, 1934; Muhammad Iqbal, *The Reconstruction of Religious Thought in Islam*, trans. Eva Meyerovitch, London: Dodo Press, 2009/Paris: Adrien-Maisonneuve, 1955, p. 63.

7. This is reminiscent of Norbert Elias's criticism of the place of the *homo clausus* of Descartes, and the larger and broader thinking of the *homo socius* that opposes it (Norbert Elias, *La société des individus: The Society of Individuals*, Paris: Fayard, 1991 [1987]).

8. Henri Bergson, *L'évolution créatrice*, in *Oeuvres complètes/The Creative Evolution*, Paris: PUF, 1984 [1959], p. 725.

9. Iqbal, *Reconstruire la pensée religieuse de l'islam*, p. 123.

10. See Note 1 of this chapter.

11. Ibid.

12. Ibid.

13. Iqbal Singh, *The Ardent Pilgrim*, Delhi: Oxford University Press, 1997 [1951], p. 52.

14. Ibid., pp. 52–3.

15. Ibid., p. 53.

16. Teilhard de Chardin, *Le Phénomène humain*, Paris: Editions du Seuil, 1963.

17. Iqbal, *Development of Metaphysics in Persia*, p. 87.

18. Ernst Mayr, *Qu'est-ce que la biologie?* (This is biology), Paris: Arthème Fayard, 1998 [1997], p. 211.

19. Ibid., p. 35.

20. André Pichot, *Histoire de la notion de vie* (History of the idea of life), Paris: Gallimard, 1993, p. 826.

21. For an introduction to this question, see Georges Pétavy, *Qu'est-ce que le dessein intelligent? Comment en réfuter les theses*, Paris: Vuibert, 2010.

22. Bergson, *L'evolution créatrice*, in *Œuvres complètes*, p. 720.

23. Ibid.

24. Emphasis added.

25. Bergson, *L'evolution créatrice*, p. 721.

26. Albert Camus, *L'homme révolté*, Paris: Gallimard, 1951, p. 213.

27. See especially Apollodore, *La bibliothèque*, trans. from the Greek under the direction of Paul Schubert, Neuchâtel: L'Aire, 2003.

28. This is what I have called 'a Muslim existentialism' (*L'islam sans soumission: Pour un existentialisme musulman*, Paris: Albin Michel, 2008).

29. Jacques Maritain, *Humanisme intégral*, Paris: Aubier, 1936.

30. Cornelius Castoriadis, *L'institution imaginaire de la société*, Paris: Seuil, p. 39.

31. Marshall Sahlins, *La nature humaine: Une illusion occidentale* (Human nature, a Western illusion), Paris, Editions de l'Eclat, 2009 [2008]

32. Castoriadis, *L'institution imaginaire de la société*, pp. 36–7.

33. Ibid., p. 220.

34. From my open letter to the Islamic world, published in French newspaper *Marianne*: http://blog.oratoiredulouvre.fr/2014/10/tres-profonde-lettre-ouverte-au-monde-musulman-du-philosophe-musulman-abdennour-bidar/

35. Particularly in French-speaking Canada. See, for example, Antoine Robitaille, *Le nouvel home nouveau: Voyage dans les utopies de la posthumanité*, Montréal: Les Editions du Boréal, 2007.

36. Singh, *Ardent Pilgrim*, p. 62.

37. Iqbal is very close, on this point, to Hinduism, which presents the self-realisation as an experience of 'Sat-Chit-Ananda': Supreme Being, Supreme Self-Awareness, Supreme Beatitude.

38. Bergson, *L'évolution créatrice*, pp. 87–8

39. G.W.F. Hegel, *Esthétique*, book 1, French translation by Charles Bénard, edited and completed by Beoît Timmermans and Paolo Zaccaria, Paris: Le Livre de Poche, 1997, p. 85: 'In the second place, man becomes to himself by his practical activity, because he has the impulsion to produce and equally to recognise himself through that which he is given immediately, that is to say that which, for him, is existing on the exterior. He achieves this end by transforming exterior things, on which he prints the seal of his interior, and in which he thus recovers his own determinations. Man acts thus, as a free subject, in order to remove for the exterior world his restive foreignness and to enjoy, only through the shape of things, of an exterior realisation of himself.' According to Iqbal's philosophy, we might add that the human recreation of the world will either be that of an ordinary ego, which already manifests this capacity only to his expectations, and according to the shape of the mediocrity of his aspirations and triviality of his needs, or be that of an ego already en route to the superior aspirations of the Supreme Ego; such an ego will want at the same time to recreate himself, and not only the exterior world, and these creations aim more at the Good, the Just, the Beautiful, as all these 'consumer goods' which we add nowadays to the world and which correspond very often to the appeasing of material and futile desires.

40. Philippe Descola, *Par-delà nature et culture*, Paris: Gallimard, 2005.

41. Claude Levi-Strauss, *Race et histoire*, Paris: Gallimard, 1987 [1952], p. 38.

42. Iqbal, *Reconstruire la pensée religieuse de l'islam*, p. 12.

43. Javeed Majeed, *Muhammed Iqbal, Islam: Aesthetics and Postcolonialism*, New Delhi: Routledge, 2009, pp. 24–5.

44. Annemarie Schimmel, *Gabriel's Wing: A Study into the Religious Ideas of Sir Muhammad Iqbal*, Lahore: Iqbal Academy Pakistan, 1963, p. 42.

45. Gilles Deleuze, 'Qu'est-ce que la philosophie?', *Revue Chimères*, 8 (May 1990).

46. For example, in *L'islam sans soumission: Pour un existentialisme musulman*, Paris: Albin Michel, 2008, I try to find a new meaning for the qur'anic verse 'I will put on earth a hãlif' (Inni jâ 'iloun fil Ardî khâlifatan, II, 30): *ha-la-fa* in Arabic means to follow/succeed/come after. Would man therefore succeed Allah?

47. Plato, *Alcibiades*, Book 1,129 e, in *Complete Works*, Book 1, Paris: Gallimard, 1950, p. 241.

48. Ibid., 128 e, p. 240.

49. Friedrich Nietzsche, *Volonté de puissance*, vol. 1, Book 2, §150, in *Vie et vérité*, Chosen texts, Paris: PUF, p. 52

50. Friedrich Nietzsche, *Ainsi parlait Zarathoustra* (Thus spoke Zarathustra), Paris: Gallimard, 1971, p. 52.

51. Iqbal, *Reconstruire la pensée religieuse de l'islam*, p. 98. Unique as Allah is 'Unique' (*Al Wâhid*): unicity of god is the symbolic key of the unicity of man.

52. Muhammad Iqbal, *Les secrets du Soi, Les mystères du Non-Moi, Muhammad Iqbal*, Lahore: Asrar-e-Khudi, Lahore, 1915; Lahore: Rumuz-e-Bikhudi, Lahore, 1918, trans. Eva de Vitray-Meyerovitch, Paris: Albin Michel, 1989, pp. 24–5.

53. Denis Matringe, *Un islam arabe, Horizons indiens et pakistanis*, Paris: Téraèdre, 2005, p. 85. See also about my book *L'islam face à la mort de Dieu: Actualité de Mohammed Iqbal*, Paris: FB Editeur, 2010: in *Samaj Review* (South Asia Multidisciplinary Academic Journal: Denis Matringe, Abdennour Bidar, L'islam face à la mort de Dieu: actualité de Mohammed Iqbal, 25 March 2011 (http://samaj.revues.org/3130).

6. THE DISSONANT POLITICS OF RELIGION, CIRCULATION AND CIVILITY IN THE SOCIOLOGY OF ISLAM

1. M. Khalid Masud and Armando Salvatore, 'Tradition and Modernity within Islamic Civilisation and the West', in Muhammad Khalid Masud, Armando Salvatore and Martin van Bruinessen (eds), *Islam and Modernity: Key Issues and Debates*, Edinburgh: Edinburgh University Press, 2009, pp. 43–5.

2. Bryan S. Turner, *Weber and Islam: A Critical Study*, London: Routledge, 1974.

3. Armando Salvatore, *Islam and the Political Discourse of Modernity*, Reading, UK: Ithaca Press, 1997.

4. Edward W. Said, *Orientalism*, New York: Pantheon, 1978.

5. Bryan S. Turner, *Marx and the End of Orientalism*, London: George Allen and Unwin, 1978.

6. Max Weber, *Gesammelte Aufsätze zur Religionssoziologie*, vol. 1, Tübingen: J.C.B. Mohr (Paul Siebeck), 1986 [1920].

7. Salvatore, *Islam*.

8. Jürgen Habermas, *The Structural Transformation of the Public Sphere*, trans. Thomas Burger, Cambridge: Polity, 1989 [1962].

9. Armando Salvatore, *The Public Sphere: Liberal Modernity, Catholicism, and Islam*, New York: Palgrave Macmillan, 2007.

10. While an exhaustive survey of this cleavage cannot be provided here, it is worth mentioning five edited collections as being broadly representative of the debate and its insufficiencies, from the viewpoint of the sociology of Islam: Ariel Mack (ed.), *Islam: The Public and Private Spheres*, Social Research 70, 3, New York: Graduate Faculty of Political and Social Science of the New School University, 2003; Armando Salvatore and Dale F. Eickelman (eds), *Public Islam and the Common Good*, Leiden: Brill, 2006; Armando Salvatore and Mark LeVine (eds), *Religion, Social Practice, and Contested Hegemonies: Reconstructing the Public Sphere in Muslim Majority Societies*, New York: Palgrave Macmillan, 2005; Nilüfer Göle and Ludwig Ammann (eds), *Islam in Public: Turkey, Iran, and Europe*, Istanbul: Bilgi University Press, 2006; Seteney Shami (ed.), *Publics, Politics and Participation: Locating the Public Sphere in the Middle East and North Africa*, New York: Social Science Research Council, 2009.

11. Marshall G.S. Hodgson, *The Venture of Islam. Conscience and History in a World Civilization*, vols. 1–3, Chicago: University of Chicago Press, 1974.

12. Norbert Elias, *The Civilizing Process*, Oxford: Blackwell, 2000 [1939; 1968].

13. Turner, *Weber and Islam*; Georg Stauth and Bryan S. Turner, *Nietzsche's Dance: Resentment, Reciprocity and Resistance in Social Life*, Oxford: Blackwell, 1988; Roy Jackson, *Nietzsche and Islam*, London: Routledge, 2007.

14. Georg Stauth, *Islam und Westlicher Rationalismus: Der Beitrag des Orientalismus zur Entstehung der Soziologie*, Frankfurt: Campus, 1993.

15. Tomoko Masuzawa, *The Invention of World Religions: How European Universalism Was Preserved in the Language of Pluralism*, Chicago: Chicago University Press, 2005.

16. Ernest Renan, *L'islam et la science; Avec la réponse d'al-Afghânî*, Montpellier: L'Archange Minotaure, 2005 [1883].

17. Michelanelo Guida, 'Al-Afghānī and Namık Kemal's Replies to Ernest Renan: Two Anti-Westernist Works in the Formative Stage of Islamist Thought', *Turkish Journal of Politics*, 2, 2 (2011), pp. 57–70.

18. Prasenjit Duara, *The Crisis of Global Modernity: Asian Traditions and a Sustainable Future*, Cambridge: Cambridge University Press, 2015, pp. 156–94.

19. Ibid., p. 138.

20. Nile Green, 'Breathing in India *c*.1890', *Modern Asian Studies*, 42, 2–3 (2008), pp. 283–315.

21. Armando Salvatore, 'Authority in Question: Secularity, Republicanism, and "Communitarianism" in the Emerging Euro-Islamic Public Sphere', *Theory, Culture and Society*, 24, 2 (2007), pp. 135–60.

22. Peter L. Berger, *The Sacred Canopy: Elements of a Sociological Theory of Religion*, Garden City: Doubleday, 1967.

23. Thomas Luckmann, *The Invisible Religion: The Problem of Religion in Modern Society*, New York: Macmillan, 1967.

24. Robert N. Bellah and Philip E. Hammond (eds), *Varieties of Civil Religion*, San Francisco: Harper & Row, 1980.

25. Clifford Geertz, *The Interpretation of Cultures: Selected Essays*, New York: Basic Books, 1973.

26. Talal Asad, *Genealogies of Religion: Discipline and Reasons of Power in Christianity and Islam*, Baltimore: Johns Hopkins University Press, 1993; Asad, *Formations of the Secular: Christianity, Islam, Modernity*, Stanford: Stanford University Press, 2003.

27. Hodgson, *Venture of Islam*.

28. Shnuel N. Eisenstadt, 'The Axial Age: The Emergence of Transcendental Visions and the Rise of Clerics', *European Journal of Sociology*, 23, 2 (1982), pp. 294–314.

29. Armando Salvatore, *The Sociology of Islam: Knowledge, Power and Civility*, Oxford: Wiley-Blackwell, 2016.

30. Bryan S. Turner, *The Sociology of Islam: Collected Essays of Bryan S. Turner*, ed. Bryan S. Turner and Kamaludeen Mohamed Nasir, Farnham: Ashgate, 2013, p. 23.

31. Ibid., p. 13.

32. Salvatore, *Sociology of Islam*.

33. Duara, *Crisis of Global Modernity*.

34. Ernest Gellner, *Muslim Society*, Cambridge: Cambridge University Press, 1981.

35. Salvatore, *Islam*.

36. Duara, *Crisis of Global Modernity*.

37. Stauth, *Islam und Westlicher Rationalismus*; Salvatore, *Islam*.

38. Bernard Lewis, *What Went Wrong? Western Impact and Middle Eastern Response*, Oxford: Oxford University Press, 2002; Dan Diner, *Lost in the Sacred: Why the Muslim World Stood Still*, Princeton: Princeton University Press, 2009 [2005]; Timur Kuran, *The Long Divergence: How Islamic Law Held Back the Middle East*, Princeton: Princeton University Press, 2011.

39. Asad, *Formations*, p. 217.

40. Ibid.

41. Elias, *Civilizing Process*; Arpad Szakolczai, *Reflexive Historical Sociology*, London: Routledge, 2000.

42. Johan Elverskog, *Buddhism and Islam on the Silk Road*, Philadelphia: University of Pennsylvania Press, 2010.

43. Arnason, *Civilizations*; Armando Salvatore, 'Eccentric Modernity? An Islamic Perspective on the Civilizing Process and the Public Sphere', *European Journal of Social Theory*, 14, 1 (2011), pp. 55–69.

44. Johann P. Arnason, *Civilisations in Dispute: Historical Questions and Theoretical Traditions*, Leiden: Brill, 2003.

45. Armando Salvatore, 'From Civilisations to Multiple Modernities: The Issue of the Public Sphere', in Modjtaba Sadria (ed.), *Multiple Modernities in Muslim Societies: Tangible Elements and Abstract Perspectives*, London: I.B. Tauris (for Aga Khan Award of Architecture), p. 33.

46. Hodgson, *Venture*, vol. 2, p. 271.

7. ISLAMIC DEMOCRACY BY NUMBERS

1. 'Pope Francis Tries to Build Bridges in Sceptical Turkey', BBC News, 2 December 2014 (http://www.bbc.co.uk/news/world-europe-30273812).

2. 'Show me just what Muhammad brought that was new and there you will find things only evil and inhuman, such as his command to spread by the sword the faith he preached', Pope Benedict XVI, 'Lecture of the Holy Father: Faith, Reason and the University Memories and Reflections', University of Regensburg, *Libreria Editrice Vaticana*,12 September 2006 (http://w2.vatican.va/content/benedict-xvi/en/speeches/2006/september/documents/hf_ben-xvi_spe_20060912_university-regensburg.html).

3. Rupert Shortt, *Christianophobia: A Faith under Attack*, London: Random House, 2012.

4. For a recent study of religious minorities in Egypt, see Saba Mahmood, *Religious Difference in a Secular Age: A Minority Report*, Princeton: Princeton University Press, 2015.

5. 'Faced with disconcerting episodes of violent fundamentalism, our respect for true followers of Islam should lead us to avoid hateful generalizations, for authentic Islam and the proper reading of the Quran are opposed to every form of violence.' Pope Francis, *The Joy of the Gospel*, London: Random House, 2014, p. 166.

6. The idea of the dangers of a 'tyranny of the majority' associated with democracy has a long pedigree in both ancient and modern Western political thought; for example, in the writings of James Madison, Alexis de Tocqueville and J.S. Mill.

7. Salafi–Wahhabism has affinities with the Hanbali school, although the nature of its precise relation to it is contested.

8. Qur'an, 2:143.

9. http://www.ammanmessage.com/

10. Mohammad Hashim Kamali, *The Middle Path of Moderation in Islam: The Qur'anic*

Principle of Wasatiyya, New York: Oxford University Press, 2015. For Ramadan's explicit inclusion of Shi'ism within his definition of classical Islam, see, among others, Tariq Ramadan, *Radical Reform, Islamic Ethics and Liberation*, New York: Oxford University Press, 2009.

11. Underlying Nasr's commitment to Sunni–Shi'a understanding is his wider attachment to the 'traditionalist' idea of universal religion and Perennial philosophy, including the influence of Frithjof Schuon. See William Chittick (ed.), *The Essential Seyyed Hossein Nasr*, Bloomington: World Wisdom, 2007.

12. In Shi'i jurisprudence, for example, *ijma* or 'consensus' is considered a source of law but not in the Sunni sense of a consensus among the people or religious scholars making something legitimate or a proof (*hujjah*) of its validity in itself. For the Shi'a, such a consensus does not necessarily lead to rectitude in an Islamic sense as all legal rulings by scholars are open to rational debate.

13. The idea of Ash'arism being tied to the 'middle path' of Islam is a common historical trope in Ash'arite apologetics. Thus, for example, in his 'The Middle Position of Al Ash'ari', Ibn Asakir (d.1175) writes, 'Al-Ash'ari took the middle road [between the *Mu'tazila* and the anthropomorphists].' See also John B. Henderson, *The Construction of Orthodoxy and Heresy: Neo-Confucian, Islamic, Jewish and Early Christian Patterns*, Albany: State University of New York Press, 1998, pp. 107–9. The position of Atharite theology, most often associated with Hanbalism though not limited to this madhab, is ambiguous when it comes to middle-way projections of Sunni orthodoxy. Here, the contemporary revival of the medieval scholar Ibn Taymiyya—himself a proponent of a 'middle way'—by both Salafi-Wahhabists and Safafi-jihadists, on the one hand, and Sufi scholars such as Hamza Yusuf, on the other, is instructive of intra-Sunni theological competition over who represents middle-way orthodoxy.

14. See, among others, Michaelle L. Browers, *Political Ideology in the Arab World: Accommodation and Transformation*, Cambridge: Cambridge University Press, 2009, pp. 48–77 and Lily Zubaida Rahim, 'The Spirit of Wasatiyyah Democracy', in Lily Zubaida Rahim (ed.), *Muslim Secular Democracy: Voices from Within*, New York: Palgrave Macmillan, 2013, pp. 1–28.

15. *The Muslim 500: The World's 500 Most Influential Muslims*, Amman, Jordan: Royal Islamic Strategic Studies Centre, 2012.

16. Available online at http://www.masud.co.uk/ISLAM/ahm/newmadhh.htm

17. 'Misleading and Defamatory: Channel 4 Accused over Documentary on Qur'an', *The Guardian*, 28 July 2008 (http://www.theguardian.com/world/2008/jul/28/islam.channel4).

18. Abdal Hakim Murad, *Commentary on the Eleventh Contentions*, Cambridge: The Quilliam Press, 2012.

19. 'The scholar reforms only because others have deformed. Adherence to Sunni Islam is acceptance of the canons of this reforming process...and of the consensual move-

ment of the Umma in the Four Schools. Only in their practices can the instruments of *ijtihad* be successfully found as simultaneously flexible and authentic. (Not) In the febrile fringes outside the Four Schools.' Murad, *Commentary*, pp. 157–8.

20. While his dismissal of the 'febrile fringes outside the four schools' alone would suggest this general criticism, his online 'Contentions' about 'Shi'ism' reinforce it. See note 25 below.

21. 'For many Rafidites, the 'Day of Judgement' refers to Zainab, while the 'Two Seas' means Ali and Fatima', Murad, *Commentary*, p. 162.

22. Ibid., p. 151. Winter occasionally uses the term *ghulat* which is itself used within Shi'i theology to denote and censure the excesses of those who ascribe divinity to the Shi'i Imams or otherwise exaggerate about them.

23. '"He will be punished severely": Free Syrian Army Vows to Hunt Down Rebel Commander Abu Sakkar Filmed Eating Government Soldier's "Heart" in Gruesome Propaganda Video', *Independent*, 15 May 2013 (http://www.independent.co.uk/news/world/middle-east/he-will-be-punished-severely-free-syrian-army-vows-to-hunt-down-rebel-commander-abu-sakkar-filmed-8615112.html).

24. For details of the initiative, see http://curriculumforcohesion.org/

25. Available at a website dedicated to his writings: http://masud.co.uk/ISLAM/ahm/contentions.htm and http://masud.co.uk/contention/contentions-9/. Here, Winter uses the term 'Shi'ism' without qualification or distinction, as a catch-all term.

26. Hassan Hassan, 'Hatred, Violence and the Sad Demise of Yusuf al Qaradawi', *The National*, 28 January 2014 (http://www.thenational.ae/thenationalconversation/comment/hatred-violence-and-the-sad-demise-of-yusuf-al-qaradawi#full).

27. http://islamopediaonline.org/fatwa/al-qaradawis-statement-shiites

28. Among major classical or pre-modern Sunni scholars who have published works in this genre or otherwise asserted Shi'ism explicitly as a heresy are Ibn Ḥazm (d.1064), Ibn al-Jawzi (d.1201), Ibn Taymiyya (d.1328), Ibn Khaldun (1406), Aḥmad Sirhindi (d.1624), Shah Abdul Aziz (d.1824) and Muḥammad Ibn Abd al-Wahhab (d.1792). The list of 'moderns' is also voluminous and notably includes the nineteenth-century founders of both Deobandi and Barelwi Sufism in India, contending strands of which stem from the Hanafi madhab, and, into the twentieth century, the Syrian pan-Islamist associate of Muhammad Abduh, Rashid Rida (d.1935).

29. Shaykh ul Islam Dr Muhammad Tahir ul Qadri, *Fatwa on Terrorism and Suicide Bombings*, London: Minhaj ul Quran, 2011.

30. These accusations have been particularly vocal among representatives of the minority Ahmadi community.

31. 'Pakistani Mob Kills Christian Couple over "Blasphemy"', BBC News, 4 November 2014 (http://www.bbc.co.uk/news/world-asia-29893809).

32. In 1996, for example, the Fatwa Committee for Religious Affairs, an official body, issued a legal opinion stating that Shi'i Muslims were deviant and asserted the sole theological legitimacy of Sunni orthodoxy in Malaysia. See also 'In Otherwise Tolerant Malaysia, Shi'ites Are Banned', Al Arabiyya News, 14 January 2011 (https://www.alarabiya.net/articles/2011/01/14/133463.html).

33. '"Controlling" Shiah Necessary for Malaysia's Sake, Says New GMM Chief', *Malay Mail*, 6 December 2015 (http://www.themalaymailonline.com/malaysia/article/controlling-shiah-necessary-for-malaysias-sake-says-new-gmm-chief).

34. See, for example, the audio CD collection, Imam Al Ghazali, *The Alchemy of Happiness*, trans. and commentary by Hamza Yusuf (Alhambra Productions, 2006) and several works by Al Ghazali edited and introduced by Tim Winter.

35. See Yahya Michot, 'Ibn Taymiyya's "New Mardin Fatwa": Is Genetically Modified (GMI) Islam Carcinogenic?', *The Muslim World*, 101: 2 (2011), pp. 130–81.

36. These surface comparisons can obscure as much as enlighten in trying to make Islamic categories fit Western ones. For example, while the Sunni scholar Tariq Ramadan has been described as 'Islam's Martin Luther' as a signifier of his role in a so-called Islamic 'Reformation', analogies are often made between Shi'i religious authority and the papacy, despite, in the case of the Twelver Shi'i *marja'iyya*, the Shi'i system being historically more voluntaristic and pluralistic than the Catholic one. This latitude for legitimate interpretative disagreement in Shi'ism is also tied to the enduring centrality of the practice of *ijtihad* (independent reasoning by a qualified scholar), which has generally made Shi'i hermeneutics historically more dynamic in exegetical terms than Sunnism. Part of the problem in positing such comparisons lies in how affinities between the aesthetics of Shi'ism and Catholicism on, for example, practices of iconography and intercession (affinities which are themselves not confined to Shi'ism but also shared with certain Sunni practices), are de-contextualised and then projected on to wider issues of religious authority where there can be substantive divergence.

37. One of the founding fathers of liberalism, John Locke, excluded Roman Catholics along with atheists from his conception of toleration. For a critical overview of the period, see John Coffey, *Persecution and Toleration in Protestant England 1558–1689*, New York: Routledge, 2013.

38. While European studies of early Islam by historical 'Orientalists' dominated by this outlook are numerous, the influential work of the late Edinburgh University academic, William Montgomery Watt, also epitomises it. See, among other works, William Montgomery Watt, *Early Islam: Collected Articles*, Edinburgh: Edinburgh University Press, 1990. In recent decades, discrete studies of early Shi'ism have emerged in Western academia to provide a degree of corrective to these accounts, some of which have also been concerned with constructing notions of Shi'i orthodoxy. For a survey of the literature, see Robert Gleave, 'Recent Research into the History of Early Shi'ism', *History Compass*, 7, 6 (2009), pp. 1593–605. As Gleave

observes, pointing to how a Shi'i perspective is still largely considered a fringe concern in the teaching of Islamic Studies in the West, 'To hire a Shi'i specialist to teach Sunni Islam is, for some reason, more controversial than hiring a Sunni specialist to teach Shi'ism'; Gleave, 'Recent Research', p. 1602.

8. BOURGEOIS ISLAM AND MUSLIMS WITHOUT MOSQUES: MUSLIM LIBERALISM AND ITS DISCONTENTS IN INDONESIA

1. Zaheer Kazmi, 'The Limits of Muslim Liberalism', *Los Angeles Review of Books*, 4 April 2014; Wael Hallaq, 'Maqasid and the Challenges of Modernity', *Al-Jāmi'ah: Journal of Islamic Studies*, 49, 1 (2011), p. 28.

2. Darul Islam was an Islamist organisation that challenged the authority of the Republic of Indonesia until the capture of its key leaders in 1962. It re-emerged under a different guise, when younger cadres returned from decades of exile to establish the Jemaah Islamiyah. For the latter, see Greg Barton, *Indonesia's Struggle: Jemaah Islamiyah and the Soul of Islam*, Sydney: University of New South Wales Press, 2004.

3. Carool Kersten, *Cosmopolitans and Heretics: New Muslim Intellectuals and the Study of Islam*, London: Hurst Publishers, 2011, pp. 53–4, 58.

4. Fazlur Rahman, 'Islam: Challenges and Opportunities', in Alford Welch and Pierre Cachia (eds), *Islam: Past Influence and Present Challenge: Festschrift in Honour of William Montgomery Watt*, Edinburgh: Edinburgh University Press, 1979, pp. 316, 323–30; Fazlur Rahman, *Islam and Modernity: Transformation of an Intellectual Tradition*, Chicago: University of Chicago Press, 1982, p. 85.

5. Rahman, 'Islam: Challenges and Opportunities', p. 323.

6. Leonard Binder, *Islamic Liberalism: A Critique of Development Ideologies*, Chicago: University of Chicago Press, 1988; Charles Kurzman, *Liberal Islam; A Sourcebook*, New York: Oxford University Press, 1998.

7. Kurzman, *Liberal Islam*, pp. 13–18; Charles Kurzman, 'Liberal Islam: Prospects and Challenges', *Middle East Review of International Affairs*, 3, 3 (September 1999), pp. 11–19.

8. Kersten, *Cosmopolitans and Heretics*, pp. 91–2.

9. Victims include Freedom Institute leaders Andi Mallarangeng, erstwhile presidential spokesman (2004–9), and ex-minister of youth and sports (2009–12); disgraced PD chairman (2010–13) Anas Urbaningrum; and JIL founder Ulil Abshar-Abdalla, who is also the son-in-law of NU General President Mustofa Bisri.

10. Benoit Challand, 'The Counter-Power of Civil Society and the Emergence of a New Political Imaginary in the Arab World', *Constellations*, 18, 3 (2011), p. 274.

11. Andrew Higgins, 'As Indonesia Debates Islam's Role, U.S. Stays Out', *Washington Post*, 25 October 2009 (http://www.washingtonpost.com/wp-dyn/content/article/2009/10/24/AR2009102402279_pf.html).

12. Carool Kersten, *Islam in Indonesia: The Contest for Society, Ideas and Values*, London, Hurst, 2015, p. 11.

13. DDII was established in the late 1960s by disgruntled former members of Masyumi and other supporters of its former leader Mohammad Natsir, who also served as its first chairman.

14. Hairus Salim HS and Muhammad Ridwan, *Kultur Hibrida Anak Muda NU di Jalur Kultural*, Yogyakarta: LKiS, 1999.

15. Kersten, *Cosmopolitans and Heretics*, pp. 95–101.

16. Hasan Hanafi is a leading Egyptian philosopher, educated at the Sorbonne, where he studied, among others, with Paul Ricoeur. Abdurrahman Wahid wrote a foreword to the Indonesian translation of Kazuo Shimogaki's study of Hasan Hanafi's 'Islamic Left': Kazuo Shimogaki, *Kiri Islam Antara Modernisme dan Posmodernisme: Telaah Kritis Pemikiran Hasan Hanafi*, Yogyakarta: LKiS, 1993.

17. Kersten, *Islam in Indonesia*, p. 39.

18. Perhimpunan Pengembangan Pesantren dan Masyarakat, or 'Society for Pesantren and Community Development'.

19. The term 'Islamic Post-Traditionalism' was first used by one of the most prominent members of the Anak Muda NU, Ahmad Baso, as the title for the Indonesian translation of a collection of essays by al-Jabri; see Muhammad 'Abid al-Jabri, *Post Traditionalisme Islam*, trans. and introduced by Ahmad Baso, Yogyakarta: LKiS, 2000.

20. Hamid Dabashi, *The World of Persian Literary Humanism*, Cambridge, MA: Harvard University Press, 2012, p. 5.

21. Imam al-Shafi'i (d.820) is considered the eponymous founder of the Shafi'i School, one of four surviving authoritative schools of Sunni Islamic law; Al-Ash'ari (d.936) and Al-Maturidi (d.944) were two leading religious scholars who were instrumental in defining orthodox Sunni theology, stripping it of much of the rationalist philosophical elements introduced by the rivalling Mu'tazila School, who relied heavily on Hellenic thinking. Al-Ghazali (d.1111) is considered the most influential classical Muslim thinker who integrated theological, philosophical, legal and mystical thinking.

22. Dabashi, *World of Persian Literary Humanism*, p. 8 (original emphasis).

23. Faisal Devji makes a compelling case for this in *Muslim Zion: Pakistan as a Political Idea*, London: Hurst, 2013.

24. Dabashi, *World of Persian Literary Humanism*, pp. 12, 21; Hallaq, 'Maqasid and the Challenges of Modernity', p. 2

25. Ahmad Baso, *NU Studies: Pergolakan Pemikiran Antara Fundamentalisme Islam dan Fundamentalisme Liberal*, Jakarta: Erlangga, 2006, pp. 15, 29–30.

26. Rumadi, 'Islam Liberal "Plus" = Post-Traditionalisme Islam', *Kompas*, 23 November 2001, n.p.. Downloaded 6 December 2012.

27. Rumadi, 'Jejak-jejak Liberalisme di NU', *Tashwirul Afkar*, 9, 2000, p. 9.

28. Ibid., p. 7.

29. Ibid.

30. Ibid.

31. Ibid., p. 9.

32. Baso, *NU Studies*, p. 159.

33. Ibid., p. 161.

34. Ibid., p. 164.

35. Ibid., p. 165

36. Ibid., p. 170.

37. Ibid., p. 172.

38. Ibid., p. 173, see also Muhammad Abid al-Jabri, *Introduction to Arab-Islamic Philosophy*, Austin: Center for Middle Eastern Studies at the University of Texas in Austin, 1999, p. 120ff.; and Mohamed Abed al-Jabri, *Democracy, Human Rights and Law in Islamic Thought*, London, I.B. Tauris, 2009.

39. Baso, *NU Studies*, p. 173. Ibn Hazm (d.1064) was a leading scholar in eleventh-century Muslim Spain (Al-Andalus) and an advocate of Zahirism; a school favouring the manifest meaning of the Qur'an and traditions of the Prophet. Al-Shāṭibī (d.1388) was also a Andalusian religious scholar, who wrote the first systematic work on the 'higher objectives of law'.

40. Baso, *NU Studies*, p. 181.

41. Nur Khalik Ridwan, *Pluralisme Borjuis: Kritik atas Nalar Pluralisme Cak Nur*, Yogyakarta: Galang Press, 2002; *Agama Borjuis: Kritik atas Nalar Islam Murni*, Yogyakarta: Ar-Ruzz, 2004.

42. Kazmi, 'Limits of Muslim Liberalism'.

43. Ridwan, *Pluralisme Borjuis*, pp. 22–5, 28–9; *Agama Borjuis*, pp. 31, 188.

44. Ridwan, *Pluralisme Borjuis*, pp. 29–31; *Agama Borjuis*, pp. 40, 187, 279.

45. Ridwan, *Pluralisme Borjuis*, pp. 192–3; *Agama Borjuis*, pp. 29, 37.

46. Ridwan, *Agama Borjuis*, pp. 32–4.

47. Ibid., pp. 302ff.

48. Ibid., pp. 322–3, 373. PPP: Partai Persatuan Pembangunan (United Development Party).

49. Ridwan *Pluralisme Borjuis*, pp. vi, xiv; *Agama Borjuis*, p. 33.

50. Ridwan, *Pluralisme Borjuis*, pp. 108–9.

51. Ridwan, *Agama Borjuis*, p. 34.

52. Ridwan, *Pluralisme Borjuis*, pp. 118–19, 237.

53. Ibid., pp. 339ff.

54. Ibid., p. 274.

55. Ibid., pp. 282, 284.

56. Ibid., p. 287.

57. Ibid., p. 293.

58. Ridwan, *Agama Borjuis*, p. 35.

59. Ridwan, *Agama Borjuis*, pp. 33–4

60. Ridwan, *Pluralisme Borjuis*, pp. 65ff.

61. Ridwan, *Agama Borjuis*, p. 42.

62. Kuntowijoyo, *Paradigma Islam: Interpretasi untuk Aksi*, Bandung: Mizan, 1991; *Islam Tanpa Masjid: Esai-Esai Agama, Budaya, dan Politik dalam Bingkai Strukturalisme Transendental*, Bandung: Mizan, 2001.

63. Kuntowijoyo, *Muslim tanpa Masjid*, pp. 112–26.

64. Zuly Qodir, *Pembaharuan Pemikiran Islam: Wacana dan Aksi Islam Indonesia*, Yogyakarta: Pustaka Pelajar, 2006, pp. 103, 126.

65. Ridwan, *Agama Borjuis*, p. 281.

66. Moeslim Abdurrahman, *Islam Transformatif*, Jakarta: Pustaka Firdaus, 1995.

67. Zuly Qodir, *Islam Liberal: Paradigma Baru Wacana dan Aksi Islam Indonesia*, Yogyakarta: Pustaka Pelajar, 2007, pp. 62–3.

68. Budhy Munawar-Rachman, *Islam Pluralis: Wacana Keseteraan Kaum Beriman*, Jakarta: Paramadina, 2001, pp. 310–11.

69. Abdul Munir Mulkhan, *Marhaenis Muhammadiyah*, Yogyakarta: Galang Press, 2010, p. 27; Qodir, *Pembaharuan Pemikiran Islam*, pp. 106–7.

70. Moeslim Abdurrahman, 'Tiga Pilar JIMM', in Pradana Boy ZTF, M. Hilmi Faiq and Zulfan Barron (eds), *Era Baru Gerakan Muhammadiyah*, Malang: Universitas Muhammadiyah Malang, 2008, pp. 195–9.

71. See Pradana Boy ZDF, 'JIMM: Sebuah "Teks" Multitafsir' and "Intelektual Sebagai Agen Perubahan"', in Boy ZTF a.o., *Era Baru Gerakan Muhammadiyah*, pp. 47–51 and 27–31 respectively.

72. Qodir, *Pembaharuan Pemikiran Islam*, p. 156.

73. Ibid., pp. 66, 102.

74. Ibid., p. 244.

75. Ibid., p. 232.

76. See Mohammed A. Bamyeh, 'Anarchist Method, Liberal Intention, Authoritarian Lesson: The Arab Spring between Three Enlightenments', *Constellations*, 20, 2 (2013), pp. 188–202.

9. ISLAMIC SECULARISM AND THE QUESTION OF FREEDOM

1. See further Arshin Adib-Moghaddam, 'The Pluralistic Momentum in Iran and the Future of the Reform Movement', *Third World Quarterly*, 26, 6 (2006), pp. 665–74.

2. On the history of democracy in Iran, see Fakhreddin Azimi, *The Quest for Democracy in Iran: A Century of Struggle against Authoritarian Rule*, Cambridge, MA: Harvard University Press, 2010.

3. I expressed this on the eve of the anniversary of the thirty-sixth anniversary of the revolution in an interview with *Tehran Times*, 'Iranians Rose against Shah to Gain Freedom', 10 February 2015, available at http://www.tehrantimes.com/component/content/article/93-interviews/121728-iranians-rose-against-shah-to-gain-freedom-justice-scholar (accessed 11 March 2015).

4. See further Mansoor Moaddel, 'Shi'i Political Discourse and Class Mobilization in the Tobacco Movement of 1890–1892', *Sociological Forum*, 7, 3 (September 1992), pp. 447–68.

5. For a recent exception, see Umar Ryad, 'Anti-imperialism and the Pan-Islamic Movement', in David Motadel (ed.), *Islam and the European Empires*, Oxford: Oxford University Press, 2014, pp. 131–49.

6. I have conceptualised the term 'transversal' and its meaning for resistance movements more deeply in Arshin Adib-Moghaddam, *On the Arab Revolts and the Iranian Revolution: Power and Resistance Today*, New York: Bloomsbury, 2013.

7. Mohammad-Hossein Jamshidi (ed.), *Andishey-e siasiy-e imam Khomeini*, Tehran: Pajoheshkade-ye imam Khomeini va enghelab eslami, 1384 [2005], pp. 245, 246 (my translation).

8. See further Arshin Adib-Moghaddam (ed.), *A Critical Introduction to Khomeini*, Cambridge: Cambridge University Press, 2014.

9. Mehdi Bazargan, 'Religion and Liberty', in Charles Kurzman (ed.), *Liberal Islam: A Sourcebook*, Oxford: Oxford University Press, 1998, p. 77.

10. Ibid.

11. Ibid., p. 79.

12. Ibid.

13. Ibid., p. 81.

14. Ibid., p. 84.

15. Ayatollah Mahmud Taliqani, 'The Characteristics of Islamic Economics', in John J. Donohue and John L. Esposito (eds), *Islam in Transition: Muslim Perspectives*, Oxford: Oxford University Press, 2007, p. 233.

16. Ibid.

17. Mahmud Taleqani, 'Taleqani's Last Sermon', in Kurzman, *Liberal Islam*, p. 47.

18. Ibid.

19. On Iran's foreign policy, see Arshin Adib-Moghaddam, 'Islamic Utopian Romanticism and the Foreign Policy Culture of Iran', *Critique: Critical Middle Eastern Studies*, 14, 3 (2007), pp. 203–16. For the impact on the region, see Arshin Adib-Moghaddam, *The International Politics of the Persian Gulf: A Cultural Genealogy*, London: Routledge, 2006.

20. 'Khomeini's Grip Appears at Its Tightest', *New York Times*, 21 November 1982.

21. Abdolkarim Soroush, 'Sense and Nonsense: About the Cultural Revolution Again', available at http://www.drsoroush.com/English/By_DrSoroush/sense&nonsense.html (accessed 11 February 2015).

22. Ibid.

23. Abdolkarim Soroush, 'Islamic Revival and Reform: Theological Approaches', in Mahmoud Sadri and Ahmad Sadri (eds), *Reason, Freedom and Democracy in Islam: Essential Writings of Abdolkarim Soroush*, trans. Mahmoud Sadri and Ahmad Sadri, Oxford: Oxford University Press, 2000, p. 33.

24. Ibid., p. 32.
25. Ibid., p. 37.
26. Abdolkarim Soroush, 'The Idea of Democratic Religious Government', in Sadri and Sadri, *Reason, Freedom and Democracy*, p. 128.
27. Ibid., p. 129.
28. Mohsen Kadivar, 'Freedom of Religion and Belief in Islam', in Mehran Kamrava (ed.), *The New Voices of Islam: Reforming Politics and Modernity*, London: I.B. Tauris, 2006, p. 119.
29. Ibid., pp. 119–20.
30. Ibid., p. 120.
31. Bazargan, 'Religion and Liberty', p. 83.
32. Kadivar, 'Freedom of Religion', p. 120.
33. Ibid., p. 142.
34. Hasan Yousefi Eshkevari, 'God's Uprooted Warriors', available at http://yousefieshkevari.com/?p=2103 (accessed 12 January 2015).
35. Kadivar, 'Freedom of Religion', p. 120
36. Soroush, *Reason, Freedom and Democracy*, p. 128.
37. Ibid., p. 128.
38. Bazargan, 'Religion and Liberty', p. 83, emphasis added.
39. Ibid., p. 84.
40. Ali Shariati, 'Humanity and Islam', in Kurzman, *Liberal Islam*, p. 193.
41. Ibn Sina, *Fontessapientiae (uyun al-hikmah)*, ed. Abdurrahman Badawied, Cairo: no publisher, 1954, p. 16.
42. Quoted in Richard Walzer, *Greek into Arabic: Essays on Islamic Philosophy*, Cambridge, MA: Harvard University Press, 1962, p. 26.

10. MILITANCY, MONARCHY AND THE STRUGGLE TO DESACRALISE KINGSHIP IN ARABIA

1. For a concise discussion of the role of historical writing in Enlightenment thought see Constantin Fasolt, *The Limits of History*, Chicago: University of Chicago Press, 2004, pp. 6–31.
2. Simon Ross Valentine, *Force and Fanaticism: Wahhabism in Saudi Arabia and Beyond*, London: Hurst, 2015; Charles Allen, *God's Terrorists: The Wahhabi Cult and the Hidden Roots of Modern Jihad*, London: Abacus, 2007; David Commins, *The Wahhabi Mission and Saudi Arabia*, London: I.B. Tauris, 2005.
4. Madawi al-Rasheed, *A History of Saudi Arabia*, Cambridge: Cambridge University Press, 2002, p. 177.
5. For an example of such scholarship, see Pascal Menoret, *Joyriding in Riyadh: Oil, Urbanism, and Road Revolt*, Cambridge: Cambridge University Press, 2014.
6. For a good discussion of this phenomenon, see B. Haykel, T. Hagghammer and

S. Lacroix (eds), *Saudi Arabia in Transition: Insights on Social, Political, Economic, and Religious Change*, Cambridge: Cambridge University Press, 2015, pp. 196–9.

7. I borrow the term jihadi-Salafism from Sadu Al-Sarhan's incisive piece 'The Struggle for Authority: The Shaykhs of Jihadi-Salafism in Saudi Arabia 1997–2003', in Haykel, Hagghammer and Lacroix, *Saudi Arabia in Transition*.

8. Stéphane Lacroix, *Awakening Islam: The Politics of Religious Dissent in Contemporary Saudi Arabia*, Cambridge, MA: Harvard University Press, 2011, p. 14.

9. Madawi al-Rasheed, *Muted Modernists: The Struggle over Divine Politics in Saudi Arabia*, London: Hurst, 2015, p. 20.

10. Madawi al-Rasheed and Carool Kersten (eds), *Demystifying the Caliphate*, London: Hurst, 2013, p. 118.

11. *Wujooh Islamiyya* (2011). Al Arabiyya. 1 August 2011. Available at: https://www. youtube.com/watch?v=BIfQLKqHleU&list=PLXk54e6gWMXXpE_QUeSl 5zu5u9988mb7j

12. Opening speech by H.R.H. Shaykh Salman bin Hamad Al Khalifa, IISS Manama Dialogue, 2014. Posted by the International Institute of Strategic Studies on 5 December 2015. Available at: https://www.youtube.com/watch?v=rIBgsazvaOE

13. This is not to deny the existence of complex codes of conduct, hierarchy or heritable privilege as well as multiple methods of generating legitimacy before the rise of the Saudi or any contemporary Arabian nation state. Rather, it is to underscore the fact that dynastic politics before the rise of such states were not conducted in the name of absolute monarchy as a differentiated, full-fledged system of authority in its own right.

14. Corey Robin, *The Reactionary Mind: Conservatism from Edmund Burke to Sarah Palin*, Oxford: Oxford University Press, 2011, p. 4.

11. ISLAMOTOPIA: REVIVAL, REFORM, AND AMERICAN EXCEPTIONALISM

1. Michael Muhammad Knight, *Blue-Eyed Devil: A Road Odyssey through Islamic America*, Brooklyn: Autonomedia, 2006, p. 14.

2. Michael Muhammad Knight, *The Taqwacores*, Brooklyn: Autonomedia, 2004, p. 72.

3. Spencer Dew, 'The Work of Michael Muhammad Knight', Rain Taxi, 2012 (http:// www.raintaxi.com/online/2012summer/knight.php).

4. Isma'il Al-Faruqi, 'Islamic Ideals in North America', In Earle H. Waugh, Baha Abu-Laban and Regula B. Qureshi (eds), *The Muslim Community in North America*, Edmonton: University of Alberta Press, 1983, pp. 259–70.

5. Ibid.

6. Kambiz Ghanea Bassiri, *A History of Islam in America: From the New World to the New World Order*, Cambridge: Cambridge University Press, 2010, pp. 318–19.

7. Al-Faruqi, 'Islamic Ideals in North America', pp. 259–70.

8. Ibid.
9. Ibid.
10. Ibid.
11. Ibid.
12. Ibid.
13. Ibid.
14. Ibid.
15. Zafar Ishaq Ansari, 'Aspects of Black Muslim Theology', *Studia Islamica*, 53 (1981), pp. 137–76.
16. Ibid.
17. Zafar Ishaq Ansari, 'Islam among African Americans: An Overview', in Zahid Hussain Bukhari et al. (eds), *Muslims' Place in the American Public Square: Hopes, Fears, and Aspirations*, Oxford: Altamira Press, 2004, pp. 222–67.
18. Ibid.
19. Ibid.
20. Ibid.
21. Ibid.
22. Ali Mazrui, 'Muslims between the Jewish Example and the Black Experience: American Policy Implications', in Bukhari et al., *Muslims' Place in the American Public Square*, pp. 117–44.
23. Ibid.
24. Ibid.
25. Sherman Jackson, *Islam and the Blackamerican*, Oxford: Oxford University Press, 2005, pp. 12–13.
26. Ibid.
27. Ibid., p. 5.
28. Ibid., pp. 31–2.
29. Ibid., p. 44.
30. Ibid., p. 43.
31. Ibid., p. 159.
32. Ibid., p. 6.
33. Ibid., p. 168.
34. Ibid., pp. 20–1.
35. Ibid., p. 111.
36. Amina Wadud, 'American Muslim Identity: Race and Ethnicity in Progressive Islam', in Omid Safi (ed.), *Progressive Muslims: On Justice, Gender, and Pluralism*, Oxford: Oneworld Publications, 2002, pp. 270–85.
37. Ibid.
38. Mitra Rastegar, 'Managing "American Islam"', *International Feminist Journal of Politics*, 10, 4 (2008), pp. 455–74.
39. Ibid.

40. Rosemary R. Corbett, *Making Moderate Islam: Sufism, Service, and the 'Ground Zero Mosque' Controversy*, Stanford: Stanford University Press, 2016, pp. 17–23.

41. Ibid.

42. Ibid.

43. Ibid., p. 37.

44. Ibid., pp. 97–8.

45. Ibid., pp. 1, 19–21.

46. Yahya Emerick, 'The Fight for the Soul of Islam in America', in Michael Wolfe and the Producers of Beliefnet (eds), *Taking Back Islam: American Muslims Reclaim Their Faith*, Emmaus: Rodale, Inc. and Beliefnet, Inc., 2002, pp. 196–202.

47. Rastegar, 'Managing "American Islam"', pp. 455–74.

48. Muqtedar M.A. Khan, 'Living on Borderlines: Islam beyond the Clash and Dialogue', in Zahid Hussain Bukhari et al., *Muslims' Place in the American Public Square*, pp. 84–114.

49. Saleemah Abdul-Ghafur, 'Introduction', in Saleemah Abdul-Ghafur (ed.), *Living Islam Out Loud: American Muslim Speak*, Boston: Beacon Press, 2005, pp. 1–6.

50. Khalida Saed, 'On the Edge of Belonging', in Abdul-Ghafur, *Living Islam Out Loud*, pp. 86–94.

51. Asma Gull Hasan, *American Muslims: the New Generation*, New York: Continuum, 2000, pp. 55–6.

52. Ibid.

53. Ibid.

54. Ibid.

55. Ibid.

56. Ibid.

57. Ibid.

58. Knight, *Blue-Eyed Devil*, p. 205.

59. Ani Zonneveld, 'It's Time for an American Islam!', Aslan Media, 2012 (http://www.aslanmedia.com/aslan-media-columns/ummah-wake-up/item/234-it's-time-for-an-american-islam).

60. Ibid.

61. Ibid.

62. Jackson, *Islam and the Blackamerican*, p. 20.

63. Ibid.

64. Richard Dwyer, 'The Matter of Whiteness', in Les Back and John Solomos (eds), *Theories of Race and Racism: A Reader*, London: Routledge, 2000, pp. 539–48.

65. Zareena Grewal, *Islam Is a Foreign Country*, New Haven: Yale University Press, 2014, p. 165.

66. Ibid., pp. 307–8.

67. Jack O'Sullivan, 'If You Hate the West, Emigrate to a Muslim Country', *The Guardian*, 8 October 2007 (http://www.theguardian.com/world/2001/oct/08/religion.uk).

68. Ibid.

69. Dwyer, 'Matter of Whiteness', pp. 539–48.

70. Grewal, *Islam Is a Foreign Country*, pp. 159–60.

71. Mahdi Tourage, 'Performing Belief and Reviving Islam: Prominent (White Male) Converts in Muslim Revival Conventions', *Performing Islam*, 1, 2 (2012), 207–26.

72. Hamza Yusuf, Facebook.com, 25 April 2014.

73. Ani Zonneveld, Facebook.com, 26 April 2014.

74. Zonneveld, 'It's Time for an American Islam!'

75. Shadee Elmasry, 'The Salafis in America: The Rise, Decline and Prospects for a Sunni Muslim Movement among African-Americans', *Journal of Muslim Minority Affairs*, 30 (June 2010), pp. 217–36.

76. Dwyer, 'Matter of Whiteness', pp. 539–48.

77. A significant exception is Umar F. Abd-Allah's outstanding biography of Alexander Russell Webb, a white American who converted to Islam in the late nineteenth century. Abd-Allah carefully situates Webb within the dominant assumptions, prejudices and intellectual currents popular within the 'white culture' of his time and place. U.F. Abd-Allah, *A Muslim in Victorian America: The Life of Alexander Russell Webb*, Oxford: Oxford University Press, 2006.

78. Dwyer, 'Matter of Whiteness', pp. 539–48.

79. Amina Wadud, 'American Muslim Identity: Race and Ethnicity in Progressive Islam', in Omid Safi (ed.), *Progressive Muslims: On Justice, Gender, and Pluralism*, Oxford: Oneworld Publications, 2002, pp. 270–85.

80. Hakeem Muhammad, 'Imam Hamza Yusuf & The Compound Ignorance of White Supremacy', Patheos, 2016 (http://www.patheos.com/blogs/truthtopower/2016/12/imam-hamza-yusuf-compound-ignorance-white-supremacy/).

12. PRELIMINARY THOUGHTS ON ART AND SOCIETY

1. Tariq Modood, 'Reflections on the Rushdie Affair: Muslims, Race, and Equality in Britain', in Modood, *Multicultural Politics: Racism, Ethnicity, and Muslims in Britain*, Minneapolis: University of Minnesota Press, 2005, p. 103. First published in 1990 as 'Muslims, Race, and Equality in Britain: Some Post-Rushdie Affair Reflections', *Third Text*, 11 (Summer 1990), pp. 127–34.

2. Saba Mahmood, 'Religious Reason and Secular Affect: An Incommensurable Divide', in Talal Asad et al., *Is Critique Secular? Blasphemy, Injury, and Free Speech*, Berkeley: University of California Press, 2009, p. 89.

3. Talal Asad, 'Freedom of Speech and Religious Limitations', in Craig Calhoun, Mark Jurgensmeyer, and Jonathan van Antwerpen (eds), *Rethinking Secularism*, Oxford: Oxford University Press, 2011, 6918 of 7924 to 6931 of 7924 (ebook location).

4. Asad's attitude towards modernism is paradoxical. For, as I have argued elsewhere,

his attitudes towards modernity and religion resonate with Eliot's own. See Chapters 3 and 4, Sadia Abbas, *At Freedom's Limit: Islam and the Postcolonial Predicament*, New York: Fordham University Press, 2014.

5. Saba Mahmood, 'Secularism, Hermeneutics, Empire: The Politics of Islamic Reformation', *Public Culture*, 18, 2 (2006), p. 346.

6. See, for instance, Mahmood's critique of Stathis Gourgouris for drawing on a 'liberal romantic imaginary through which we are routinely asked to recognize our most profound commitments' in 'Is Critique Secular? A Symposium at UC Berkeley', *Public Culture*, 20, 3 (2008), p. 447.

7. See Patrick Eisenlohr, *'Na't*: Media Contexts and Transnational Dimensions of a Devotional Practice', in Barbara D. Metcalf (ed.), *Islam in South Asia in Practice*, Princeton: Princeton University Press, 2009.

8. http://tune.pk/video/862062/meri-janib-bhi-ho-ek-nigah-e-karam-exclusive-umm-e-habiba- (accessed 23 November 2014).

9. Eisenlohr, *'Na't*: Media Contexts and Transnational Dimensions of a Devotional Practice'.

10. Constitution of Pakistan (Second Amendment) Act 1974, art. 3, http://www.pakistani.org/pakistan/constitution/amendments/2amendment.html (accessed 28 November 2014).

11. Muhammad Iqbal, 'Qadianis and Orthodox Muslims', in A.R. Tariq (ed.), *Speeches and Statements of Iqbal*, Lahore: Gulam Ali & Sons, 1973, p. 92. On Iqbal and the Ahmadis, see Chapter 3, Naveeda Khan, *Muslim Becoming: Aspiration and Skepticism in Pakistan*, and Chapter 4 of Faisal Devji's, *Muslim Zion: Pakistan as a Political Idea*, Cambridge, MA: Harvard University Press, 2013 and Chapter 4 of *At Freedom's Limit*.

12. Asiya Nasir, 'Speech in Parliament following Shahbaz Bhatti's Murder', 'Dedicated to Shaheed Shahbaz Bhatti', https://www.youtube.com/watch?v=cT4oGIWXfQ4 (accessed 26 August 2014).

13. Nasir, 'Speech'.

14. On the importance of electronic dissemination of the *na't*, see Eisenlohr, *'Na't*: Media Contexts and Transnational Dimensions of a Devotional Practice'.

15. See Chapter 4, *At Freedom's Limit*.

16. See, for example, Ayesha Jalal, Partisans of Allah.

17. Email correspondence with painter, 30 August 2014.

18. On F.N. Souza, see, for instance, Geeta Kapur, 'Francis Newton Souza: Devil in the Flesh', *Third Text*, 3, 8–9 (1989), pp. 25–64.

19. Email correspondence with painter, 30 June 2014.

20. For a more detailed discussion of the term, see Chapters 5 and 6 in Sadia Abbas, *At Freedom's Limit*.

21. See Asma Jahangir and Hina Jilani, *The Hudood Ordinances: A Divine Sanction? A Research Study of the Hudood Ordinances and their Effect on the Disadvantaged Sections of Pakistan Society*, Lahore: Rhotas Books, 1990.

22. Nusrat Fateh ali Khan, *Tum Ek Gorakh Dhanda Ho*, https://www.youtube.com/watch?v=alMEZfaAYq4 (accessed 24 December 2014).

23. Syed Akbar Hyder and Carla Petievich, 'Qawwali Songs of Praise', in Metcalf, *Islam in South Asia in Practice*, and Esinlohr, '*Na't*: Media Contexts and Transnational Dimensions of a Devotional Practice'.

24. On devotional forms such as the *marsiya* and the *nauha*, see Syed Akbar Hyder's wonderful *Reliving Karbala: Martyrdom in South Asian Memory*, New York: Oxford University Press, 2006, particularly Chapter 1.

25. See particularly the chapter 'Lyrical Martyrdom' in *Reliving Karbala* for a discussion of the way the *qawwali* treats the martyrdom at Karbala.

26. Email correspondence with painter, 21 March 2014.

27. For instance, in his talk at Rutgers-Newark on 20 October 2014, trying to give a sense of the kind of authentic and unmediated response to his work he liked, Shafi mentioned his carpenter who he then seemed to feel necessary to point out was also 'the cook's son'.

13. THE POLITICAL MEANINGS OF ELIJAH MUHAMMAD'S NATION OF ISLAM

1. For an introduction to 1960s US liberalism, see 'The Rise and Fall of the New Liberalism', in Jeanne Boydston et al., *Making a Nation: The United States and Its People*, Upper Saddle River: Pearson Prentice Hall, 2002, http://wps.prenhall.com/hss_boydston_makinganat_1/1/434/111105.cw/index.htmlhttp://wps.prenhall.com/hss_boydston_makinganat_1/1/434/111105.cw/index.html (accessed 15 April 2014). Compare Alonzo L. Hamby, *Liberalism and Its Challengers: From F.D.R. to Bush*, 2nd edn, New York: Oxford University Press, 1992.

2. See Reinhard Schulze, *Islamischer Internationalismus im 20. Jahrhundert: Untersuchungen zur Geschichte der Islamischen Weltliga*, Islamic Internationalism in the Twentieth Century: Studies on the History of the Muslim World League, Leiden: Brill, 1990.

3. Hishaam D. Aidi, *Rebel Music: Race, Empire, and the New Muslim Youth Culture*, New York: Pantheon, 2014, pp. 237–40.

4. Eric C. Lincoln, *Black Muslims in America*, Boston: Beacon, 1961; E.U. Essien-Udom, *Black Nationalism: A Search for an Identity in America*, Chicago: University of Chicago Press, 1962.

5. See Manning Marable, *Malcolm X: A Life of Reinvention*, New York: Viking, 2011.

6. Andrew Clegg III, *An Original Man: The Life and Times of Elijah Muhammad*, New York: St. Martin's Press, 1997, pp. 135–6, 189.

7. *Chicago Daily Defender*, 3 October 1959; Lincoln, *Black Muslims in America*, p. 143.

8. Robert A. Hill, *The FBI's RACON: Racial Conditions in the United States*, Boston: Northeastern University Press, 1995, p. 4.

9. Ernest Allen Jr, 'When Japan was "Champion of the Darker Races": Satokata

Takahashi and the Flowering of Black Messianic Nationalism', *Black Scholar*, 24 (Winter 1994), pp. 23–46.

10. Clegg, *An Original Man*, pp. 70, 72–3, 82, 90–1, 172, 181, 182, 187, 283.

11. Penny von Eschen, *Race against Empire: Black Americans and Anticolonialism, 1937–1957*, Ithaca: Cornell University Press, 1997, p. 174.

12. Mattias Gardell, *In the Name of Elijah Muhammad: Minister Louis Farrakhan and the Final Call*, Durham: Duke University Press, 1996, pp. 72–6; Sean McCloud, *Making the American Religious Fringe: Exotics, Subversives, and Journalists, 1955–1993*, Chapel Hill: University of North Carolina Press, 2004, pp. 55–95.

13. This story is told in great detail in Robert A. Caro, *The Years of Lyndon Johnson: Master of the Senate*, New York: Knopf, 2002; Caro, *The Years of Lyndon Johnson: The Passage to Power*, New York: Knopf, 2012.

14. Edward E. Curtis IV, *Black Muslim Religion in the Nation of Islam, 1960–1975*, Chapel Hill: University of North Carolina Press, 2006, p. 36.

15. See further William L. van DeBurg, *New Day in Babylon: The Black Power Movement and American Culture, 1965–1975*, Chicago: University of Chicago Press, 1992.

16. Frank T. Donner, *The Age of Surveillance: The Aims and Methods of America's Political Intelligence System*, New York: Knopf, 1980, pp. 178, 212–13.

17. Essien-Udom, *Black Nationalism*, p. 276.

18. Curtis, *Black Muslim Religion*, pp. 43–4.

19. Ibid., pp. 4–5, 35–65.

20. See Edward E. Curtis (ed.), *Columbia Sourcebook of Muslims in the United States*, New York: Columbia University Press, 2008, pp. 18–22, 53–8; A.J. Toynbee, *Civilization on Trial*, New York: Oxford University Press, 1948, p. 205; Edward E. Curtis IV, 'Islamism and Its African American Muslim Critics: Black Muslims in the Era of the Arab Cold War', *American Quarterly*, 59, 3 (2007), pp. 695–6.

21. Curtis, 'Islamism and Its African American Muslim Critics', pp. 683–709.

22. For an account that traces the remaking of American religions along conservative and liberal political lines, see further Robert Wuthnow, *The Restructuring of American Religions: Society and Faith since World War II*, Princeton: Princeton University Press, 1988.

23. Edward E. Curtis IV, 'Islamizing the Black Body: Ritual and Power in Elijah Muhammad's Nation of Islam', *Religion and American Culture*, 12, 2 (2002), pp. 167–96.

24. Quoted in Manning Marable (ed.), *Dispatches from the Ebony Tower: Intellectuals Confront the African American Experience*, New York: Columbia University Press, 2000, p. 227.

25. Curtis, *Black Muslim Religion*, pp. 24–31, 136–53.

26. Ibid., pp. 109–18, 167–74.

27. Ibid., pp. 118–127.

28. The use of the law by the Nation of Islam is covered in Sarah Barringer Gordon, *The Spirit of the Law: Religious Voices and the Constitution in Modern America*, Cambridge, MA: Harvard University Press, 2010, pp. 96–132.

29. See the pioneering account of Kathleen M. Moore, *Al-Mughtaribun: American Law and the Transformation of Muslim Life in the United States*, Albany: State University of New York Press, 1995, pp. 69–102.

30. Curtis, *Black Muslim Religion*, pp. 26–7, 106–7, 141–3.

31. Ibid., pp. 102–9.

32. Ibid., pp. 11–12.

33. Chancellor Williams, *The Destruction of Black Civilization*, Dubuque: Kendall/Hunt, 1971; in ibid., pp. 86–93.

34. 'Black Muslim', *New York Times*, 28 February 1975, p. 32.

35. Nathan Irvin Huggins, *Black Odyssey: The African-American Ordeal in Slavery*, New York: Vintage, 1990, p. xlviii.

36. Curtis, *Islam in Black America*, pp. 113–27.

37. This story is told in Gardell, *In the Name of Elijah Muhammad*.

14. POST-ISLAMISM AS NEOLIBERALISATION: NEW SOCIAL MOVEMENTS IN THE MUSLIM WORLD

1. In the case of Indonesia, the Justice and Prosperity Party (PKS) occupies a position on the spectrum of Islamist politics somewhere between a traditional Ikhwani orientation and the 'new Islamist' approach represented by the AKP in Turkey.

2. See Vali Nasr, 'The Rise of "Muslim Democracy"', *Journal of Democracy*, 16 (2005), pp. 13–27; Ray Baker, *Islam without Fear: Egypt and the New Islamists*, Cambridge, MA: Harvard University Press, 2003; and Augustus Richard Norton, 'Thwarted Politics: The Case of Egypt's Hizb al-Wasat', in Robert Hefner (ed.), *Remaking Muslim Politics: Pluralism, Contestation, Democratization*, Princeton: Princeton University Press, 2005, pp. 133–61.

3. Jillian Schwedler, *Faith in Moderation: Islamist Parties in Jordan and Yemen*, Cambridge: Cambridge University Press, 2006.

4. Carrie Wickham, 'The Causes and Dynamics of Islamist Auto-Reform', *ICIS International*, 6 (2006), pp. 1–3.

5. John R. Bradley, 'Cairo's Failing Fundamentalists', *Prospect*, 147 (2008).

6. Saba Mahmood, *Politics of Piety. The Islamic Revival and the Feminist Subject*, Princeton: Princeton University Press, 2005.

7. Quintan Wiktorowicz, 'The Salafi Movement: Violence and Fragmentation of Community', in Miriam Cooke and Bruce Lawrence (eds), *Muslim Networks from Hajj to Hip Hop*, Chapel Hill, NC: University of North Carolina Press, 2005.

8. Ronald Inglehart, *The Silent Revolution: Changing Values and Political Styles among Western Publics*, Princeton: Princeton University Press, 1977.

9. My omission of militants from this 'portfolio' of contemporary Islamism should not be taken to imply that I discount the continued relevance of violent extremism in the name of Islam. Indeed, according to recent interviews conducted by Fawaz Gerges, there has been a marked upsurge in support for and interest on the part of young men in North Africa to serve as volunteer fighters in Iraq: 'If there were not so much attention being paid to border crossings these days, the flow of Arab fighters to Iraq would be much greater than the number who went to Afghanistan in the 1980s.' Gerges notes that this phenomenon is not a by-product of the classic model of urban, professional Islamism but rather that it correlates strongly with socioeconomic disaffection in the urban slums of large cities (personal conversation, June 2008).

10. Ted Gurr, *Why Men Rebel*, Princeton: Princeton University Press, 1969.

11. Charles Hirschkind, 'What Is Political Islam?', *Middle East Report*, 27, 4 (1997), pp. 12–14.

12. Ibid., p. 14. Note that he is not rejecting the idea of a relationship between socioeconomic status and Islamic social activism, only the notion that the totality of the latter can be comprehended through the former.

13. See Asef Bayat, 'Islamism and Social Movement Theory', *Third World Quarterly*, 26, 6 (2005), pp. 891–908. Sara Lei Sparre and Marie Juul Petersen, 'Youth and Social Change in Jordan and Egypt', *ISIM Review*, 20 (2007), pp. 14–15.

14. Hirschkind, 'What Is Political Islam?'

15. Bayat, 'Islamism and Social Movement Theory', p. 899.

16. Ibid., p. 898.

17. Ibid.

18. Steven M. Buechler, *Social Movements in Advanced Capitalism*, Oxford: Oxford University Press, 1999.

19. See Dale Eickelman and Jon Anderson (eds), *New Media in the Muslim World: The Emerging Public Sphere*, Bloomington, IN: Indiana University Press, 1999; and Armando Salvatore and Dale Eickelman (eds), *Public Islam and the Common Good*, Leiden: Brill, 2006.

20. Alberto Melucci, *Nomads of the Present: Social Movements and Individual Needs in Contemporary Society*, Philadelphia: Temple University Press, 1989.

21. Henri Lefebvre, *Critique of Everyday Life*, 3 vols, London: Verso, 2008 [1947]; Michel de Certeau, *The Practice of Everyday Life*, Berkeley: University of California Press, 2002 [1974].

22. Alberto Melucci, *Nomads of the Present: Social Movements and Individual Needs in Contemporary Society*, Philadelphia: Temple University Press, 1989, p. 7.

23. Ibid.

24. Ibid., p. 6.

25. Ibid., p. 4.

26. Olivier Roy, *Globalized Islam: The Search for a New Ummah*, New York: Columbia University Press, 2004, p. 99.

27. Ibid., p. 172.
28. Bayat, 'Islamism and Social Movement Theory', p. 901.
29. Robert D. Benford and David A. Snow, 'Framing Processes and Social Movements: An Overview and Assessment', *Annual Review of Sociology*, 26 (2000), pp. 611–39.
30. Bayat, 'Islamism and Social Movement Theory'.
31. Unless otherwise indicated, all basic information on Khaled and his career development are taken from Lindsay Wise, '"Words from the Heart": New Forms of Islamic Preaching in Egypt', M.Phil thesis, Oxford University, 2003; and Wise, 'Amr Khaled: Broadcasting the *Nahda*', *Transnational Broadcasting Studies*, 13 (2004).
32. As recounted by Shawkat Warreich, director of Amr Khaled's UK office, personal interview, February 2008.
33. Steven Covey, *The Seven Habits of Highly Effective People: Powerful Lessons in Personal Change*, New York: Free Press, 1990.
34. Wise, 'Amr Khaled'.
35. Ibid.
36. Benedict Anderson, *Imagined Communities: Reflections on the Origin and Spread of Nationalism*, London: Verso, 1998.
37. Sara Lei Sparre and Marie Juul Petersen, 'Islam and Civil Society: Case Studies from Jordan and Egypt', *DIIS Report*, 13 (2007), Copenhagen: Danish Institute for International Studies.
38. Personal interview with Shawkat Warreich, executive director of Amr Khaled's UK office, February 2008.
39. Wise, 'Amr Khaled'.
40. Hossam Tammam and Patrick Haenni, 'Egypt's Air-Conditioned Islam', *Le Monde Diplomatique*, September 2003.
41. Wise, 'Amr Khaled', pp. 15–16.
42. Although Khaled's staff claims that, through the use of 'viral marketing' techniques involving, for example, mass SMS text messaging, they can fill a stadium with just one day's notice (personal interviews, Birmingham, February 2008). In the past, popular Indonesian preacher Aa Gym, whose profile is remarkably similar to that of Khaled's, has made similar claims. He once said, for example, that given ten minutes he could get 100,000 of his supporters from the Istiqlal Mosque in downtown Jakarta to the US embassy. 'With God's will I could use that power', he says. 'But I won't. My program is for Indonesians to control themselves, to not be emotional. If we are emotional we have problems'. See Simon Elegant and Jason Tedjasukmana, 'Holy Man', *Time*, 4 November 2002.
43. Charles Tilly, *From Mobilization to Revolution*, New York: McGraw-Hill, 1978.
44. Amel Boubekeur, 'Cool and Competitive: Muslim Culture in the West', *ISIM Review*, 16 (2005), pp. 12–13.

INDEX

INDEX